RICHARD MEIER

kenneth frampton

Electaarchitecture

editorial coordination
Giovanna Crespi

layout and cover design
Tassinari/Vetta

page layout
Eva Bozzi

editing
Gabriella Cursoli

technical coordination
Paolo Verri
Andrea Panozzo

Distributed by Phaidon Press
ISBN 1-9043-1313-2

www.phaidon.com

www.electaweb.it

Contents

7 Meier's Style
Francesco Dal Co

9 Forty Years of Practice
Kenneth Frampton

Works and Projects 1965–2002
28 Smith House, Darien,
Connecticut, 1965–67

34 On Materiality
Richard Meier

36 Hoffman House, East Hampton,
New York, 1966–67
38 Westbeth Artists' Housing, Greenwich
Village, New York, 1967–70
40 Saltzman House, East Hampton,
New York, 1967–69
46 Project for a House in Pound Ridge,
New York, 1969
50 House in Old Westbury, New York,
1969–71
54 Twin Parks Northeast Housing, Bronx,
New York, 1969–74
58 Bronx Developmental Center, Bronx,
New York, 1970–77
64 Maidman House, Sands Point,
New York, 1971–76
66 Douglas House, Harbor Springs,
Michigan, 1971–73
74 Branch Office Prototypes for Olivetti,
United States, 1971
76 Project for a Dormitory for the Olivetti
Training Center, Tarrytown, New York, 1971
80 Project for Olivetti Headquarters
Building, Fairfax, Virginia, 1971
82 Shamberg House, Chappaqua,
New York, 1972–74
86 Project for the Cornell University
Undergraduate Housing, Ithaca,
New York, 1974
88 The Atheneum, New Harmony,
Indiana, 1975–79
96 Sarah Campbell Blaffer Pottery Studio,
New Harmony, Indiana, 1975–78
100 New York School Exhibition, State
Museum, Albany, New York, 1977
102 Aye Simon Reading Room,
Solomon R. Guggenheim Museum,
New York, New York, 1977–78
104 House in Palm Beach, Florida,
1977–78
108 Hartford Seminary, Connecticut,
1978–81
114 Giovannitti House, Pittsburgh,
Pennsylvania, 1979–83
120 Museum für Kunsthandwerk,
Frankfurt am Main, Germany, 1978–85
128 Project for Somerset Condominiums,
Beverly Hills, California, 1980

130 High Museum of Art, Atlanta,
Georgia, 1980–83
140 Project for Renault Administrative
Headquarters, Boulogne-Billancourt,
France, 1981
144 Project for International
Bauausstellung Housing, Berlin,
Germany, 1982
146 Des Moines Art Center Addition,
Iowa, 1982–85
152 Siemens Headquarters Building,
Munich, Germany, 1983–88
160 Competition Project for the Lingotto
Factory Conversion, Turin, Italy, 1983
162 Westchester House, New York,
1984–86
168 Siemens Office and Research Facilities,
Munich, Germany, 1984–90
170 Ackerberg House, Malibu,
California, 1984–86
178 Bridgeport Center, Connecticut,
1984–89
180 Grotta House, Harding Township,
New Jersey, 1985–89

186 On the Road Again
Richard Meier

192 The Getty Center, Los Angeles,
California, 1985–97
212 Competition Project for the Supreme
Court Building, Jerusalem, Israel, 1986
214 Bicocca Competition Project,
Milan, Italy, 1986
216 Exhibition and Assembly Building,
Ulm, Germany, 1986–93
222 City Hall and Central Library,
The Hague, Netherlands, 1989–95
228 Project for the Eye Center
for Oregon Health Sciences University,
Portland, Oregon, 1986
230 Project for Naples, Italy, 1987
232 Competition Project for Santa Monica
Beach Hotel, California, 1987
234 Competition Project for the Madison
Square Garden Site Redevelopment,
New York, New York, 1987
240 Weishaupt Forum, Schwendi,
Germany, 1987–92
246 Royal Dutch Paper Mill Headquarters,
Hilversum, Netherlands, 1987–92
252 Museum of Contemporary Art,
Barcelona, Spain, 1987–95
260 Project for the Cornell University
Alumni and Admissions Center, Ithaca,
New York, 1988
262 Canal+ Headquarters, Paris,
France, 1988–92
268 Espace Pitôt Residential Housing,
Montpellier, France, 1988–93

273 On White
Richard Meier

274 Daimler-Benz Research Center, Ulm, Germany, 1989–93
278 Project for an Office Building for Quandt, Frankfurt am Main, Germany, 1989
280 Competition Project for the Bibliothèque de France, Paris, France, 1989
284 Hypolux Bank Building, Luxembourg, 1989–93
292 Project for the Museum of Ethnology, Frankfurt am Main, Germany, 1989
298 Competition Master Plan for the Sextius Mirabeau Area, Aix-en-Provence, France, 1990
300 Project for the Jean Arp Museum I, Rolandswerth, Germany, 1990
304 Euregio Office Building, Basel, Switzerland, 1990–98
308 Camden Medical Center, Singapore, 1990–99
312 Rachofsky House, Dallas, Texas, 1991–96
320 Swissair North American Headquarters, Melville, New York, 1991–94
328 Competition Master Plan for Potsdamer Platz, Berlin, Germany, 1992
330 United States Courthouse and Federal Building, Islip, New York, 1993–2000
338 Museum of Television and Radio, Beverly Hills, California, 1994–96
342 Gagosian Gallery, Beverly Hills, California, 1994–95
344 Project for the Jean Arp Museum II, Rolandseck, Germany, 1995

346 What Good are Critics?
Richard Meier

348 Sandra Day O'Connor United States Courthouse, Phoenix, Arizona, 1995–2000
356 Neugebauer House, Naples, Florida, 1995–98
366 Museum of the Ara Pacis, Rome, Italy, 1996–

368 Jubilee Church
Richard Meier

372 Jubilee Church, Rome, Italy, 1996–2004

380 Crystal Cathedral Hospitality and Visitors Center, Garden Grove, California, 1996–2003
384 Tan House, Kuala Lumpur, Malaysia, 1997–2002
386 Peek & Cloppenburg Department Store, Düsseldorf, Germany, 1998–2001
388 Rickmers Reederei Headquarters, Hamburg, Germany, 1998–2001
396 Canon Headquarters, Tokyo, Japan, 1998–2002
398 Project for the Cittadella Bridge, Alessandria, Italy, 1998
400 Friesen House, Los Angeles, California, 1998–2001
402 San Jose Civic Center, California, 1998–2003
404 Southern California Beach House, Malibu, California, 1999–2001
410 Project for Office Buildings in Chesterfield Village, St. Louis, Missouri, 1999–2003
412 173/176 Perry Street Condominiums, New York, New York, 1999–2002
418 Project for New York House, Katonah, New York, 2000
424 Master Plan for Pankrac City Office Buildings, Prague, Czech Republic, 2000–05
426 Project for a Performing Arts Center, Bethel, New York, 2001
432 Wijnhaven Kwartier Master Plan, The Hague, Netherlands, 2001
434 Project for Santa Barbara House, California, 2001
438 Yale University History of Art and Arts Library, New Haven, Connecticut, 2001–06
442 Burda Collection Museum, Baden-Baden, Germany, 2001–04
446 Peek & Cloppenburg Department Store, Mannheim, Germany, 2001
450 The Urban Facility – Downtown Manhattan Project for the New York Times, New York, New York, 2002

452 Turning Point
Richard Meier

Appendices

456 Chronology of Works
479 Biography
480 General Bibliography
484 Project Bibliography
502 Acknowledgements
502 Collaborators
504 Photograph Credits

Meier's Style
Francesco Dal Co

In 1948 the Museum of Modern Art in New York embarked on a program of exhibitions dedicated to contemporary architecture. The idea behind the project was that each year an architect would be invited to build the prototype of a house in the garden of the museum, at that time accessible from the 53rd Street as well as from the museum, "demonstrating how much good living and good design can be purchased for how many dollars." After seeing it, visitors would be able to buy the design and build the house wherever they thought fit. Marcel Breuer was the architect chosen to inaugurate the series of exhibitions. His house (the roof had upside-down pitches; the front was generously glazed; the garden with well-cropped grass was bounded by low walls; the plan was organized around the fireside; the fireplace was built out of rough stone; and the internal surfaces were in wood and white plaster) was a well-made representation of the American dream, in an absolutely domestic key. The house was not, however, bought by a discerning family man: designed as a mirage for the middle class, it was transferred directly from MoMA to the garden of a property of the Rockefellers, in the vicinity of New York.

In 1961, Richard Meier, twenty-seven-years old at the time and with a short curriculum behind him after finishing his training at Cornell University, joined Breuer's studio, where he worked until 1963. The decision that brought the young architect into the studio of the man who had contributed more than most to shaping the domestic stereotypes of the American postwar dream was neither fortuitous nor devoid of consequences. In fact Lambert House, which Meier had just finished (1962) on Fire Island, New York, was the fruit of a curious mixture of ideas drawn from Breuer himself and from what architects active in California had been experimenting with in various ways.

Shortly afterward, Meier opened his own studio in New York. One of the first projects he drew up was for the competition held for the construction of a monumental fountain on the Franklin Parkway in Philadelphia (the project also bore the signature of Frank Stella and marked the beginning of a partnership that was to continue to this day). From this moment on, Meier's career developed along enviably straightforward lines. Completing the Saltzman House at East Hampton and working on the ones at Pound Ridge and Old Westbury, again in New York State, between 1967 and 1971, Meier laid the foundations of the success that he was to enjoy in the following years, in the United States and Europe.

These constructions were also emblematic expressions of a renewed version of the American dream. Naturally, things had changed since 1948: the average American, which MoMA had set out to turn into a client for good architecture, available at a reasonable price, was the citizen of a nation that was emerging from the war and moving toward McCarthyism. Very different were the clients who permitted Meier, with these early experiences, to develop a style that he went on to cultivate tenaciously, suited to the invention of continually varied *mises-en-scène* of the aspirations that are summed up in the word refinement.

Meier's style, whose structure is revealed in the essay by Kenneth Frampton serving as an introduction to this volume, is the result of a procedure similar to the one adopted by Breuer, in the years of his maturity. If Breuer had been successful, it was because he had been able to graft the ingenuous stereotypes of American domesticity onto the worn-out stock of the avant-garde, and Meier has carried out a symmetrical operation. He adapted to totally American structural conceptions, modes of construction and typologies, a language that reduced to a manner what had been produced by the European avant-garde, which he had studied through the distorting lens represented by the historical and methodological popularizations of Colin Rowe. Fruit of a work of continual contamination, Meier's style has been created by sterilizing the materials that he blends, obsessively cleansing every form of any trace of depravity, assigning to each construction a reassuring, familiar and gratifying appearance, aimed at satisfying, with tried-and-tested professional efficiency, the expectations of the ever broader public that is unified by the cult of sophistication.

Translation by Christopher Evans

Forty Years of Practice
Kenneth Frampton

As much time has elapsed in Richard Meier's forty years of practice as that which now separates the formulation of a purist architecture in Le Corbusier's Maison Cook of 1926, from the completion of Meier's neopurist Smith House, at Darien, Connecticut in 1967.

Thirty years later we may ask, what was it that was transferred from one to the other in the course of four decades? While an overall cubic mass was a trope that they shared in common, it is evident that the *free plan* of the Smith House did not correspond to the *free plan* of the Maison Cook. The Meier plan was open, rather free in its fundamental character, a quality that suggests its partial derivation from the American domestic tradition (cf. Vincent Scully's account of the evolution of Prairie Style from Bruce Price to Frank Lloyd Wright)[1] rather than from the Le Corbusier's latent neo-Palladianism as this determines the frontalized format of the Maison Cook. Although one encounters dramatic spatial displacements in both houses, the space-form of the Maison Cook is spiraling in its development as opposed to the layered spaces of the Smith House. Needless to say, the respective context of the two works was also totally different, for where the Maison Cook presented its discreet front to a verdant street in Boulogne-sur-Seine, the Darien dwelling was posited as a panoramic belvedere overlooking the rocky shoreline of the Long Island Sound.

The partially purist origin of Meier's architecture is possibly more apparent when we compare the Smith House to Le Corbusier's Villa Stein de Monzie completed at Garches in 1927, for in this instance, aside from the common freestanding cylindrical columns, we encounter a similar categoric differentiation between an approach façade, which is largely closed and a garden façade which is open; a gesture that is comprehensible in picturesque terms but rather hermetic from the point of view of representation; that is to say, the more expressive façade is situated to the rear of the building rather than the front. While making this observation one should note other differences, above all the fact that where the opaque façade of the Villa Stein de Monzie consists of a

thin membrane cantilevered in front of a reinforced concrete skeleton, the entry elevation of the Smith House comprises a thick volume of balloon frame construction entirely divorced from the freestanding, tubular steel, Lally columns supporting the roof of the double height living volume overlooking the sea. The full height, panoramic glass wall of this last could hardly be more removed from Le Corbusier's steel-framed "free façade" held tight against the outer limits of the Villa Stein de Monzie. By way of contrast the plate-glass fenestration at Darien is articulated through the thickness and the rebates of the timber frame that holds it in place while simultaneously serving to sustain cantilevered glazing at the corners. The glass returns at the ends of the living volume in order to ensure a panoramic prospect over the Sound. The fact that a void adjacent to the entry runs as a vertical space through the three floors of the house, linking the dining on the lower ground floor, to the entry level and the sleeping level above, only serves to reinforce an incipient pinwheeling character which is implied by the freestanding chimney set in front of the ocean façade. Asymmetrically placed in respect of the mass, this feature is balanced by a dogleg stair leading from the first floor dining room to a narrow greensward running along the shore. Although this stair may be compared as a sculptural element to the straight-flight garden stair in the Villa Stein de Monzie, it performs a different spatial function. At Garches it corresponds to the layering of the internal space, while at Darien it serves as a rotational addendum to the relatively static focus of the living volume. This alternating shift from frontality to rotation seems to have exerted a strong influence over the way in which Le Corbusier's purist syntax was received by the American neo-avant-garde of the mid-sixties, not only in the work of Meier but also in the early houses of Michael Graves and Charles Gwathmey dating from the same period.

Meier's next house of consequence, his Saltzman House completed in East Hampton in 1969, partially derives its composition from the "head vs. tail" format of the Anglo-Saxon, Arts and Crafts house of the last quarter of the nineteenth

Saltzman House, East Hampton,
New York, 1967-69.

century, wherein a double-height living volume serves as the *head* while the *tail* comprises a series of lower, ancillary volumes. Although truncated in the Saltzman House, this *head/tail* syndrome still constitutes the basic configuration of the plan.

The spatial character of this house has perhaps never been better characterized than by Stan Allen, when he wrote: "Curves in Meier's other early works often appear as incidents or quotations in an otherwise regular fabric, while this curve is fully integral and distorts the fabric itself. However, it does not undermine the essentially cubic form of the house: the massing reads as a cube with rounded corners rather than a quarter circle joining two arms. The plan is compact, not an aggregation of parts. Finally in the handling of the base, which is eroded in layers, he achieved an effect of weightlessness without relying on the more obvious, or referential, strategy of pilotis ... The interior space of the house reads at once as a dense plastic mass, swelling the walls outward but at the same time it is allowed to flow continuously out into the translucent air and space of the site itself. Meier has created this effect in part through his arrangement and detailing of the exterior openings. Looking at the south elevation, the first element on the left is the rounded planar enclosure of the spiral staircase, floating above the base and pressing slightly forward. To its immediate right is the recessive void of the terrace/balcony, more or less solid above and open below. Next to this, an enormous glass pane runs the full three-story height. In this sequence of solid/void/plane, Meier has taken full advantage of the changeable character of glass as a material. By detailing the glass without intermediate mullions, and by framing it very close to the enclosing skin he has created a shifting scrim. Charged to near opacity by reflection of the sky, it continues the stretched surface of the enclosing skin, but at other times it nearly disappears, creating the visual effect of dissolving large chunks of the exterior skin, leaving the interior vulnerable and exposed."[2]

Apart from its Arts and Crafts affinities the Saltzman House is also the first of a series of houses by Meier to be influenced by the Cooper Union Nine Square exercise as developed by John Hejduk, who was Meier's close colleague at Cooper Union during the years 1962 to1973 when Meier was teaching there. As in Hejduk's houses, both the Saltzman and Meier's Pound Ridge house of 1969 will be partially based on a neo-Palladian nine square format.

Both the Saltzman House and the next canonical residence, the Douglas House—built on a spectacular, wooded site overlooking Lake Michigan in 1973—served to consolidate and enrich Meier's plastic repertoire. In reworking and extending the *parti* of the Smith House, the Douglas House took on a certain refinement through the rounding of its arises on the landward side of the house. The tubular steel balustrading of the Douglas House would serve to enrich the expressive repertoire of the Smith House, in part through an aerial *passerelle*, spanning between the upper part of a steeply sloping site and the entry level at the top of the house and in part through an exposed straight flight, linking this level with its bedrooms to the double-height living space below. This stair, ornamenting the large plate-glass fenestration of the house through the filigree of its handrails, is a trope that Meier will repeatedly apply in subsequent works, most immediately in The Atheneum built at New Harmony, Indiana in 1979, wherein tubular steel balustrading, at multiple levels, appears both to festoon and erode the dynamic mass of the building.

The baroque, cacophonic character of The Atheneum derives in part from the fact that it is generated by the superimposition of the two intersecting squares in plan, one of which is rotated 45 degrees. The other energizing figure is the central ramp, drawn as an essential element from Le Corbusier's Villa Savoye of 1929. Set against one side of a small auditorium, this last functions as the dynamic kernel of the entire composition. Cubist painting seems to be the direct formal inspiration behind this enterprise, particularly when it is viewed from the southwest, when the rupture between the rotated cube and the larger orthogonal volume is repaired, as it were, by a freely undulating wall. Here, the reference is to Juan Gris rather than to Le Corbusier. Meier will return to similar synthetic Cubist strategies in his Renault Administrative Headquarters projected for Boulogne-Billancourt in 1981.

A particularly significant but often underestimated work between the Saltzman House of 1969 and The Atheneum of 1979 is the Bronx Developmental Center New York (1970–77) wherein Meier was first commissioned to design at an institutional, quasi-urbanistic scale. Projected for some 380 physically and mentally handicapped children this facility challenged the technological capacity of the office and Meier's response was not only to project a rational plan but to clad the structure in metal paneling made out of rolled aluminum sheets. This system of gasketed panels, previously restricted to the facing of industrial structures was adapted by Meier as a form of generic revetment, the main virtue of which was not only its modular, prefabricated, character and its ease of erection but also the self-cleansing nature of its surface. Prefigured in two utilitarian projects of virtually the same date—the Fredonia Health and Physical Education Building and the Charles Evans factory prototype—this system would greatly augment the technical capacity of the office. Once the standard aluminum panel came to be replaced by bright white panels of enameled steel, the "signature style" of the architect was virtually crystallized. Meier's ubiquitous glistening membrane first shines forth with vibrant intensity in The Atheneum, but thereafter it will become, along with a certain plastic repertoire, the touchstone of the office.

The Bronx Developmental Center remains a seminal piece in Meier's *oeuvre* for herein he tackles for the first time the theme of the "city in miniature" to which he will return in numerous projects and realizations throughout the eighties. Perhaps the most remarkable aspect of this complex are the four dormitory blocks, as these are arranged in staggered formation in front of the horizontal continuity of the gymnasium and the classroom/admin block, that enclose the central plaza on its northern face. Two modular tropes typical of the house style are also initiated with this work; the first of these turns on the use of gasketed, round-cornered "television" windows and air-conditioning grills. These impart to the metallic envelope a marine-cum-aeronautical character, much as we find this in Norman Foster's Sainsbury Center at the University of East Anglia, Norwich, England of 1978. The second stems from the semi-transparent *passerelles* that serve to both modulate and enclose the multi-level, planted space of the plaza.

The highly reflective ambience of this complex in the Bronx, particularly as this is embodied internally in the glass block wall of an indoor swimming pool, will afford the architect an occasion in which to set shining metal handrails and scintillating surfaces against the undulating turbulence of water and the luminescence of opaque glass.

Elsewhere, at this time, Meier's neo-Corbusianism gravitates towards loosely aggregated "cubistic" fragments as we find these in the house at the Old Westbury of 1971 which bears, however coincidentally, an uncanny resemblance to the Brewer House that Le Corbusier projected for Olivet College, near Chicago in 1935. This tendency towards disaggregation will be somewhat checked in the next three projects; the Maidman House (1976), the Palm Beach House (1977) and, above all, in the exceptionally ingenious Giovannitti House, realized outside Pittsburgh in 1983, of which he wrote: "The overall plan consists of an eroded double square, with one square elevated into a three-story cubic volume and containing most of the program, and the other square devoted to the service functions of garage and kitchen on the ground level and an open terrace above. The three-story volume is carved away on the ground level to provide a second terrace, this one shielded from view and partially roofed by the projecting volume of the third floor. Inside, the program is organized vertically, giving all the spaces of this small house an unexpected amplitude. The dining room and guest room, located on the first level, are accessible from the garage and kitchen. The living room and the formal entry to the house, on the second level, are contiguous to the parapeted terrace over the garage. The library and master bedroom are on the third level. A wood stair adjacent to the entry area connects all three floors. On the façades, porcelain-enameled steel panels and stucco protect the private spaces from view, while a delicate, steel-framed glass skin allows light to penetrate the public spaces. The openness of this skin permits views to the outside which are balanced and framed by more massive solid forms, as well as by the large existing trees on the property, which have been left intact. Throughout this small house there is a subtle dialogue between open and closed spaces, private and public realms with each element enhanced by the play of contrasts and transitions."[3]

This is Meier at his diminutive domestic best before the overall scale of his work shifts via the Hartford Seminary towards large scale civic structures, first with the Frankfurt am Main Museum für Kunsthandwerk of 1978–85 and then with the High Museum of Art, Atlanta, Georgia in 1980.

While Meier had enjoined the task of designing an urban intervention in contextual terms before, above all in his UDC Twin Parks Northeast Housing built in the Bronx in 1974, the Frankfurt Museum introduced two fundamental shifts in the substance of his architecture, for this is not only his first European commission of consequence but also his first work of an unequivocally civic character. It not only represents a fundamental paradigmatic shift but it also brings with it a fundamental change in terms of the conceptual and presentation methods adopted in bringing the work to fruition, although the syntax and the overall conceptual strategy had been hinted at previously, first in The Atheneum where the cruciform square window first appears and then in the Giovannitti House where a square grid determines every element. All of this is further inflected in Frankfurt through the use of an axial ramp and through the introduction of certain subtle alignments in the orientation of the four squares that make up the basic *parti*. Thus once again a square format is the operable motif both in terms of plan and the skin.

We are also witness to the way in which, as Jean Louis Cohen reminds us, the *promenade architectural* becomes the prime mover in all of Meier's public buildings from The Atheneum to the Museum of Contemporary Art in Barcelona, wherein, as he puts it, we are confronted with an inversion of Louis Kahn's hierarchy in which, as opposed to the work of Kahn, pride of place is reserved for the *servant* rather than the *served*.[4]

Circulation aside, everything stems in the Frankfurt Museum from four basic cubes of which the existing Villa Metzler facing onto the Schaumainkai is the aboriginal quadrant determining the dimensional order of the entire scheme, however much of this is also inflected by the topography of the site. Thus as an office description puts it: "The site is on the southern edge of the Main River, in proximity to several other museum buildings which together form the *museum-surfer*, a venerable embankment of buildings fronting the

Douglas House, Harbor Springs,
Michigan, 1971-73.

13

water. Since the program readily fits into the east end of the site the rest is given over to a landscaped park … The organizational grid of the new complex is derived primarily from two geometries: that of the Villa Metzler, a near-perfect cubic volume, and that of the slightly skewed angle to the site of the river bank and existing buildings. The villa is enscribed into one quadrant of the larger square plan, a sixteen-square grid that takes in the entire new complex. This grid is overlaid by another of the same size, but rotated 3.5 degrees to establish a frontal relationship with the other buildings on the embankment … The villa's 17.60-metre width and height become the basis for the exterior dimensions of each quadrant, while its elevational dimensions become the source of the 1.10-metre width and height of the metal panel grid; similarly, the proportions of windows in the villa generate those of the new building."[5]

In terms of its basic organization the High Museum in Atlanta, Georgia, designed at the same time, was also structured around four squares in plan, three of which were distanced from each other by a module of equal dimension, thereby assuming a disaggregated L-shaped formation, while the fourth square was rotated through 30 degrees in order to correspond to the main approach entering from the southeast corner of the site. The vacant space remaining at the center of this "nine square" assembly was filled by a full-height ramp hall linking all four cubes, the ramp ascending around the outer perimeter of a top-lit atrium. This peripheral ramp was surely inspired, in some measure, by Frank Lloyd Wright's Guggenheim Museum of 1959. Here the trope comes to be overlaid by a free-form in plan, plus a dogleg stair and a number of freestanding screen walls, all of which are deployed so as to animate and resolve the picturesque cacophony of the whole.

Whatever the importance of the High Museum on the home front, the realization of the Museum of Decorative Art in Frankfurt was crucial as far as Meier's subsequent European career was concerned, for it afforded consummate proof of his capacity as an architect who could be trusted with major civic commissions. Although some of Meier's European work came through direct commission as with the project of 1981 for the Weishaupt industrial complex completed at Schwendi in 1992, the main part of Meier's continental practice was acquired through a series of limited competitions. First among those after Frankfurt was the Ulm Exhibition and Assembly building designed in 1986, a project that combined Meier's late modern syntax with an extremely sensitive approach to the urban scale and context; above all with regard to the overwhelming presence of Ulm Cathedral. Apart from its contextualism, the Ulm project is also the first occasion in which Meier would employ a cylinder as a principal unifying element. Significantly it was also the first time that Meier had to respond to a major architectural

monument, the cylinder affording a diminutive counter-form to the cathedral through its syncopated relationship to an inner cubic mass. This last capped by a tripartite, sawtooth monitor roof light embodied two contextual gestures in a single form; namely, on the one hand, a consolidated mass and, on the other, three successive triangular gables that not only echo the traditional gable fronts of the square but also present a set of peaks which seem to allude to the pinnacles of the cathedral. At the same time the piloti under the drum help to establish the limit of the Munsterplatz, while the nine-square inner cube, faced in stone, stands in strong contrast to the plastered surface of the drum.

The Hague City Hall and Central Library, won in the same year, could hardly be more removed from the scale of Ulm, for the Hague amounts, in effect, to the redesign of an entire quarter. Aside from its unusual size (approximately 820 feet by 330 feet) one of the most remarkable things about this project is the way in which it comes to fulfill an eighty-year-old ambition to erect a city hall on this site. It says something for the colossal scale of Meier's city hall that what had been projected by Kalf and Wils in 1925 as an ornamental water garden flanked by low-rise municipal offices would be recast some sixty years later as a twelve-story megastructure enclosing a vast atrium. Almost twice as big as the concourse of New York's Grand Central Terminal, this space remains, as of now, the largest enclosed public space in Europe.

As a seminal work Meier's City Hall and Central Library in The Hague is not only indebted to Frank Lloyd Wright's Larkin Building of 1904 but also to Giuseppe Mengoni's Galleria Vittorio Emanuele in Milan of 1867. With regard to this last, we may say that both the Mengoni and the Meier galleries exhibit political affinities, with the former proclaiming the triumph of the Risorgimento and the latter consolidating the reawakening of the Dutch capital from its earlier genteel incarnation, as it attempts to rival, in terms of high-tech, high-rise construction, the booming skyline of Rotterdam. Meier's mandate, although never stated as such, was to unify and consolidate the city's new metropolitan character. Thus the city hall is rendered as a megaform of sufficient height and horizontal continuity to hold its own against the random, mediocre office slabs that had already been loosely superimposed upon the preexisting low-rise urban fabric.

While on the one hand it would be difficult to imagine a building more removed from the Netherlands than this large structure clad in an enameled skin, on the other this new municipality seems to be uncannily sympathetic to Dutch culture—which may be explained somewhat by the Dutch assistants who worked on the project. Thus, one feels that the tradition of the pre-war Dutch "new objectivity" was somehow implicit in this work from the beginning. In addition, while the fenestration provides, in accordance with Dutch law, a specific number of operable windows both within and without the atrium, these lights do more than meet the legal requirement since their detailing recalls both the profile and the proportion of the cabinetmaker Gerrit Rietveld. Aside from these references, Meier's design conforms to Dutch tradition in other respects, most notably with regard to the optimization of natural light. Moreover, the general use of tubular-steel and wire-mesh balustrading seems to be equally native in as much as these items recall the work of Herman Hertzberger. Last but not least, the aerial *passerelles,* which traverse the atrium to provide convenient access from one side of the office complex to the other, are reminiscent of the glazed conveyor belts we find in the canonical Brinkman's and Van der Vlugt's Van Nelle factory of 1929, an evocation that tends to be reinforced by the freestanding glazed elevator shafts.

Equally Dutch is the sense of communality that pervades the atrium, for here most of the public amenities are immediately accessible, and even where access is restricted, mutually interpenetrating lines of sight prevail. This popular panoptic dimension is equally part of the Dutch tradition for it goes along with that particular mixture of conformism and anarchy that pervades the Netherlands at every turn. All of this seems to be summed up by the giant portico that spans between the central library and Hulshoff's furniture emporium. This largely transparent, elevated rotunda and trapezoid are also penetrated by sight lines, whereby one may catch a glimpse of the library from the elevated corridors and bridges of the galleria. The library, flooded with light on all levels, is equipped with a continuous escalator bank running between floors; a provision which makes for unceasing movement on every level, bestowing a measure of accessibility rarely found in contemporary libraries, where the omnipresent book-lined volumes, artificially lit, often convey a sense of exclusion and claustrophobia.

On entering through the monumental southwestern portico of this civic galleria one passes into the cubic, all-glass lobby, which is deftly inserted into the twelve-story, glazed wall that closes this end of the atrium. This structural *tour de force*, made out of square-sectioned tubular steel, at once imparts a feeling of monumental grandeur to the ensuing space. It is also the first in a series of permeable planes extending for the full height of the atrium. These become, in effect virtual veils, produced by the superimposition of stacked balustrades and *passerelles*, which generate a scrim-like haze in the middle of the space that counters the false perspective created by the 10.5-degree difference between the flanking walls of the atrium. While delaying the foreshortening of the space, they also assume the character of a mirage for as one passes under each stack, it subsequently reappears behind one, hovering in the air with a persistence resembling sea mist. This effect recalls Moholy-Nagy's light-space modulator of 1930, since each dematerialized stack of walkways induces a varying proliferation of light and shade at different scales.

In a similar way the overall volume is constantly transformed by an ever-changing pattern of light and shade, first through the way in which the full-height curtain wall casts its shadow on the drum of the council chamber and then through the way the deep beams, carrying the skylights over the atrium, modulate the vast volume through a constantly changing shadow pattern. This alternating aesthetic is complemented by the white-enameled panels of the flanking walls which produce a series of highlights and reflections that further diffuse the ephemerality of the aerial walkways. This modulation of space by light, so typical of Meier, is further enhanced by the cantilevered balconies that open off the elevator lobbies on each floor, providing vantage points from which to contemplate the spatial spectacle. At the same time these anthropomorphically scaled elements bestow upon the vast space a reassuring intimacy. They encourage our active perception of its volume, which at one instant appears to be vast and at another, relatively small; a perceptual instability that is often an indication of architectural quality.

The central vista collapses once one views the space traversely across the axis; a re-orientation which only serves to confirm one's perception of the building as a "city in miniature." On one side, one sees a café terrace together with a long public service counter followed by two shops; a sequence that is terminated by the drum of the wedding hall while, on the other, one looks down on the information center together with a curved stair leading up to the council chamber. At the first floor a wide gallery runs along the northwestern side of the atrium, giving access to a series of private offices and interview rooms. These private suites are subtly illuminated during the day by full-height glass-block walls. Finally, one of the prime virtues of this building is to allow the citizen to overlook the various activities of the city hall from an elevated position. Thus one may survey the roof of the council chamber, where the general public meets with councilors on a one-to-one basis. This elevated semipublic arena is set by the recessed four-story café terrace which lets into the opposing atrium. The other primary point of focus in the atrium is by the recessed, cubic loggia, situated at the first floor reserved solely for municipal employees.

It is important to note that Meier had to insist on a council chamber being included in the final brief, arguing that a municipality without such a representational space could hardly be regarded as a city hall at all. Meier had to do something of the same in the case of the Hartford Seminary, where at his insistence a chapel was finally incorporated. Is it not symptomatic of our instrumental age that the clients in both instances were initially indifferent to the presence of the traditional symbolic element?

While this galleria is ultimately more of a bureaucratic clearing house than a city hall in the old sense it is still nonetheless readable as a major civic symbol, in the first instance because of its character as a *res publica* in which all sorts of civic rituals, public displays and performances may be enacted while protected from the weather; in the second because it has introduced a gargantuan horizontal scale into the city that more than compensates for its excessive size by helping to unify the rather piecemeal urban development by which it is attended, including Rem Koolhaas's dance theater, Herman Hertzberger's cinémathèque and a hotel designed by Carol Weber.

As we have already seen, Meier has created some of his finest works to date in Europe. Unlike Frank Lloyd Wright, who invariably dealt with the endemic "placelessness" of the average American city by inserting into its fabric, totally introspective, semipublic buildings, Meier's more extroverted approach has hardly served him quite as well when confronted with the universal *motopia* of the States. This much is suggested by his design for the Santa Monica Beach Hotel (1987), which attempts to establish its own micro-urbanity against the random contours of the coast and the vast expanse of the sea. On the other hand Meier seems to have proven himself in Europe as the only American architect of his generation capable of working at a civic scale, as we may judge, say, from the low-rise, high-density housing scheme that he designed for the International Bauausstellung, Berlin in 1982. This regrettably unrealized perimeter development, following the sweep of the Landwehrkanal, was, in my view, one of few truly seminal schemes projected for IBA in that it demonstrated how the generous low-rise scale of Bruno Taut's legacy on the outskirts of Berlin's nineteenth-century core, could be introduced into the center of the city.

Since the early eighties Meier has had the fortune to be recognized by European corporate clients as an architect of world stature. This much is confirmed by a series of industrial commissions beginning, in 1981, with the brilliant, microurban perimeter office complex, projected for Renault on a triangular leftover site in Boulogne-Billancourt; a work which unfortunately was not to be built. Bounded on one side by the Seine and a grove of trees and on the other by dense urban fabric, this was an exceptionally rational, multi-courtyard scheme, animated by the undulating form of the main reception building.

While Meier's comparable bureaucratic campus, projected for Siemens in the center of Munich, was not developed to the same level of resolution as Renault, despite the generous layout of the initial proposal of 1983, the disused Pirelli Bicocca site in Milan provided an occasion for a project that was equally dynamic in its urbanistic scope. Meier's Bicocca was broken down into a series of courtyard blocks available for different kinds of use. Meier's subsequent proposal for the transformation of the disused Fiat plant at Lingotto originally designed by engineer Mattè Trucco as a particularly compelling reinforced concrete megaform was to afford an equally fertile point of departure. Ironically enough, given the iconographic role that this particular factory played in the prehistory of the modern movement, Meier proposed to transform this once exemplary automobile plant into a *unité d'habitation!*

Given the private patrons who have formed the main body of Meier's domestic clients in the past, the last thing one would expect from a practice of this genre is that the architect should respond to the challenge of low-cost housing. It is paradoxical that of the twenty-two projects designed by a whole slew of prestigious architects for Naples in 1987, Meier's in-fill housing for the perimeter of the Spanish Quarter should prove to be one of the more sensitive and modest projects for the redevelopment of the city. As Meier wrote of in his interstitial proposal: "Faced with the critical problem of how to put a new building in a historical context we have proposed constructing a series of housing units situated so that the existing fabric of the site is preserved. Contrary to the Corbusian vision of housing slabs isolated from their context, we have responded to the given fabric by literally extruding the building volume from the current street plan." Meier's ribbon housing was projected as a suture in the urban fabric, linking a congested slum back into the fabric of the city.

Historically and topographically Barcelona is perhaps the most delicate urban fabric in which Meier has been asked to intervene to date, and the resulting mass of the municipal Museum of Contemporary Art seems to have been appropriately inflected with regard to the surrounding pattern of streets and squares. The central drum together with its attendant concave walls functions as a kind of pedestrian valve between the garden court at the rear of the museum and the Plaça dels Angels onto which the building opens. This partially concealed passage forms part of a labyrinthine promenade that runs through the Gothic *barrio* in such a way as to connect a number of different cultural institutions. While Meier's figurative syntax reappears here against an insistently horizontal façade, this work nonetheless remains one of the most sensitively scaled urban interventions that the office has achieved to date.

The Getty Center for Art and Humanities in Los Angeles (1985–97), under continual development in Meier's office for thirteen years, will prove to be his ultimate "city in miniature," not only with respect to the States, but also in comparison with his European work. Amounting to a 110-acre site with panoramic views over Los Angeles the Getty Center has become the ultimate cultural focus for the entire region. Carefully laid into the undulating contours of a spectacular

Museum für Kunsthandwerk,
Frankfurt am Main, Germany, 1978-85.

following pages
City Hall and Central Library,
The Hague, Netherlands, 1989-95.

site, the Getty comprises an organic complex of buildings, with adjacent courts and gardens, covering some 24 acres, together with a 5-acre "propylea" situated at the northern end of the site.

The main complex is organized about two converging ridges separated by a ravine. This last is partially filled with earth, taken from the site, since one of the conditions of the development permit was that all soil had to remain within the confines of the site. The new topography produced by this vast earth-moving enterprise resulted in a spectacular landscape, closely integrated into the original scrub vegetation covering the lower reaches of the acropolis. The dominant axial shift running through the entire plan corresponds to the 22-degree angle of the San Diego Freeway as it travels north in a straight line from the Los Angeles County Airport. A countering secondary axis, running through the center of the museum, compounds and parallels the line of the freeway before it veers eastwards away from the longitudinal body of the main ridge. The principal public access is from the north where automobiles coming off the Sepulveda Boulevard pass under the freeway into a "propylea" reception arena where visitors leave their cars in a sixteen hundred-vehicle subterranean garage. They are then transported by light rail to the top of the acropolis, ascending some 246 feet in the process. A two-car shuttle traversing the three-quarter mile run in five minutes is capable of moving eighty people per trip. The seven hundred-man staff, comprising scholars, administrators and service personnel, take the undulating access road to the top of the acropolis where they park in an undercroft immediately below the main entry court. This court, established at the convergence of three axial routes, serves as the main distribution point for the entire complex. From this agora visitors and staff proceed on foot according to the three itineraries. The first of these conducts the visitor in a reverse direction up a monumental stair to the portico of the main four hundred-seat auditorium, the second leads straight up a stepped causeway into the museum and a third leads, after a short rise, into the terraced access way of a stepped garden, culminating in a planted amphitheater at the lowest point of the site.

In terms of its overall assembly the complex divides up along two ridges as follows: first, a continuous cranked sequence along the eastern ridge comprising the Auditorium and Trust Building, the Getty Conservation Institute and the Museum; second, at the crest of the short western ridge, the largely cylindrical form of the Center for the History of Art and the Humanities. Between these two ridges lies the principal garden while at the highest point, close to the entry court, there is a freestanding food services building housing restaurants and café facilities, having panoramic views, over Brentwood to the west. The most consolidated cluster of this entire complex is appropriately enough the museum itself comprising a set of opaque, top-lit prisms containing the galleries, the cornices of which do not rise beyond the permitted 65-foot height above the crest of the hill. The outer stone-faced walls of these galleries, readily visible from the San Diego Freeway, rise some 100 feet or so above their apparent foundations. Largely planned on a square grid, the museum sequence is organized in section so as to allow the visitor to pass easily through the top-lit chronological arrangement of the main collection. The other gallery spaces, the bookstore, the decorative arts sequence, the temporary exhibition space and the photographic gallery are woven between those floors of the museum, largely devoted to painting and sculpture.

Aside from the main auditorium, the executive offices and the Center for Conservation, the other primary mass-form is the Center for the History of Art, situated on the opposing ridge. This complex is organized around a top-lit centroid that penetrates into a vast irregular undercroft containing the stacks. The central part of this vast, two-story podium, housing nearly one million volumes, together with its three-story "crown" of scholars' offices, seminar rooms and a two-hundred seat lecture hall, are all concentrically organized as circumferential volumes, subdivided by partitions that radiate out from the center of the largely top-lit, cylindrical reading room.

The civility of this "hill-town" derives, as one would expect, not so much from the volumetric sequences within the buildings themselves as from the open space between them, and one senses that almost as much time has been lavished on the picturesque setting as on the organization and accommodation of the building programme. It is to be regretted, in this regard, that due to local culture politics and an accommodating act of patronage on the part of the client, Meier's original concept for a stepped garden leading down to the amphitheater at the lowest point of the site was not executed. This descent, broken up by fugal sequences to either side of a central axis, was originally conceived as a reinterpretation of the Villa d'Este. In the event it was replaced by an "artistic" set piece designed by the Californian artist Robert Irwin.

From an architectonic standpoint, it may be claimed that this is Meier at his most "baroque," wherein dispersed architectonic fragments are collaged together in such a way as one can no longer clearly perceive the "figure" of one element against the "ground" of another. And while one may argue that this conforms to the prevailing sensibility of our time, one would also have to admit that after a short while, the game loses any sense of significant articulation so that one's interest flags before the endless differentiation of one form from the next. The facing of the entire steel-framed complex in cream-colored, enameled steel panels combined with split travertine slabs, deployed as a rain shield over windowless masses, does little to enhance the overall legibility of the form.

Despite its refusal to allow Meier's design for the central gardens to prevail, the Getty Center clearly belongs to that long tradition of cultural enclaves in America, whereby the economic maximization that otherwise rules the entire continent finds itself momentarily suspended. Like Stanford, Harvard, Wellesley, and Cranbrook, to cite only a handful of the more idyllic campuses, the Getty Center is a heterotopia that harks back to the patrician values of a bourgeois America prior to rise of the military/industrial complex and the dominance of the media. As Meier is only too aware, it is unlikely that such an extravagant act of patronage will ever be repeated, for the commodified surplus of our digital, telematic age is hardly inclined towards this kind of elitist culture. And yet, besides being a topographic tour de force and one of the most well-stocked centers of cultural study in the world, the Getty is also, as of now, a place of enormous popular appeal, with hundreds of tourists and regular visitors coming to the site every day.

From the late eighties onwards, while the Getty was under development, the emphasis in the other commissions received by the office seems to have shifted to the outer membrane, where the image of a work would depend on its appearance as a luminous membrane animated by horizontal fenestration and brise soleil. At this juncture the dominant image becomes that of a shallow relief, suffused with light. In these works the tessellated elevation is often offset by an opaque cylindrical or conic element that is either placed in front of or behind the façade. This formula is already evident in the Museum of Contemporary Art, Barcelona (1987–95) where a free form is played off against the horizontal fenestration and a cylinder appears as a counterform to the rear of the building.

In the Canal+ Television Headquarters, Paris (1988–92) the syncopated surface of a gently curving wall derives solely from the pattern of the glazing while the rotund element assumes the form of a truncated cone encompassing a screening room. In a similar way, syncopated glazing and projecting horizontal louvers are combined to form a particularly dynamic relief, on the northwestern elevation of Meier's Royal Dutch Mills building erected in Hilversum of 1992, while in the Rachofsky House, Texas, dating, as a design, from 1991, thin paneled walls are animated by a neoplastic spatial play that is interwoven, as in Meier's earlier houses, with neo-Corbusian elements, most notably, in this instance, a free-standing cylindrical column grid. The Rachofsky House is a luminous prism designed for bachelor living and the exhibition of art. Based on a double square in plan, its lightweight aestheticism is taken to such an extreme that it borders on the effete. By way of contrast, the Federal Building and Courthouse at Islip, New York (1993–2000) transposes the format of the Barcelona museum into a large slab block in which the "figure" of a monumental cone is obtrusively situated before the "ground" of a syncopated neo-Corbusian façade.

In three successive works developed during the last five years of the century, Meier's latter-day emphasis on the membrane will finally come to be combined with tectonically expressive structural form; first in the Federal Office Building and Courthouse, projected for Phoenix, Arizona in 1995, then the Neugebauer House, Naples, Florida, dating from the same year, and finally in the Jubilee Church, Rome, designed in 1995 and still under construction. Where the Sandra Day O'Connor Courthouse, as it is now called, is in effect a hi-tech "green" shed set against the fierce Arizona sun, the Neuegebauer House departs from Meier's habitual syntax through the adoption of a butterfly roof, resting on hollow steel framework thereby covering a monumental dwelling, some 280 feet in length. A comparable technical and tectonic shift is evident in the Phoenix Courthouse, which is essentially a seven-story, 350 by 150-foot concourse, covered by a steel space-frame and closed on the south and west by courtrooms and other supplementary court facilities. In an equally sweeping manner the Neugebauer residence is in effect a giant loggia, beneath which is accommodated the body of an exceptionally luxurious four-bedroom house. In both works an exposed steel frame is an essential part of the building's expression.

The Phoenix Courthouse occupies a unique place in Meier's architecture in as much as it is his first sustainable hi-tech work. It amounts in fact to nothing more than ingeniously louvered glass shed, in which air entering below the roof is treated at the sixth floor level with jets of atomized water vapor, which immediately have the effect of cooling the air, thereby causing it to gradually descend toward the floor. It becomes further cooled on its descent by conditioned air issuing from the courtrooms and the access galleries flanking the atrium space. It then passes out of the "greenhouse" volume several feet above the floor, by virtue of natural convection. A brief technical assessment reads: "Exploiting this low-cost passive technology along with various shading devices, the temperature on the floor of the atrium during hot summer days is generally 20 degrees cooler than on the street. For the majority of the year, the atrium can be maintained at a very comfortable 75 degrees Fahrenheit, a significant achievement for a large glass-enclosed open space designed for one of the hottest places in the United States."[6]

Of all of Meier's buildings to play with the theme of a cylinder set against an orthogonal form, this is surely the most successful, since in this instance a freestanding, glazed drum in the middle of the atrium serves to house the large special proceedings courtroom which is, in effect, the symbolic heart of the building. It is hard to imagine anything more appropriate as an integrated artwork than the suspended ceiling that roofs this space, designed by the American glass artist James

Neugebauer House,
Naples, Florida, 1995-98.

following pages
Sandra Day O'Connor
United States Courthouse,
Phoenix, Arizona, 1995-2000.

Carpenter who, for this occasion, created a shallow inverted dome of opaque glass; a particularly intimate form which has proven to be a particularly fitting treatment for the honorific character of the major courtroom.

One can hardly ignore the Scandinavian affinities of the Jubilee Church in as much as its concrete shell roof inevitably recalls the elaborate concrete shells of Jørn Utzon's Sydney Opera House (1956). This particularly striking departure from Meier's established repertoire may be due to the fact that Meier has never designed a church before. However, unlike the more complex additive geometry of Utzon's shells, Meier's overlapping spherical segments are derived from shifted circles of the same diameter. Conceived as a "city crown" for the displaced center of a somewhat isolated housing scheme on the outskirts of Rome, the original *parti* for this parish center was divided into sacred and secular zones, with the church precinct being situated to the south and the secular community center to the north. The dividing east-west line between these two zones is still registered by the east-west alignment of the nave, which is slightly inclined toward the southeast. Along with the rhythm established by the concentric shells, this axial inclination seems to have been response to the topography, above all to a small hill situated to the northwest of the church and to the organic formation of the housing blocks that flank the sides of the paved *sagrato* on its southern and northern boundaries. This inflected arrangement is reinforced by a roadway and a parking lot to the south and by a tree-lined boundary to the north, culminating in a square, formal cluster of fifteen trees to be planted adjacent to the *sagrato* entrance. The hierarchical and secular connotations of this organization in section and plan are evident from the fact that the *sagrato* extends into the heart of the housing complex, providing an open plaza for public assembly.

As in the other two tectonic works, a double lenticular truss of welded tubular steel serves as the ultimate crown of the church. It is situated within the apex of the nave, where it helps to sustain a canted roof light coming off the highest, innermost shell as it slopes down onto the roof of the community building below. Like Le Corbusier's Ronchamp, one can well imagine the concentric shells of this church radiating out as a formal concatenation over the surrounding landscape, while maintaining its serrated mass-form as the terminus of an axis passing through the center of the housing.

Apart from certain neo-Corbusian affinities which are an all too familiar aspect of Meier's career, something needs to be said here about other affinities which, directly or indirectly, present themselves as a series of sub-themes running throughout his work; themes that do much to account for a changing spectrum of undeclared, subliminal intentions. In the first instance, one has to acknowledge the truly uncanny capacity of Meier's architecture to serve as a device for the modulation of light, so much so that rather than being merely received as a hermetic *white* architecture, it should be more perceptively seen as an architecture of *light* in as much as it not only responds to every imperceptible change in the nature of the ambient light, but it also at times attains such a level of luminosity as to dematerialize before one's eyes. The affinity here, apart from the propensity for immateriality in the late modern world, is surely the South German Baroque and above all the work of Balthazar Neumann with whose architecture Meier was exceptionally impressed during his sojourn in the American Academy of Rome in 1974.

The second most unacknowledged generic character in Meier's architecture comes from his absolute obsession with the principle of cladding which first comes definitively to the fore with the Giovannitti House of 1983. Here the *quadrat*, endlessly repeated at both a macro and a micro scale, determines every conceivable element. This total revetment of the entire surface in square porcelain steel panels inescapably recalls the work of the Austrian Jugendstil master Otto Wagner, for whose work Meier's displays an understandable affinity at more than one level. Apart from their common emphasis on tessellated cladding, (see Wagner's penchant for *Bekleidung),* this affinity seems to be confirmed by the use of Wagnerian figures in the perspectival renderings of both the Frankfurt and the High Museums, not to mention the presence of collaged trees drawn from K.F. Schinkel's *Sammlung Architektonischer Entwurfe* of 1840 to whom, as it happens, Wagner was indebted in his turn. Further confirmation of this romantic Germanic connection may be found in Meier's furniture designs for Knoll, beginning in the late seventies, wherein one may detect not only shades of Wagner but also the "ladderback" furniture of C.R. Mackintosh, who surely exercised a passing ornamental influence on the architecture of Wagner.

That Meier's aesthetic is as much ornamental in its deeper affinities as it is volumetric and spatial, testifies to the latent presence of Frank Lloyd Wright lying beneath the surface of his work; for while he has abjured any direct emulation or elaboration of Wright's architectonic syntax, his entire output is predicated on a vision of the world which is inescapably transcendental and, in that sense, quintessentially American; Wright's perennially progressive midwestern belief, let us say, that all ultimately is destined for the best in the best of all possible worlds. Thus, despite their occasional civic displacement, his prismatic luminous spaces, aspirationally opening onto endlessly rolling picturesque landscapes à la Wright, are redolent with the myth of a pluralist democracy set in an infinitely benevolent nature, restorative by definition, no matter what instrumental ruthlessness may threaten in the interim to lay the world to waste. There is nothing here of that implacably tragic Greek vision that ultimately touches

everything that Le Corbusier projected, particularly after the apocalypse of the Second World War. In his tectonic, painterly exuberance, Meier keeps a safe distance from the unnerving, demoralizing Gramscian prospect that the old is dying and the new cannot be born and that in this interregnum many morbid symptoms appear.

1 Scully, Vincent. *Frank Lloyd Wright*. New York: Braziller, 1960.
2 Allen, Stan. "Richard Meier's Working Space: The Uses of Abstraction." In *Richard Meier Architect*. New York & Los Angeles: Monacelli & MOCA, Los Angeles, 1999, pp 17-18.
3 See *Richard Meier Architect 1964–1984*. New York: Rizzoli, 1984, p. 97.
4 Cohen, Jean Louis."Creative Repetition." In *Richard Meier Architect*. New York & Los Angeles: Monacelli & MOCA, Los Angeles, 1999, p. 36.
5 See *Richard Meier Architect 1964–1984*. New York: Rizzoli, 1984, pp. 269-70.
6 *Sandra Day O'Connor, United States Courthouse.* Brochure. Washington: GSA, US General Services Administration, Public Buildings Service, 2000, p. 16.

Bronx Developmental Center, Bronx,
New York, 1970–77.

Works and Projects

1965–2002

1965
1967

Smith House

Views of the house from the east
and of the rear facing onto the sea.

View of the back of the house,
facing onto Long Island Sound,
from the southwest.

Site plan and plans of the third,
second and ground floors.

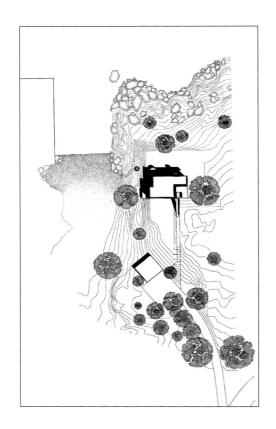

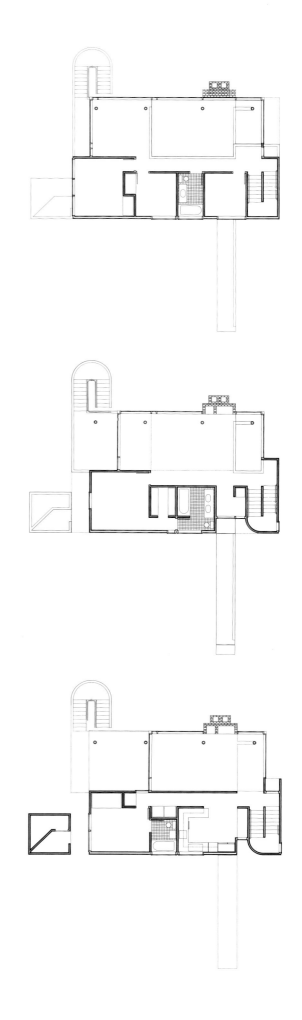

Northwest and southeast elevations
and longitudinal and cross sections.

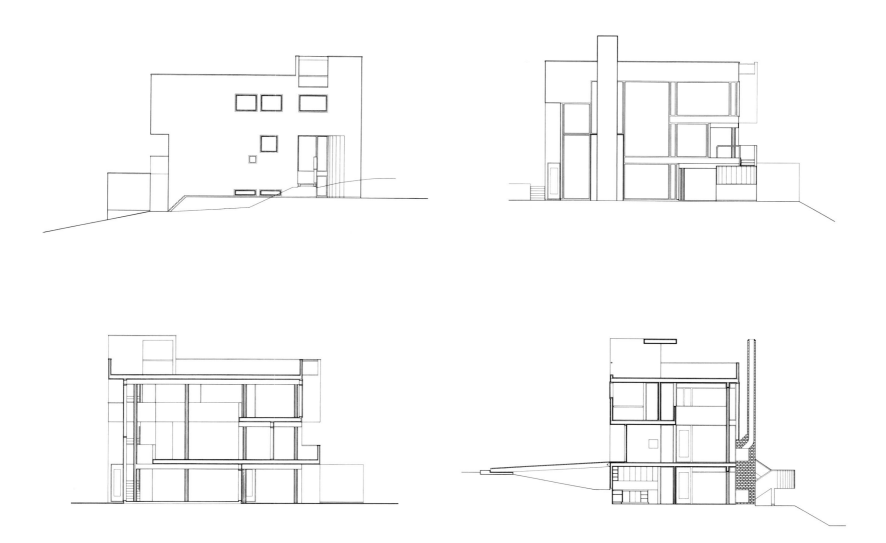

On Materiality
Richard Meier

Several years ago I had occasion to return to the Smith House in Darien, Connecticut, with a photographer commissioned to document the building for publication. The particular day of our visit was quite extraordinary: a brilliant October day of very intense and colorful light, very sharp and clear as a fall day of little humidity is apt to be. I was pleased that we had this opportunity to see and record the house in such favorable conditions. When we arrived, however, and the photographer began to set up his equipment, a sudden change in wind direction brought a great cloud of smoke from an adjoining property where a neighbor was burning leaves. As the smoke thickened and enveloped the house—and as my frustration rose with the irony of such a beautiful light consumed in this gray fog—I noticed the photographer furiously taking pictures. My immediate reaction was one of alarm. I encouraged him to stop. He waved me off, insisting this was a fleeting and exceptional moment.

Several weeks later I had a chance to review these photographs. They were incredible. The image of the house as a clear composed presence in light had been fundamentally modified. In many of these prints, the house was visible as if through an irregular scrim, circumscribed by a strange glow as the light radiated through the smoke. Its contours were only partially discernable and its precision as an object very much obscured. But this was not an image for which the house was designed; not, in any event, in the conscious operations of either myself or the owners as we had conceived the building. As the photographer took his pictures, I had been alarmed at the prospect of it being documented so uncharacteristically. In fact, it revealed to me something quite extraordinary about the building and its relationship to site.

I recall this particular experience because it illustrates to me one of the essential understandings we must all come to as architects. One likes to think that the architect has the ability to plan everything, but this is not so. In my work, I have come to rely more and more on the juxtaposition of that which one makes against that which one does not. This has to do with the play of architecture's inherent artificiality against an unpredictable and dynamic context. I believe this dynamic quality of natural and urban phenomena is very much a part of man's experience of architecture. This is true not simply in the appreciation of the object from without—as this experience at the Smith House illustrates—but in the actual occupation of the building's interior spaces as well.

This sense of the building is conditioned by many things—rotating shadows, changing seasons, expanding and contracting light, the world of change that takes place outside its limits—in such a way that the building acquires a life much more complex than the architect could ever hope to control. I believe that there is an important moment in an architect's life when one gives up one's attempts at such control. Perhaps this is when a very real dialogue with context may begin.

My particular understanding of that dialogue has led me to occupy a somewhat controversial position within the world of architectural criticism. I have been figuratively accused of placing buildings as if by helicopter onto the landscape. One might interpret this suggestion to mean that the buildings remain alien from their context; that they do not literally share the animate or organic qualities of their place. I confess that I cannot see how this might be otherwise. To the extent that buildings are made up of materials that, in a strict sense, cease to live—that are fallen and no longer grow, that are unearthed and are no longer part of a fluctuating and metamorphic cycle—one is engaged in an act of willful artificiality. Architecture is not the product of a natural process. It simply is what you make it. I have always thought this was a

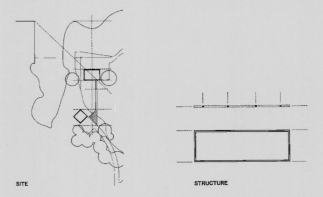

SITE

STRUCTURE

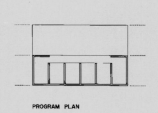

PROGRAM PLAN

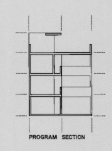

PROGRAM SECTION

compliment being paid to me, this suggestion of the artificiality of the structure, this man-made presence that the buildings have. For some, this creates a distance between the view and the work, which I very much regret. I do not wish to alienate people from the landscape they choose to inhabit, nor do I wish them to feel in conflict with my work. It has simply been my intention to propose an alternate form of integration.

In my earlier work, this integration was pursued through a very intentional process of dematerialization. This has to do with an attempt to subvert the specific character of the framed, which is that much more intense. I am committed, however, to a rigorous investigation of the physical consequences of such an operation. To dematerialize does not mean to remove from weather and time. One must accept these things and let them inform one's construction. In this sense, the inevitability of enclosure comes to bear, and the continuity of inside and outside that was so important to early masters of the modern movement must be questioned.

I have gone through this exercise myself. In a very early house I wanted to develop this free relationship of inside and outside space. To that end—and very much in the spirit of Frank Lloyd Wright at Fallingwater, an architect and a building I continue to admire very much—I proposed a brick wall running continuously through a living space to the adjacent garden. The house was constructed as such and in the end proved unsatisfactory to me. In the garden this brick wall rapidly began to show the effects of water and wind, to assume a thin layer of moss, to stratify, so to speak, as its lower portion soiled and its parapet weathered. Within the house itself, the wall remained as it was at the time of construction. The two halves—one inside, the other outside—had acquired two lives. The myth was destroyed.

I have come to appreciate the completeness of this separation that occurs along the plane of the building enclosure. Glass does not change this fact. A wall of glass is as strong and as powerful a membrane as any material in describing the limits of enclosed space—in setting up two futures, as it were, for one wall.

With that understanding, I am no longer in pursuit of this conceptual interpenetration of interior and exterior space. My work has proceeded with an investigation of what it means to create enclosed space; in some cases, simply to create a room. I am fascinated by the interior world of light and shadow that exists free of the degenerative qualities of weather. I believe this to be the promise of architectural space. It is perhaps the promise of white as well. But I am also intrigued by the very different way in which a building exists in the natural or urban worlds beyond its control.

Again, the Smith House comes to mind. Here the project was conceived so as to sit between two trees very close to the base of the building. It was very important to us that it be sited this way, and we took many precautions to insure that these trees were not lost during construction. We did this with a simple ambition: to preserve the landscape which had prompted its inhabitation. But we could not have anticipated the precise way in which those trees have grown and affected the house over time. The have, in fact, created a virtual umbrella over both sides of the building, filtering light differently depending on the time of the year and modeling its colors in ways much more intricate than we could ever have planned. I believe the success of the house lies in the capacity to absorb and enter into a dialogue with temporal phenomena of light and context. They are, in the end, its material.

October 1987

Richard Meier. "Essay." In *Perspecta* 24. New York: Rizzoli, 1988, pp. 104-105.

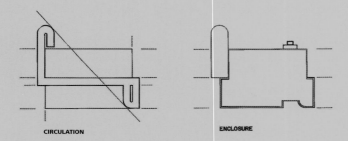

CIRCULATION

ENCLOSURE

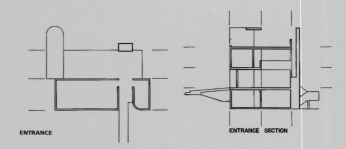

ENTRANCE

ENTRANCE SECTION

1966
1967

Hoffman House

Views of the northwest front,
of the southwest end
and entrance front.

Site plan and plans of the ground
and second floors.

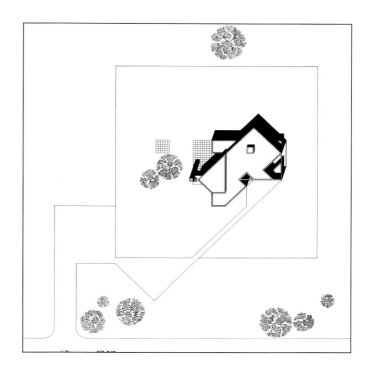

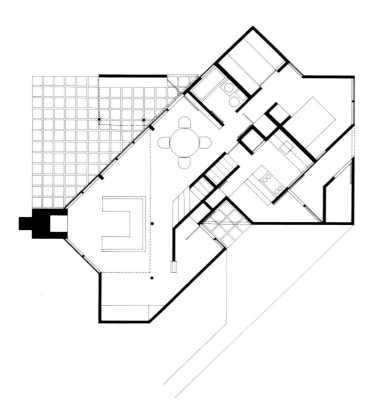

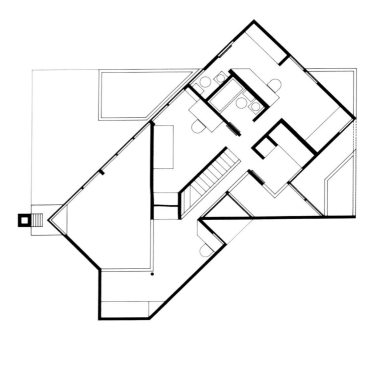

1967
1970
Westbeth Artists' Housing

Views of the courtyard inside the block.

Plans of the second and ground floors.

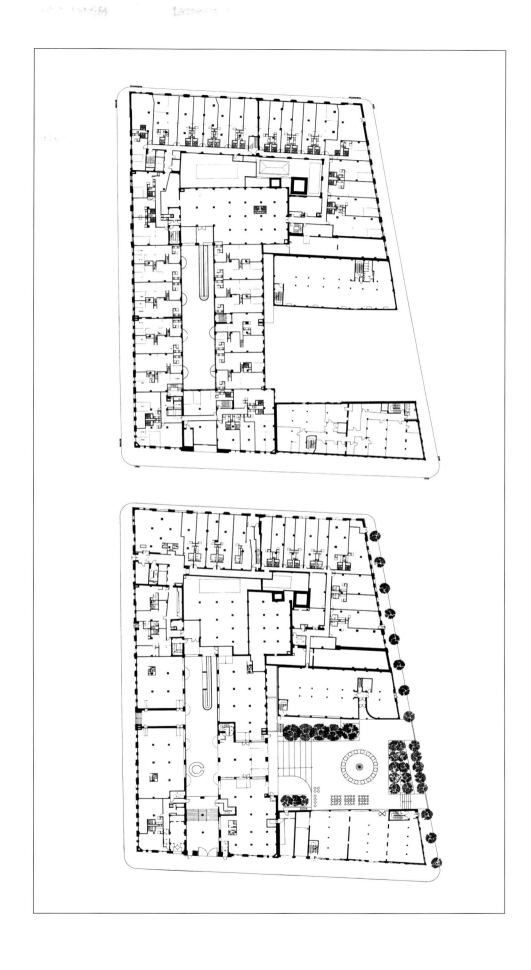

1967
1969

Saltzman House

View of the south front.

Views of the north façade, the raised
external walkway and the west end.

View from the southwest.

Site plan and diagram by Richard Meier.

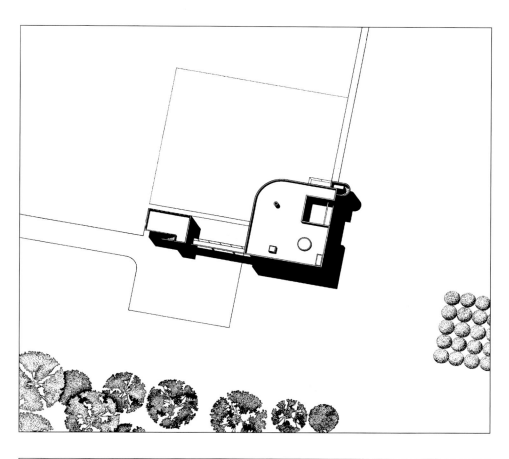

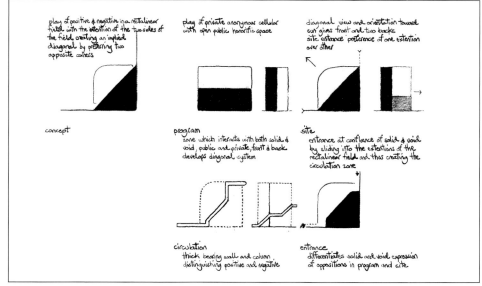

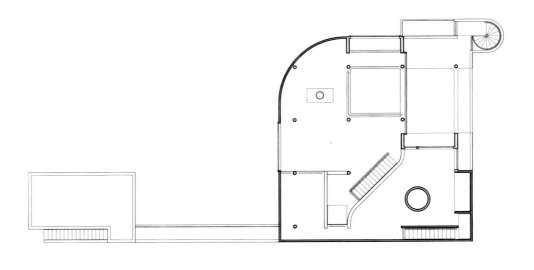

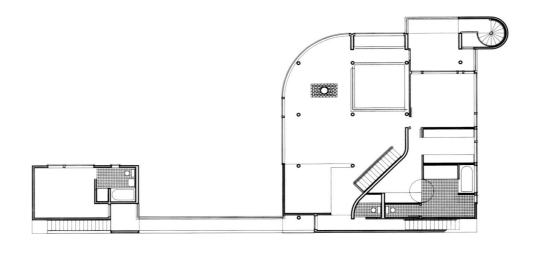

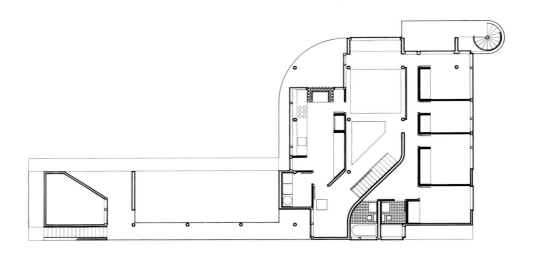

Plans of the third, second
and ground floors.

North and south elevations
and longitudinal section.

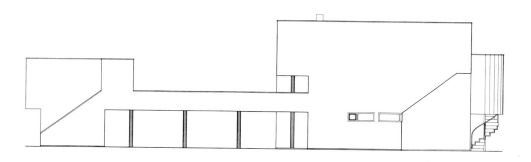

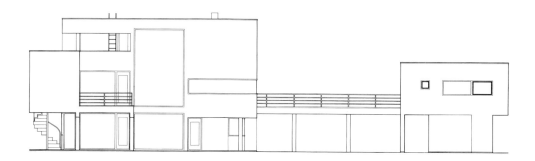

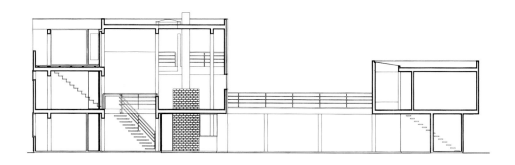

Views of the model.

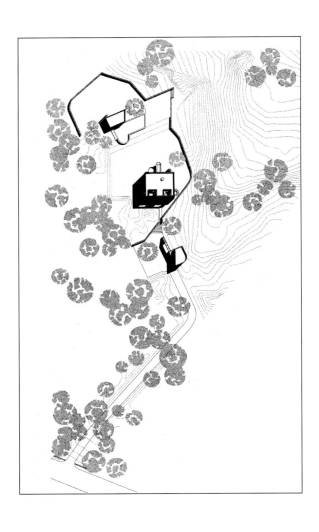

General plan.
Plans at the level of the roof terrace
and of the second and ground floors.

Cross section and axonometric cutaways.

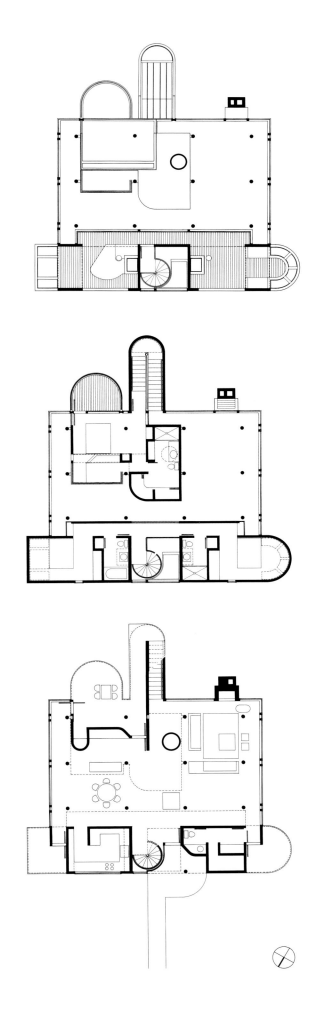

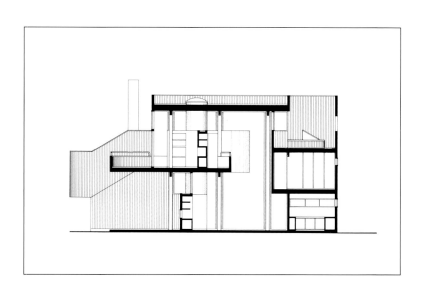

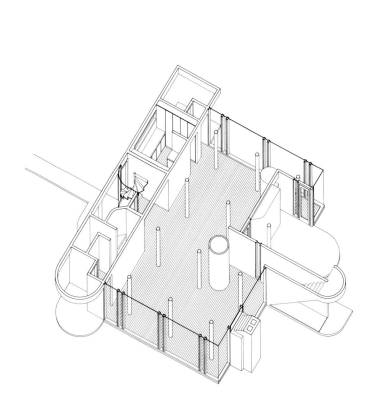

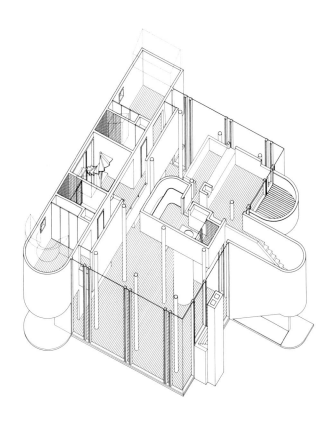

1969
1971

House in Old Westbury

Views from the southwest and the north,
with the caretaker's house
in the foreground.

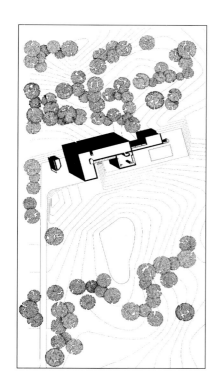

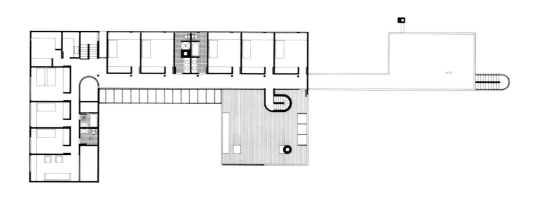

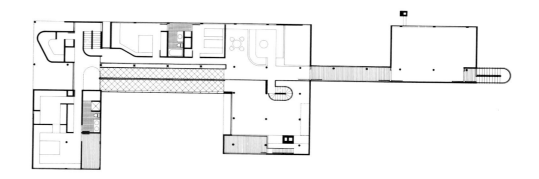

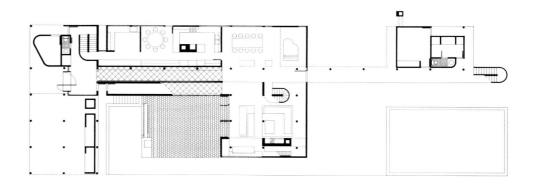

Details of the pavilion on the south end.

Site plan, plans of the third, second and ground floors and longitudinal section through the internal ramp.

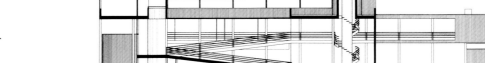

1969
1974

Twin Parks Northeast Housing

Views of the internal plaza from
the northwest and southeast.

Views of the tall block on Southern
Boulevard and the internal plaza
from the south.

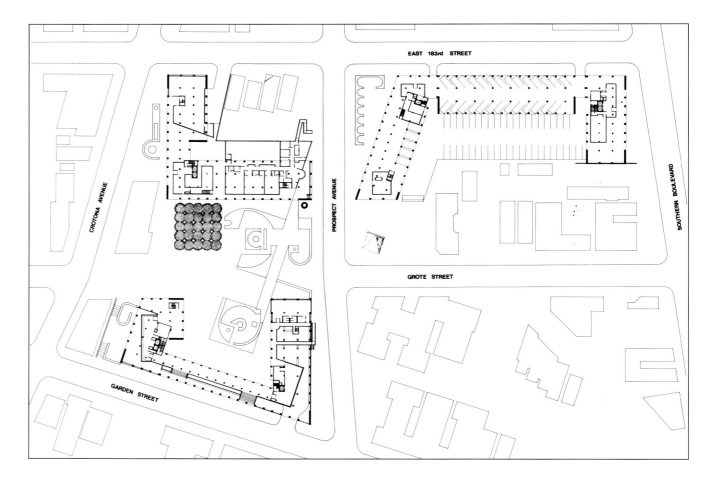

EAST 183rd STREET

CROTONA AVENUE

PROSPECT AVENUE

SOUTHERN BOULEVARD

GROTE STREET

GARDEN STREET

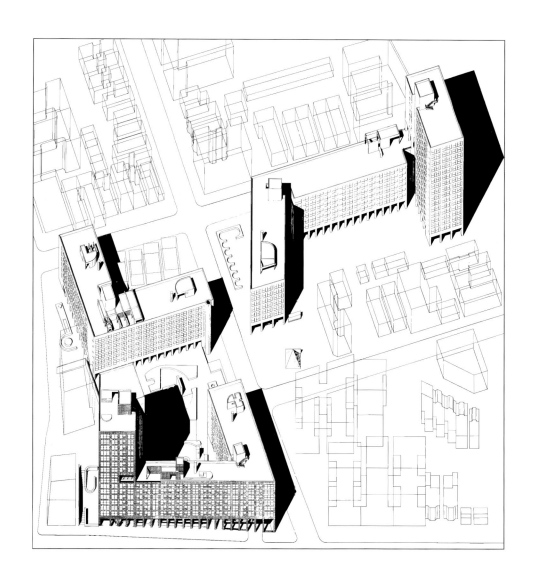

Area plan and plan of the ground floor.

General axonometric projection.

1970
1977

Bronx Developmental Center

View of the complex from the
Hutchinson River Parkway to the east.

Views of the residential wing
to the southeast, and of the block
of the health facilities to the northwest.

View of the southern inner courtyard and detail of the central gallery linking the two wings of the complex.

Details of the modular facing aluminium paneling.

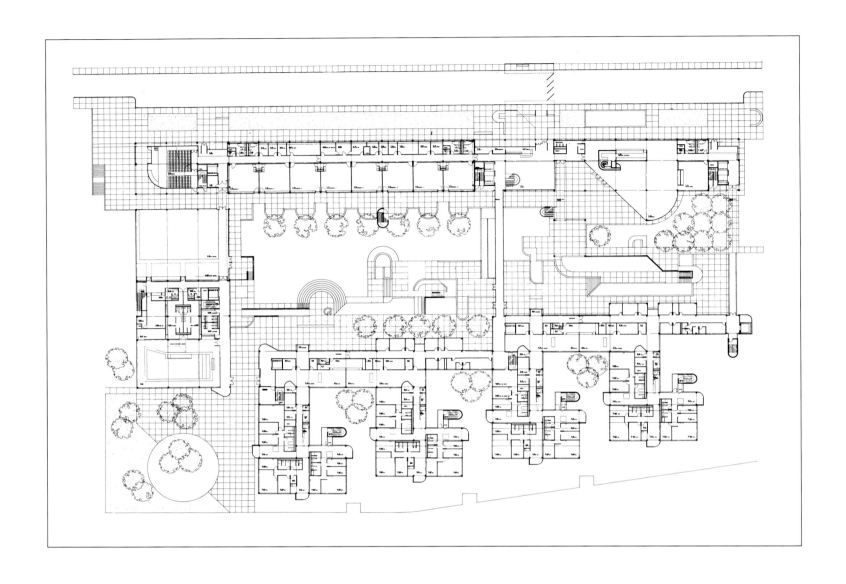

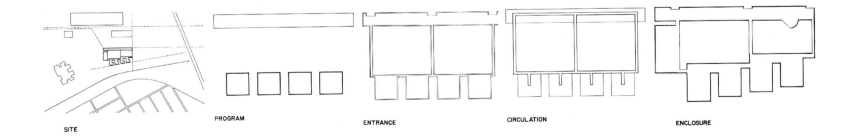

SITE

PROGRAM

ENTRANCE

CIRCULATION

ENCLOSURE

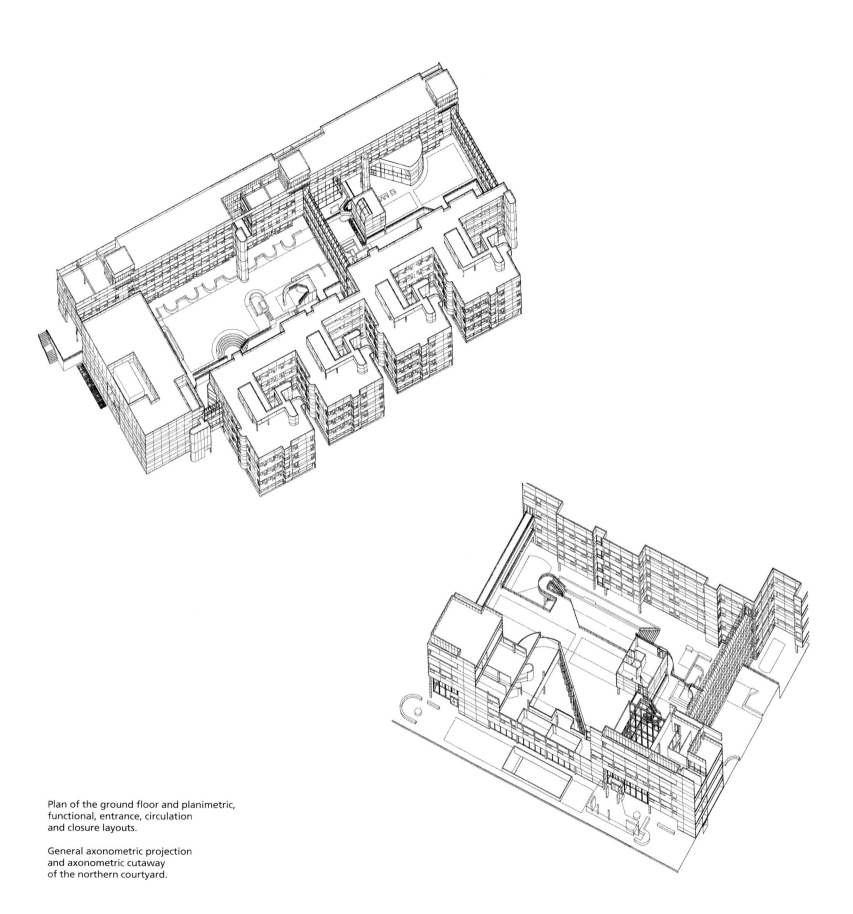

Plan of the ground floor and planimetric,
functional, entrance, circulation
and closure layouts.

General axonometric projection
and axonometric cutaway
of the northern courtyard.

1971
1976

Maidman House

View of the entrance end
and the west front. General plan.

View from the southeast,
plan of the ground floor
and axonometric cutaway.

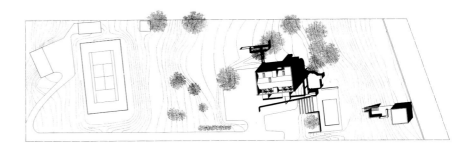

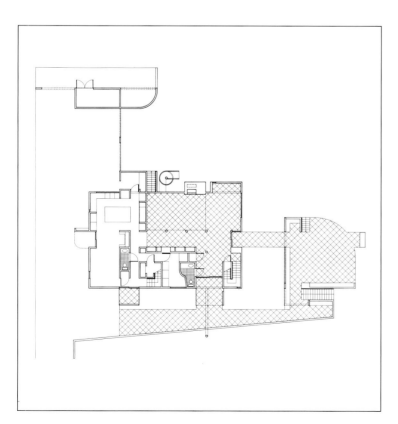

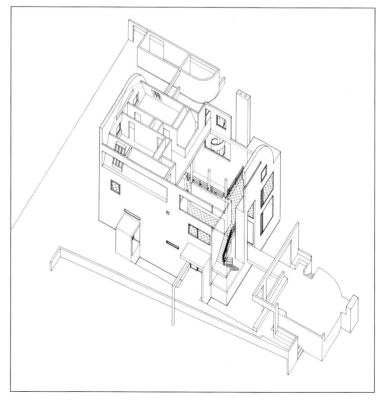

1971
1973

Douglas House

Details of the external passageways
and of the terraces overlooking
the lake.

Views of the double-height living room.

Site plan.

Plans of the roof levels and third, second and ground floors, south elevation and cross section.

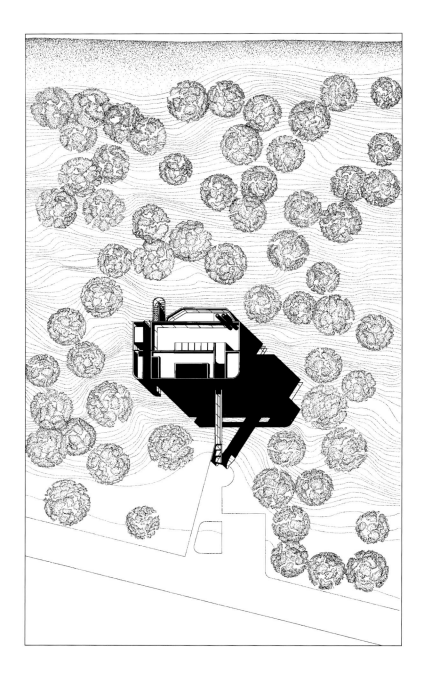

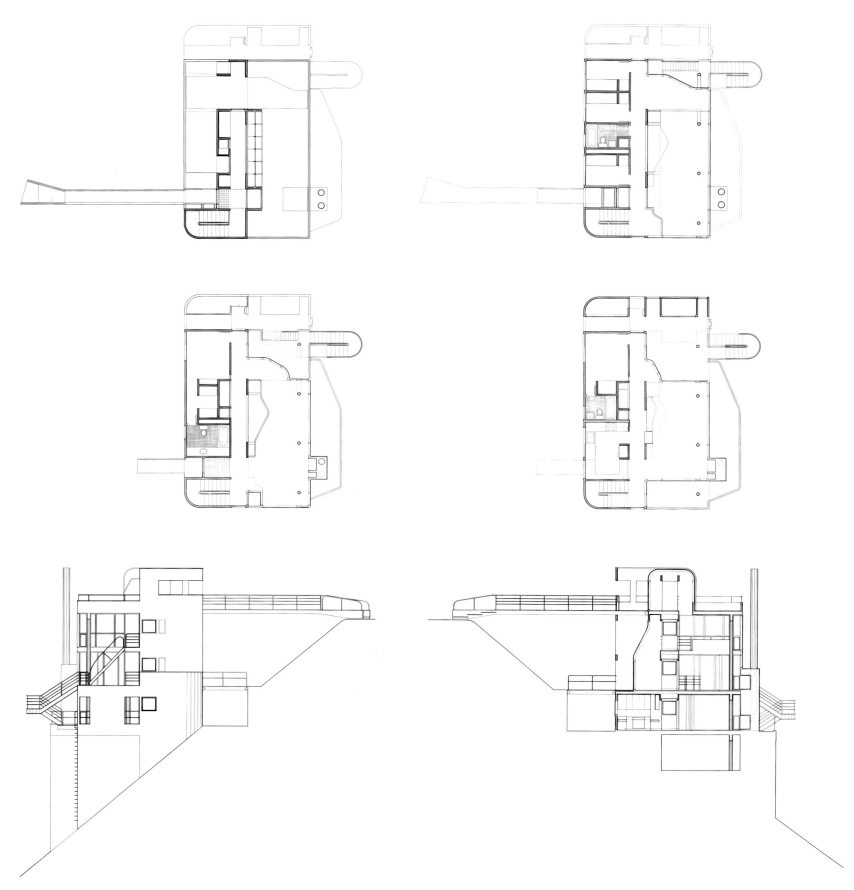

1971 | Branch Office Prototypes for Olivetti

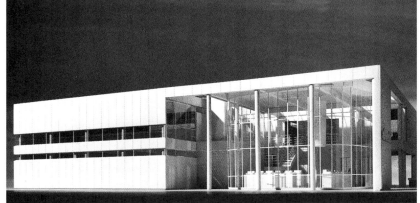

Views of the model.

Layouts and standard plan.

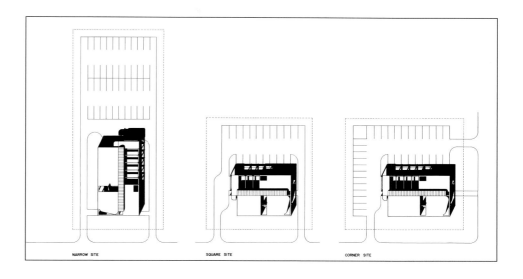

NARROW SITE   SQUARE SITE   CORNER SITE

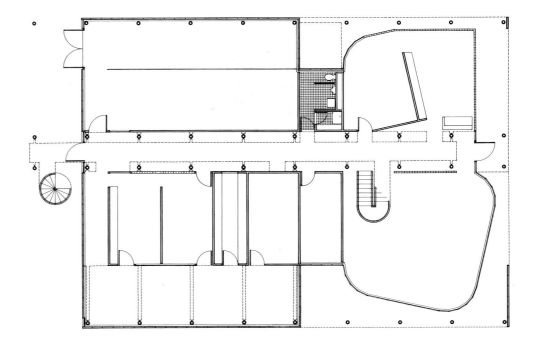

Views of the model.

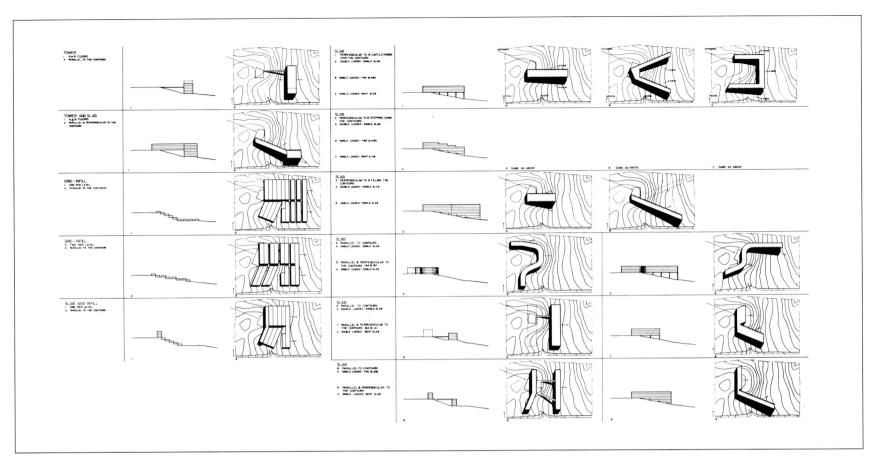

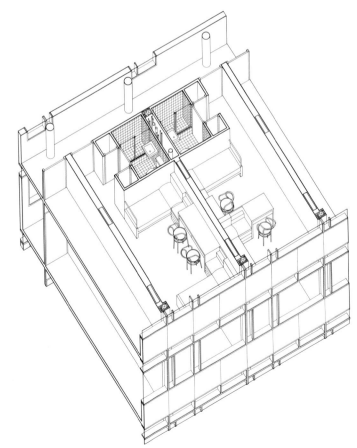

78

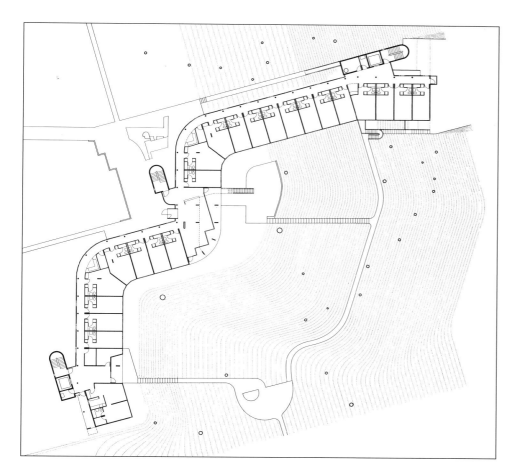

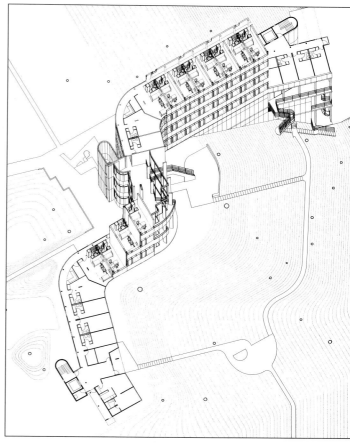

Variants in layout and disposition
of masses and axonometric cutaway
of standard bedrooms.

Plan at the level of the entrances
and axonometric cutaway.

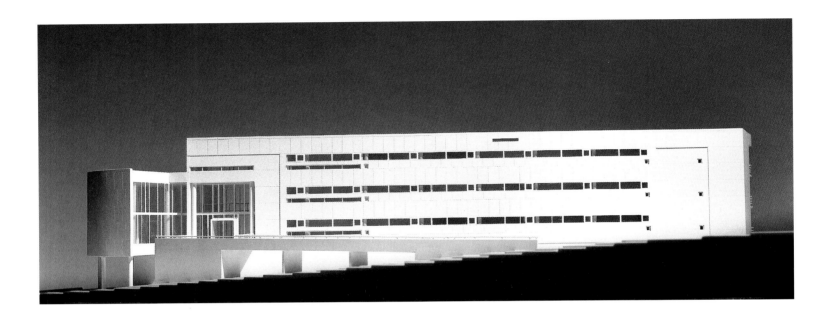

Views of the model.

Axonometric cutaway of the end
with the entrance.

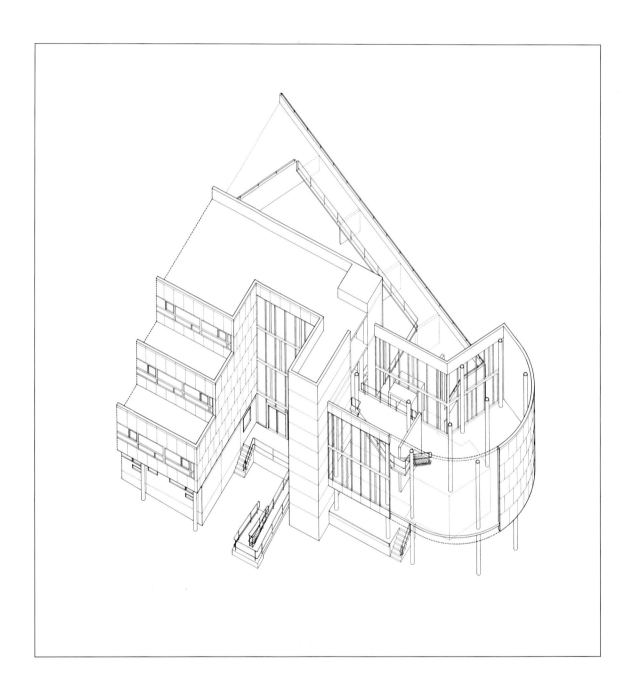

1972
1974

Shamberg House

Partial view of the north front of the house.

Views of the double-height living room and of the east façade with the terrace and the external staircase.

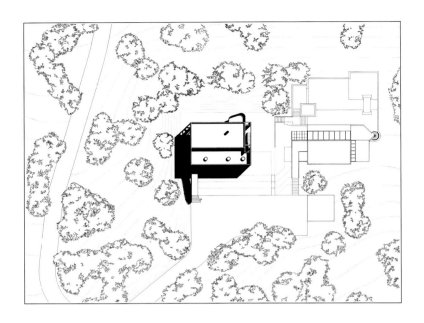

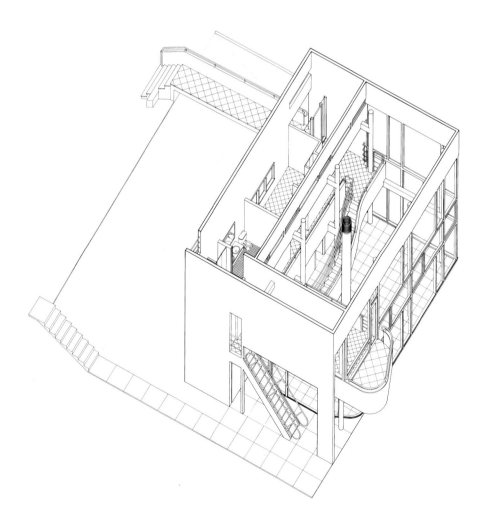

Site plan and axonometric cutaway.
Plans of the second and ground floors
and cross section.

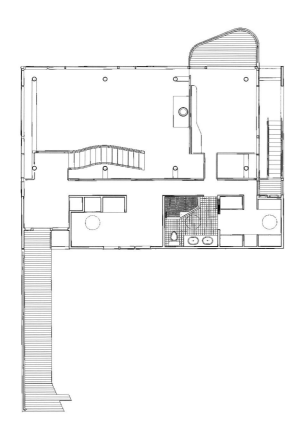

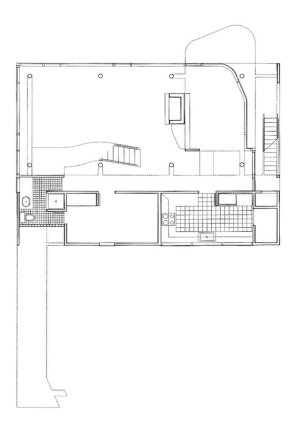

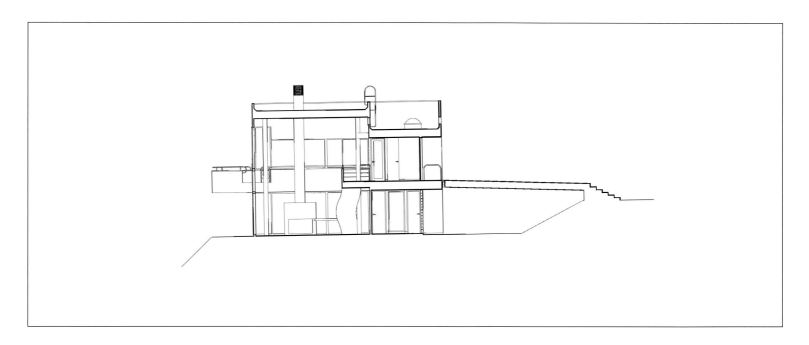

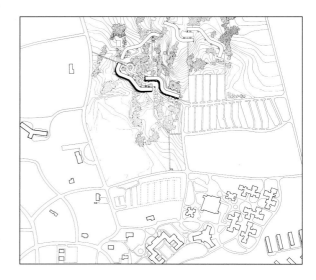

Views of the model, area plan
and perspective drawing
of the internal plaza.

Views from the south, west
and southwest.

Detail of the external access ramp.

Details of the west front
and the external vertical connections.

View of the entrance hall
and the internal ramp.

Details of the layout
of the internal ramp.

Plans of the third, second
and ground floors.

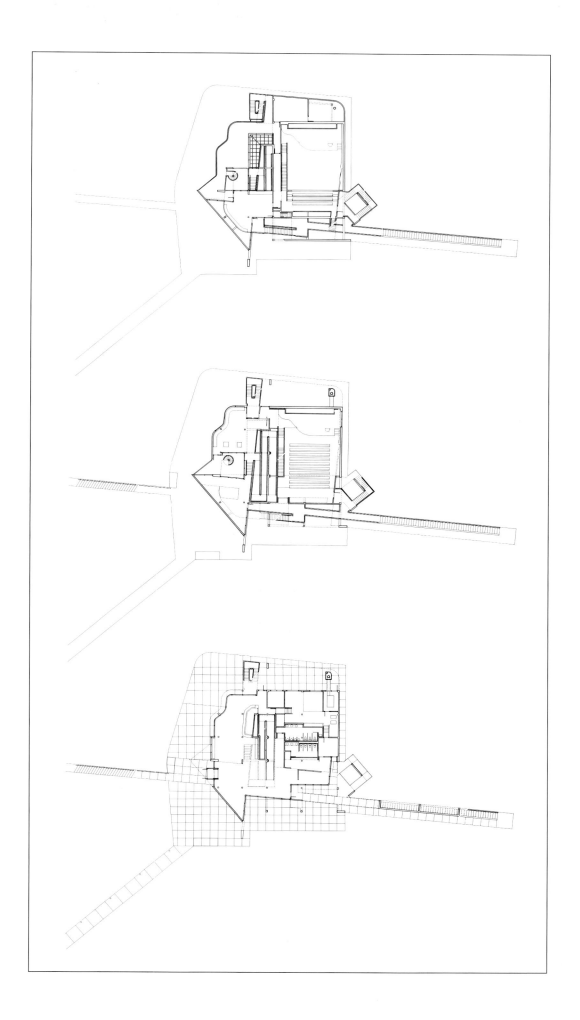

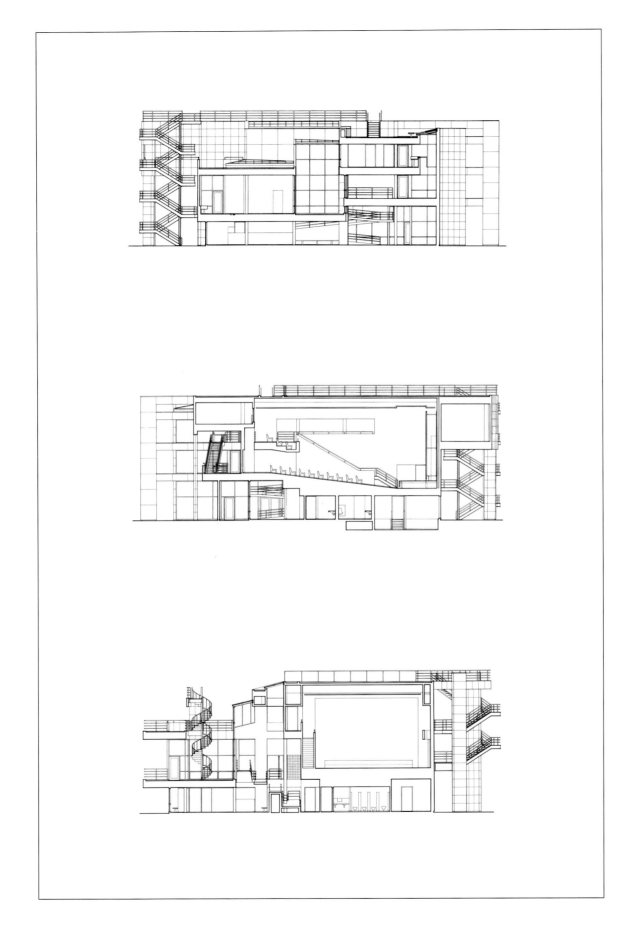

Sections through the entrance front
and the auditorium.

Axonometric cutaway and axonometric
projection of the open-air auditorium
that was not built.

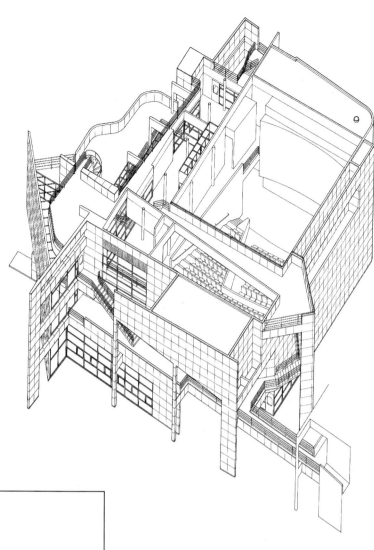

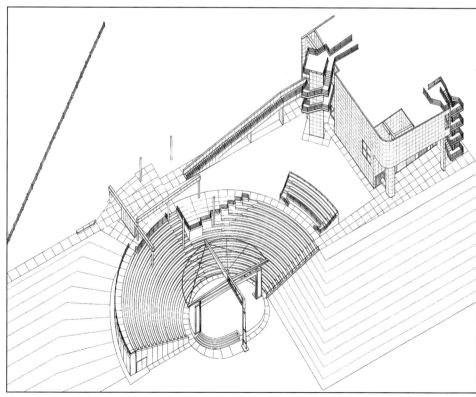

1975
1978 | Sarah Campbell Blaffer Pottery Studio

Views from the northeast, east and south.

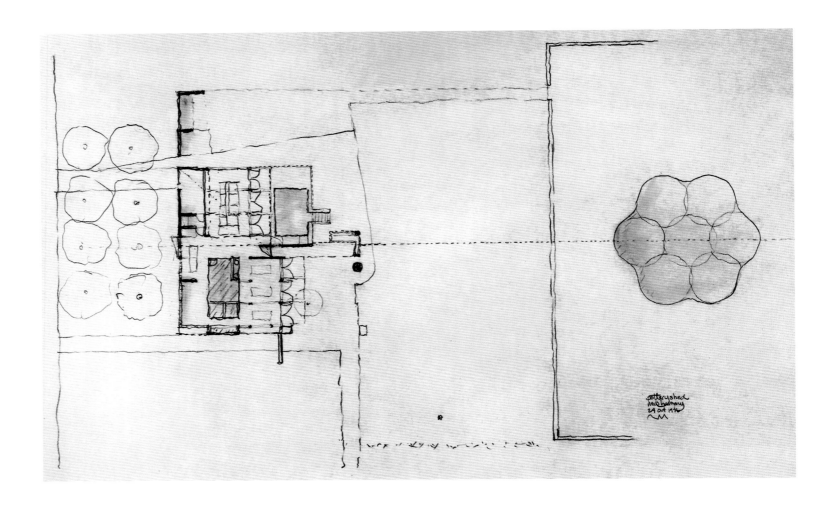

potteryshed
new harmony
24 oct 1996

Study drawing by Richard Meier,
plan and axonometric cutaway.

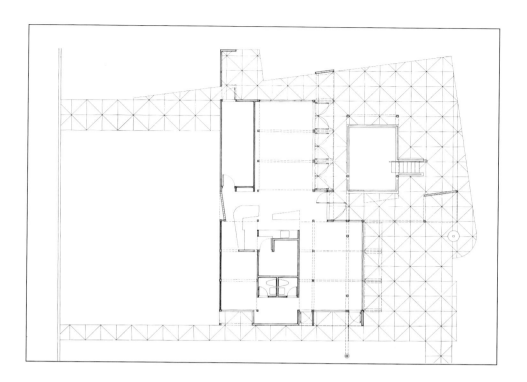

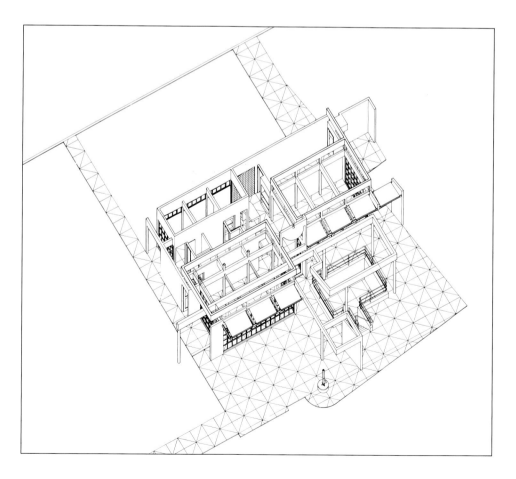

Details of the preparation.

Axonometric projection and study
drawing for the plan by Richard Meier.

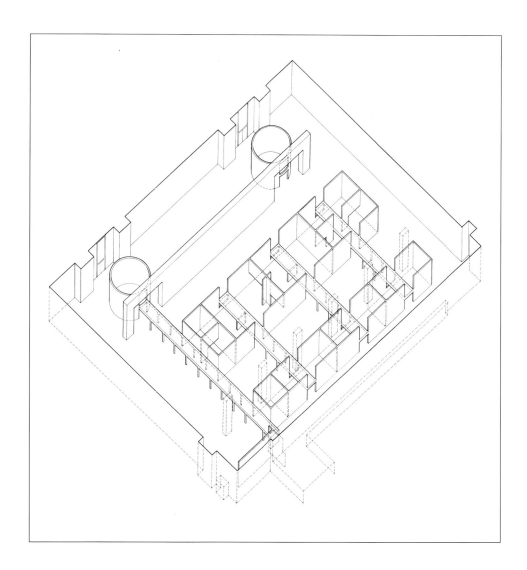

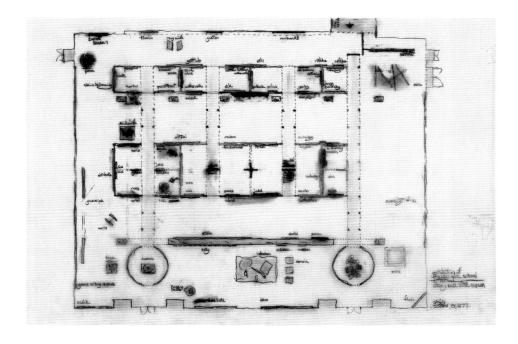

1977
1978

Aye Simon Reading Room, Solomon R. Guggenheim Museum

Internal view.

Detail of the entrance, plan
and axonometric projection.

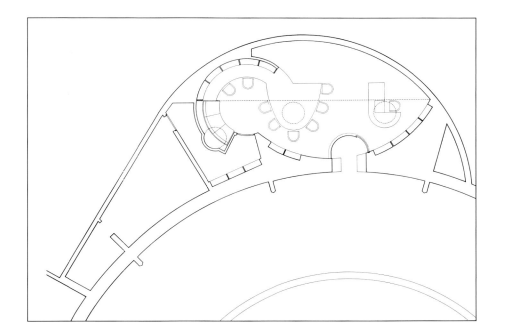

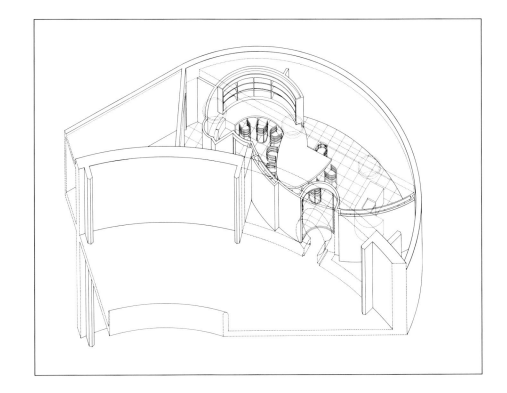

Views of the west and east façades.

Detail of the entrance.

Details of the courtyard with
the swimming pool and the volume
of the living room.

Site plan, axonometric cutaway
and plans of the ground
and second floors.

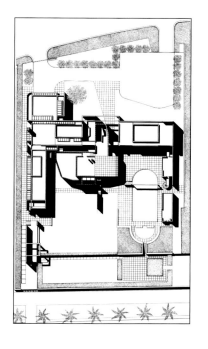

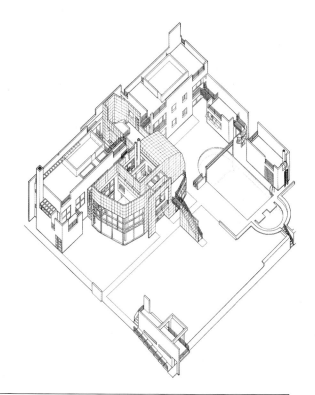

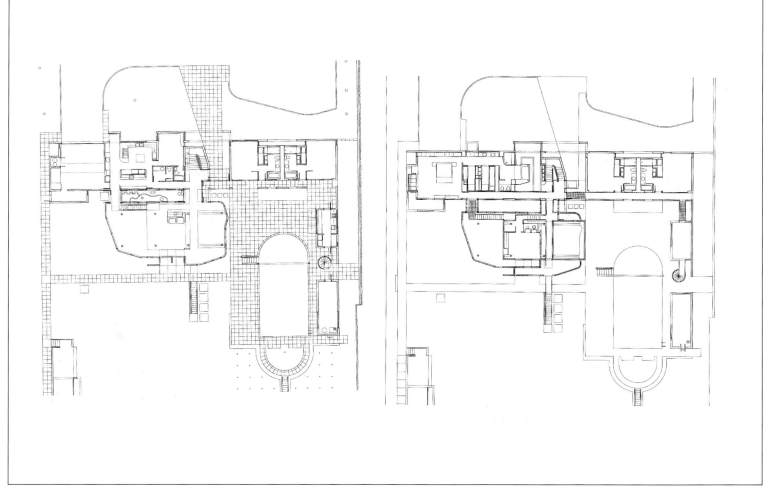

1978
1981

Hartford Seminary

View of the east front and details
of the entrance court.

Detail of the east façade and view
of the building from the northeast.

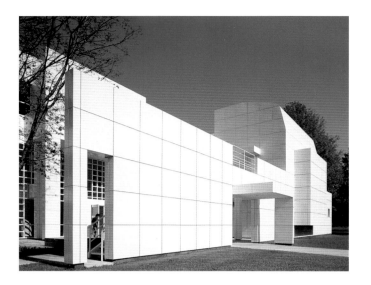

Views of the interior of the chapel
and of the auditorium.

Site plan and plan of the ground floor.

Axonometric cutaways of the whole
building and of the chapel.

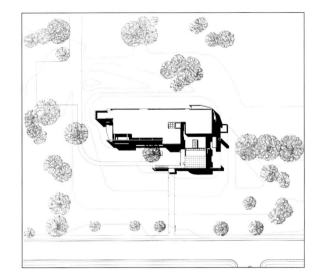

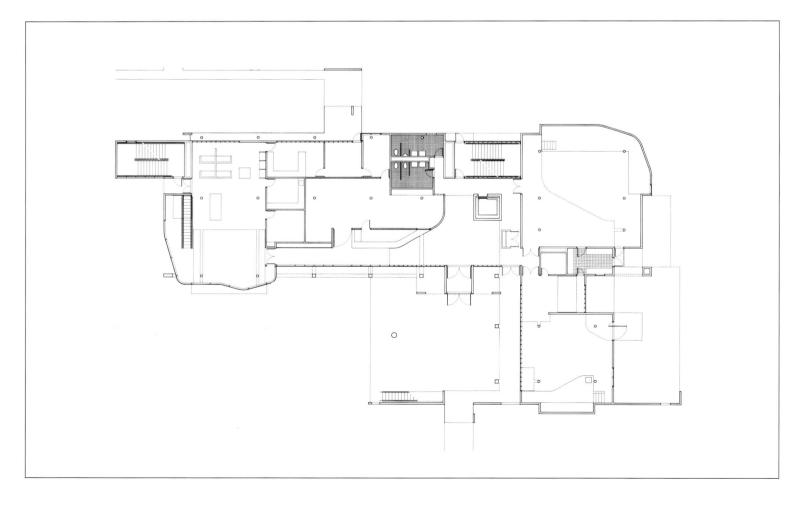

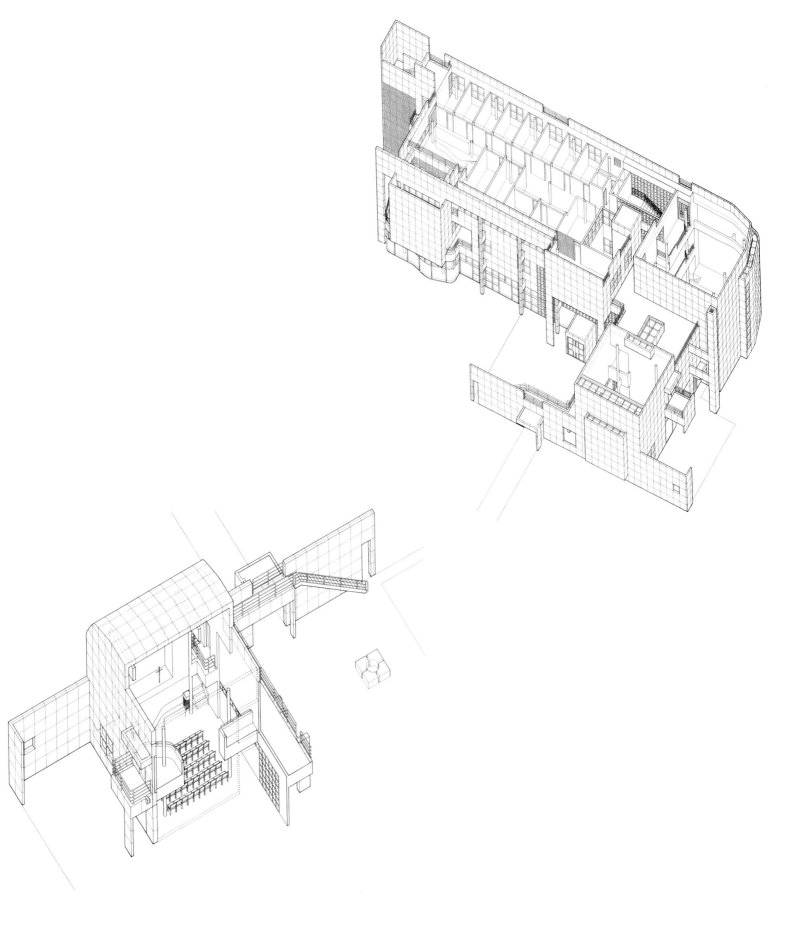

1979
1983

Giovannitti House

Views of the east front onto the garden,
from the southeast and of the entrance
front facing west.

The porch and the large glass wall facing south.

View of the living room.

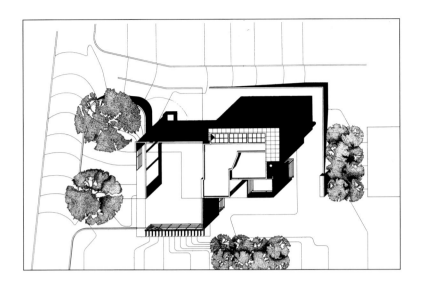

Site plan, plans of the ground and second floors, sections and axonometric cutaway.

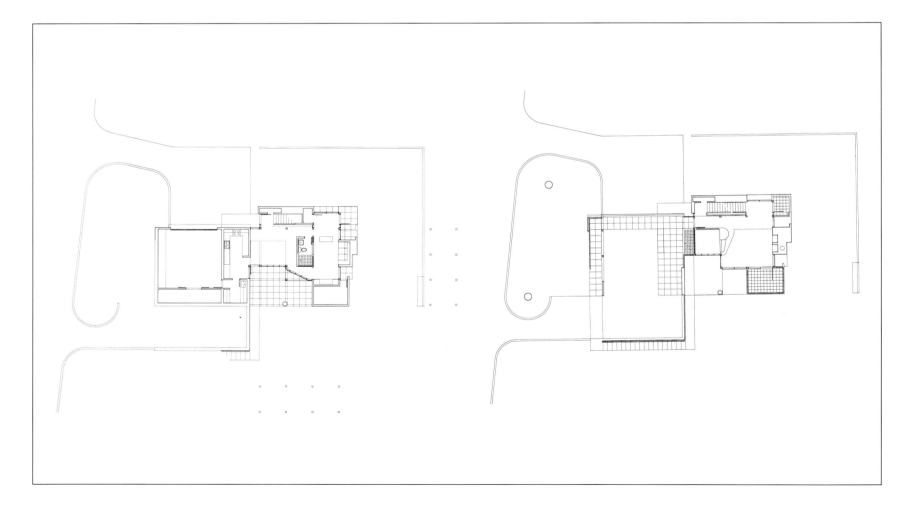

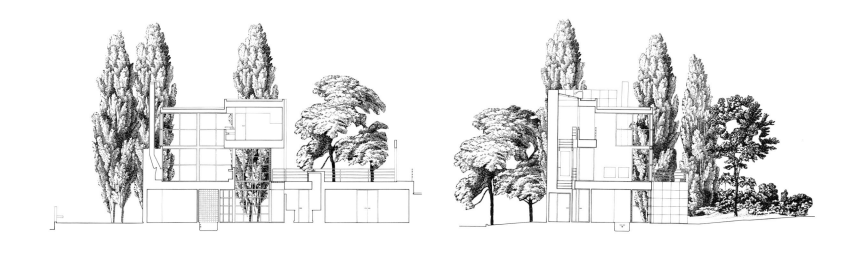

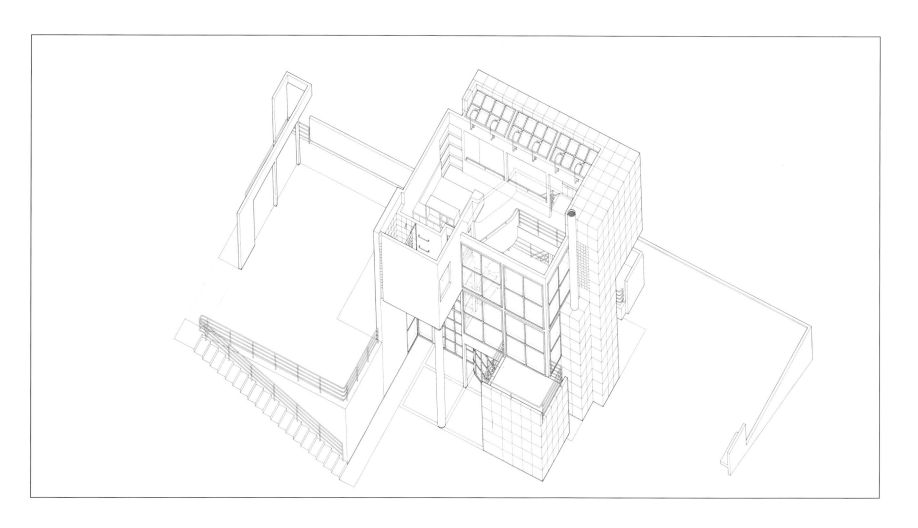

1978
1985

Museum für Kunsthandwerk

View of the front onto the Main River.

View from the garden to the southwest
and detail of the entrance.

Details of the southwest
and southeast façades.

Views of the bridge linking Villa Metzler
and the new buildings.

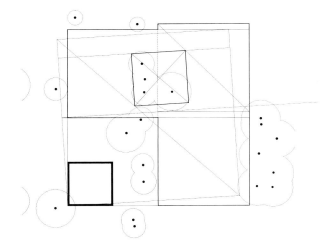

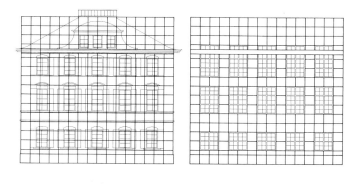

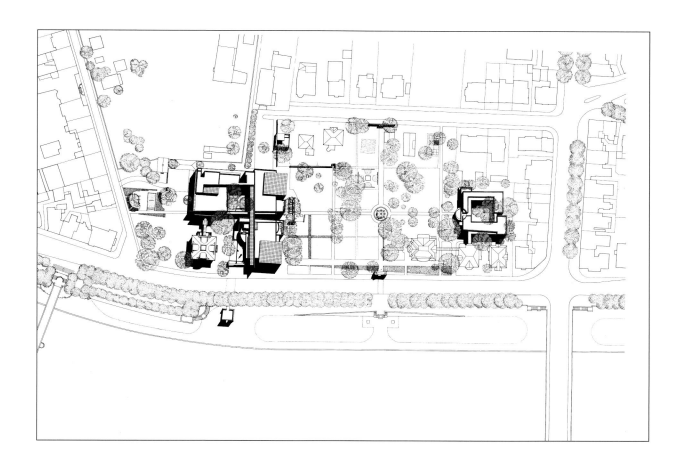

Details of the internal ramp.

Geometric diagrams of the plan,
of the façade and general plan.

Plans of the third, second and ground floors.
General axonometric projection.

Perspective section through the ramp and rooms.

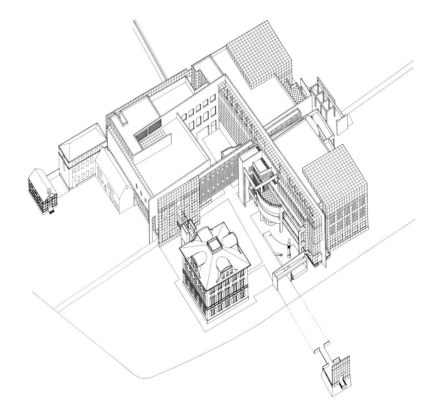

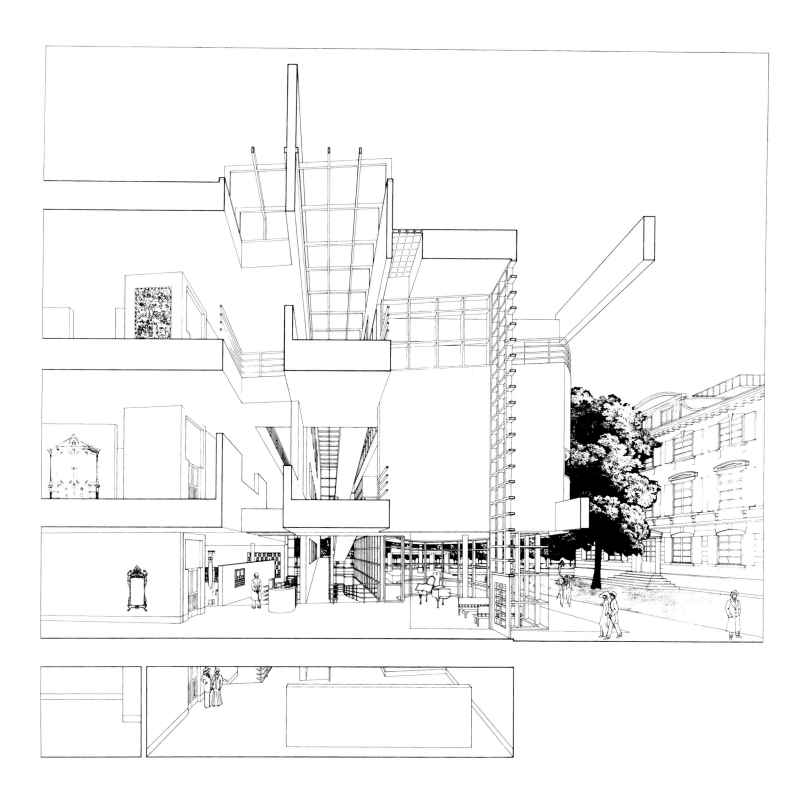

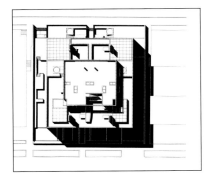

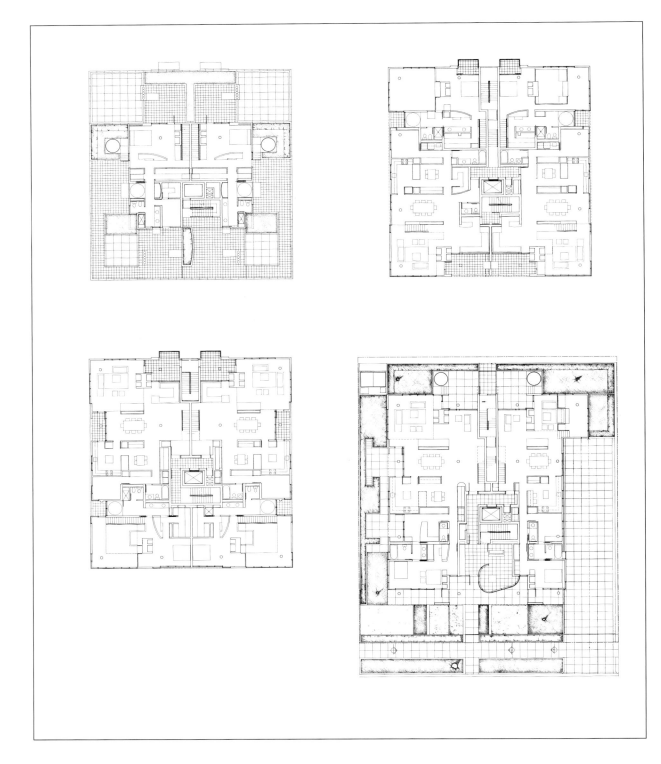

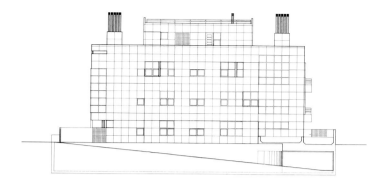

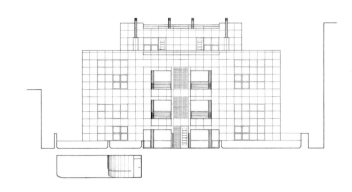

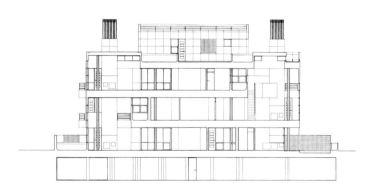

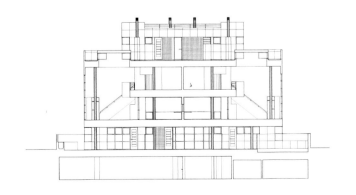

Site plan and plans of the fourth, third, second and ground floors.

North and west elevations, longitudinal and cross sections, axonometric cutaway.

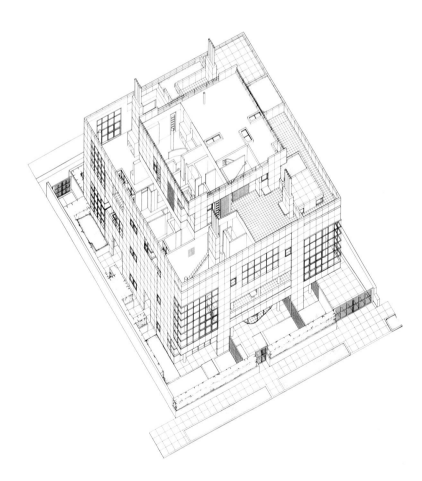

1980
1983

High Museum of Art

Views of the entrance front facing west.

Details of the ramp and the outer wall
of the entrance rotunda.

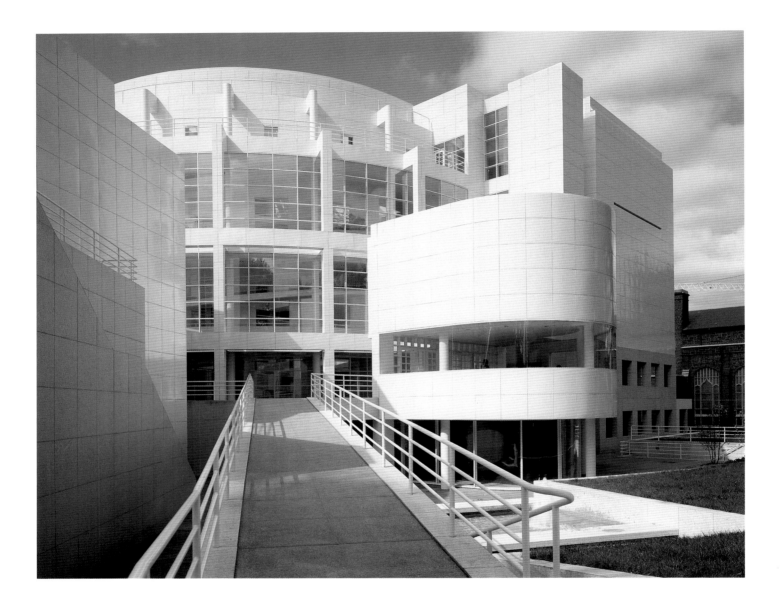

The large, four-story-high central atrium.

Details of the systems of ramps inside the museum and the glazed roof structure.

View of the museum by night.

Plans of the fourth, second, ground and basement floors.

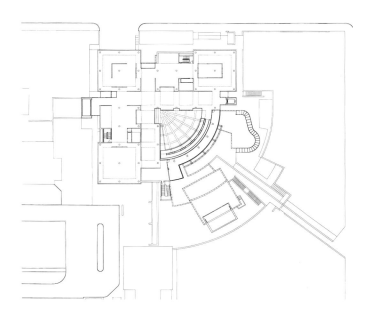

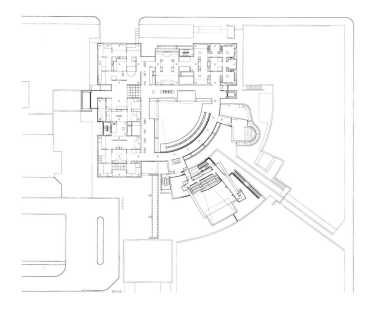

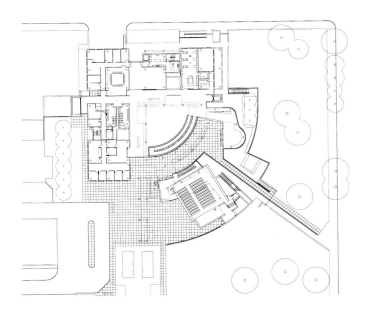

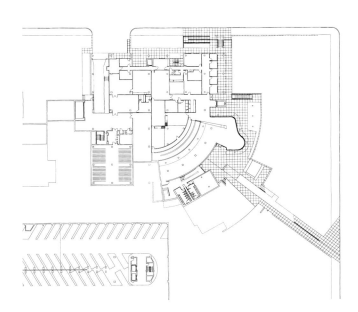

Perspective section of the atrium
and axonometric projections.

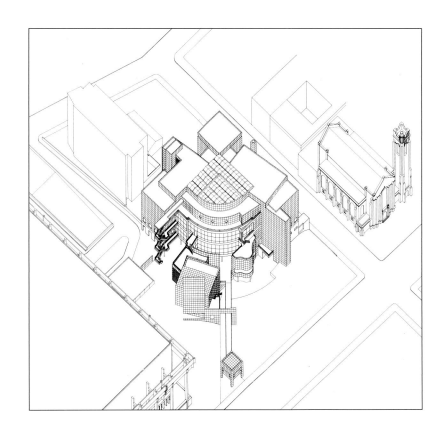

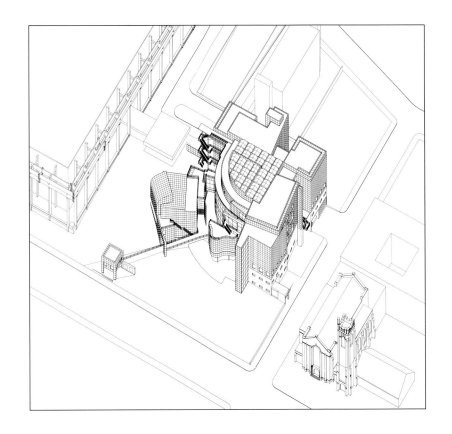

Views of the model.

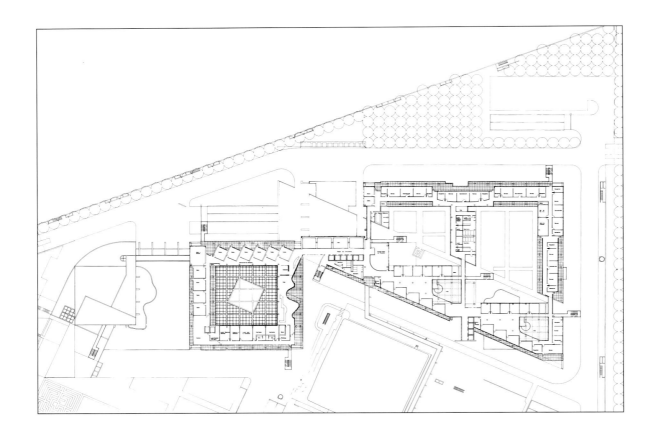

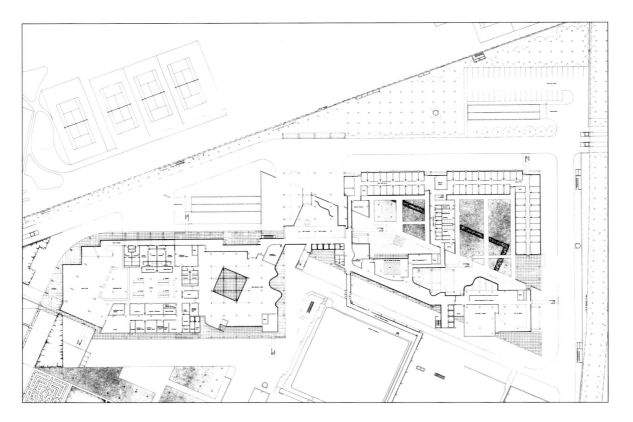

Plans of the eighth and ground floors.

General axonometric projection
and axonometric cutaway
of the east building.

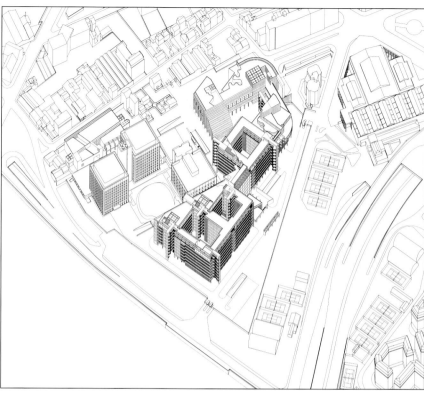

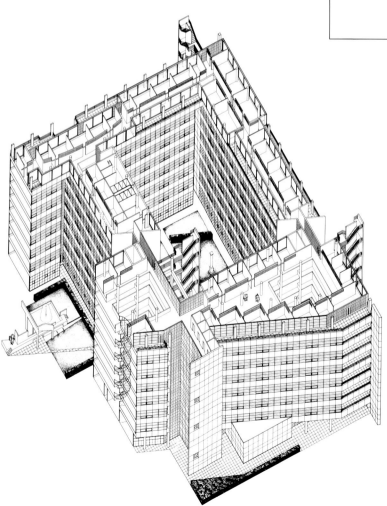

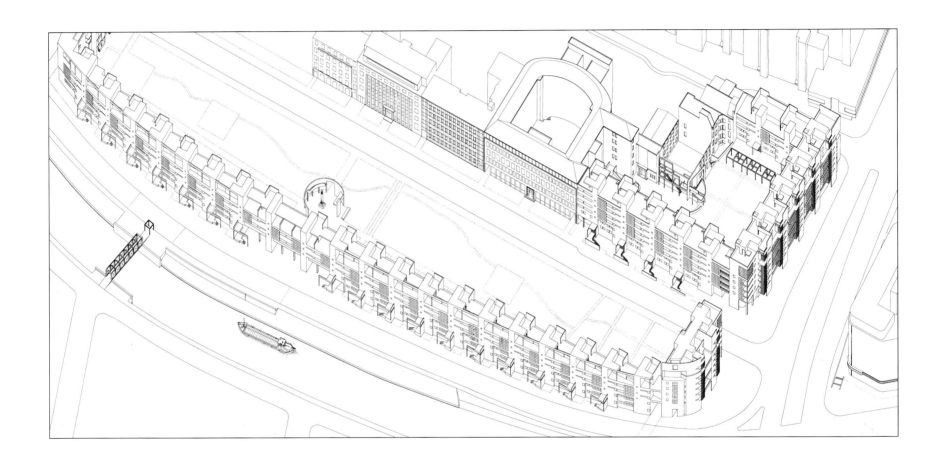

Axonometric projection
and general plan.

Plan of the ground floor
and view of the model.

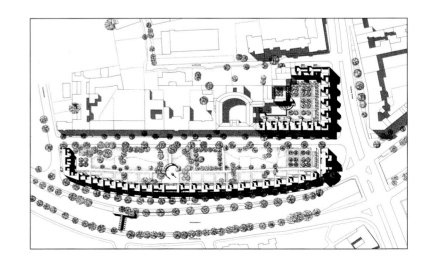

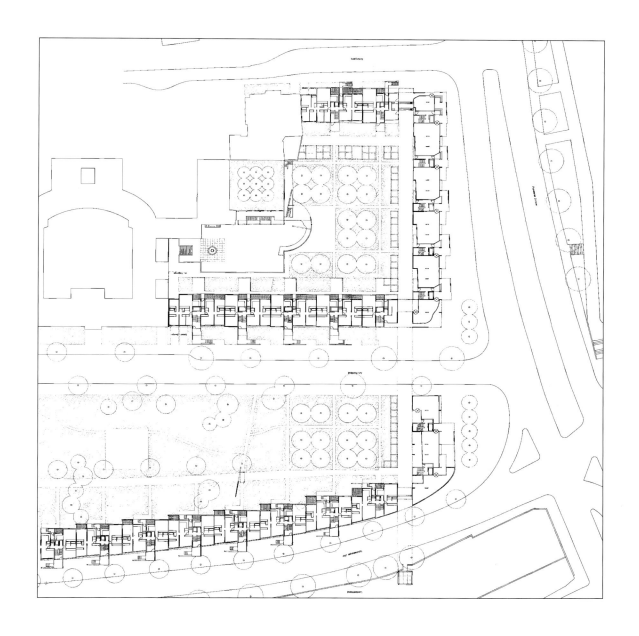

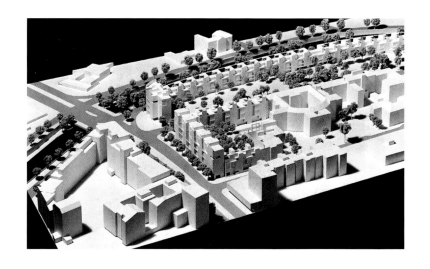

1982
1985

Des Moines Art Center Addition

Views from the north and west.

Views of the east front of the new exhibition wing showing the glazed corridor linking it to the preexisting core of the museum.

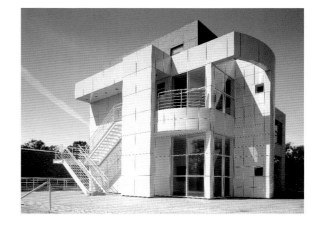

The café-restaurant
in the entrance court.

Plans of the second, ground
and basement floors and general plan.

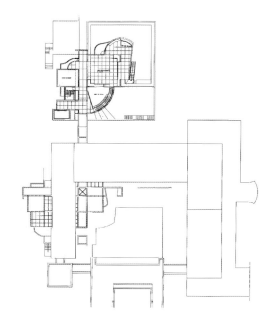

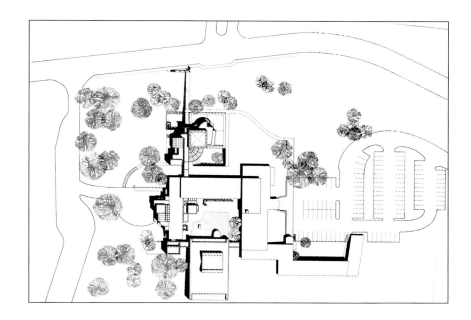

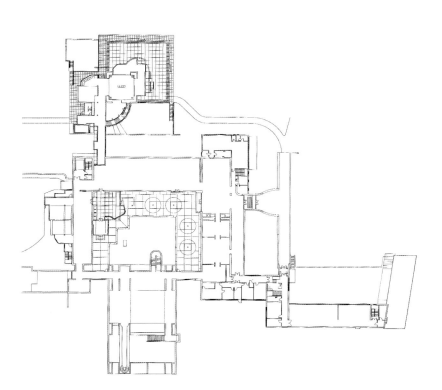

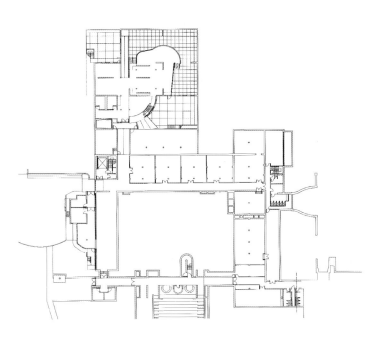

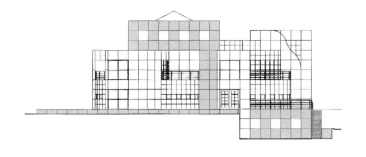

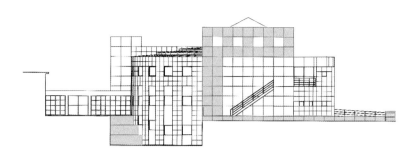

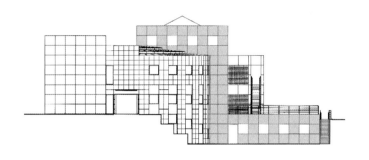

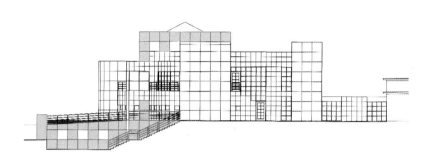

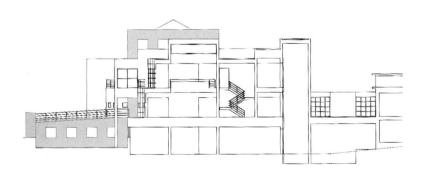

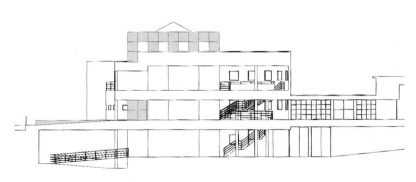

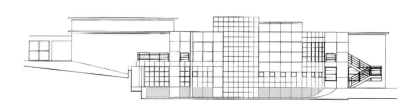

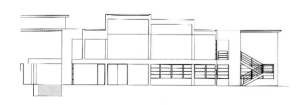

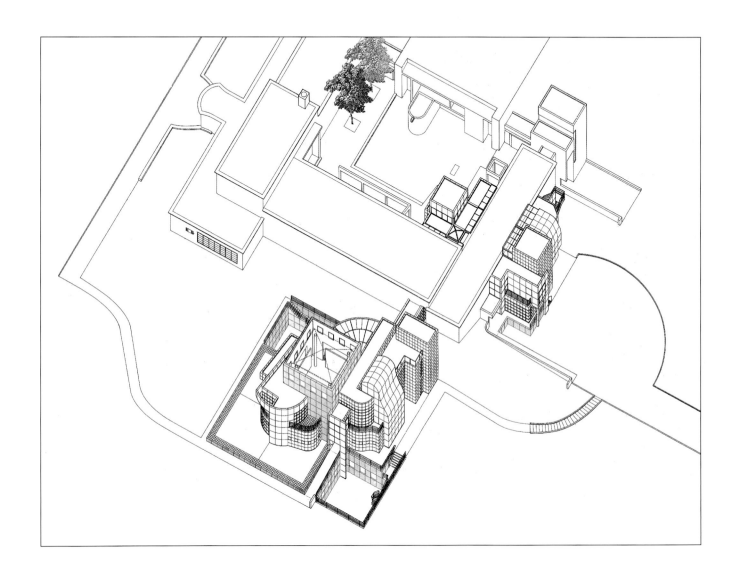

General axonometric projection.

North, east, south and west elevations
and sections of the new northern wing.
West elevation and section
of the southern addition.

1983
1988

Siemens Headquarters Building

View of the entrance block
on Oskar-von-Miller-Ring
and detail of the north courtyard.

Views of the east and north fronts
and external detail of the cylindrical
hall on the roof.

154

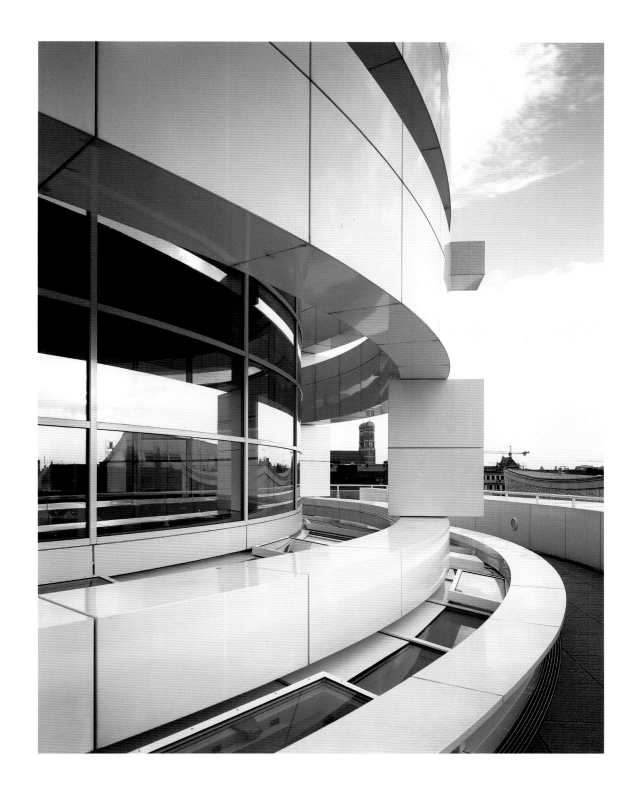

Views of the west façade
and of the staircase inside
the central spine
of distribution.

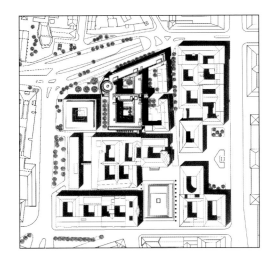

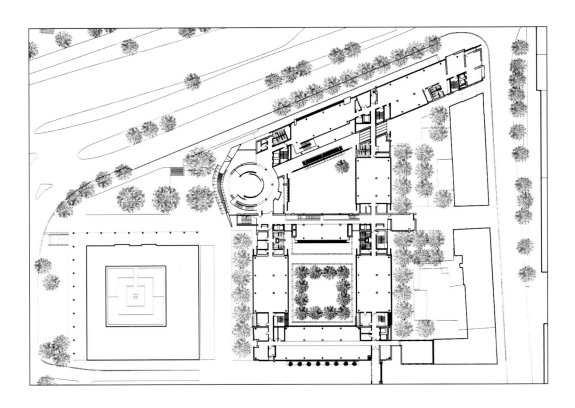

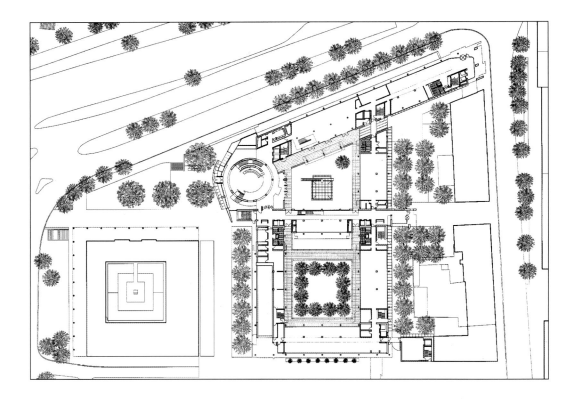

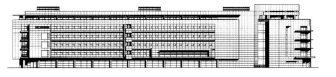

158

Area plan, plans of the second
and ground floors, west
and north elevations.

Plans of the sixth and third floors
and sections.

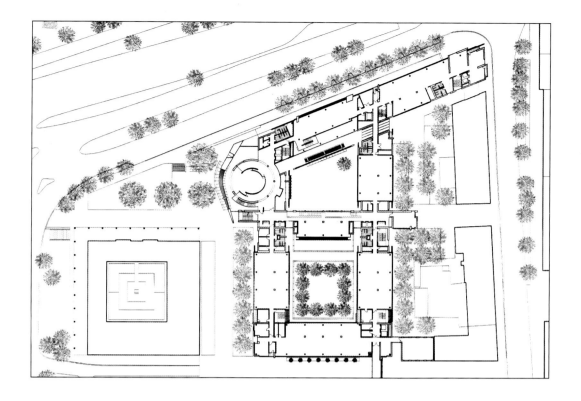

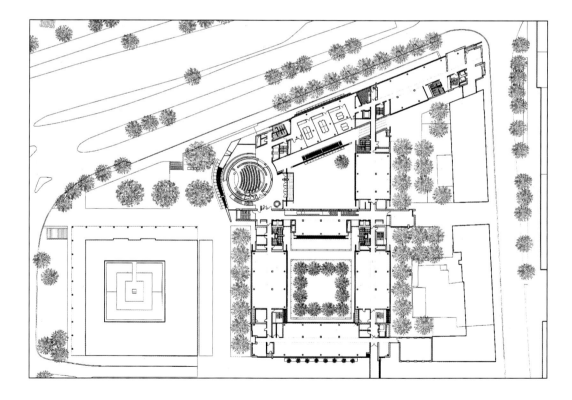

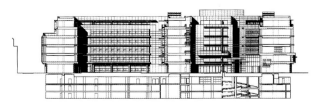

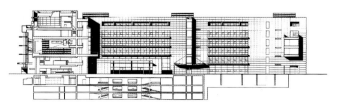

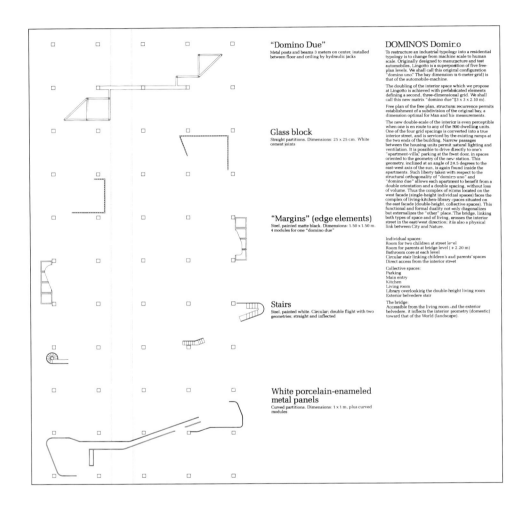

"Domino Due"
Metal posts and beams 3 meters on center, installed between floor and ceiling by hydraulic jacks

Glass block
Straight partitions. Dimensions: 25 x 25 cm. White cement joints

"Margins" (edge elements)
Steel, painted matte black. Dimensions: 1.50 x 1.50 m. 4 modules for one "domino due"

Stairs
Steel, painted white. Circular; double flight with two geometries; straight and inflected

White porcelain-enameled metal panels
Curved partitions. Dimensions: 1 x 1 m, plus curved modules

DOMINO'S Domino

To restructure an industrial typology into a residential typology is to change from machine scale to human scale. Originally designed to manufacture and test automobiles, Lingotto is a superposition of five free-plan levels. We shall call this original configuration "domino uno". The bay dimension (a 6-meter grid) is that of the automobile-machine.

The doubling of the interior space which we propose at Lingotto is achieved with prefabricated elements defining a second, three-dimensional grid. We shall call this new matrix "domino due" (3 x 3 x 2.10 m).

Free plan of the free plan, structural recurrence permits establishment of a subdivision of the original bay, a dimension optimal for Man and his measurements.

The new double-scale of the interior is even perceptible when one is en route to any of the 800 dwelling units. One of the four grid spacings is converted into a true interior street, and is serviced by the existing ramps at the two ends of the building. Narrow passages between the housing units permit natural lighting and ventilation. It is possible to drive directly to one's "apartment-villa", parking at the front door, in spaces oriented to the geometry of the new station. This geometry, inclined at an angle of 24.5 degrees to the east-west axis of the sun, is again found inside the apartments. Such liberty taken with respect to the structural orthogonality of "domino uno" and "domino due" allows each apartment to benefit from a double orientation and a double spacing, without loss of volume. Thus the complex of rooms located on the west facade (single-height individual spaces) faces the complex of living-kitchen-library spaces situated on the east facade (double-height, collective spaces). This functional and formal duality not only diagonalizes but externalizes the "other" place. The bridge, linking both types of space and of living, crosses the interior street in the east/west direction; it is also a physical link between City and Nature.

Individual spaces:
Room for two children at street level
Room for parents at bridge level (+ 2.20 m)
Bathroom core at each level
Circular stair linking children's and parents' spaces
Direct access from the interior street

Collective spaces:
Parking
Main entry
Kitchen
Living room
Library overlooking the double-height living room
Exterior belvedere stair

The bridge:
Accessible from the living room and the exterior belvedere, it inflects the interior geometry (domestic) toward that of the World (landscape).

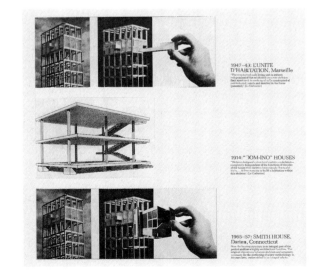

1947–43: L'UNITÉ D'HABITATION, Marseille

1914: "DOM-INO" HOUSES

1965–57: SMITH HOUSE, Dariea, Connecticut

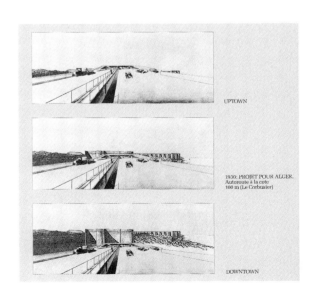

UPTOWN

1930: PROJET POUR ALGER, Autoroute à la cote 100 m (Le Corbusier)

DOWNTOWN

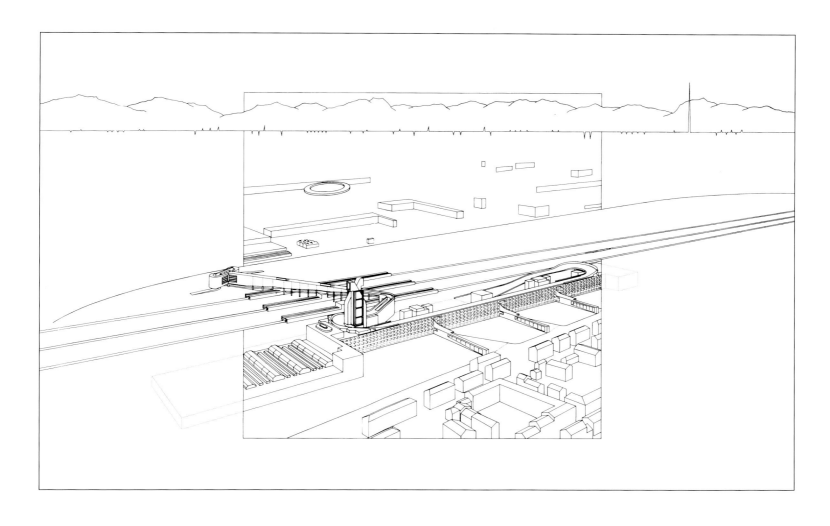

Diagram of the structural elements
of a housing module.
Illustrations of the design references.

Aerial perspective of the intervention
and plans of the two internal levels
of a villa-apartment.

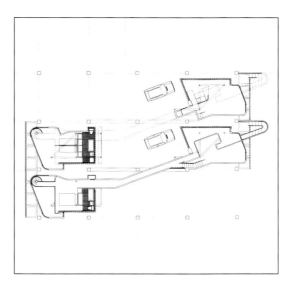

1984
1986 | Westchester House

South façade and view
from the northeast.

Views of the east front, with the stairs
leading down to the swimming pool,
and north front.

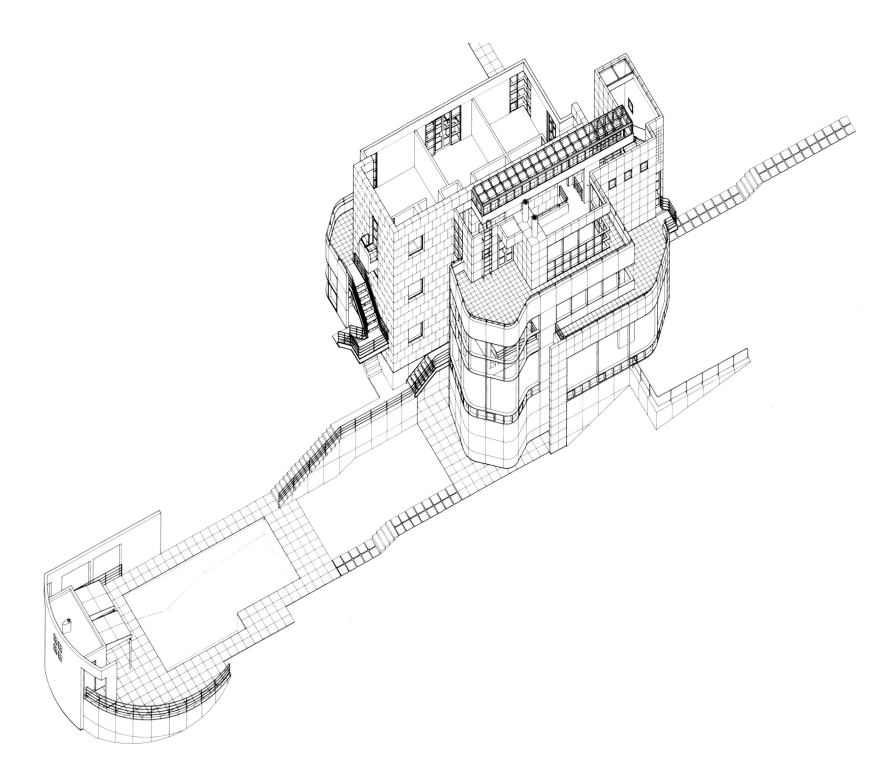

Site plan and axonometric cutaway.

Plans of the third, second
and ground floors.

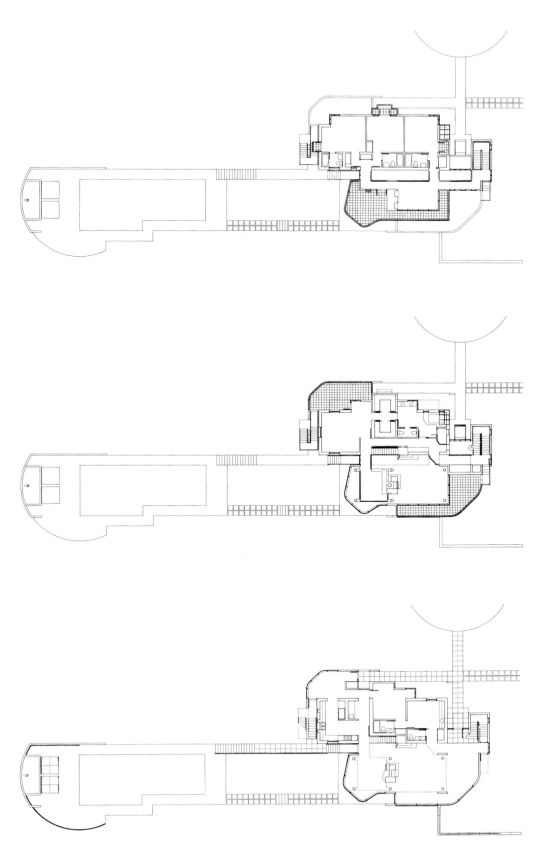

1984
1990 | Siemens Office and Research Facilities

View of one building of the complex.
Detail of an entrance.

Axonometric projection
and general plan.

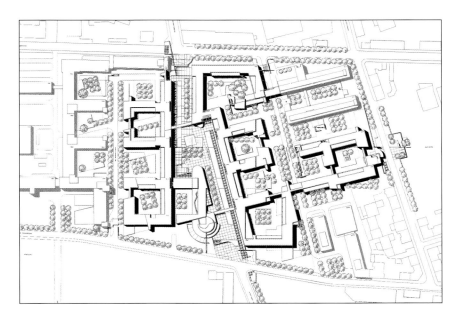

1984
1986

Ackerberg House

The north front facing onto the road.

Details of the east side of the living
room and the entrance porch
in the inner courtyard.

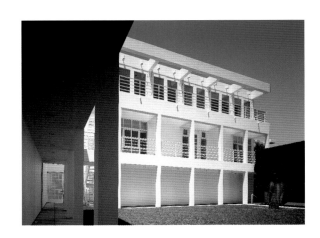

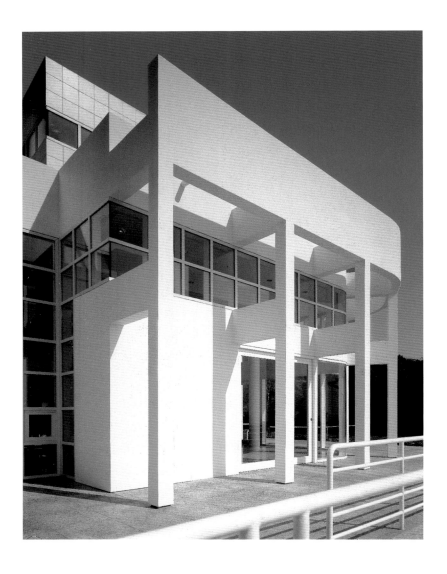

Detail of the brise-soleil around
the glass-walled living room
and view from the north entrance
onto the terrace overlooking the sea.

The volume of the living room
in the central patio.

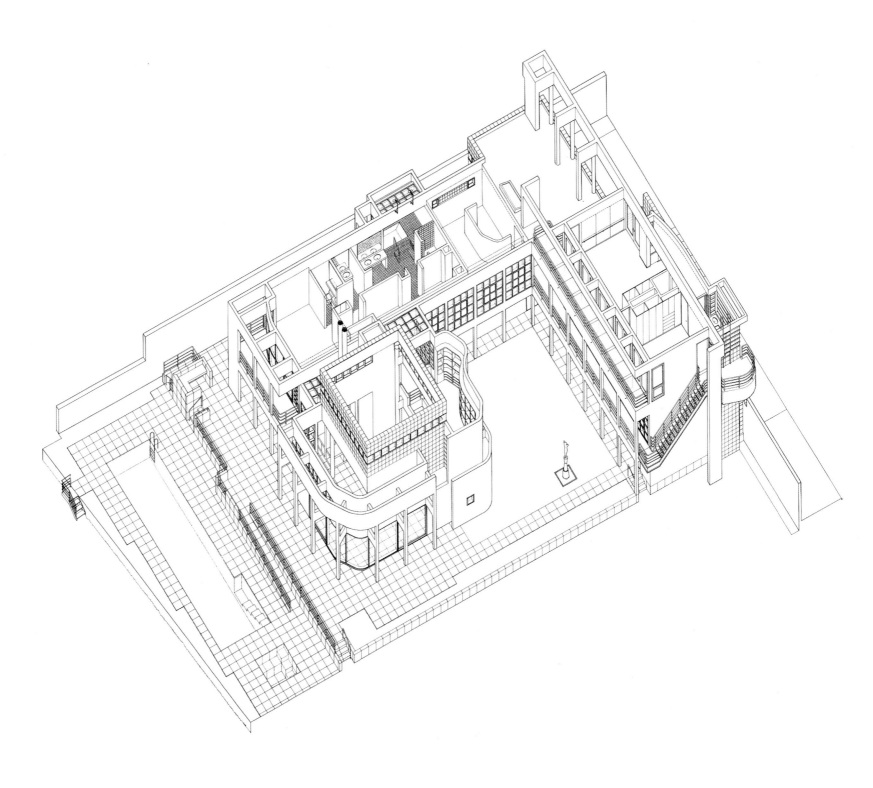

Axonometric cutaway.

Plans of the second and ground floors.

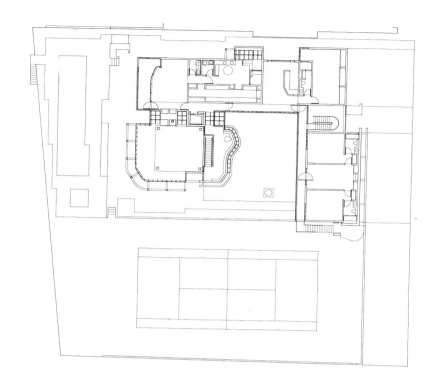

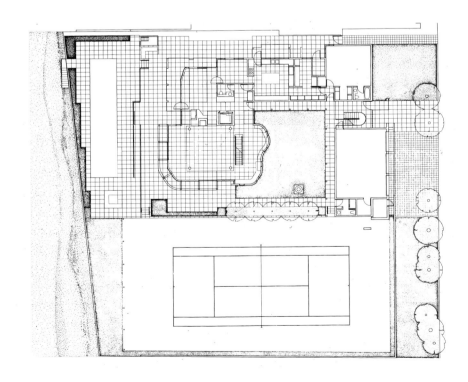

1984
1989

Bridgeport Center

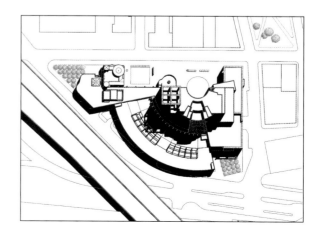

View of the complex from the harbor
and site plan.

View of the front on Main Street
and cross section.

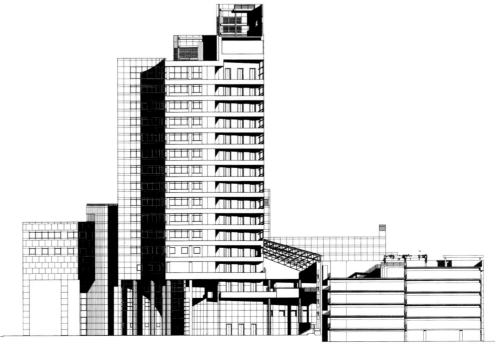

1985
1989

Grotta House

Views from the east and south
and detail of the entrance bridge.

following pages
View of the east front of the house.

View of the living room.

Axonometric projection and plans
of the ground and second floors.

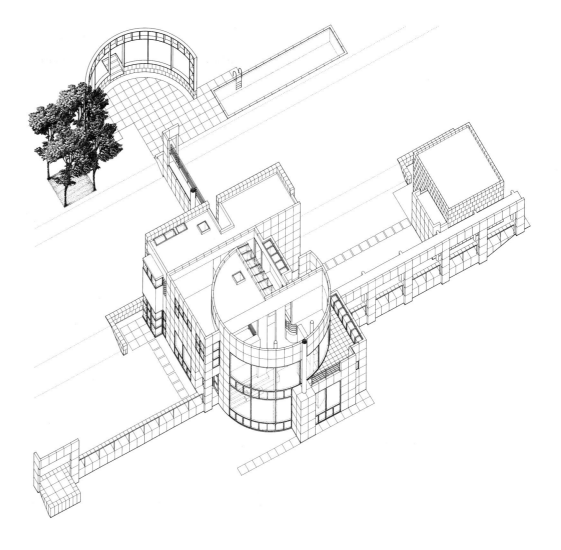

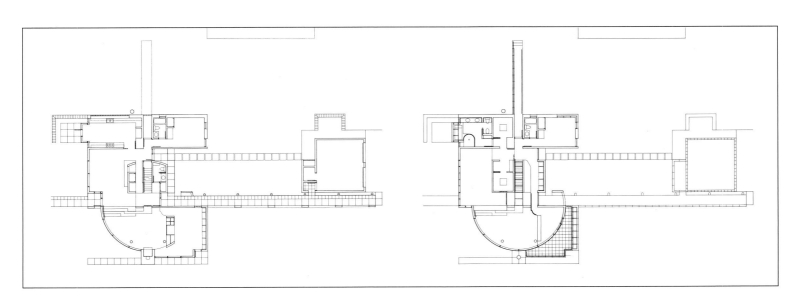

On the Road Again
Richard Meier

Not too long ago someone asked me what I would choose as the one building type that I would like to do for the rest of my life. My answer was museums. It seems I got my wish, for I have had an involvement with art and with museums for a long time. The relationship between art and architecture has always been a part of my work.

In all of my work, I am expanding or elaborating on what I consider to be the formal basis of the modern movement. What happened in the twentieth century was the creation of a crack, the breaking open of the classically balanced plan. The spirit of the twentieth century is allowed to go through and enter that crack so that the experience of being in a building is not static but is ever-changing. This twentieth century fissure, made possible by the free plan, the free façade, the separation of skin and structure, and the whole formal basis of the modern movement, has fostered a new kind of volumetric exploration, one that still holds a great number of possibilities.

It seems to me that the promise and richness of the formal tenets of modernism have almost unlimited areas of investigation. My work does not lie within the neoclassical tradition. I reject the representational. I embrace the abstract. Mine is a preoccupation with space—not scaleless space, but space whose order and definition are related to light, to human scale, and to the culture of architecture.

I work with volume, with surface. I try to manipulate forms in light and also deal with changes of scale, view, movement through the building, and spaces. My sources include many from the history of architecture, but my quotes and allusions are never literal. My meanings are always internalized, and the metaphors are purely architectural. I am still taken with the poetics of modernism and the beauty, the utility, of technology.

My primary ordering principles have to do with a kind of purity. The purity derives, in part, from the inherent distinction between that which is man-made and that which is natural. This relationship between the man-made and the natural I see as complementary. I see man's intervention as an aesthetic organization of the environment, and I try to impose a coherent system of mutually dependent values, a harmonious relationship of parts.

I believe that buildings should speak, and in my work the use of a specific and internally consistent vocabulary of elements and themes has, over the years, allowed me to have a coherent and evolutionary means of expression. The process by which I manipulate and assemble this vocabulary within the urban and historical contexts has perhaps become a bit more complex. One might say that this is an intellectual progression that has coincided with the growing scope and increased size of some of the commissions.

In the beginning, private houses allowed me to have a very good opportunity to develop my ideas about architecture because, within them, I have been able to find and test my vocabulary and my set of values. The contexts have varied a great deal, and they have ranged from virtually freestanding and autonomous buildings to ones that existed within the urban fabric. Nevertheless there are, within all of them, interrelated ideas about the basic dialogues between public and private space, between the building and its context. There is also the notion of architectural promenade, of spatial sequence, which has also been a constant in my work.

City Hall and Library, The Hague

The City Hall and Library in The Hague is part of an urban design scheme that incorporates existing buildings and relates to the urban texture of the surrounding area. It is a rather complicated project in that it is a city hall and main library. It is a competition that we won and since then it has been debated among the councilmen for three reasons. First, they asked if The Hague would be the right place for a city hall. Second, they were concerned whether the program for the city hall with a central library would satisfy all the needs and requirements for the next twenty-five or forty years. And third, they questioned whether the building was within the budget. As the budget is based on preliminary drawings, that is a very difficult thing to ascertain. No less than ten companies

attempted to determine it, and they all assured the city fathers that it was within the budget.

The main space within the city hall is the large atrium. This would be the center of the city, the hall of the people, a place where people come for their marriage licenses, for their building permits, and to pay for their parking tickets. But the atrium is also very important as a covered plaza, and with the city hall and the library, which draw thousands of people every day, it becomes a place to move through on the way from one part of the city to another. Because of the number of offices and bureaucrats in The Hague, it is also a large office building. But the center hall, the atrium, is a place where people can come together, where musical events can occur, where there is nightlife, where demonstrations against city government can take place, where everything except ice-skating is possible. It is a plaza, but because of the climate in Holland, it is glazed and covered, much like the Galleria in Milan.

The High Museum, Atlanta

During the Enlightenment, the museum came to have educational as well as collection and display functions, and I would like to think that the High Museum in Atlanta is in that tradition. It not only houses art, but it contributes to the museum's educational role in the broadest sense. It is intended to provide an ambience that is conducive to viewers' contemplative moments as well as their appreciation and discovery of the collection's aesthetic values.

The High Museum is a public building, so the quality of light, the proportions of the openings and the enclosures are made to have some intimate spaces within this rather large public realm. The museum is intended to encourage the discovery of aesthetic values and to convey a sense of purpose as a public place and also as a contemplative place.

By its circulation, its lighting, its spatial qualities, the museum encourages people to experience the art of architecture as well as the art that is displayed within. The design is a series of architectonic responses to the site on Peachtree Street and also to the programmatic and typological concerns. Because of its location in a residential area and the pedestrian-oriented character of the neighborhood, the role of this building as an urban and cultural symbol became an important influence on the design.

The corner site affords a number of entrances. One way is from a subway station, so the building becomes a thoroughfare for people going to work or coming back from work in the residential neighborhood. One can walk around the building or walk through the building, without actually entering into the gallery space. It becomes a place for people to move through during the day and at night.

For those who come in through the main entry, there is a compression of spaces, narrowing until you come in through the lobby, past the information counters, into the top-lit atrium space. The atrium space, the main hall, is really the center of the High Museum, and it is a place that has all kinds of activity. It is rented out almost every evening for cocktail parties or for fashion shows. It is a cultural center, but it is also a social center.

Around the atrium space, there is a ramp from one level to another. The reference here to the Guggenheim Museum in New York is obvious because at the Guggenheim there is the same focus on monumental central space and curved ramp circulation. But I would like to think that the High Museum overcomes certain shortcomings of the Guggenheim as a place for the display and viewing of art because it has a clear

Design diagrams of the High Museum
in Atlanta.

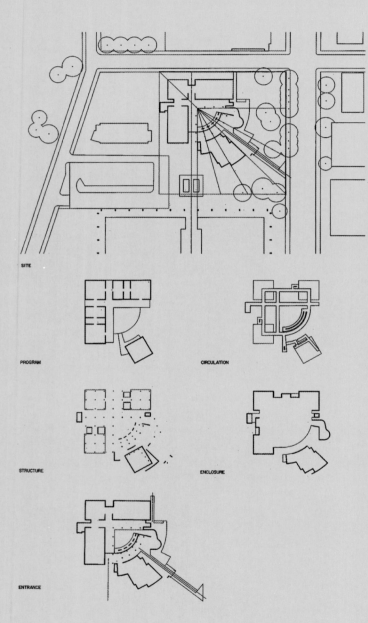

SITE

PROGRAM

CIRCULATION

STRUCTURE

ENCLOSURE

ENTRANCE

distinction between the path, or the ramp, and the destina-
tion, or the galleries. At Atlanta, we tried to reinterpret some
of the values of the Guggenheim Museum. By the manner in
which we have separated the vertical circulation from the
gallery space, we have been able to maintain the idea of continual references to the central space filled with light. But the
gallery walls are flat, they are not on sloped walls.

Apart from its purely functional role, light in this building is a
constant preoccupation. In fact, light is a symbol of the museum's purpose, it is basic to the architectural conception. The
museum is meant to be both physically and metaphysically
radiant. The building is intended both to contain and reflect
light, expressing the museum's purpose as a place of enlightenment as well as the center of the city's cultural life.

Des Moines Art Center
The original Des Moines Art Center was designed by Eliel
Saarinen and was built in 1948. We were asked to do an addition, an enlarged gallery space, because the 1948 building did
not anticipate the large-scale painting and sculpture that
would come to the collection. In 1965, Ieoh Ming Pei was commissioned to do a sculpture gallery. What he did was really
very logical; he took Saarinen's U-shaped plan, which was
open to a park, and he closed it with the sculpture gallery,
making a continuous square doughnut and completing the
circulation route within the museum. That was very logical,
and if I had been asked to do that commission, I probably
would have done the same thing. But by closing the open
plan with his sculpture gallery, Pei made any future addition
quite problematic. The building was complete, so any further
additions had to be pavilions separate from and connected to
the existing buildings. Since it was impossible to mimic either
the stone material of Saarinen or the concrete work of Pei, it
seemed to me that the best way to relate to the existing buildings was by scale.

Our gallery addition is a connected pavilion. Unlike the
Saarinen portion, which is beautiful and small-scale, in our
addition natural light becomes an important element that
enhances the museum experience. The three levels of gallery,
the main level of which is below ground, are interconnected
through a stairwell that is filled with light. This becomes the
main circulation space, so that one comes through the connected passage into the stairwell and circulates within the
new exhibition pavilion, viewing works of art, looking into

the stairwell, then going back into the older parts of the building.

In fact, my addition is really three pieces. There is the gallery addition. There is the renovation of the whole underground storage part of the museum, which has more needs today than it did forty years ago. And there is also the addition of a small meeting room-café within the courtyard. When Pei closed the courtyard, it became a dead space. The small café now reanimates that area.

The Museum für Kunsthandwerk

I believe that the city, like smaller works of architecture, consists primarily of public and private spaces and also the spaces in between. Unlike architectural works of lesser scale and complexity, urban design contains the dynamic of history. History is a given for the architect. It is a veritable confrontation; the city forces a historical spatial dialogue. This museum for decorative art is an attempt to make historical spatial dialogue within the city as articulate as one can. Here the notion of context is expanded to take in not only the physical and the programmatic concerns, but the historical

context of the site and of the building type.

There is an existing neoclassical building called the Villa Metzler, which is a stately relic from the age of Goethe and Schinkel. Since the end of World War II, it has contained the city's decorative arts treasures, I might add that it is one of eight museums on the Main River overlooking the center of Frankfurt. This three-story stuccoed mansion, which was built in 1803, provided elegant but insufficient gallery space for an extensive collection of European and non-western decorative arts. The new building, which is an addition, is roughly nine times the size of the old museum, so one wonders which one is adding onto which. But we had to preserve and connect the Villa Metzler as well as relate to all of the other museums along the riverside embankment.

At Frankfurt, we took the actual proportions, the size of the window openings, the proportions of the Villa's plan, the pattern of the façades, and we repeated them as modules in the new design. The accompanying diagram shows how the proportions and scale of the villa are abstracted into the new building and how that abstraction is derived from all the elements of the villa—its width, its height, its cornice

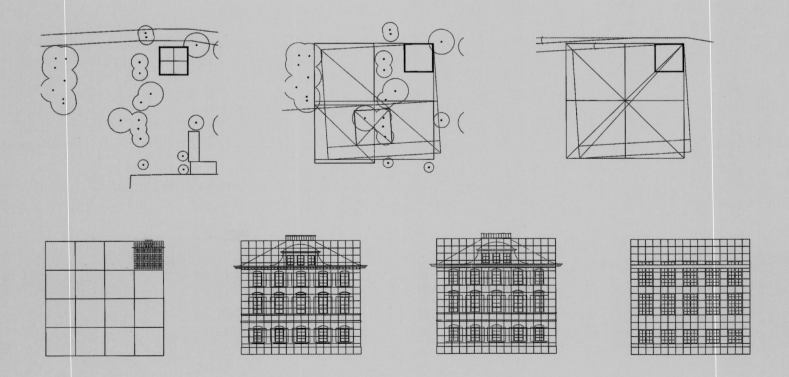

line and window proportions. Although the new building does not look like the villa, it takes its dimensions as a basis for organization.

In addition to relating to the villa, the design had to consider the seven other museums along the riverbank. It just so happens that there is a bend in the road at the site, and that bend is 3.5 degrees. By bending the plans and rotating them 3.5 degrees, we were able to open up the building to the city to the north, open it up to the park to the west, and also align the façade of the new building with the façades of the other seven museums along the street. The diagonal tension that is produced by rotating the square plan within the orthogonal grid allows for a compressing of spaces in some places and an opening of spaces in others, and this rather subtle tension allows different things to happen within the building.

The museum is also an urban bridge, a pedestrian link between the residential area of the city, called Sachsenhausen, to the south, and the commercial area of Frankfurt, to the north. As they come from the residential portion of Sachsenhausen, people can move through the building, under the building, through the courtyards, and can also see the changing exhibitions. As in the High Museum in Atlanta, the building becomes part of the daily route from home to work, and that route goes through the building across the pedestrian bridge, which links the residential area on one side of the Main River with the commercial business area on the other.

The route within the building is by a ramp up through the center of the building, which is open on one side with views out toward the city. At the opening ceremonies, the mayor of Frankfurt stood on the top level of the ramp, looked down, then said to me, "You know, Frankfurt is not this awful place that people say it is. It looks quite well from here." I think that this is an important part of the museum experience—to see the city, to be related to areas outside. There are always shifting views to the city beyond—and these reinforce the experience of the museum as a bridge. It is a bridge between home and work as well as between the past and the present.

The Getty Center

J. Paul Getty made it all possible when he left 11 percent of his wealth to the Getty Museum in Malibu. He spent his youth in Los Angeles and lived in a house in Malibu. Getty began collecting art in the 1930s, mainly Greek and Roman antiquities, but also some Renaissance and Baroque paintings as well

as a very good collection of European decorative arts.

In 1953, he established his Malibu house as a museum. By the sixties, the house could not accommodate his vast and ever-growing collection, so he commissioned another building that is a re-creation of an ancient Roman country house, the Villa dei Papiri. The villa was buried when Mount Vesuvius erupted in 79 A.D., so the museum is a replica based on a loose interpretation of what the building was like. The museum, designed by the architects Langdon and Wilson, was completed in 1974.

When I first visited this rather charming building, I was struck by something that I had never seen before—the relationship of interior to exterior space. The way in which one can go outside and inside, the flow from garden to gallery, is something that I think is special to the climate here in Southern California. Although one can argue about the style of the building, the beauty has to do with this free flow of space, this movement from outside to inside. This is one of the things that was very important to me in the design of the new Getty Center, the way in which there is a free flow of space, the relationship between building and garden.

The Getty Center is more than a museum, it is also a Center for the History of the Arts and Humanities, a very important art history library, and the Conservation Institute. The Conservation Institute is not only concerned with conservation of works of art, but with conservation of architecture and of monuments throughout the world.

The site in Brentwood is an astounding piece of land. It was tough because there was nothing to hang your hat on, nothing to relate to. The property was formerly owned by a developer who used to spend his weekends on a Caterpillar tractor moving the earth around for fun. So even the topography is

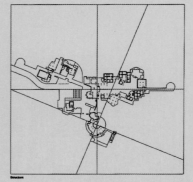

not very sacred, since it has been treated like putty, pushed here and there. On the top there was only chaparral; there were no trees. The views are in every direction—to downtown Los Angeles, to the mountains, to the desert, to the ocean.

The freeway, as it comes straight from the airport, then toward the San Fernando Valley to the north, bends 22.5 degrees at about the point where you enter the site. To me, that seemed a powerful element. It happens, also, that there are two ridges on the site: one that parallels the freeway and the other that is roughly at 22.5 degrees, paralleling the way in which the San Diego Freeway turns.

So the freeway became one of the generating elements in the organization of the buildings of the Getty Center. The public side of the site is adjacent to the freeway, and the more private side of the site is the one on the west, which looks out to the Pacific Ocean. The scheme, then, is that the museum side, the public side, is also the San Diego Freeway side, while the Center for the History of Arts and Humanities, the scholarly place, is on the other ridge, and in between the two is a public garden. This was to be a Villa d'Este-type water garden, which would have connected the museum to the center.

Visitors experience the museum, the clusters of buildings around the courtyard, and then move out to the garden to the café. The trust offices, art history information program, and Conservation Institute are much more private, with different outlooks to the site. With its unique location in Los Angeles, its view to the city, this is a place where people come to view the gardens as much as to visit the museum.

To me, architecture is an art of substance, of material ideas about space. There are many demands on the architect—program, site, location, and others—but buildings are for the contemplation of the eyes and the mind and must be experienced and savored by all human senses. Form in architecture cannot be unrelated to human experience. One cannot approach an understanding of experience in terms of architecture without a strongly sensuous and tactile attitude about form and space.

I believe it is possible to see my work as a sequence of investigations into the spatial interchange between the public and the private realms. This interchange expresses itself in a variety of ways, but it is always related to the idea of architectural promenade, to the idea of passage. My work is an attempt to find and to redefine a sense of order, to try to understand a relationship between what has been and what might be. I try to extract from our culture both the timeless and the topical, and this, to me, is the basis of style. The decision of what to include and what to exclude is the final exercise of the individual will and intellect.

My mediations are on space, form, and light, and how to make them. My goal is presence, not illusion, and I pursue it with unrelenting vigor. I believe that it is the heart and soul of architecture.

February 1989

Richard Meier. "On the Road Again." In *Architecture: Shaping the Future – A Symposium and Exhibition with Legorreta, Maki, Meier & Rogers.* Introduction by Allan Temko. San Diego: University of California, 1990.

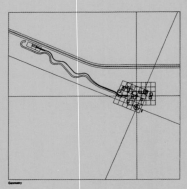
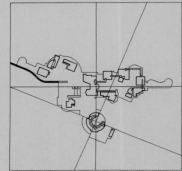
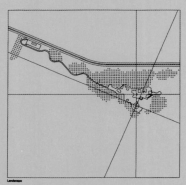
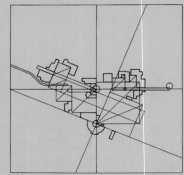

The Getty Center

Views of the complex from the northwest
and from the San Diego Freeway
to the east.

The entrance to the auditorium.

The plaza providing access
to the museum at the cableway
terminal and the end of the service road.
The entrance to the museum
from the streetcar terminal.

Views of the Foundation building
to the north, the Institute
of Conservation to the northeast
and the cafeteria
from the entrance plaza.

following pages
View of the plaza and the flight of steps
leading to the museum.

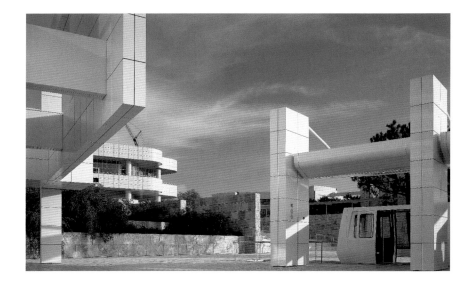

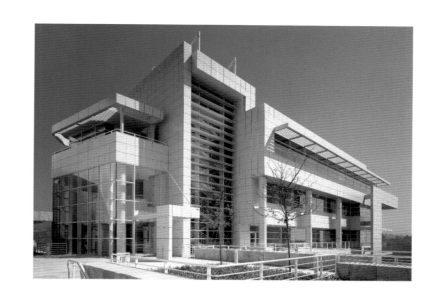

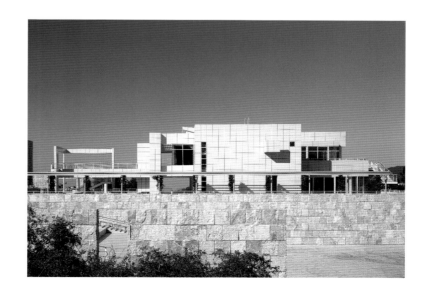

197

Views of the café-restaurant
from the west and south.

Views of the Institute of Art History
and Humanities to the southwest
of the complex.

View of the gardens
and of the exhibition pavilions
from the west.

The ramp leading to the plaza
of the museum from the southwest.

Views of the museum courtyard
and detail of the south entrance.

Views of the interiors of the auditorium
and a pavilion of the museum.

Views of the interior of the entrance
rotunda leading to the museum
and the Institute of Conservation.

View of the interior of the Institute
of Art History.

Planimetric diagrams for the analysis
of the design elements and criteria:
context, structure, geometry,
circulation, landscape, external spaces.

Site plan showing the disposition
of masses of the complex.

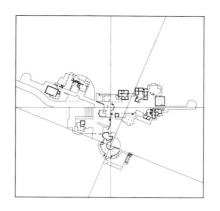
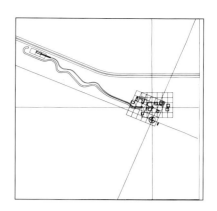

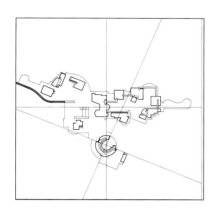
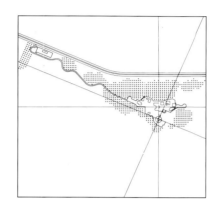
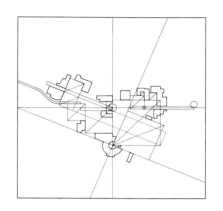

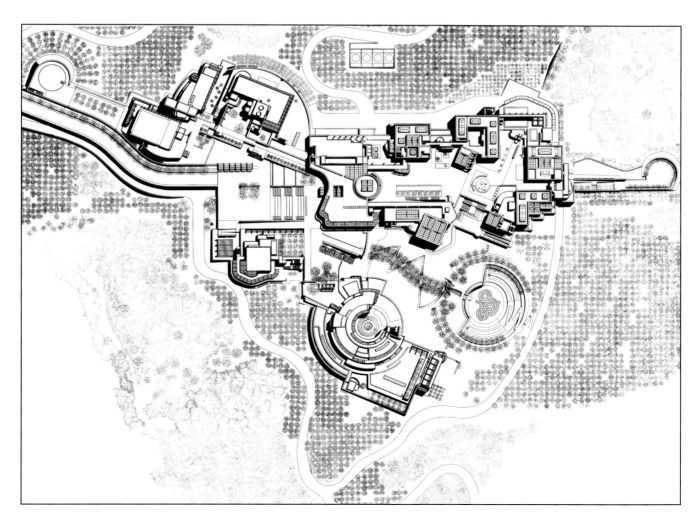

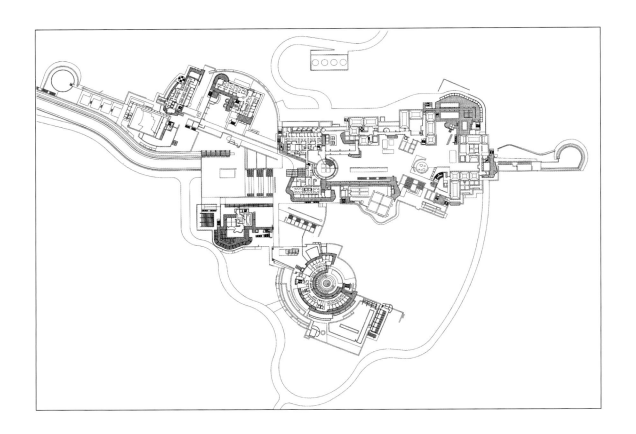

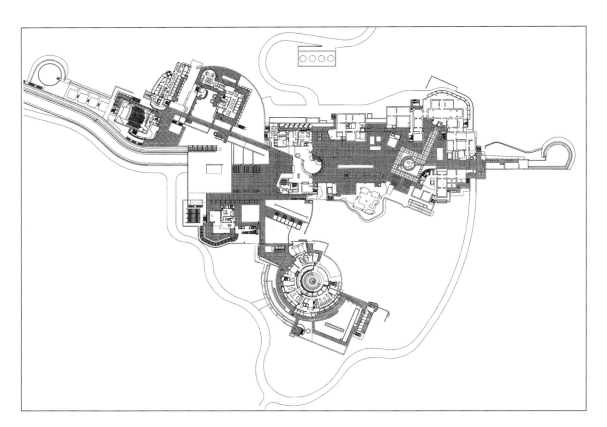

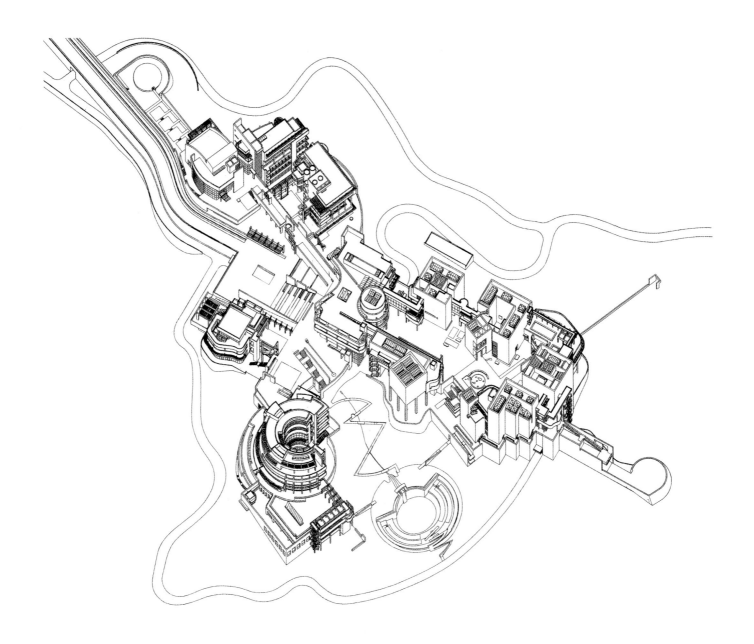

Plans of the upper floor
and of the entrance level.

General axonometric projection.

Details of the *brise-soleil*
and the facings of the façade.

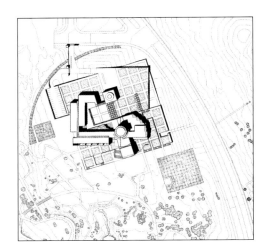

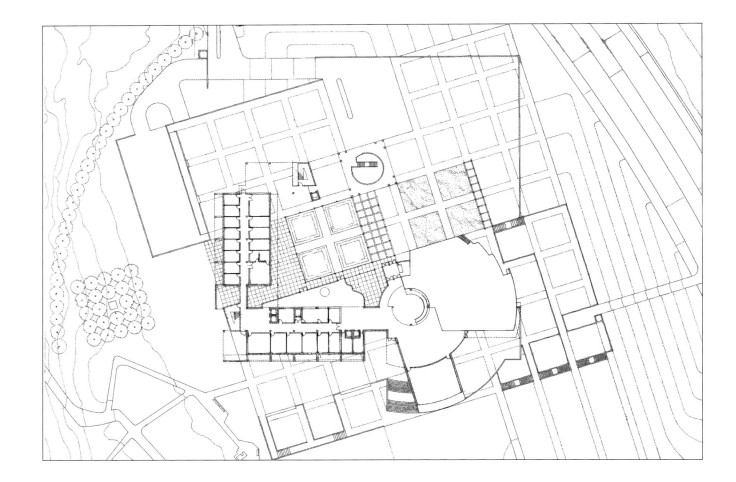

Site plan showing the disposition
of masses and plan of the ground floor.

Perspective drawing from the entrance
court, north elevation and section
through the assembly hall.

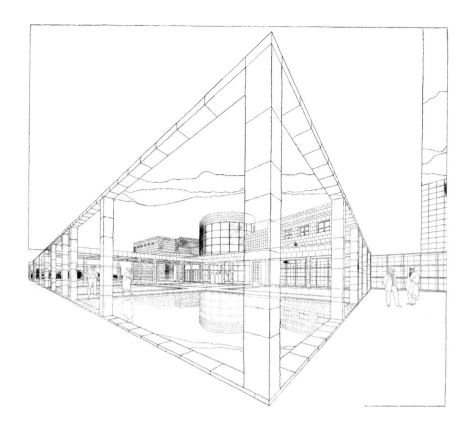

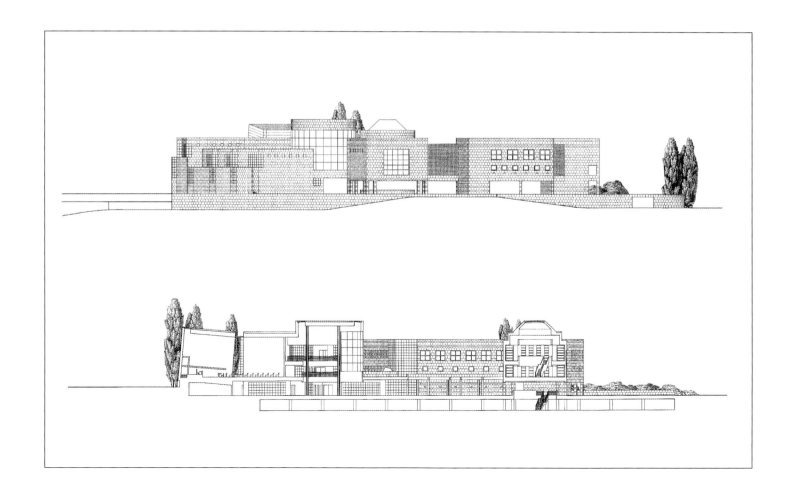

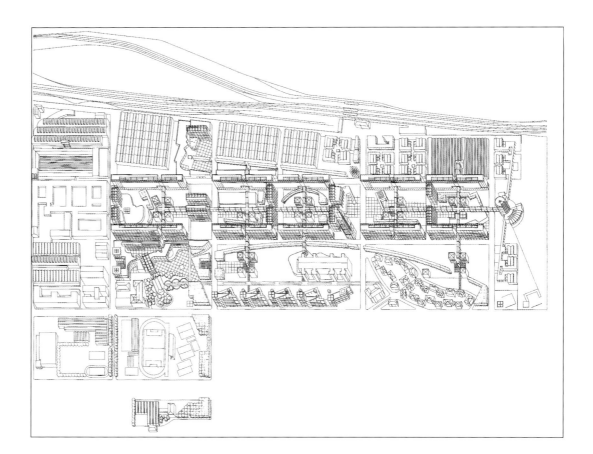

Area plans of the existing situation, the project proposal and general axonometric projection.

Aerial view from the south.

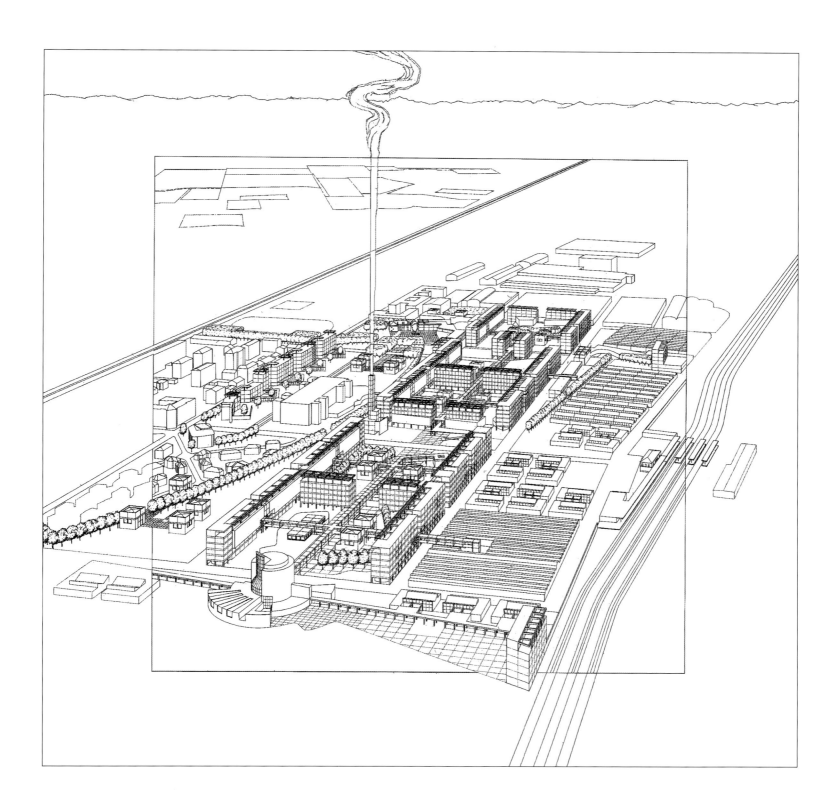

1986
1993

Exhibition and Assembly Building

View from Hirschstrasse.

The main front on Münsterplatz.

217

Views of the passages
and the exhibition rooms
on the two upper floors.

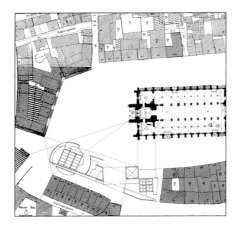

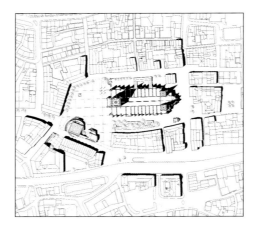

Scheme showing the visual impact of the new volumes on the square. Site plan and general axonometric projection.

Richard Meier's studies for plans at various levels.

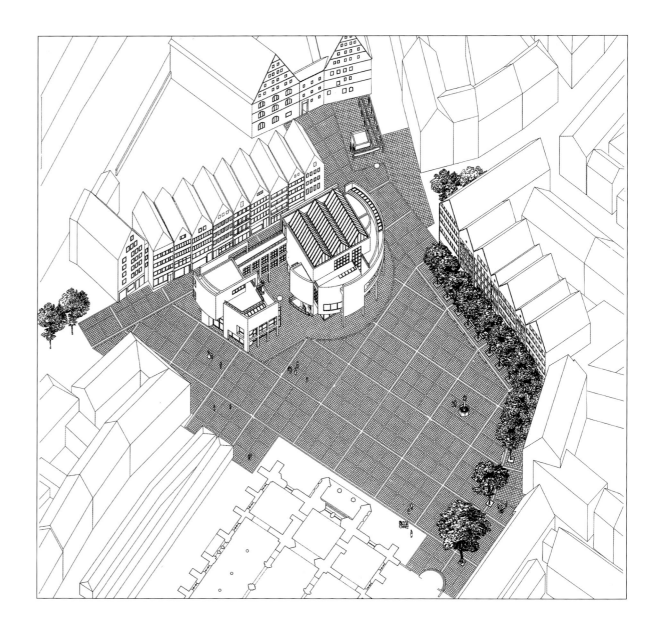

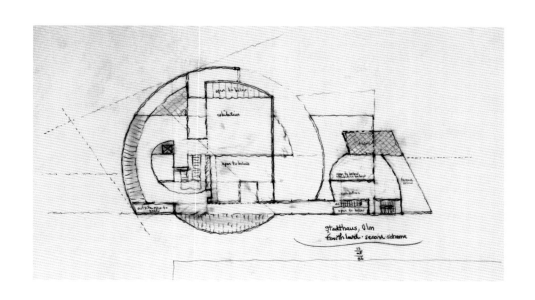

Stadthaus, Ulm
fourth level · second scheme

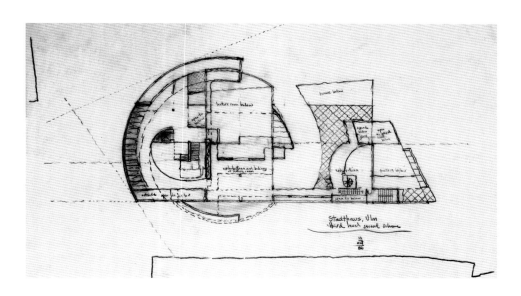

Stadthaus, Ulm
third level · second scheme

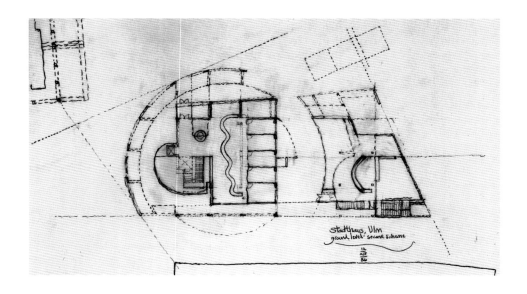

Stadthaus, Ulm
ground level · second scheme

221

1989
1995

City Hall and Central Library

View of the corner between
Kalvermarkt and Turfmarkt
from the west.

The entrance from the urban square
to the southeast.

Views of the internal covered plaza.

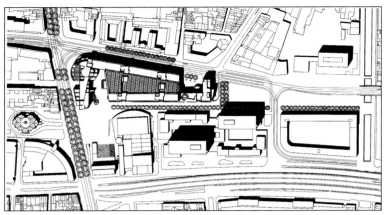

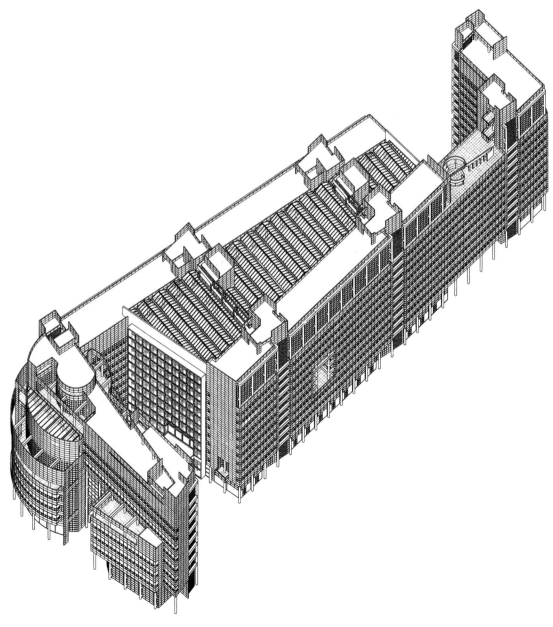

General plan and axonometric
projection.

Plans of the fifth and ground floors.

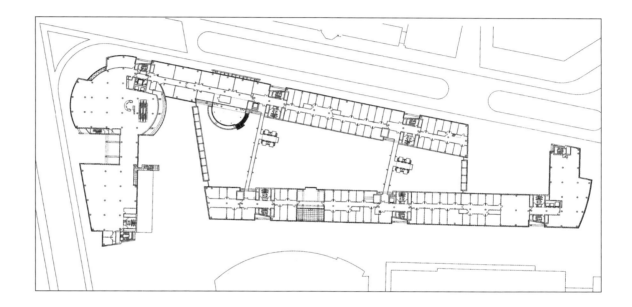

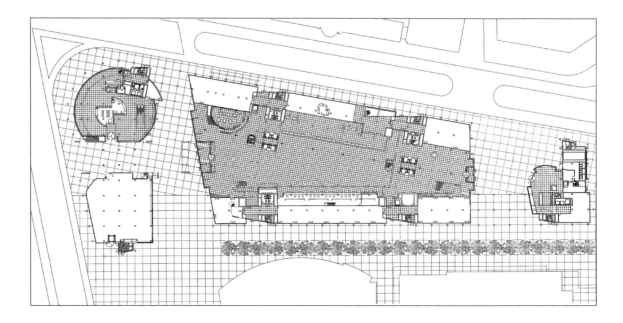

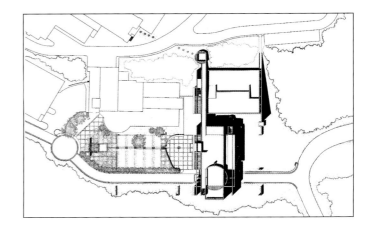

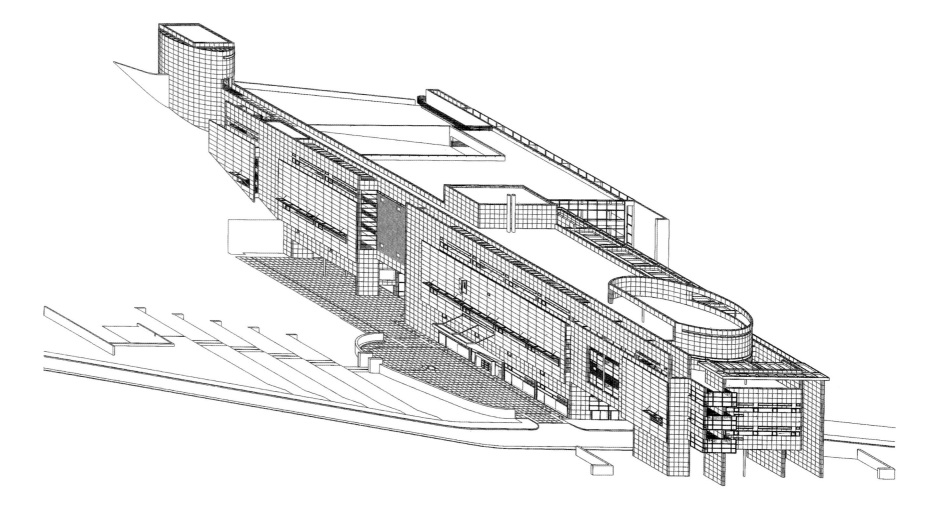

General plan and axonometric
projection.

Views of the model.

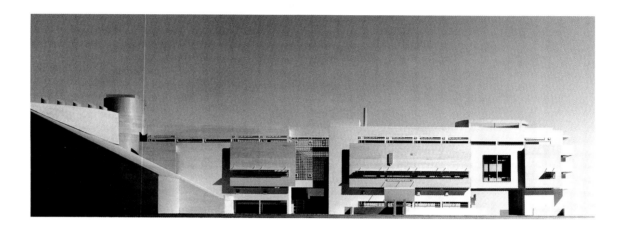

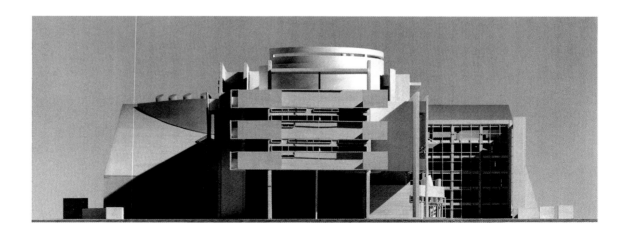

1987 | Projects for Naples

Photomontages and design sketches
by Richard Meier.

Site plan and perspective study
of the zone of the Quartieri Spagnoli.

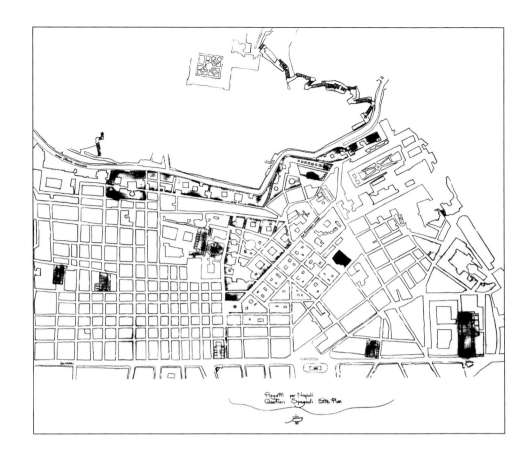

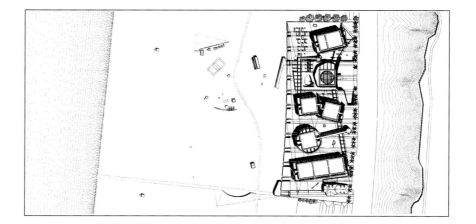

Plan of the ground floor and plan showing the disposition of masses.

Views of the model.

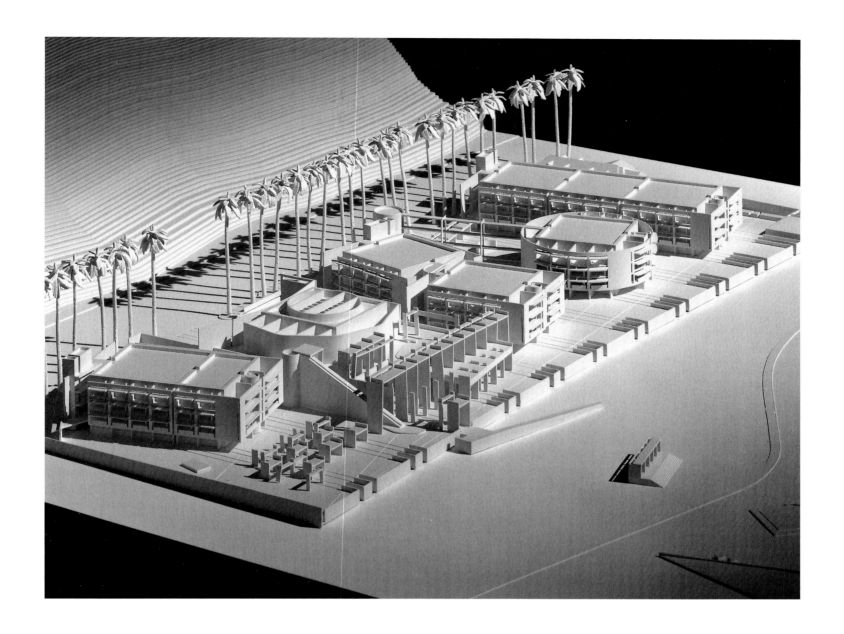

233

Views of the model.

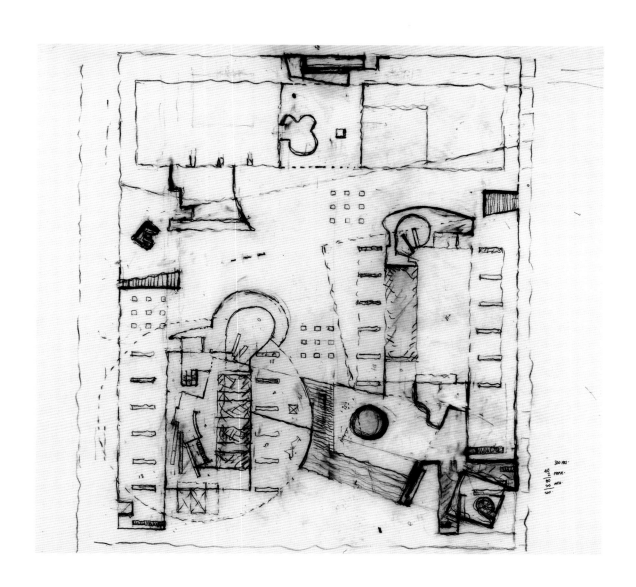

View of the model and study
by Richard Meier for the ground floor.

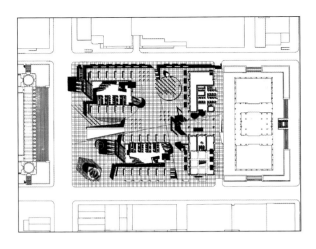

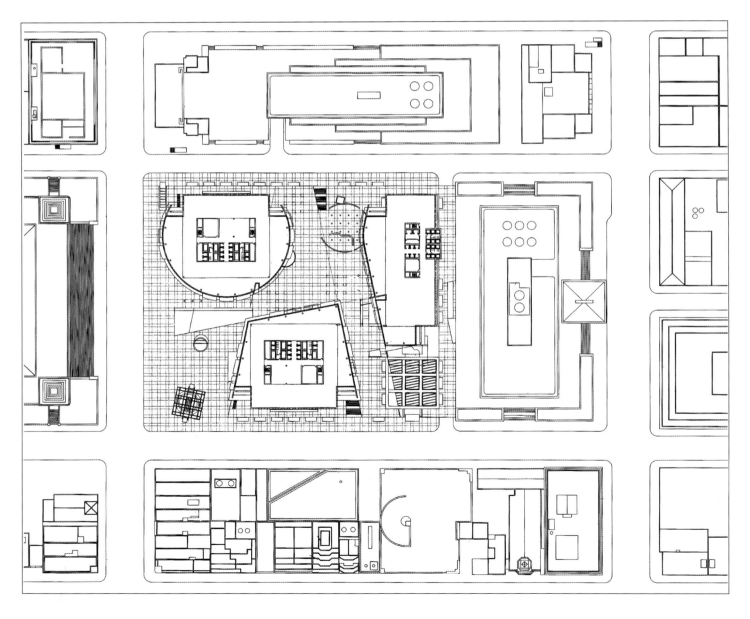

Plans of the ground floor with shadows
and of a standard floor.

South and west elevations and sections.

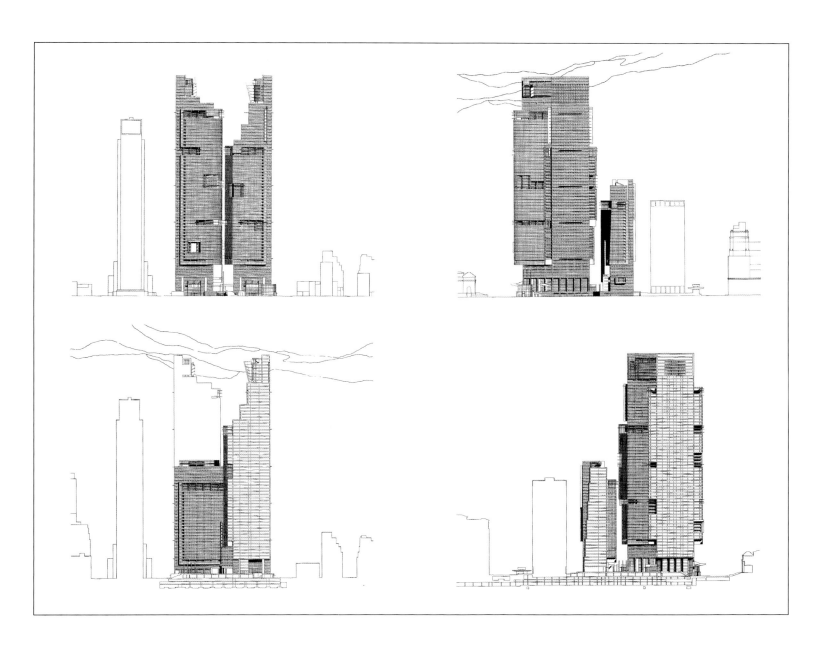

Views of the south front,
of the courtyard and detail
of the arcade facing onto the road.

Details of the ends of the arcade
and view of the canteen interior.

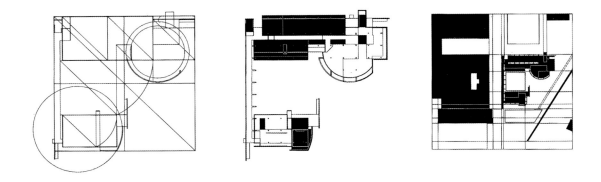

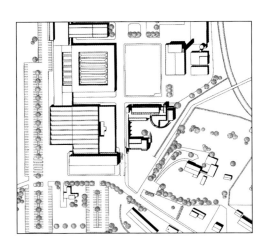

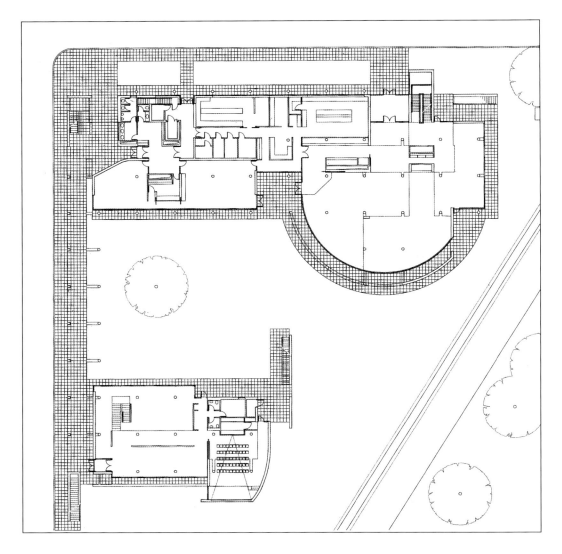

Geometric diagrams of the relationship
between solids and voids
and the relations with the site.
General plan and plan of the ground
floor.

Axonometric projection.

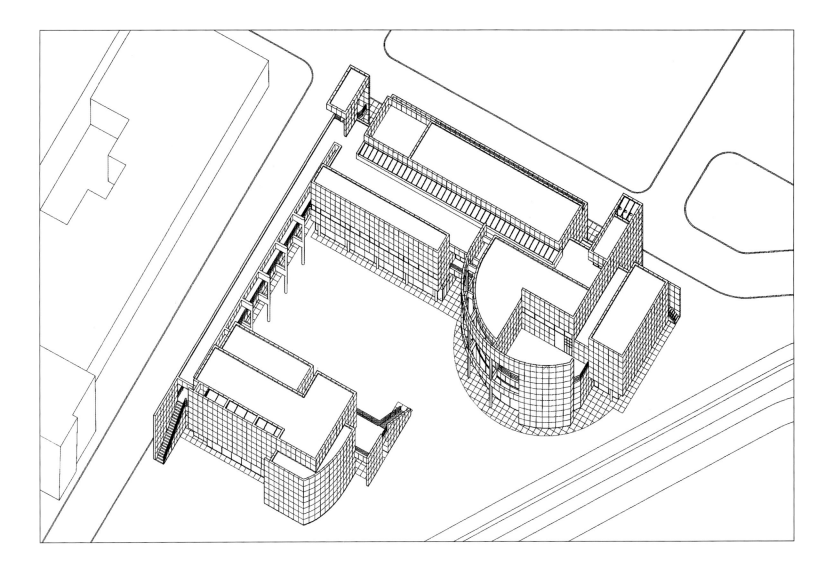

1987
1992

Royal Dutch Paper Mills Headquarters

The entrance to the northeast
and the southwest façade
of the reception building.

Details of the office block
and of the top of the reception building.

View of the reception building by night
showing the meeting room
on the top floor.

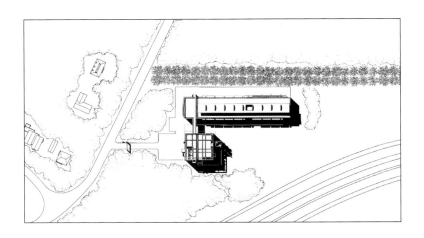

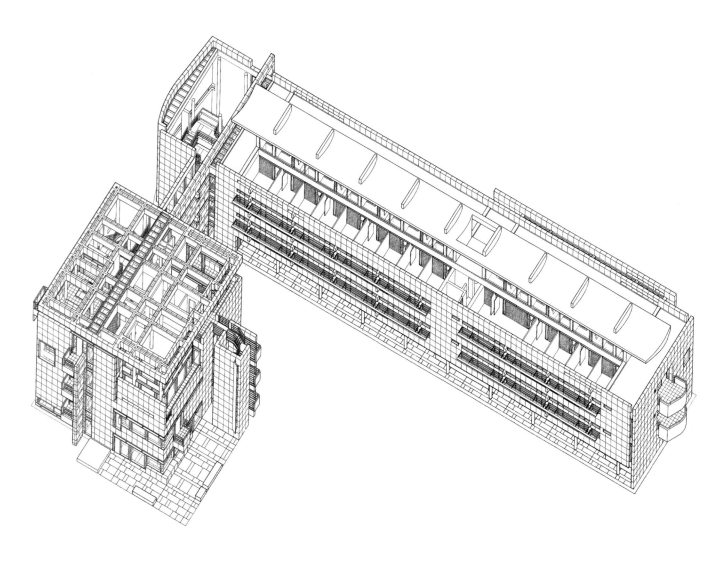

General plan and axonometric
projection.

Plans of the third, second
and ground floors.

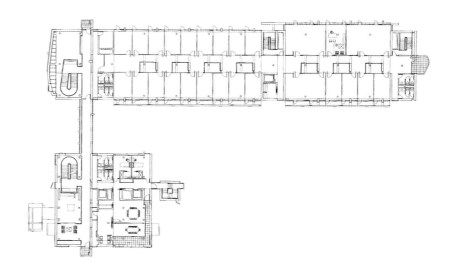

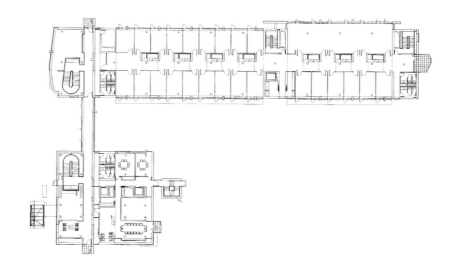

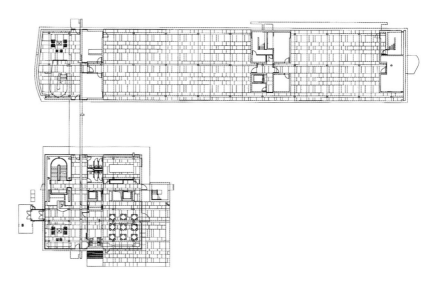

1987
1995

Museum of Contemporary Art

Views of the entrance of the museum,
on Plaça dels Angels.

Details of the exterior and view
of the entrance from the southwest.

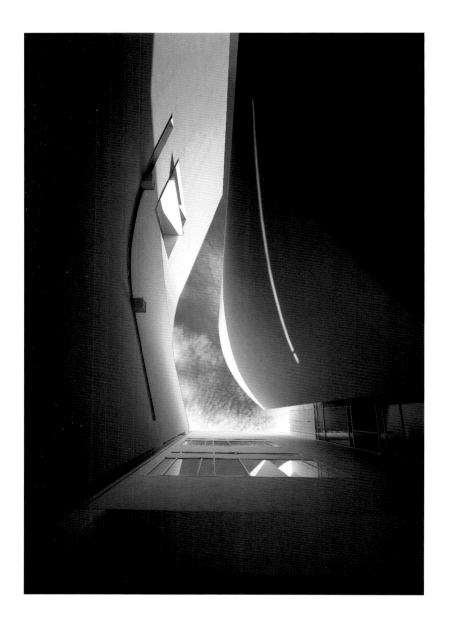

Views of the internal ramp
in the three-story-high atrium.

The exhibition gallery on the top floor
and detail of the skylight
in the multifoil hall.

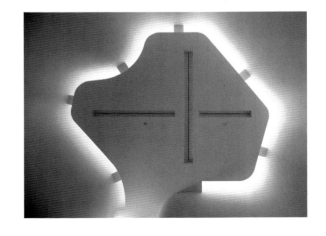

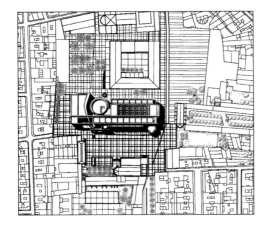

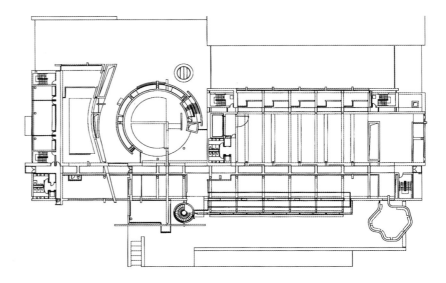

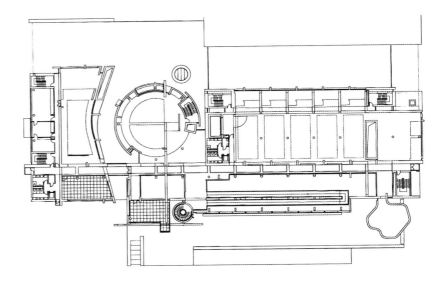

General plan of the museum set
in the block of the former convent
of the Casa de la Caritat.
Plans of the third, second
and ground floors.

Cross section through the entrance
and general axonometric projection
set in the urban context.

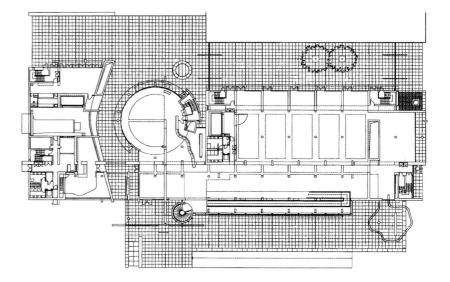

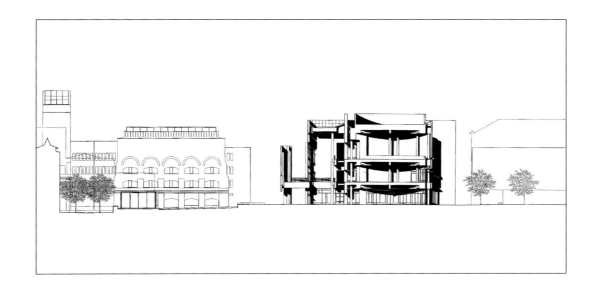

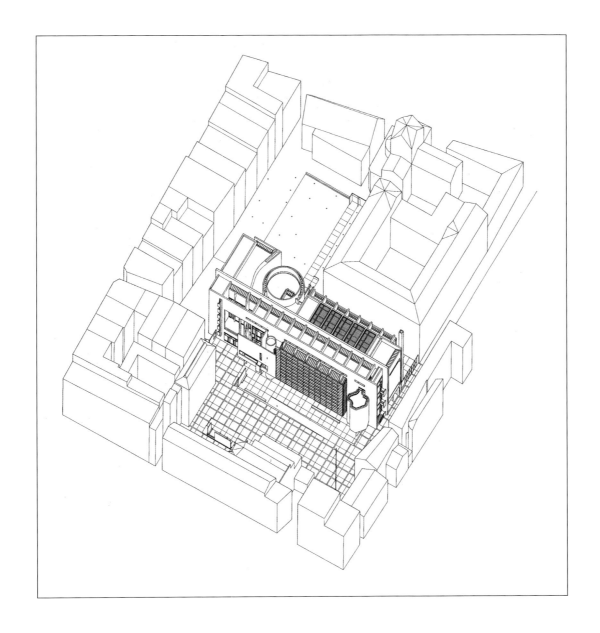

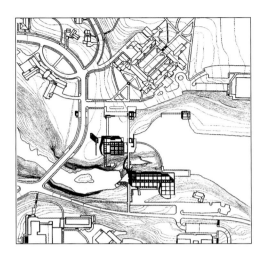

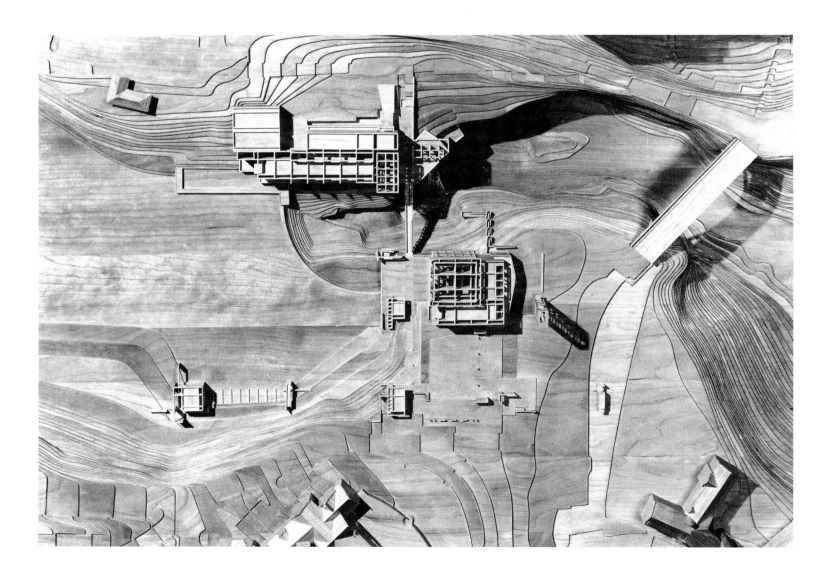

General plan and views of the model.

Views of the northwest
and northeast façades.

The building on the bank of the Seine.

View of the wing of the administrative
offices from the north.

Northwest, southeast, northeast
and southwest elevations,
at different times of day.

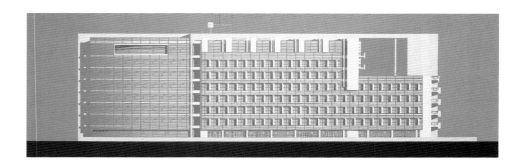

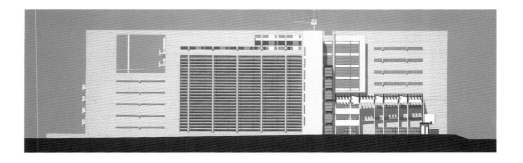

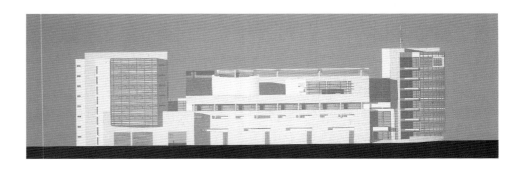

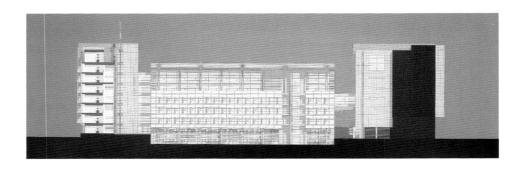

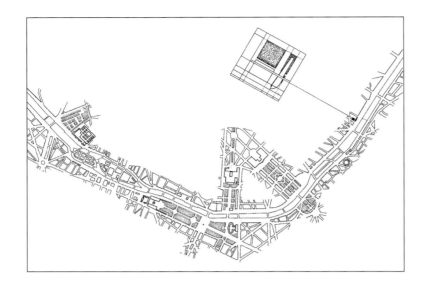

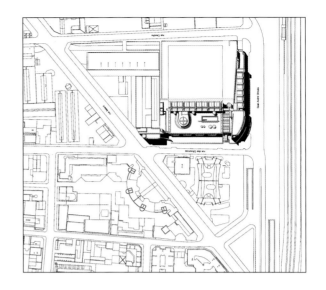

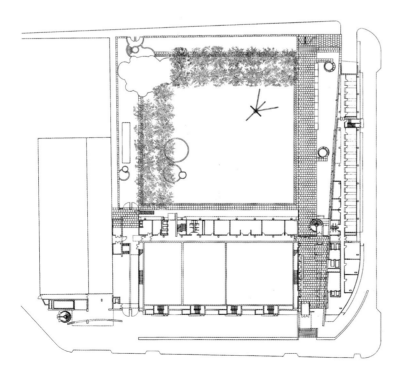

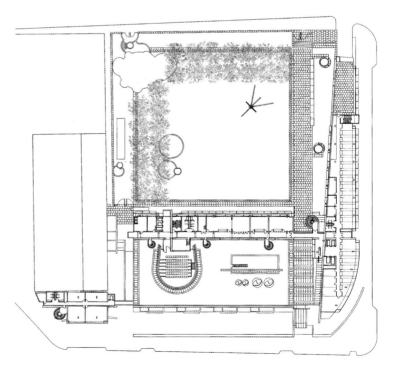

Urban location on the Seine
embankment and general plan.
Plans of the ground and sixth floors.

Axonometric projection.

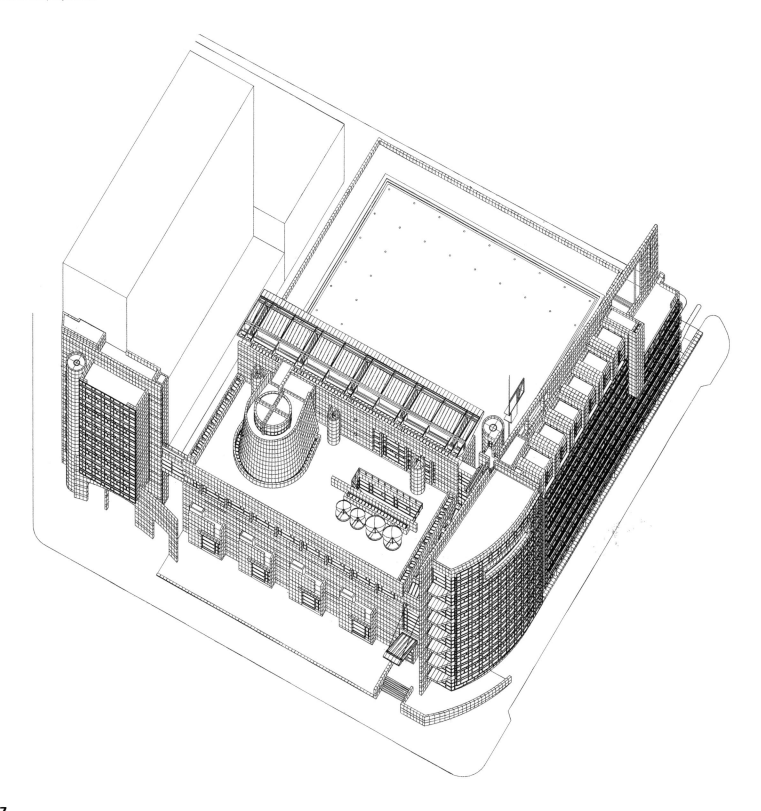

View of the front on Rue Pitôt
from the east and view
of the inner courtyard.

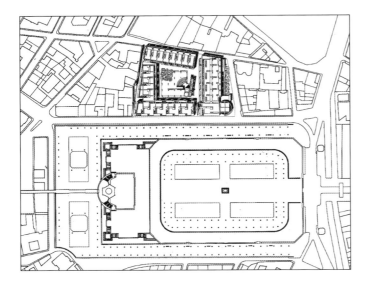

Plan set in the urban context
and plan of the intervention showing
the disposition of masses.

Plans at the levels of the underground
car parks, ground floor
and inner courtyard.
South, east and north elevations
and sections.

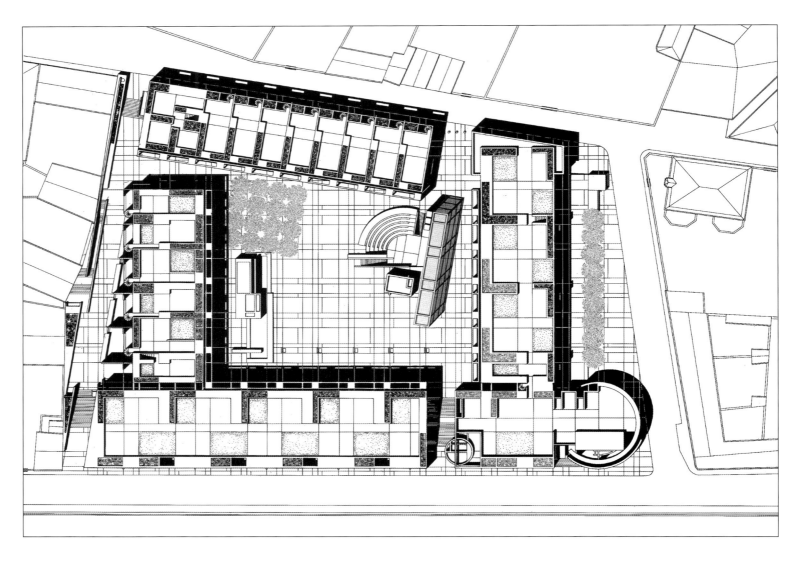

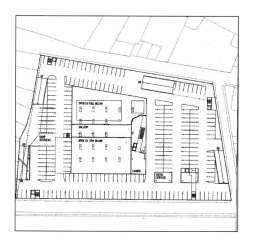

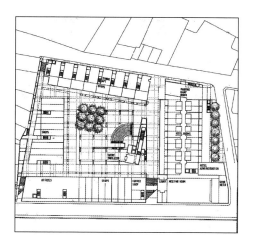

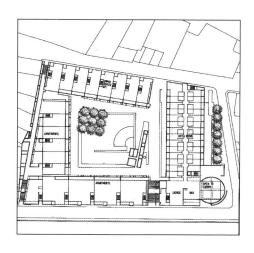

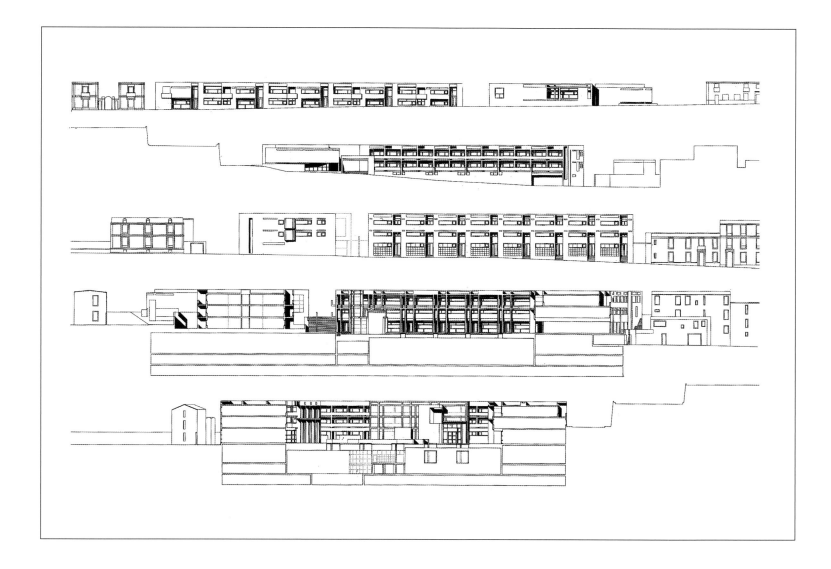

On White
Richard Meier

"Or is it, that as in essence whiteness is not so much a color as the visible absence of color; and at the same time the concrete of all colors …?"
Herman Melville, *Moby Dick*

The question I am most often asked by students of architecture following a lecture is "Why white?" I am always surprised by this question because having just completed a lecture illustrating many current and past projects I assume that the answer to this question is self-evident. But given the frequency of this inquiry, it is now clear to me that for many, the concreteness of white is not always as obvious as one would think, and so I am pleased to have the opportunity with the publication of this book to attempt to shed some light on the subject.

For me, white encompasses all colors. It most effectively reflects the passing colors of nature: the green grass, the blue sky, the autumn leaves. It is in that sense then that white is all colors. It is an expanding color, not a limiting one. Rather than choosing one color, which would remain static, white allows for the full spectrum of colors to manifest itself in a building. The contents of the building, be it people or art or books, present their own myriad set of colors as well. And with the changing light and seasons these things are in constant flux, resulting in architecture that can look different depending on the time of day or weather when they are experienced.

In architectural terms white is the color that most easily allows the fundamentals of building—space, volume, material—to be expressed in the most direct and clear way. With the use of white the differentiation between materials and the differentiation between solids and voids are most clearly articulated. The whiteness allows one to perceive the difference between transparent, translucent and opaque surfaces more easily. White enhances one's perception of the basic architectural elements.

I am fascinated by the world of light and shadow that exists free of associations with specific colors or materials. The whiteness creates a neutral surface on which to build an experience of a space. It heightens one's awareness of the organization and ordering principles of the space. It allows the powerful play of light and shadow to expression in the most expansive way. It allows the architecture to be flooded with light—light pervades, light is everywhere—and therefore to be experienced at its purest and most fundamental level.

There are other aspects of white and Melville is very descriptive about them as he looked at white in a special way: "This elusive quality it is, which causes the thought of whiteness, when divorced from more kindly associations, and coupled with any object terrible in itself, to heighten that terror to the furthest bounds … Bethink thee of the albatross, whence come those clouds of spiritual and pale dread, in which that white phantom sails in all imaginations? … Therefore, in his other moods, symbolize whatever grand or gracious thing he will by whiteness, no man can deny that in its profoundest idealized significance it calls up a peculiar apparition to the soul."
Herman Melville, *Moby Dick*

Ultimately, the use of that "white-light whiteness" allows me to pursue my basic concerns of creating space, form and light in architecture.
February 2002

Views of the constructed part
from the west and north.

Views of the southeast front
and the interior of the café-restaurant.

Ground-floor plan of the constructed
parts and general plan of the project.

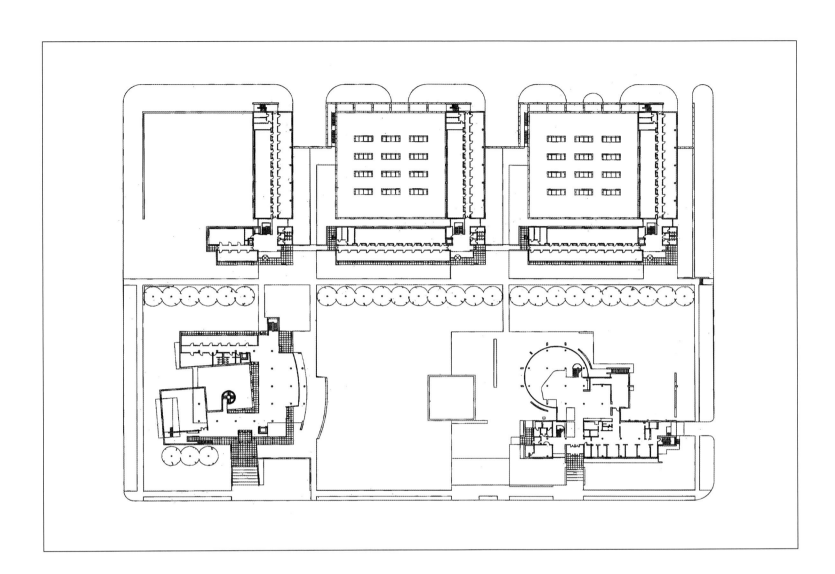

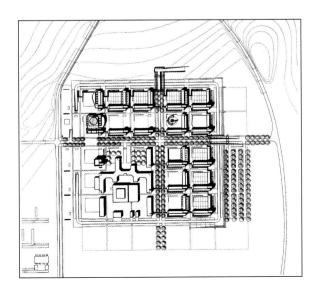

Views of the model.

Ground-floor plan, south and west elevations and section.

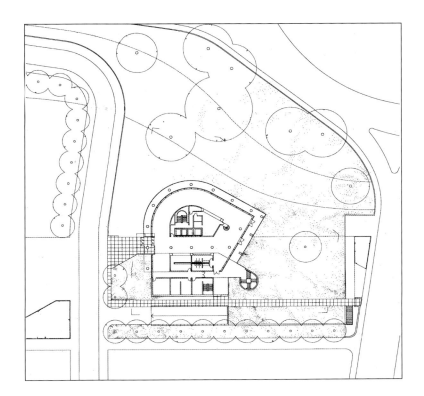

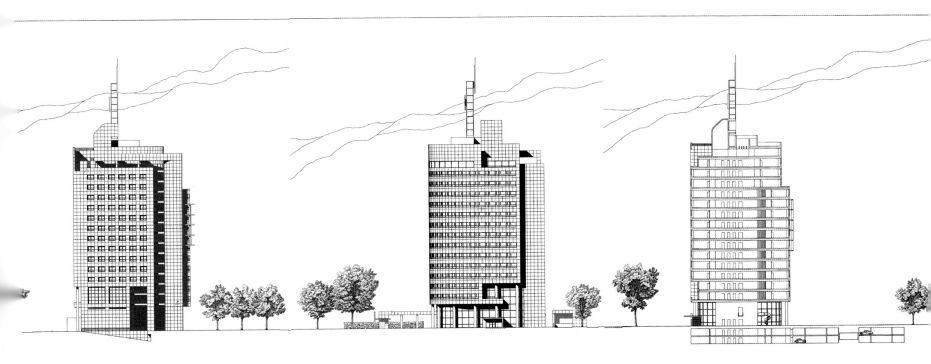

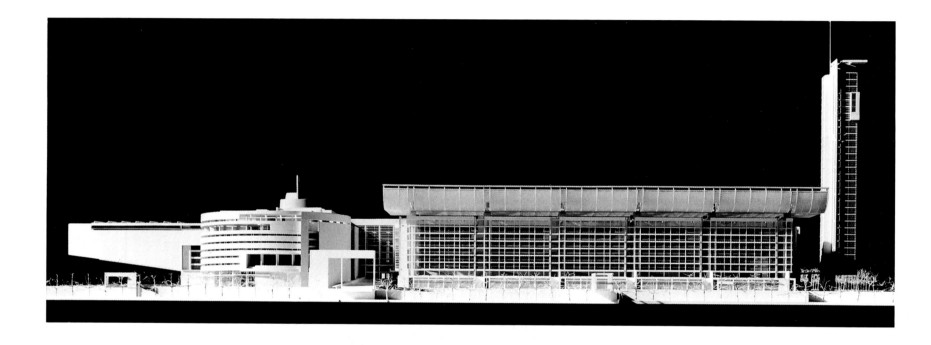

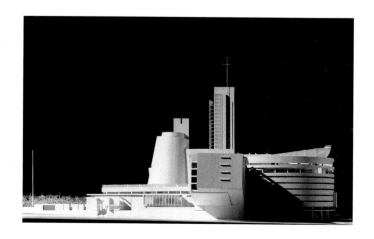

Views of the model.

General plan showing the disposition
of masses and elevation facing
onto the river.

Urban location along the Seine.

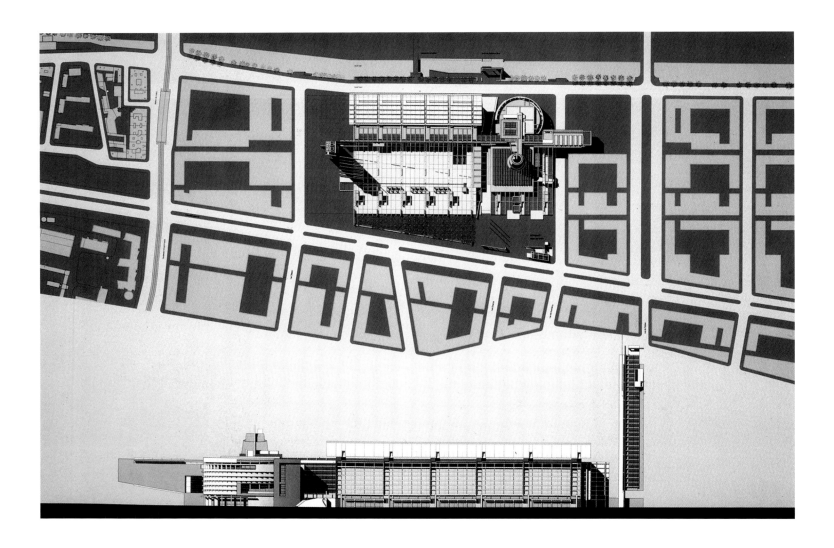

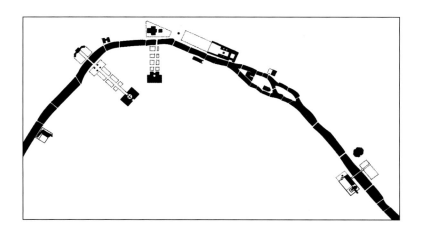

Plan at the level of the reading room
and southwest elevation-section.

Cross section.

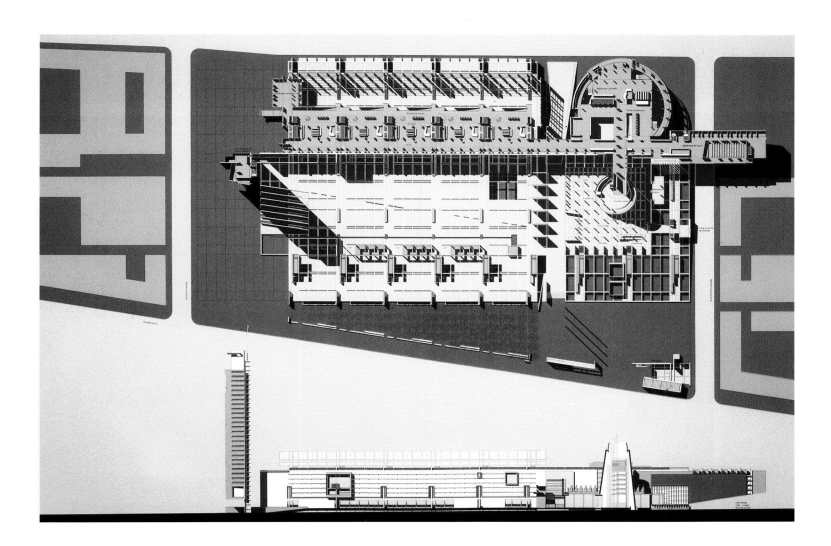

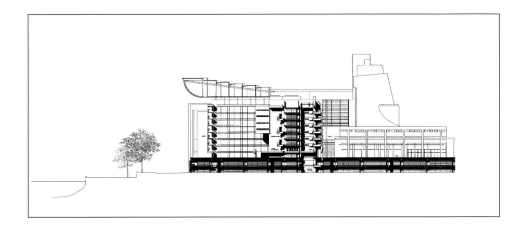

1989
1993

Hypolux Bank Building

View of the main front
facing northeast.

View of the northwest wing
from the entrance court.

Views of the southeast end
and the cylindrical volume
of the premises open to the public.

The modular grid of the sunscreens
on the southwest and northwest façades.

The gallery linking the spaces open
to the public and the office wing.

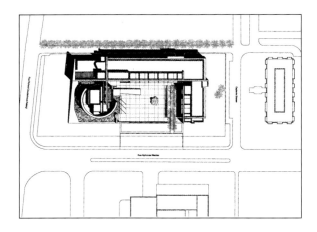

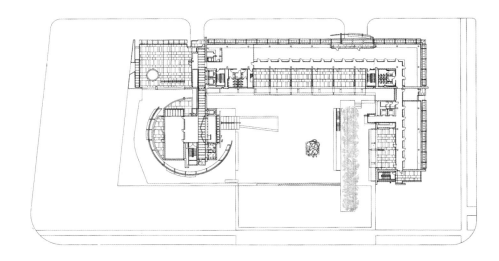

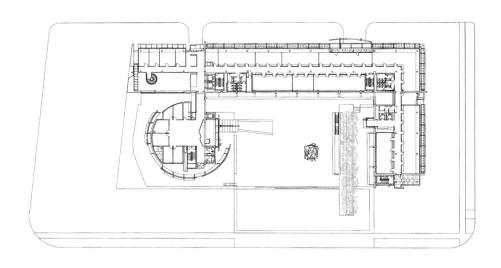

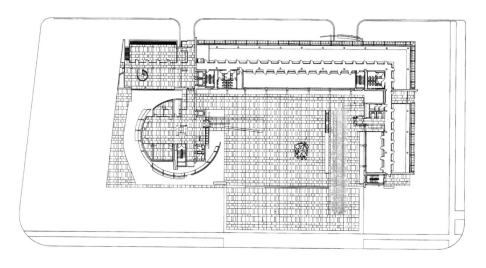

Site plan and plans of the fifth, fourth
and ground floors.

Northeast, southwest and southeast
elevations and cross section.

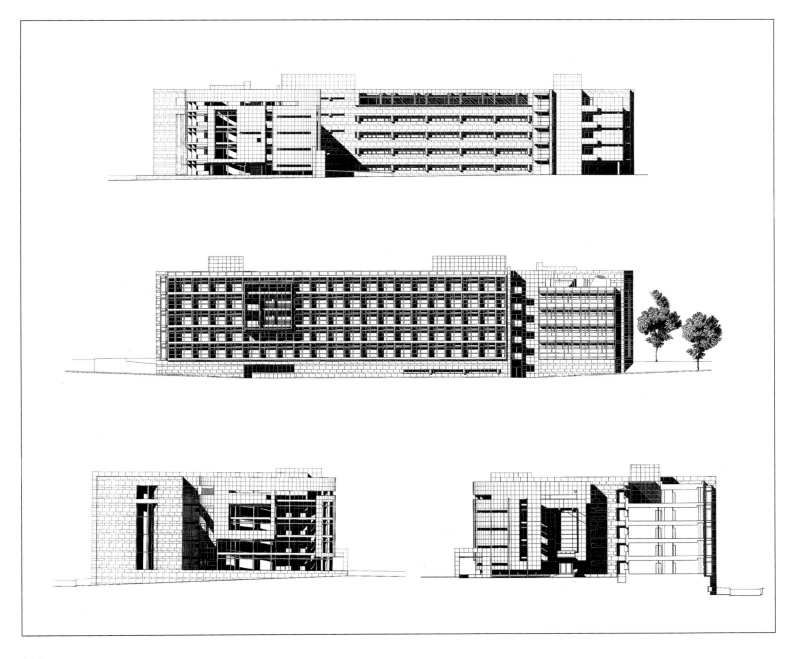

Views of the model.

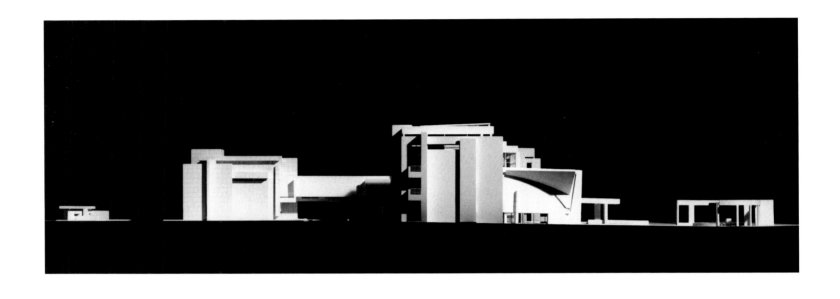

Views of the model.

General plan of the ground floor
with the Museum of Decorative Arts.

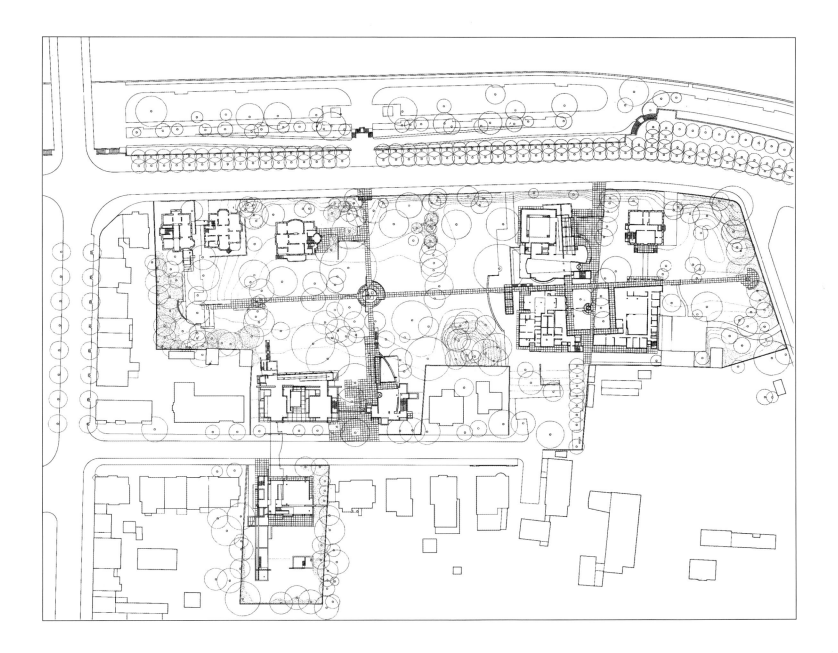

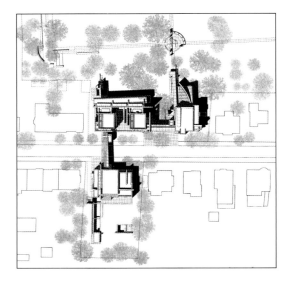

Site plan showing the disposition of masses and plans of the ground and third floors.

General axonometric projection.

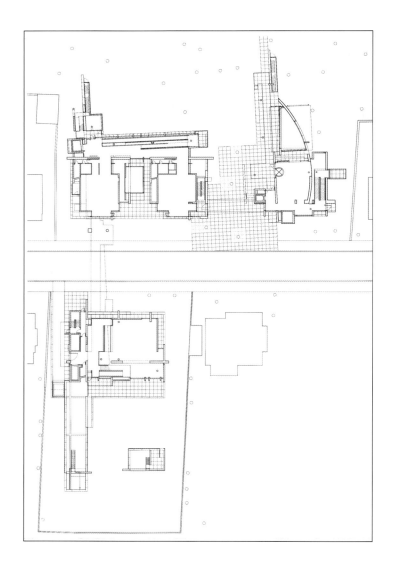

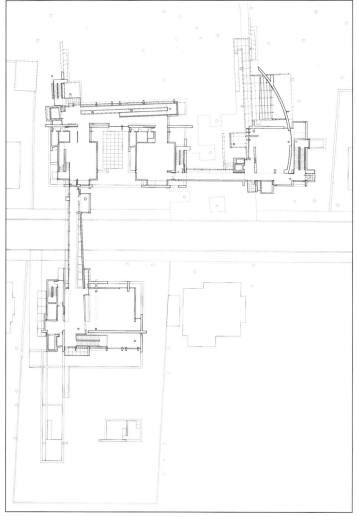

View of the model.

Diagrams of insertion of the plan
in the urban context: networks, limits,
spaces and routes, fabric.
General plan showing the disposition
of masses.

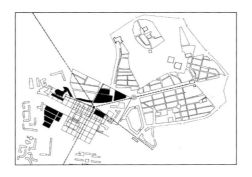

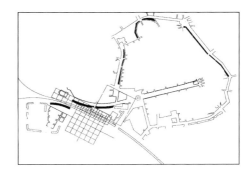

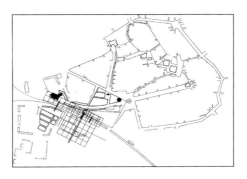

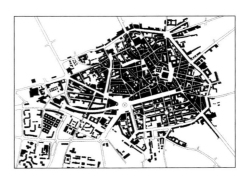

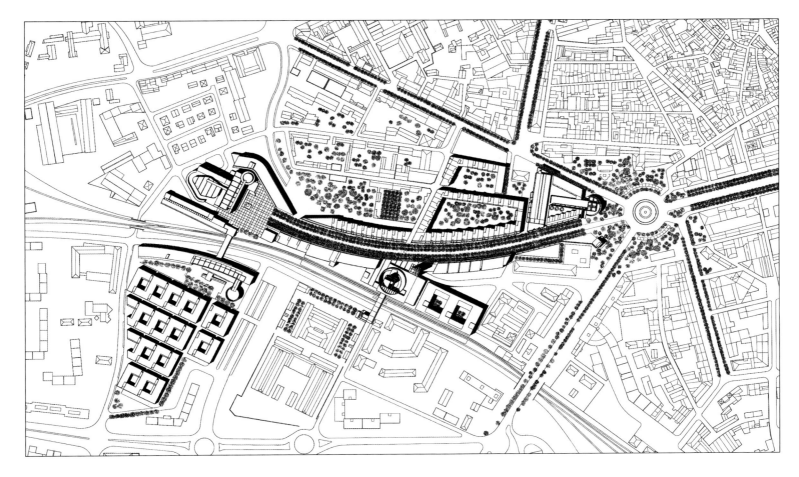

Views of the model from the river
and overhead.

Axonometric projection.

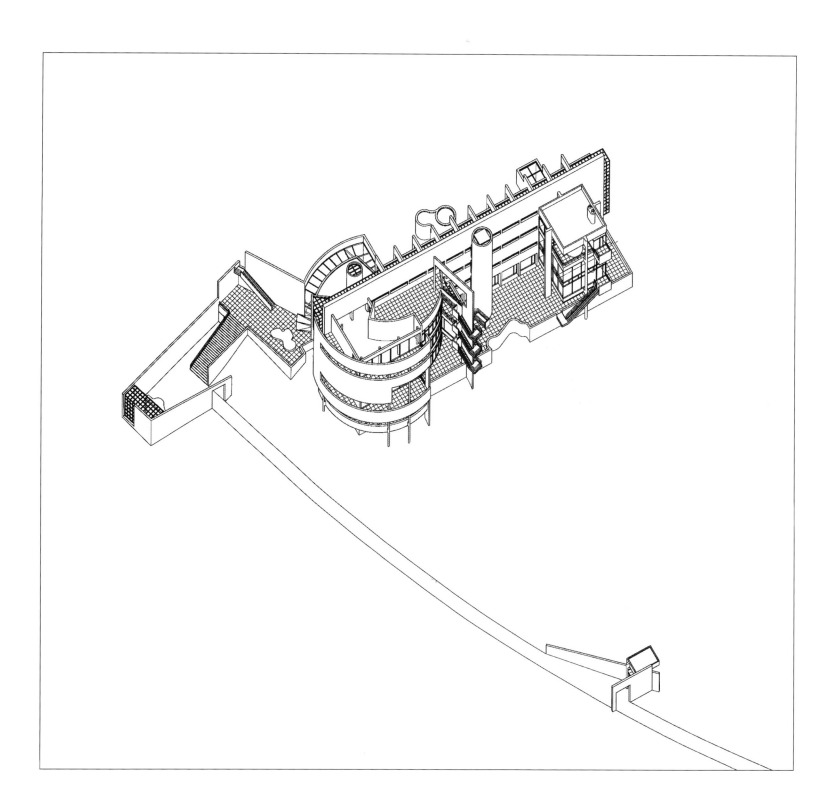

Plans of the third, second, ground
and basement floors.

Longitudinal and cross sections.

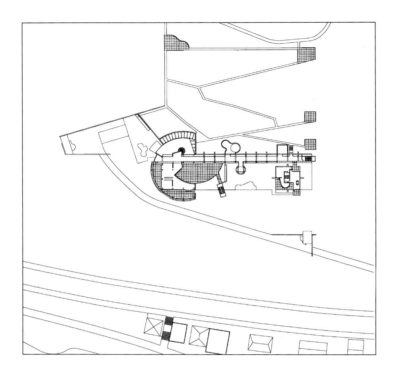

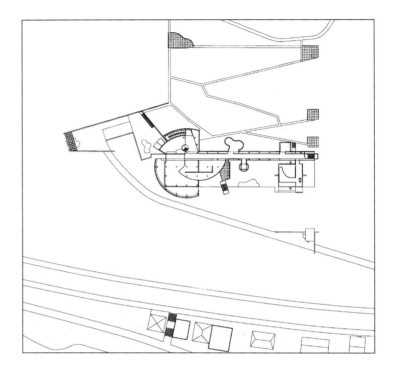

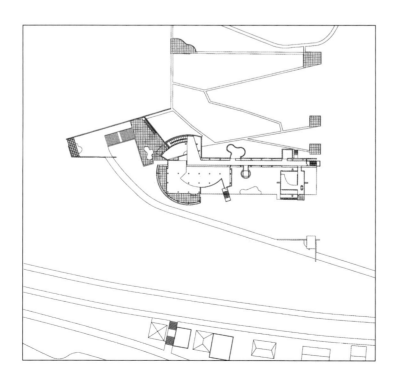

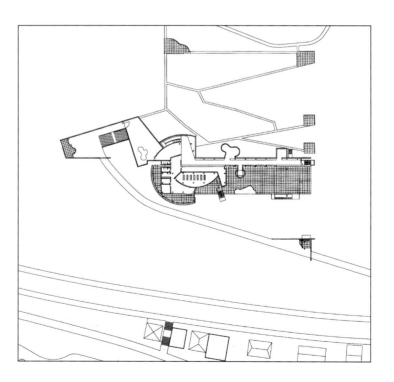

1990
1998

Euregio Office Building

Views of the bank from the southeast
and of the northwest front.

Detail of the entrance court
from Viaduktstrasse.

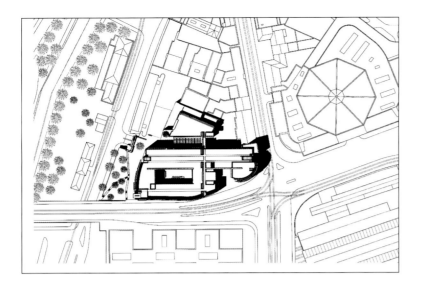

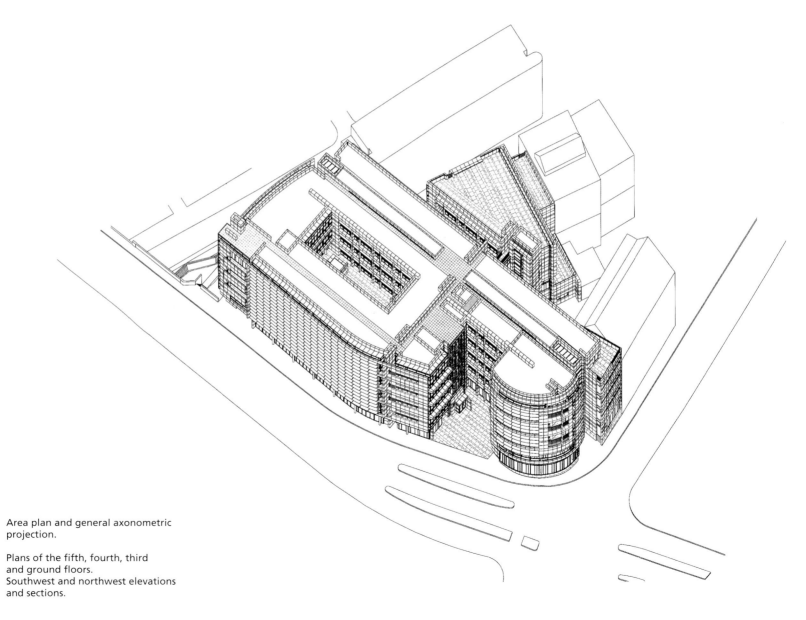

Area plan and general axonometric
projection.

Plans of the fifth, fourth, third
and ground floors.
Southwest and northwest elevations
and sections.

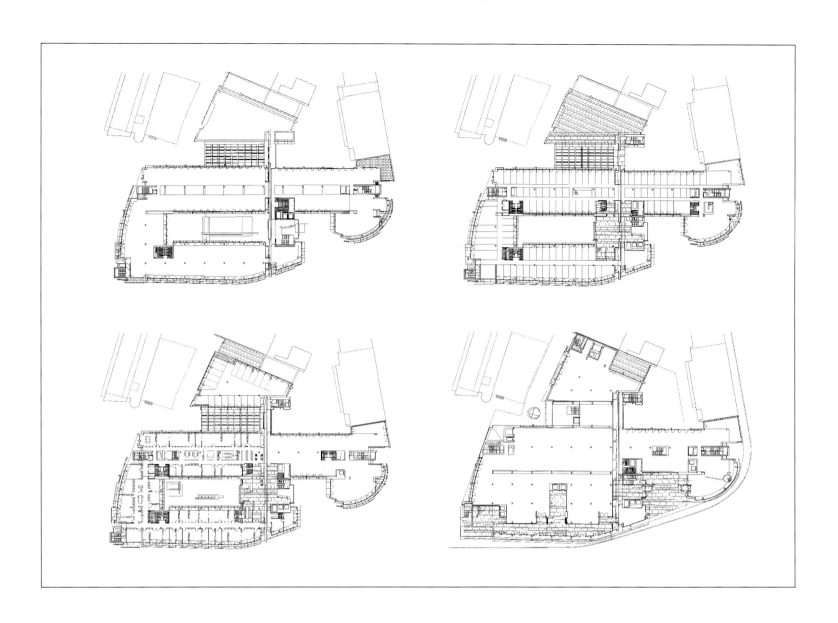

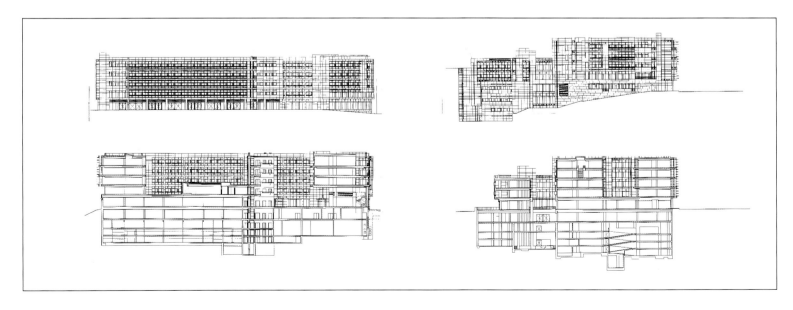

Perspective view from below.

Detail of the entrance
and view from the northeast.

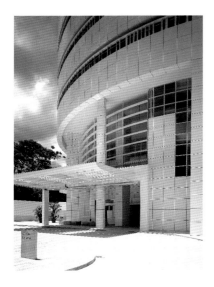

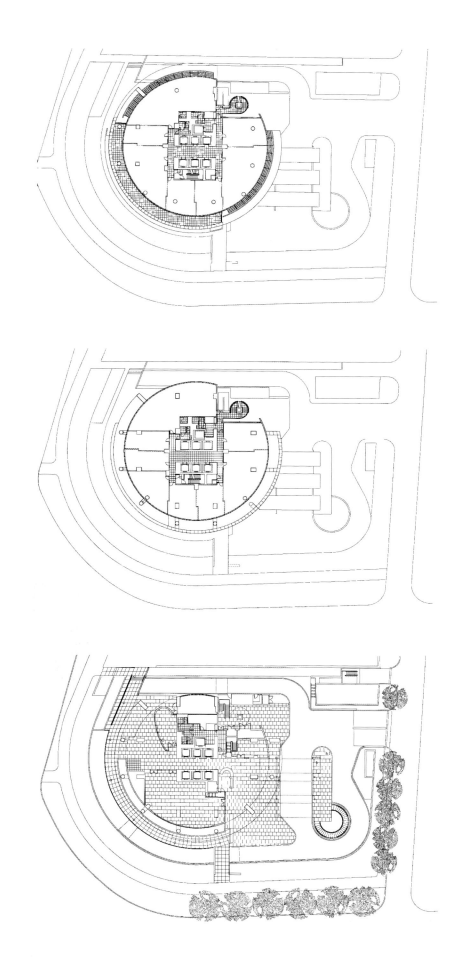

Plans of the fifteenth, ninth
and ground floors.

North and east elevations.

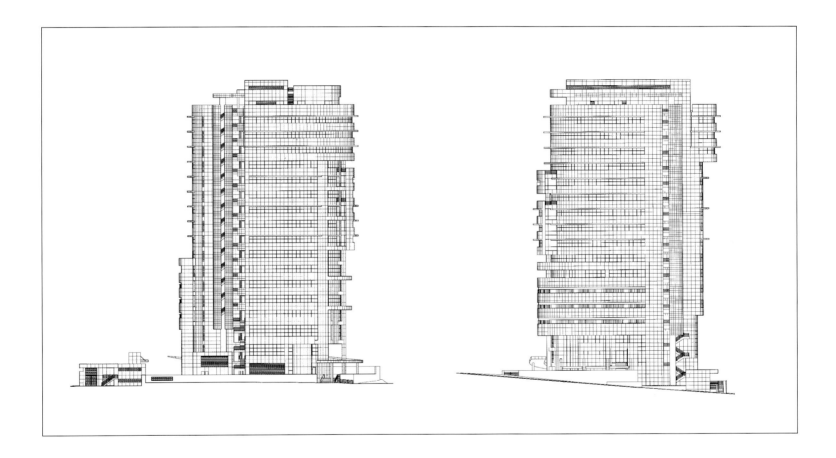

Views of the west front
onto the garden.

Details of the block of stairs
on the south end and the pavilion
of the swimming pool.

The entrance front viewed
from the east.

The glass wall of the living room from the northwest and detail of the atrium-internal gallery.

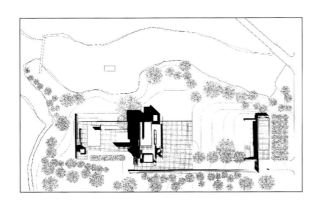

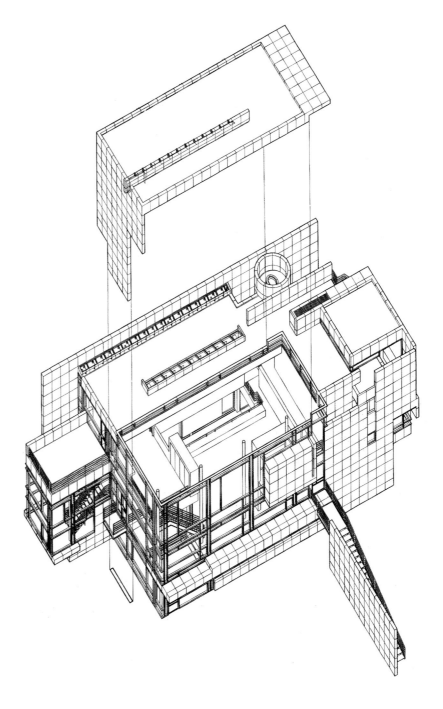

General plan and axonometric
exploded diagram.

Plans of the ground and second floors.
West and south elevations and sections.

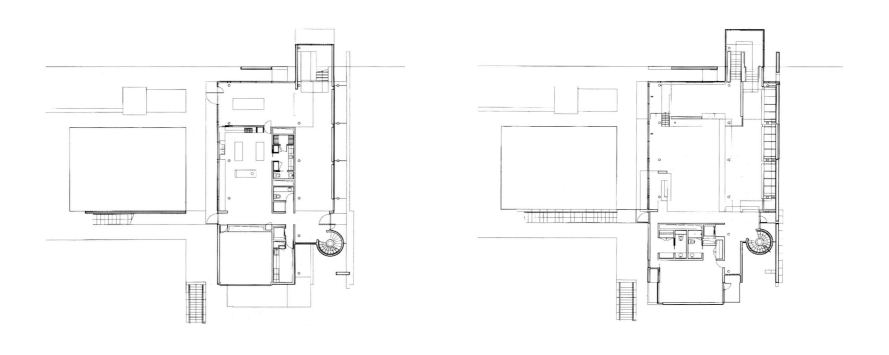

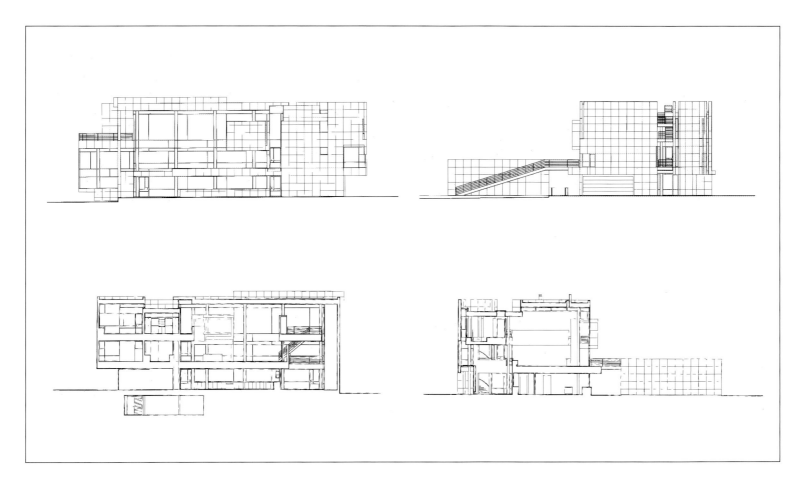

1991
1994

Swissair North American Headquarters

Views of the south, north
and east fronts.

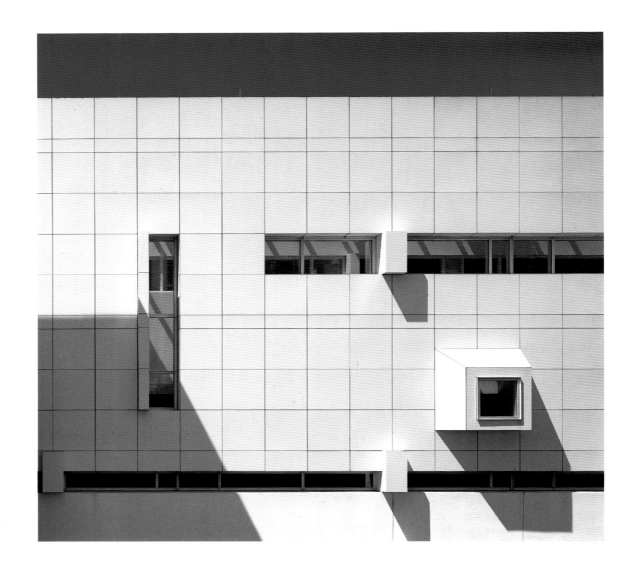

Details of the south front facing
onto the expressway.

View of the two-story-high
gallery running through
the building and detail
of the entrance hall.

General axonometric projection.

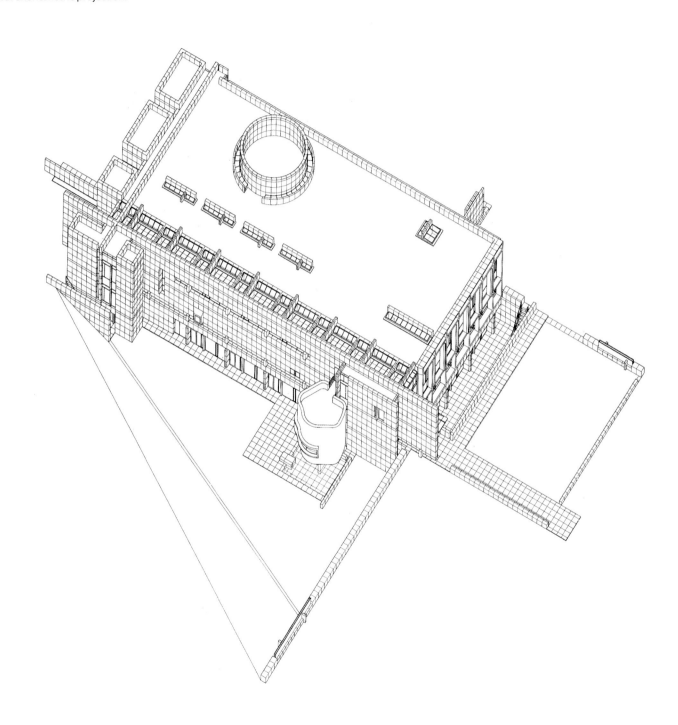

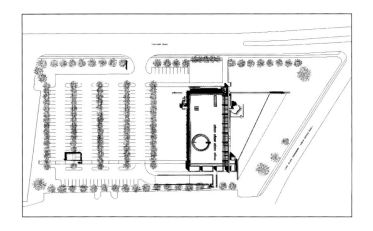

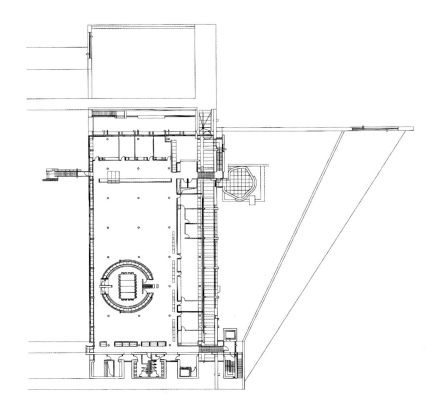

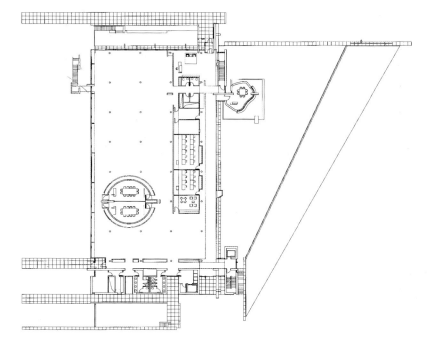

General plan and plans of the second and ground floors.

North, south, west and east elevations and sections.

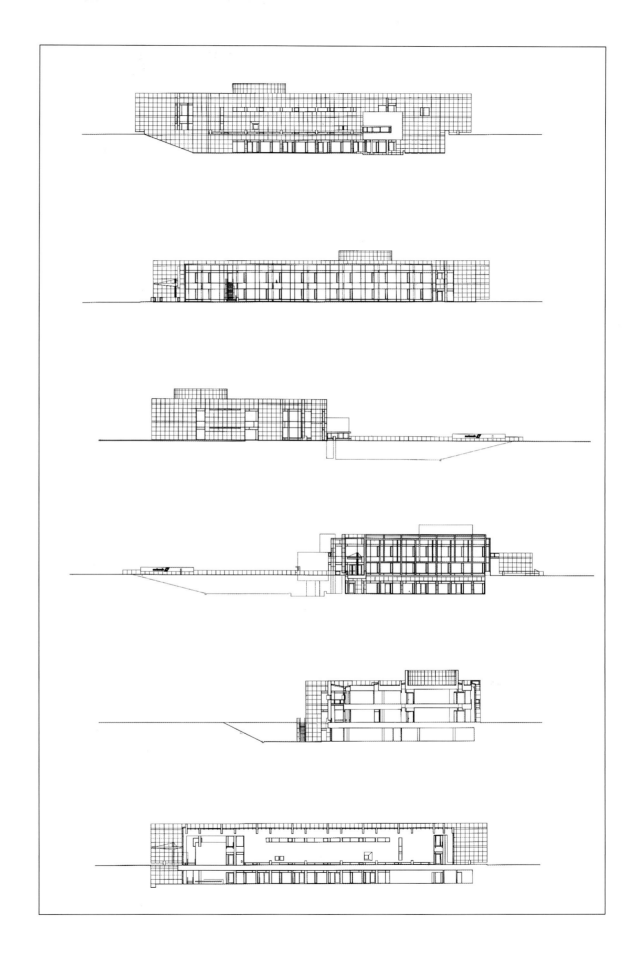

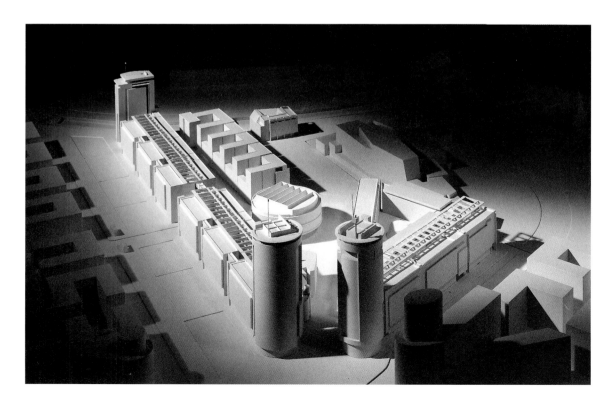

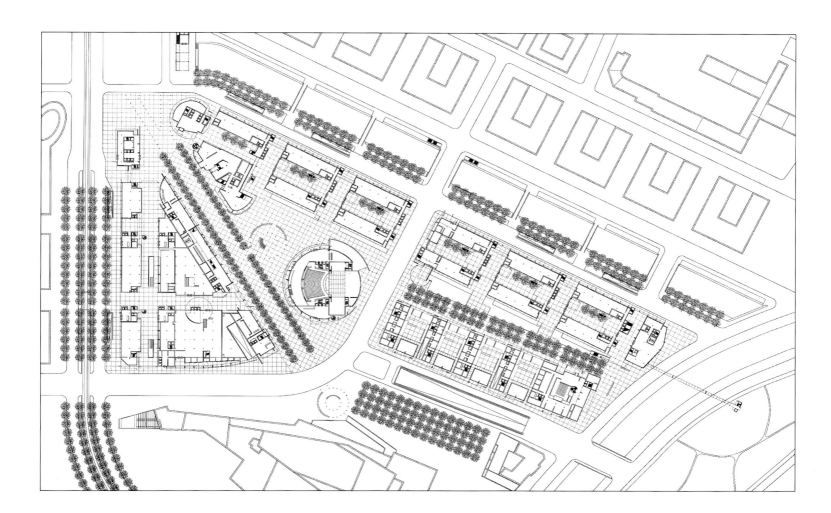

Views of the model.

Plan of the ground floor
and west elevations.

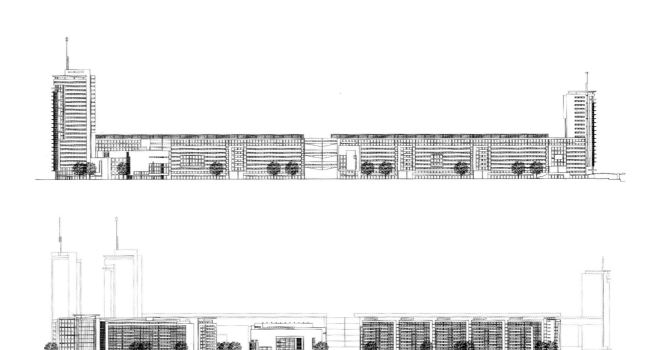

View from the expressway and detail
of the southeast entrance.

Views from the southwest
and of the rotunda.

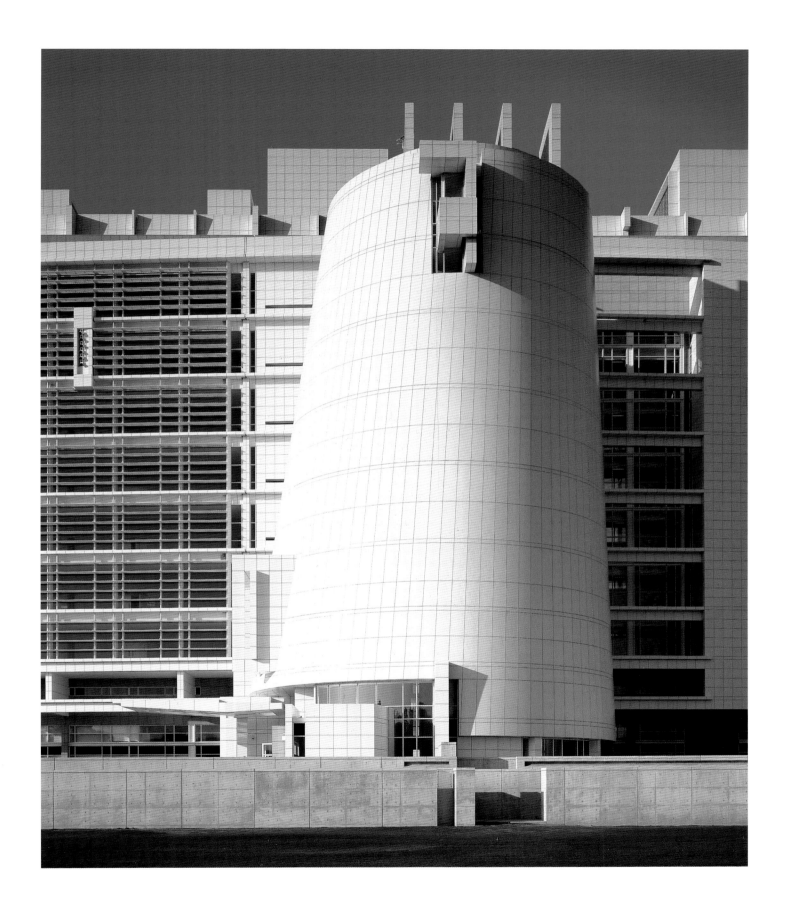

Details of the interior of the rotunda and of the full-height atrium.

Compositional, functional and structural diagrams.
General plan.

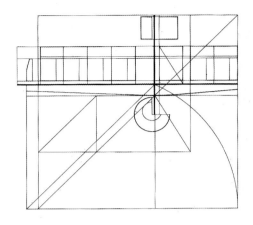

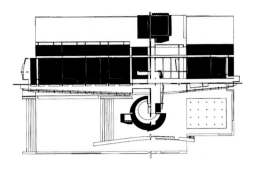

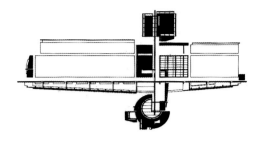

Geometry

Figure/Ground

Elements

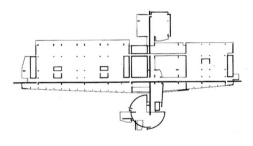

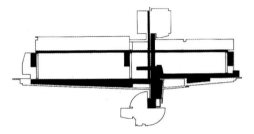

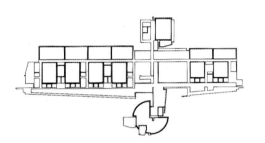

Structure

Circulation

Program

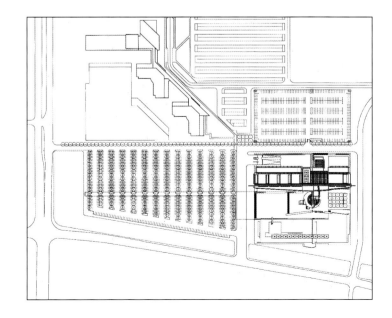

Plan of the ground floor, north
elevation and cross section
of the atrium.

Plans of the second and eighth floors
and cross sections.

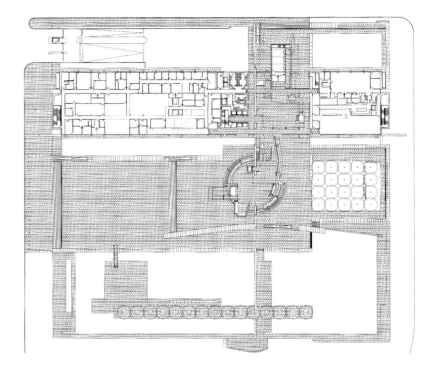

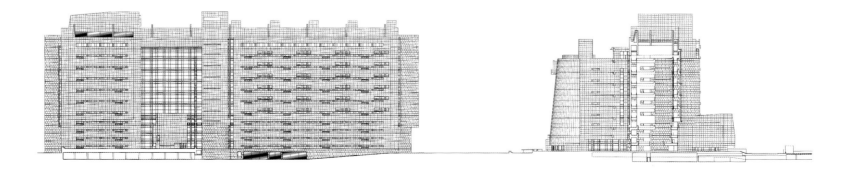

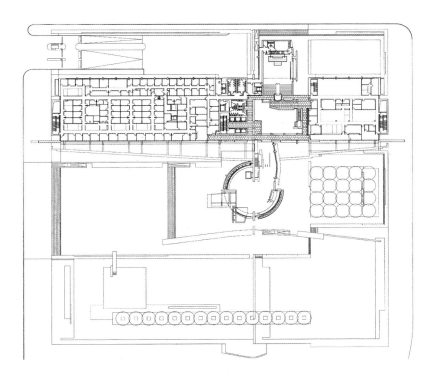

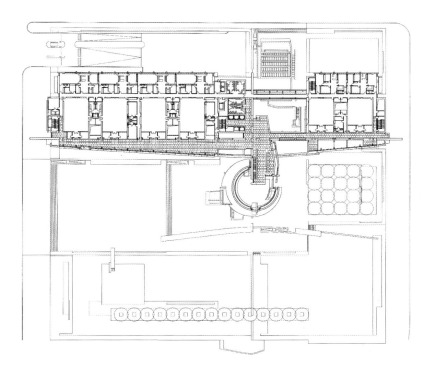

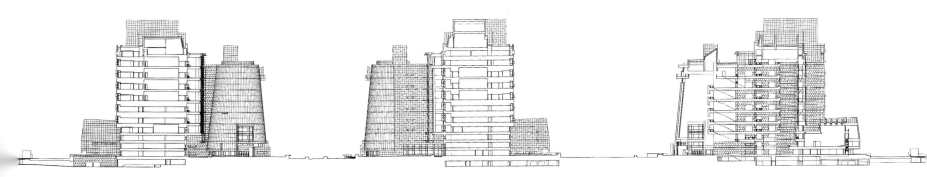

1994
1996

Museum of Television and Radio

The main façade on North Beverly Drive.

View of the interior of the atrium.

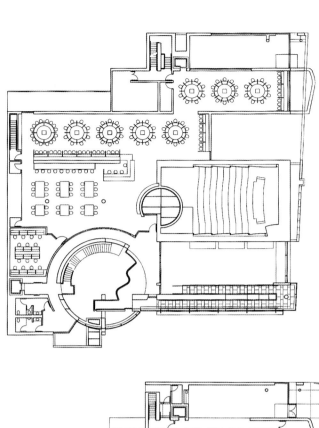

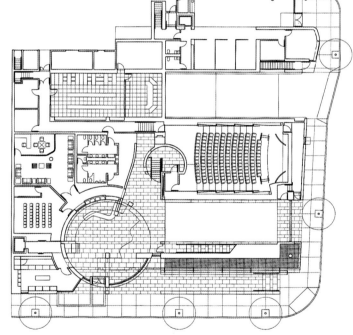

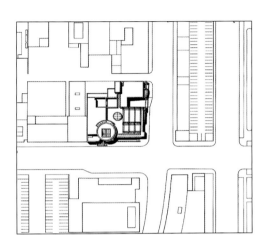

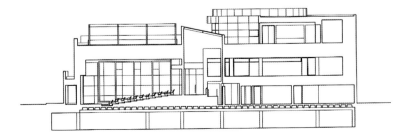

Details of the internal ramp.

Area plan, plans of the second and ground floors and section through the conference hall.

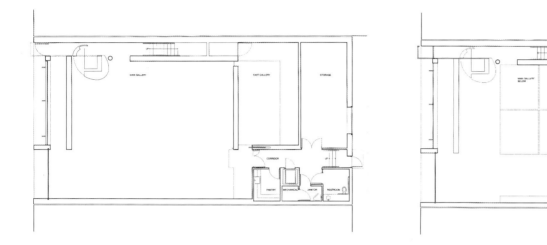

Plans of the ground and mezzanine floors.
View of the street front.

Views of the exhibition halls.

1995

Project for the Jean Arp Museum II

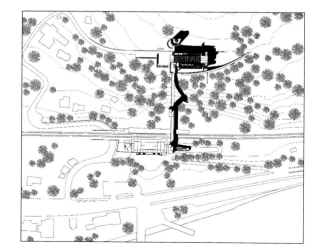

Photomontage showing the museum
on its riverside site and area plan.

Plans of the basement
and ground floors.
West, north and east elevations
and cross section.

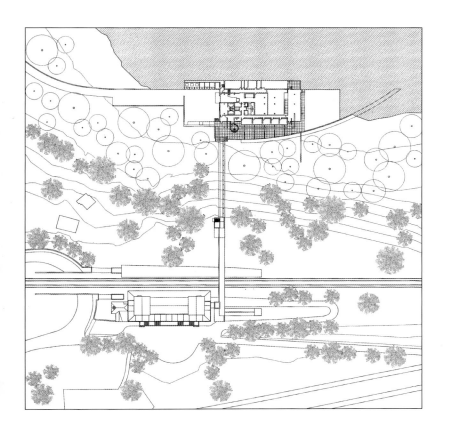

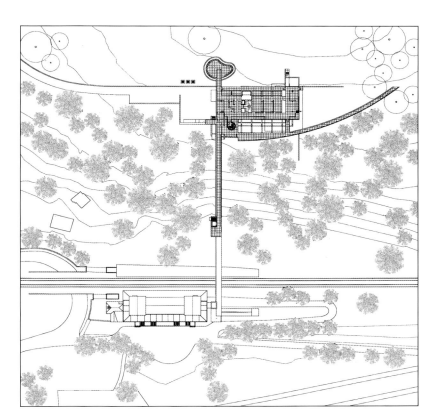

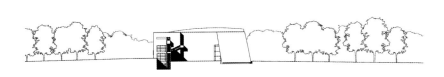

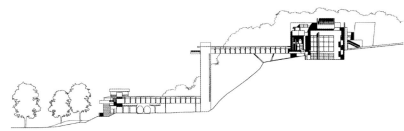

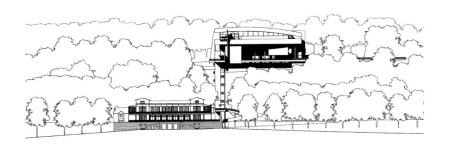

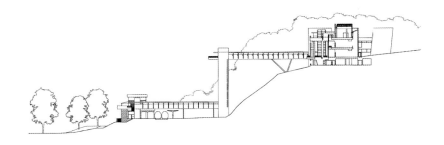

345

What Good Are Critics?
Richard Meier

There is not an architect that I know of who does not read his or her own press—contrary to what they may profess on the subject. But my personal recommendation is to read it and forget it. A negative article can put me in a bad mood for an hour or so, but it has never affected my work in any meaningful way. During the height of Postmodernism in the 1980s and the concomitant criticism of Modernism and my work, critical discussion only served to strengthen the resolve of my convictions. Architectural criticism is not for the benefit of the designer being discussed but for the public at large—professional and lay. Certainly Herbert Muschamp's 19 December 1999 article in *The New York Times*, "Trump, His Gilded Taste, and Me," addressed this issue including the role of architectural criticism, and was more stimulating than any of Mr. Trump's buildings. From Muschamp's point of view "criticism is partly an art of complicating simple things. And beauty, historically, has topped the list of things critics like to worry about." Too few architectural critics are currently preoccupied with how architecture forms, provokes, and enhances the culture of our cities.

Usually I find the criticism of architects whose work I respect and admire to be of benefit in thinking about my own work. Because I travel a lot there is ample opportunity to visit the recently completed work of my peers. The experience of visiting a building always brings a unique understanding that is not possible through reading or looking at photographs. For that reason I try to encourage students and younger architects to visit and look carefully at buildings. One of the roles of good critics is to encourage this by creating an atmosphere of excitement and/or controversy about an individual building. Luckily, however, they do not have the powers of theater critics who can close a show after the opening night.

On occasion, I have found myself criticized for not writing more about my own intentions for a design. This continues to surprise me, as I do not feel that it is the role or the requirement of an architect to explain his own work. Perhaps it is naïve to say that the work should stand for itself but I believe it should. It would have little meaning for me to tell people what I was trying to achieve in a building if they could not reach the same conclusions on their own. It is the role of the critic and the historian, not the architect, to codify and interpret the work. The strongest works of architecture and art are those that can stand up to multiple readings. The most meaningful buildings of the past are those that have resonance for current issues not those that simply have historical value. The works that force us to reconsider our preconceived notion of a particular building type or space, are the ones that will stand the test of time. The buildings, for instance, that traditionally receive the AIA Twenty-Five Year Award were not only respected but debated when they were first completed—such as the Seagram Building or the Guggenheim Museum in New York. My Smith House of 1967 received an Honor Award from the AIA in 1968 and this year's Twenty-Five Year Award, but it was also the subject of much discussion and dissension.

The true benefit of much architectural criticism lies in its ability to promote buildings as works of architecture, rather than as mere buildings and ultimately to elevate the level of popular taste. A critic identifies the qualities that make a building a work of architecture, a distinction that should be based on intrinsic quality and timely significance. The value of good criticism (and by that I do not necessarily mean positive criticism) is that it excites and provokes people to go and look at the work. The most important role of architectural criticism is to create a receptive audience for good architecture, which is why the quality of criticism should be important to all of us who practice architecture, as well as those concerned with the quality of our built environment.

In the past there were more clearly defined differences among publications featuring architectural criticism. Professional journals, such as this one, tended to merely present current work by leading practitioners and were prey to the vagaries of the marketplace and advertisers. While still accountable to the bottom line, professional journals in recent years have moved away from a vanity press role to a more analytical and critical presentation of works. It is a move in the right direction but one that could go even further. Critical journals such as the now defunct *Oppositions* presented theoretical and historical views and contributed to the discourse about contemporary architecture often in compelling and challenging ways. Serious debate continues sporadically in various university publications from Columbia, Harvard, Yale and other universities, and although the discussion can tend to be too esoteric or academic its role for practitioners should not be minimized. It is in the architecture schools and the academies that many of the current directions in architecture are formulated and argued and it behooves all of us to remain involved with the academic aspect of the profession.

It is surprising and disturbing that in the United States there are only two major architectural journals, *Architectural Record* and *Architecture*, while in Europe there are dozens. It would seem to me that there is more than enough good work being produced today to fill the pages of at least one more architecture publication in this country. Or is the professional audience lacking? Assuming the audience exists, I think there is also a demand for presenting more buildings in the project stage. At most there is meaningful coverage of only one project per issue. More often unbuilt work is represented by a model photograph or two in the news section. As this is the stage of a project's development where there is room for *constructive* criticism, it would seem to me to be an area to be greatly expanded.

Another outlet for architectural criticism is newspapers and it is newspaper criticism that seems to me most in need of a strong shot of adrenaline. Most American newspapers (with the exception of *The New York Times*, which is read as much outside New York as inside) tend to do little more than report on the latest new local building, and they address themselves to the lowest common denominator. Many newspapers in major cities do not even have a full-time architecture critic and are not given regular space for their articles. Even the venerable *Sunday New York Times* does not have a predictable, weekly architecture review.

If we as architects wish to have our work better respected and understood by the public we should work towards seeing it more regularly represented in the popular press and given the same weight as other cultural endeavors. It is only by making architecture a topic of popular discussion and debate that we as a profession will be able to fully engage the much-needed support of policy makers and the business community in urban design and development issues.

March 2000

Richard Meier. "What good are critics? We need them to excite and provoke the public." *Architectural Record*, March 2000, pp. 57-58.

1995
2000

Sandra Day O'Connor United States Courthouse

Views from the northeast
and northwest.

View of the west façade.

View and detail of the east front.

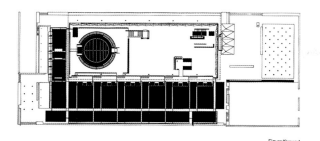

Figure/Ground

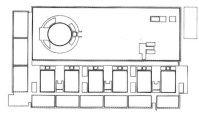

Program

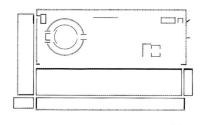

Enclosure

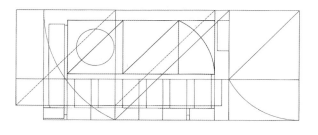

Geometry

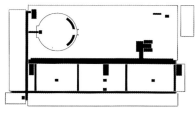

Circulation

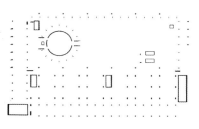

Structure

Views of the interior of the covered plaza with the cylinder of the room for special hearings.

Compositional, functional and structural diagrams and general plan.

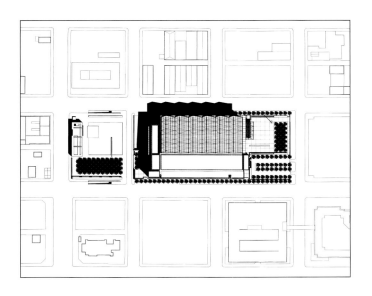

Plans of the second and ground floors
and longitudinal section.

Plans of the fifth and third floors
and cross section.

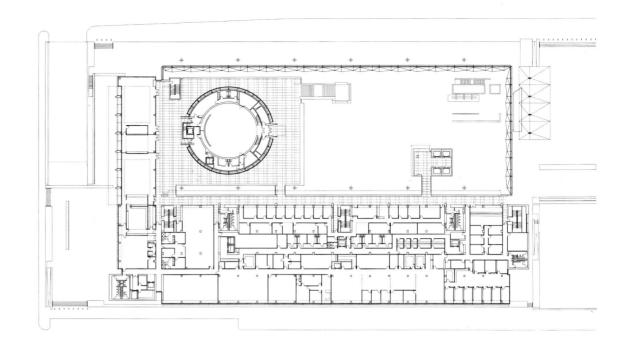

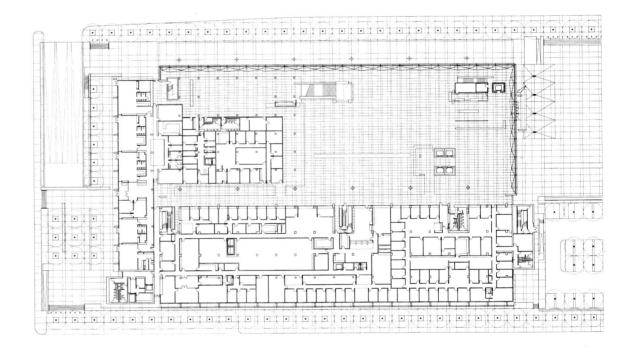

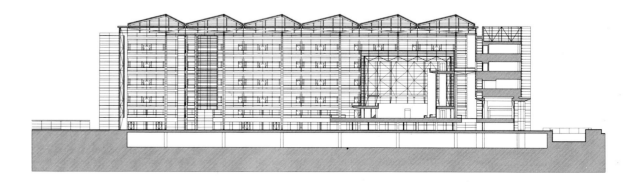

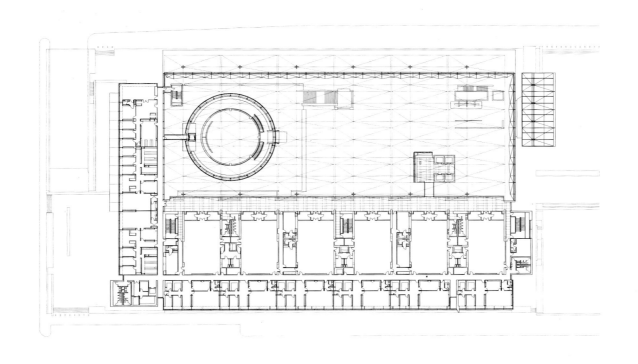

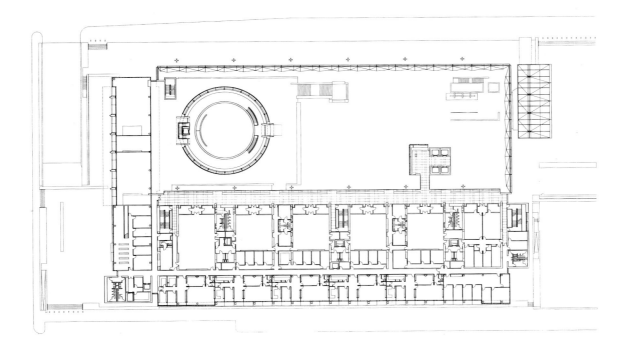

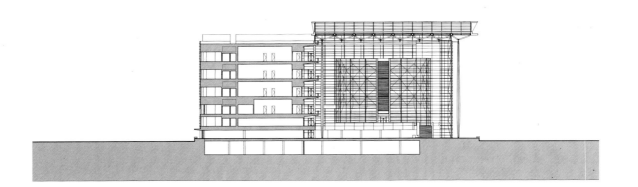

1995
1998

Neugebauer House

Views from the west and of the entrance
front facing northeast.

The north end.

following pages
The west façade overlooking the ocean.

View of the swimming pool solarium
from the south veranda.

The veranda of the living room
and the two aligned entrances,
from the sea garden and from the road.

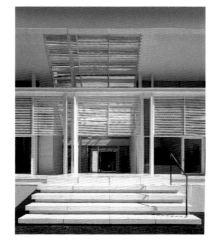

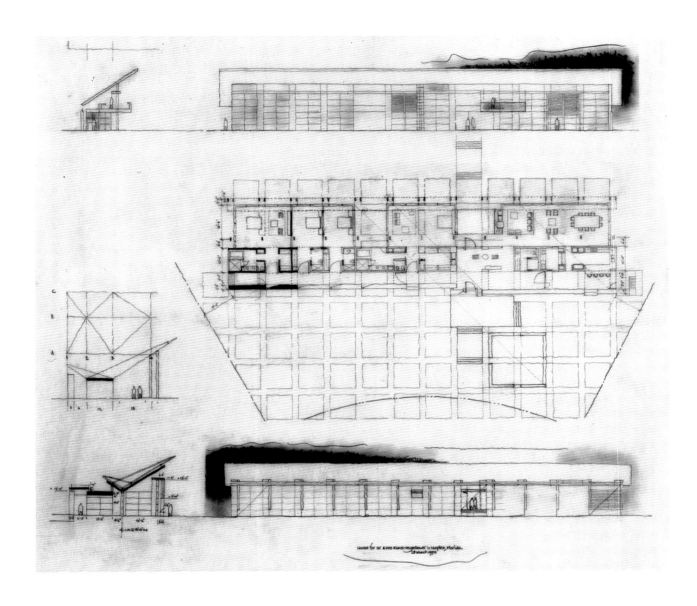

Views of the gallery of distribution
running along the east side
of the house.

Project drawing by Richard Meier.

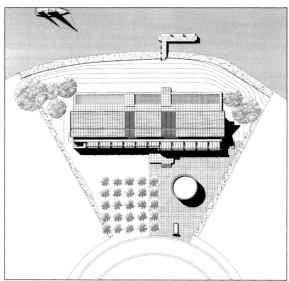

General plan and axonometric cutaway.

Plan, west and east elevations
and cross section.

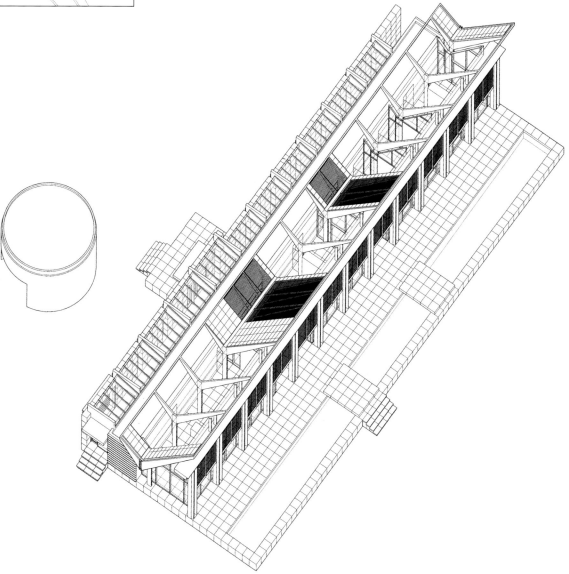

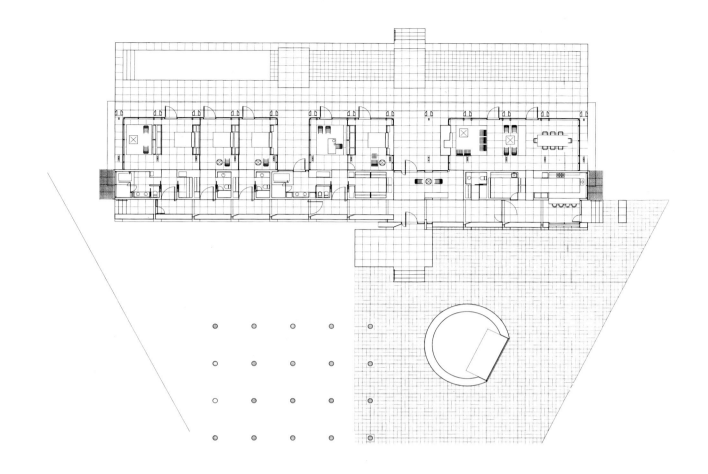

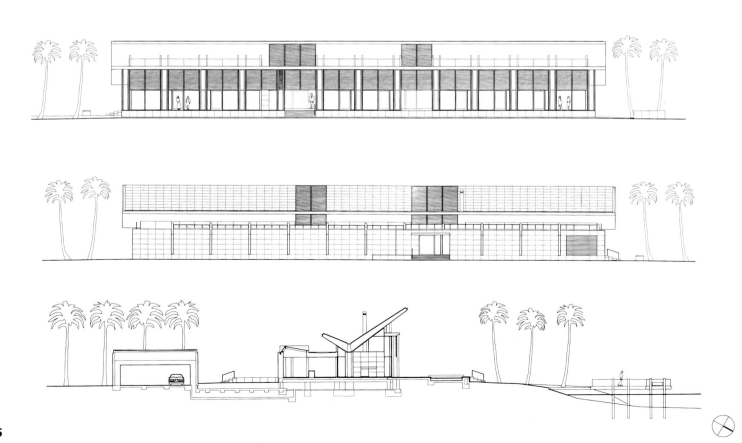

365

1996–

Museum of the Ara Pacis

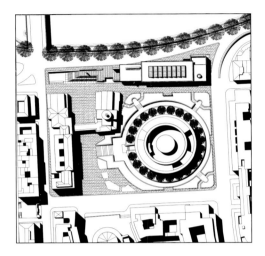

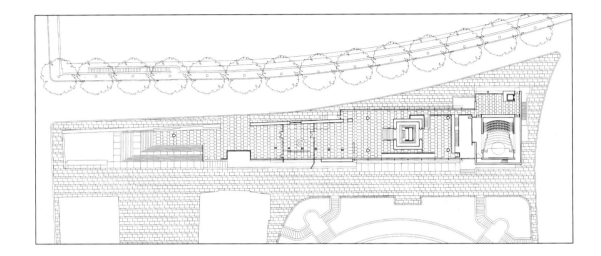

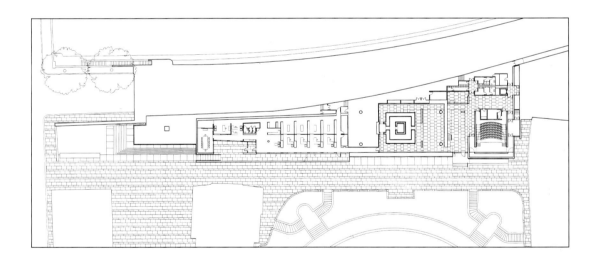

General plan.
Plans of the ground and basement floors.

East, north, west and south elevations,
sections and photomontage showing
the building on its site on the bank
of the Tiber.

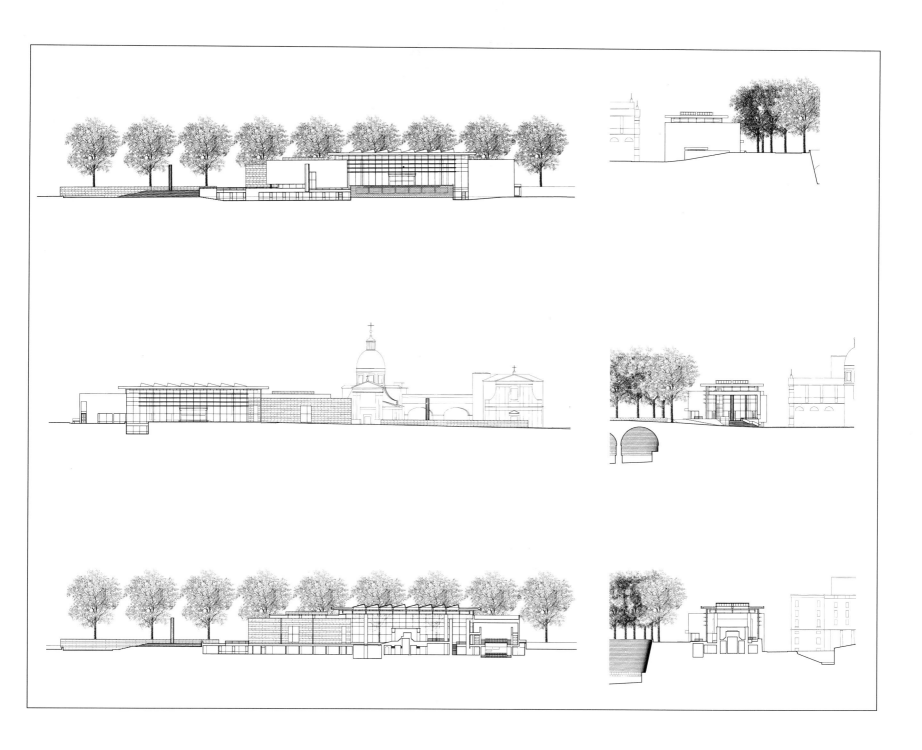

Jubilee Church
Richard Meier

The Catholic Church has an extraordinary history of artistic patronage; indeed, this history constitutes one of the most sustained and enriching relationships in the history of Western art. In this age of extreme positions and instantaneous communication of images and ideas, such relationships have become increasingly rare, the histories of artworks and architecture increasingly divorced from the circumstances of their origins. The Sistine Chapel, while still an ineluctable symbol of both Renaissance Rome and man's aspirations to the heavens, has itself become a marketable commodity, to the point that Michelangelo's divine vision has become salable, with rights to publish ceded to a foreign telecommunications company.

I have spent a good part of my career as an architect applying my language to places for art, striking the delicate balance between assertive form and empty vessel. Building this new church is a joyous next step, a timeless place for people and for God, a space unfettered by the comparatively mundane requirements of our new, sometimes transient cultural artifacts. While some might say that these are inevitable consequences of our age, I have always believed in an architecture that stands apart from the artifices of time: categories, labels, appropriations. A church cannot be divorced from the imperatives that first guide its building. It is timeless, despite the effects of time on stone or tile, despite the knowledge of the long years that went into its creation. What makes a church timeless is the simple act, preordained by open, bright space, of looking up. Giving one's self over to a gesture of humility inspired by both faith and the faithful application of hand and mind.

This church has been conceived in opposition to the isolation of the site. It has been devised as an enclosure, part sacred, part secular in order to help the populace re-situate themselves in the world. It does this largely through the way in which it allows the community to represent itself through the process of ritual, play and celebration.

The church and the community center are located on the southern and northern sides of the buildable area of the site. Both components are accessible from the east via a paved entrance plaza (*sagrato*) which is situated on the side of the site nearest to the effective center of the housing estate. A minimal landscape treatment of the park flanking the terrain of the church to the north serves to articulate the church through two intermediary elements: a square of trees just south of the hill and a serpentine path that eventually leads to a greensward from the *sagrato*.

Within the precinct established by a bounding bench/wall, the unbuildable western side of the church site is laid out as two courts separated from each other by a paved causeway running between the community center to the north and the church to the south. This causeway runs east-west and is coextensive with an ambulatory running around the two courts. The first of these courts situated to the north has been treated as a recreational garden with a paved café terrace adjacent to the community center. The second court which is furnished with a large reflecting pool, has been arranged as a meditation space with a small paved area set aside for this purpose.

Some reorganization of the Largo Serafino Ceyasco parking lot, which has been enlarged by the addition of almost 1,400 square meters along the western perimeter of the site is also contemplated so as to accommodate a special parking space for the priest's car and for the accommodation of processional cars used in connection with weddings and funerals.

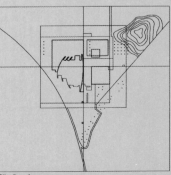

Site/Landscape

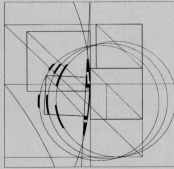

Geometry

The southern curb of the *sagrato* fronting onto Via Francesco Tovaglieri has been gently curved so as to both accommodate and represent this ceremonial approach by automobile.

The proportional structure of both the church and the precinct is predicated on a series of displaced squares and four circles. Three circles of equal radius are the basis of the three shells that, together with the spine-wall, make up the body of the nave. The whole discretely implies the Holy Trinity. At the same time, the enclosure of the church by water symbolizes the way in which the faith of the community arises out of the life-giving waters of baptism.

The stone of the portico, the paving, the liturgical furniture and the wall cladding has a dichotomous significance as on the one hand it alludes to the masonry of the residential fabric in which the parishioners live, on the other hand it symbolizes the living stone which constitutes the body of Christ's Church. The architectural concrete of the shells also serves, in this instance, as a surrogate for stone.

The approach to the church is via the paved *sagrato* at the eastern side of the site with the front of the church and the portico jointly symbolizing the welcome that the church offers to the community. In addition to the main portico two other entrances from the *sagrato* are provided between the two outer shells. These afford independent access to the weekday chapel and the baptistery respectively. Rather than fully enclose the *sagrato* with a fence we have opted for an open plaza framed by carefully placed elements—benches, fountain, trees and a water "source" at the southwest edge of the *sagrato*.

Passing under the trellis portico and a symbolic stone portal one enters the atrium via a pair of double doors made out of wood. These entrance doors are opposed by a single pair of ceremonial doors set in a stone wall on the axis of the church. These are only intended to be used on special occasions such as weddings, festival processions and funerals.

The nave comes into being through the interplay between the straight north wall and the concave shells on the southern side of the volume. Where the former is faced in stone and acoustic wood paneling, the latter is executed out of architectural concrete. The floor, the altar, the President's chair, and the ambo are all executed in stone in both the main nave and the side chapel. Only the pews are furnished in wood.

The organ and choir loft at the east end of the nave and the opposing sanctuary with the sacristy "tower" at the west end rise toward a translucent roof compounded out of clear glass with integral light-diffusing louvers.

The perceptual volume of the church is directly influenced by natural light since the zenith light and the glazed skylights between the successive shells are continually responsive to the changing pattern of light and shadow as the sun moves across its trajectory. According to the season, the weather, and the time of day, light is variously graduated down the inner surface of the shells thereby imparting to the Church, the Chapel and the Baptismal Fount a particular character. This light is complemented by the light coming through the vertical glass walls executed in translucent glass which is carefully modulated to illuminate but not overwhelm. A narrow band of clear glass is provided along the whole perimeter of the church.

The weekday chapel is separated from the baptistery by a rectangular block of three reconciliation rooms which are entered directly from the chapel. While the necessary separation

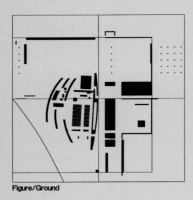

Figure/Ground

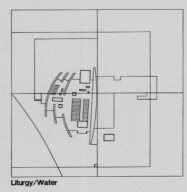

Liturgy/Water

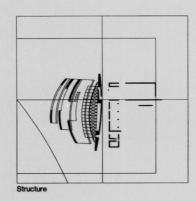

Structure

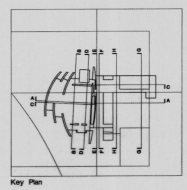

Key Plan

between the chapel and the sanctuary is effected by a curved wall, a view of the altar from the chapel is maintained by an aperture.

If one takes into consideration the two courts to which it gives access, the garden court to the west and the paved assembly court to the east, one sees that the community center occupies the entire northern half of the site. It does so in the form of an L-plan formation loosely attached by first and second level bridges to the northern side of the church. These bridges give enclosed walkway access to the atrium and sanctuary in the first instance and to the organ loft and sacristy in the second. A top-lit foyer connects the priest's office and meeting rooms on the ground floor of the community center to the catechism classrooms on the second floor.

The main approach to the community center from the *sagrato* is through the narrow east-west conservatory separating the church from the center, although it may also be approached incidentally from the two courts that flank its north/south wing. These courts have been expressly provided so as to accommodate both informal and formal communal assemblies, that is to say, on the one hand the garden court with a café terrace that may be spontaneously shaped by all, by socializing adults and the play of children; on the other an enclosed paved court appropriate for the blessing of palms on Palm Sunday or for the formation of the various processional assemblies that are an integral part of the annual church ritual.

In the planning of both the church and the community center with its respective courts we have borne in mind Hans-Georg Gadamer's views with regard to the absolutely fundamental role of play and ritual in all forms of human culture. Indeed we may further claim that in our deliberate exposure of the entire complex to the simultaneous play of both light and movement we have echoed his words only too directly, when he wrote in his essay on *The Relevance of the Beautiful*: "It is worth looking more closely at the fundamental givenness of human play and its structures in order to reveal the element of play as free impulse and not simply negatively as freedom from particular ends ... We only have to think of certain expressions like the 'play of light' and the 'play of the waves' where we have such a constant coming and going, back and forth, a movement that is not tied down to any goal."

Elsewhere in the same text, Gadamer assimilates the idea of human play as living self-representation to the concept of the festival or the festive celebration that always at its root is fundamentally theological. We have thus conceived of this entire complex as a site for both formal and informal festive celebration wherein the act of symbolic remembrance is to be enacted through prayer and the orchestration of human movement.

The acoustical design of the church is based upon meeting the need for intelligible speech in the giving of sermons, readings, and announcements while at the same time providing a reverberant volume for congregational singing, liturgical choir, instrumental and organ sound. This has been achieved by providing a sound reinforcement system suitable for a large, highly reverberant worship space such as the one proposed. This "pewback" system consists of small ten-centimeter diameter loudspeakers in small wooden enclosures, mounted on the back of the pews. One loudspeaker serves three occupants and provides for clear, low-level reinforcement of the spoken word. The large volume and the hard concrete, stone and glass surfaces will support a live, rich sound from the choir and particularly the organ. The acoustic paneling of the north wall of the nave eliminates flutter as does the uneven (cleft) surface of the stone cladding on the convex wall separating the atrium from the nave together with the stone on the lower portion of the north wall.

Energy consumption of the church, in terms of heating, cooling and ventilating will be greatly reduced by a number of features that have been specifically designed to limit the thermal peak loads inside the space. The large thermal mass of the concrete walls effectively moderates the internal heat gain. By balancing out the peaks and troughs in the daily temperature variation it eliminates the need for mechanical air-conditioning inside the nave and the chapel, and at the same time reduces the extent to which it will be necessary to use mechanical equipment for heating the space in the winter.

Due to its thermal mass, the building has a capacity to be naturally ventilated within both the nave and the chapel. Fresh air is introduced through intake louvers in the upper part of the northern wall of the church and transmitted at a low velocity through an acoustically lined shaft. The thermal stack effect within the main space promotes upward air movement, naturally drawing air through the congregational hall via fresh air inlets at low level, while exhaust air is discharged at the upper part of the volume.

Overhanging concave-shaped walls at the south perimeter of the building serve as shading devices for the glazed parts of the roof and walls, thereby protecting the internal volume from the direct solar penetration of radiation and glare.

An underfloor system will be installed to provide radiant heating in the congregation hall and chapel during winter.

This system will be divided into two circuits: one for the nave and one for the chapel. Energy to heat the building will be drawn from a modular boiler which is accommodated in the mechanical equipment room. In summer, the same system can also be used for cooling by pumping filtered water from the reflecting pool through the pipe circuits. The Community Center has a conventional radiator circuit along its perimeter wall. The artificial illumination of the church volume is divided into three zones: the main congregational space, the chapel and the altar. Since electric light cannot rival the sun, such light will emanate mainly from below, making the church most intimate in the evening.

The duty of architecture, the responsibility of the architect, is to create a sense of order, a sense of space and a sense of relationships. Hopefully, the Jubilee Church will be a place for interaction and communion with God and for personal reflection, in this time of conflicted and chaotic conditions.
February 1997

Richard Meier. "The Church of the Year 2000." *Politecnico*, 25 February 1997, pp. 13-23, and *a+u – Architecture and Urbanism* 319, April 1997, pp. 40-53.

Views of the construction site.

Views of the exterior and interior
of the model.

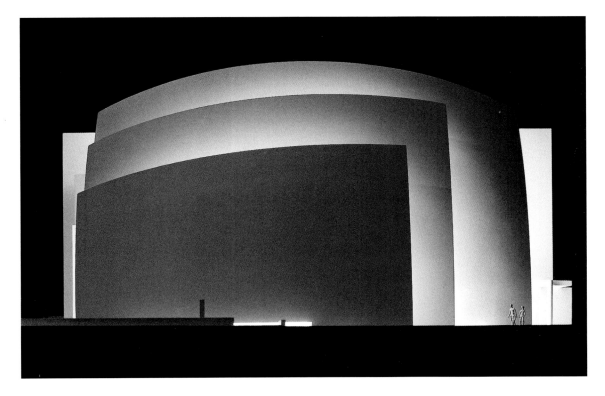

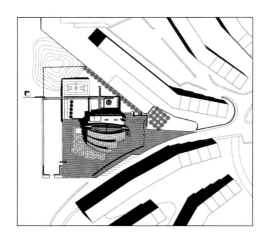

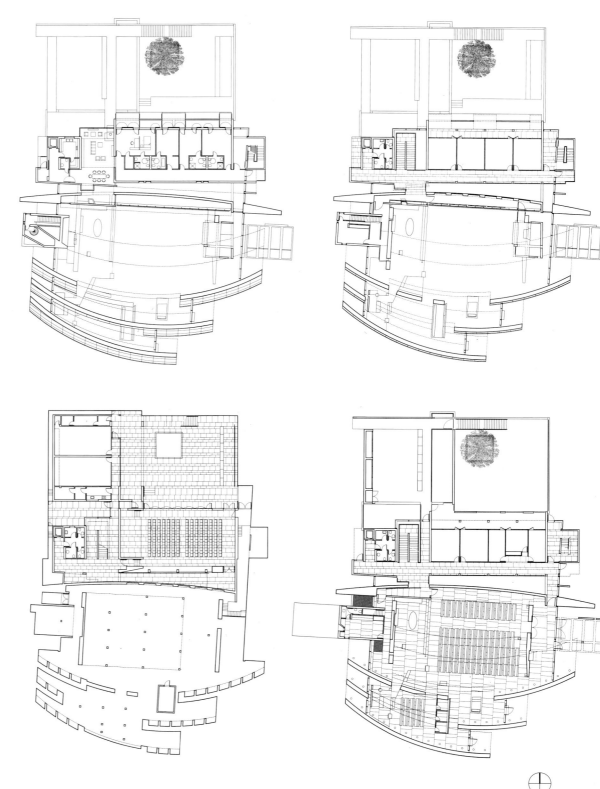

General plan.
Plans of the third, second, ground
and basement floors.

Study by Richard Meier for the plan.

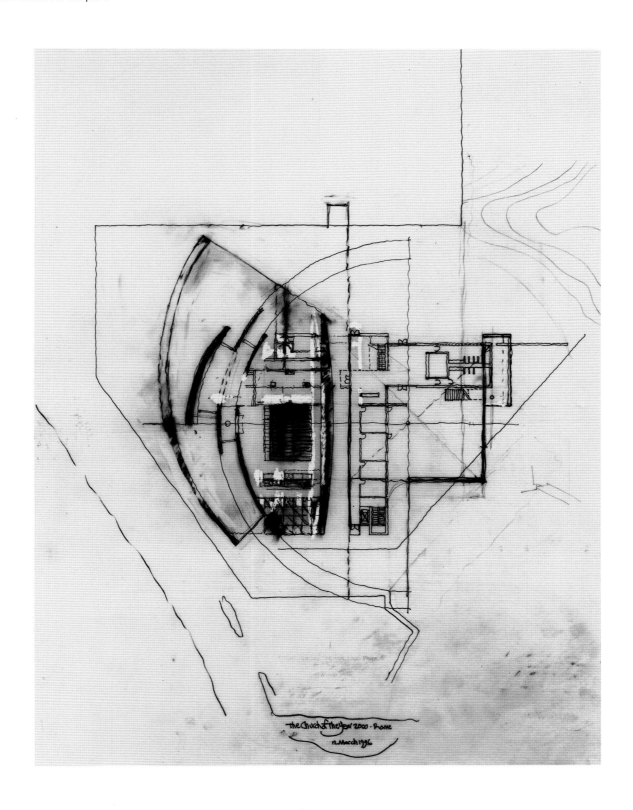

Studies by Richard Meier for the south
elevation and the cross section.

North, south, east and west elevations
and corresponding sections.

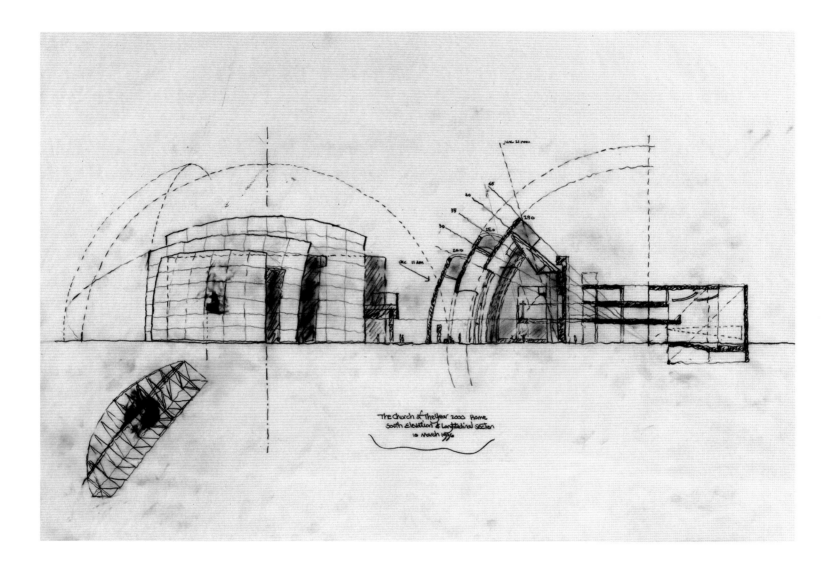

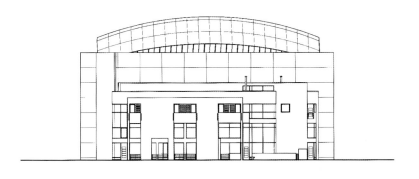

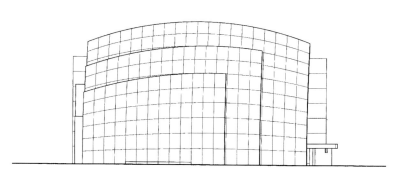

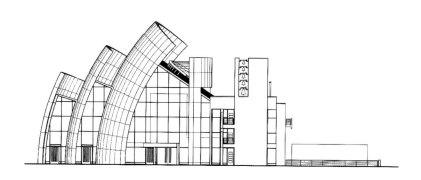

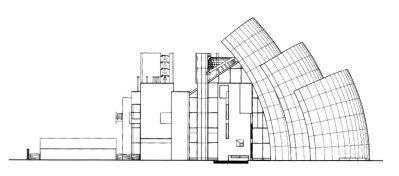

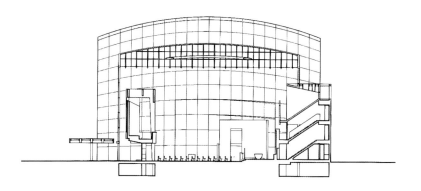

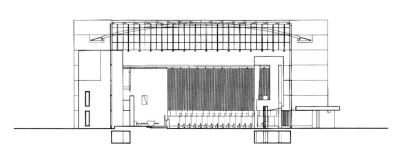

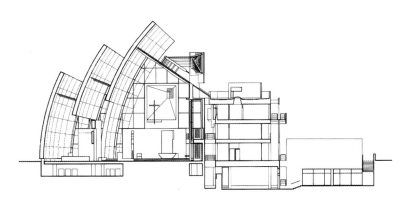

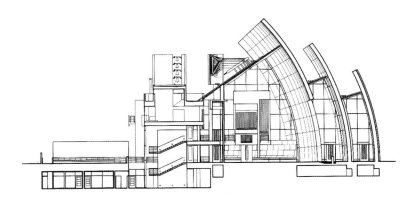

1996
2003

Crystal Cathedral Hospitality and Visitors Center

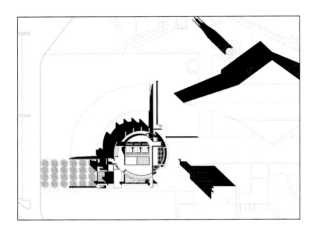

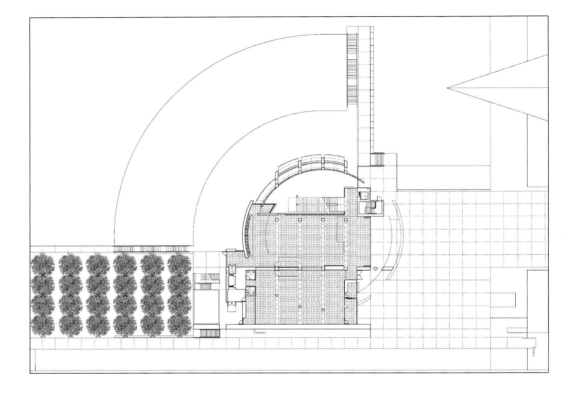

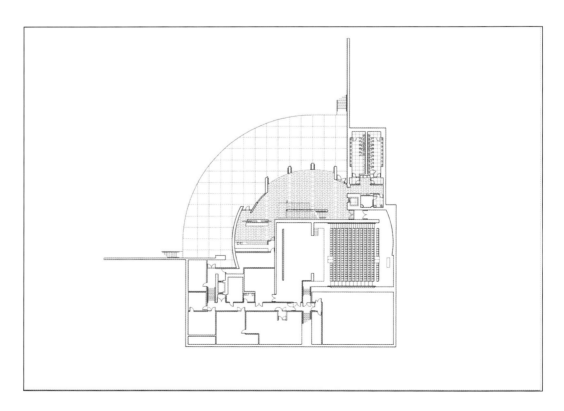

General plan and plans of the ground
and basement floors.

Plans of the fourth and second floors.

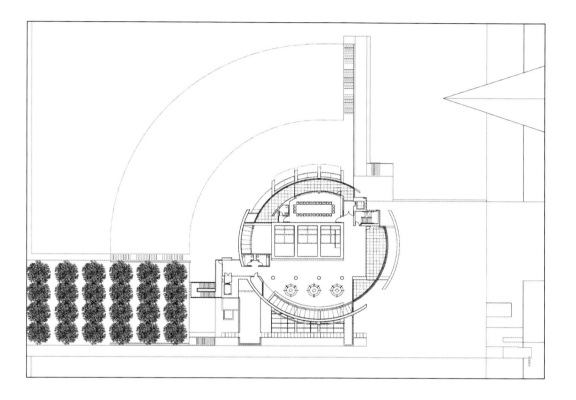

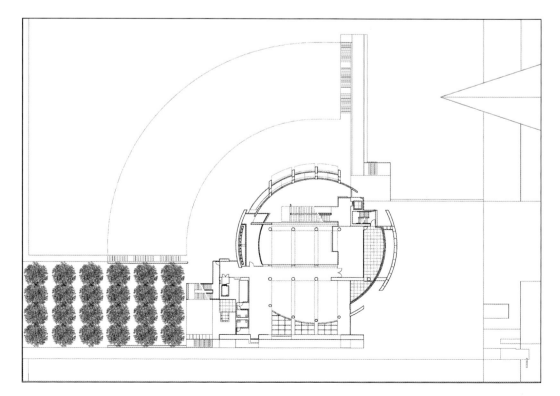

North and south elevations
and sections.

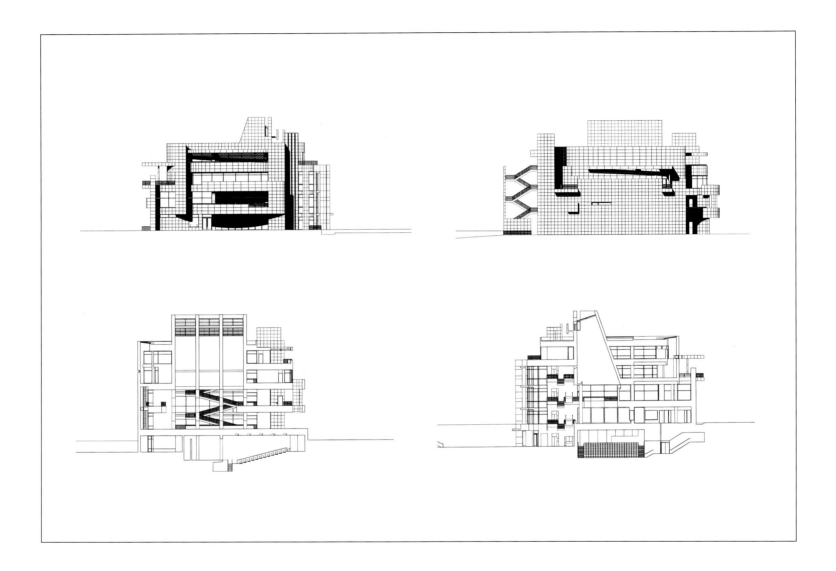

Views of the model.

1997
2002 | Tan House

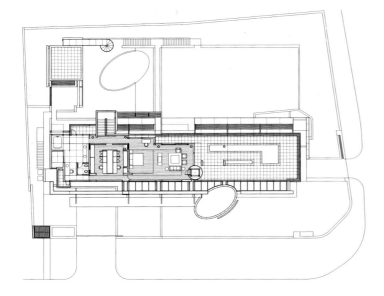

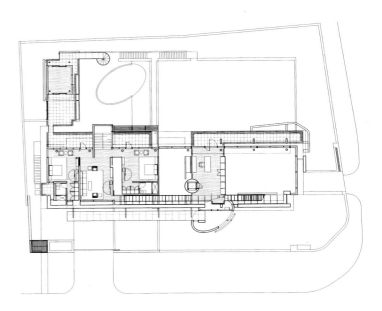

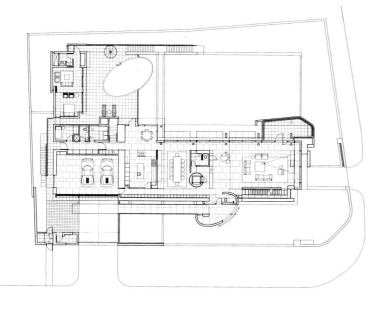

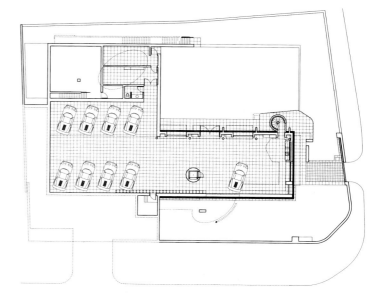

Plans of the third, second, ground
and basement floors.

Site plan showing the disposition
of masses and view of the digital model.
North, south and east elevations
and sections.

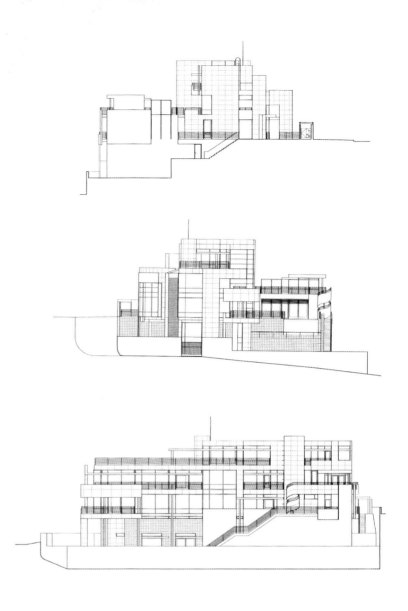

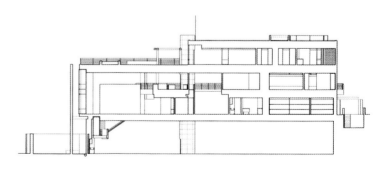

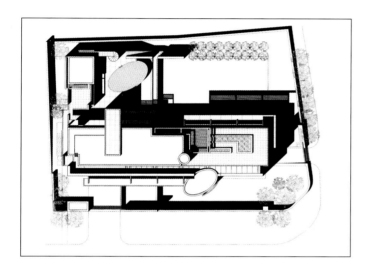

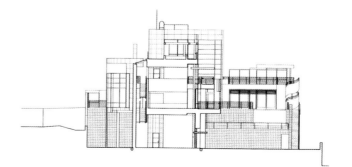

1998
2001

Peek & Cloppenburg Department Store

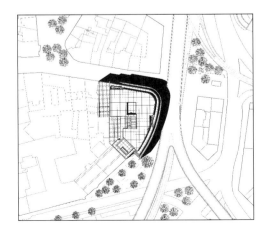

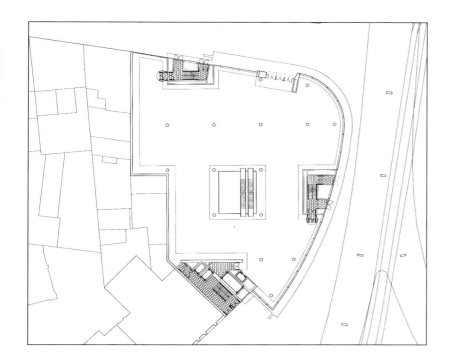

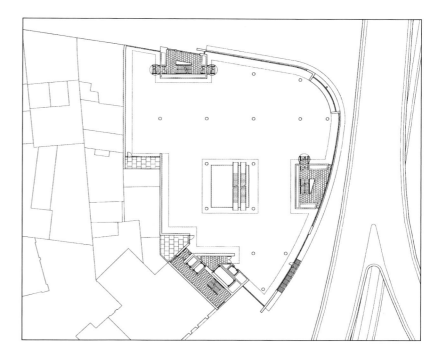

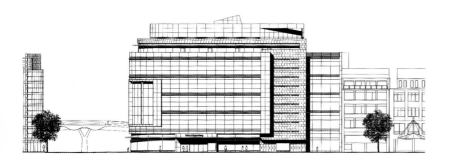

Plans of the third and ground floors,
north elevation and section.

View from the east and area plan.

1998
2001

Rickmers Reederei Headquarters

Views from the south and northeast.

Details of the side terrace on the roof.

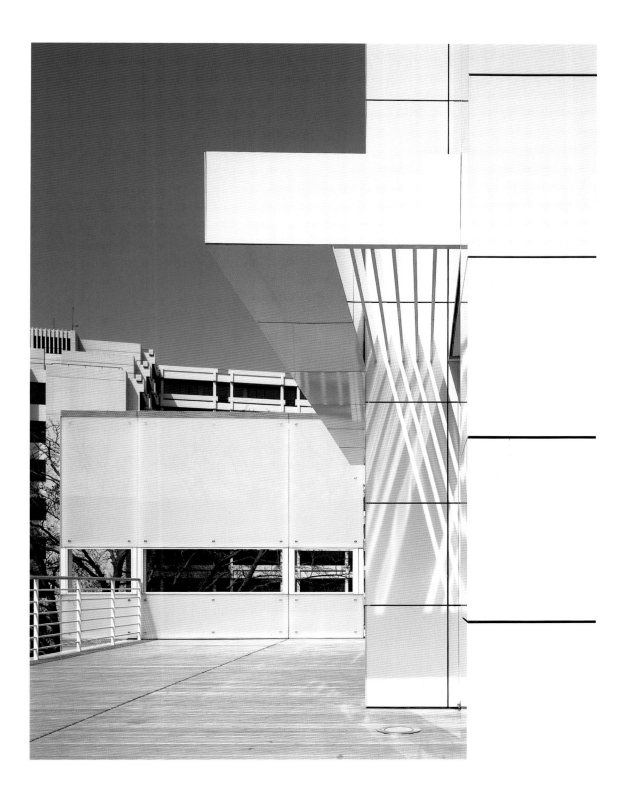

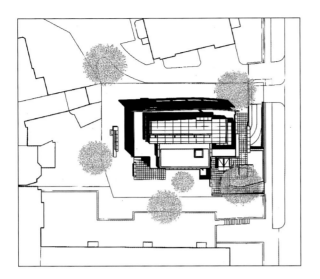

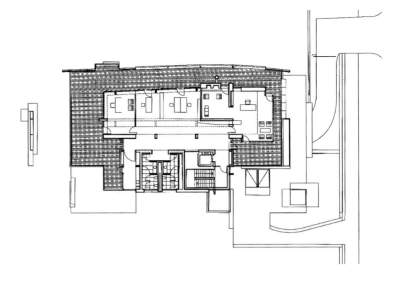

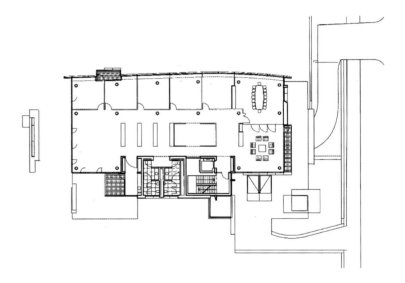

Site plan and plans of the fourth, third
and ground floors.

North, south, east and west elevations
and sections.

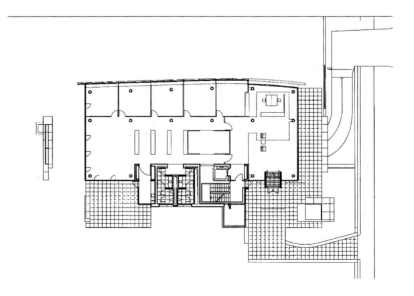

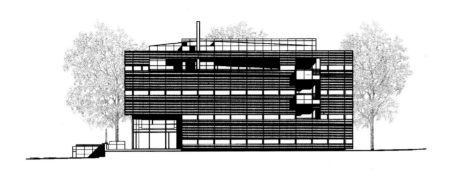

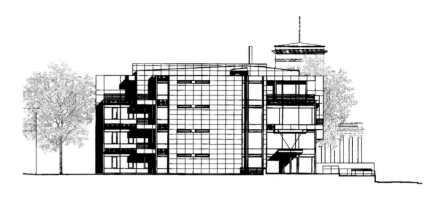

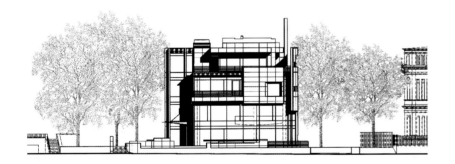

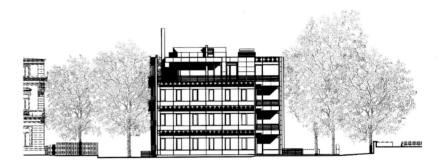

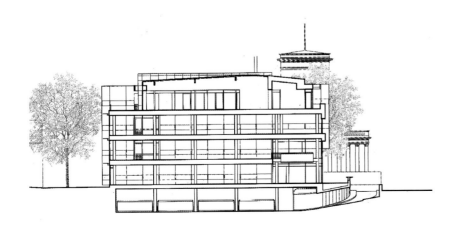

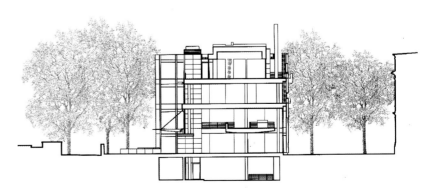

1998
2002

Canon Headquarters

Views of the entrance front facing south
and one of the three-story-high spaces
inside.

Plans of a standard floor,
of the ground floor
and cross section.

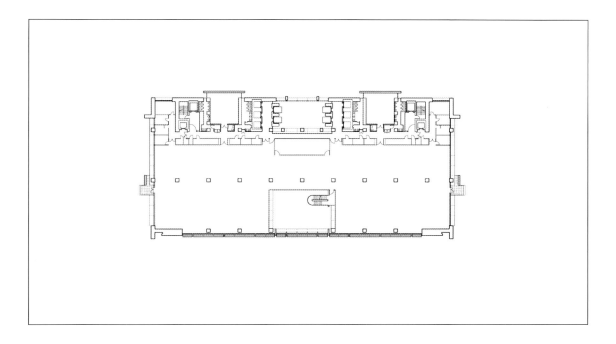

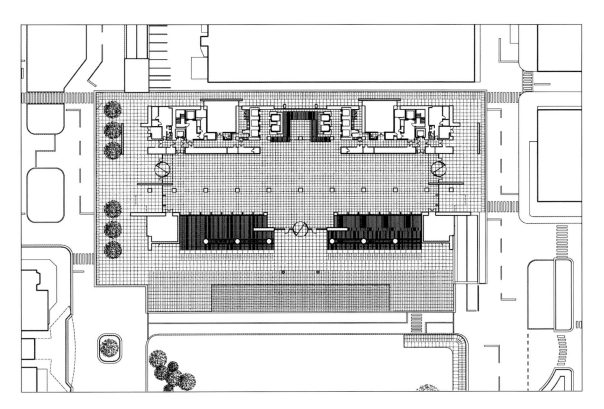

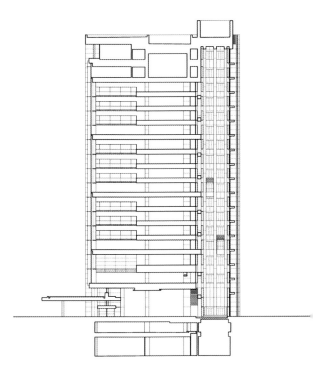

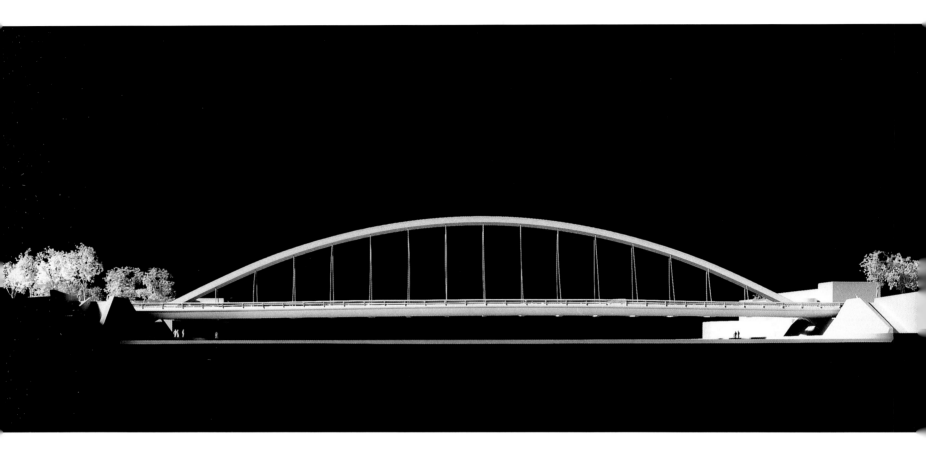

Views of the model.

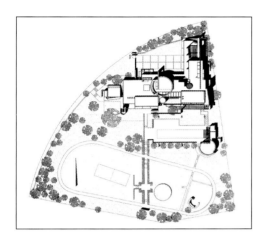

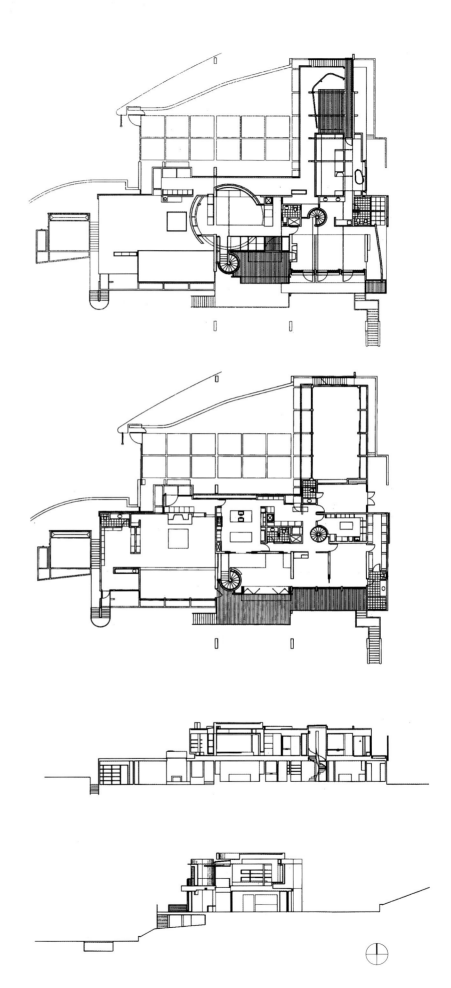

View of the rear courtyard to the north.

General plan, plans of the second
and ground floors and sections.

1998
2003

San Jose Civic Center

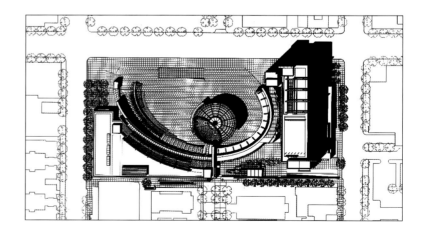

View of the digital model
and general plan.

Plans of the ground floor
and of a standard floor
of the tower.
East elevation and section.

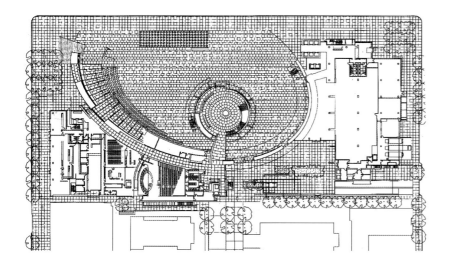

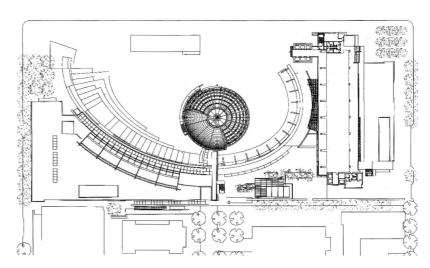

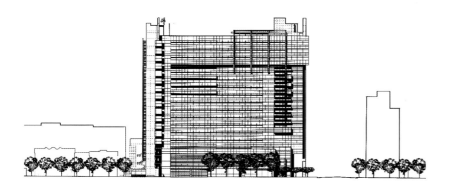

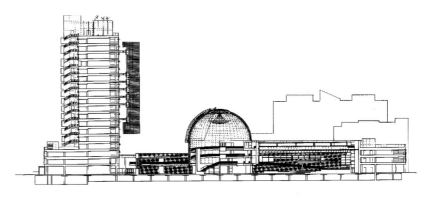

Southern California Beach House

The terrace facing onto the beach
viewed from the southwest.

Views of the south front, facing the sea,
and the north front, facing the road.

The side garden.

Details of the entrance running
through the house and the living room.

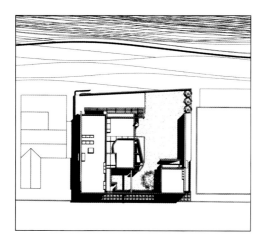

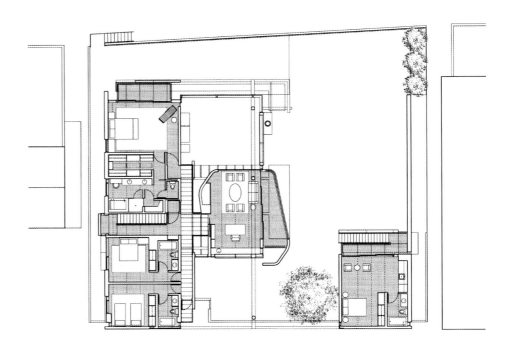

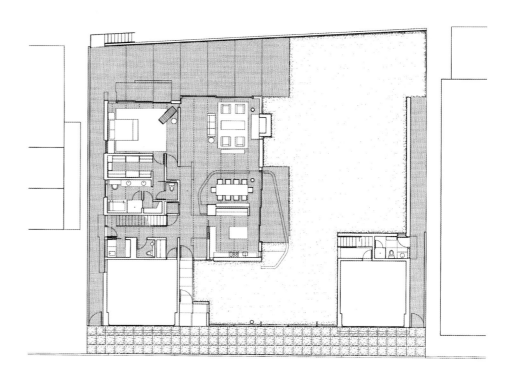

Site plan and plans of the second
and ground floors.

North, south and west elevations
and longitudinal and cross sections.

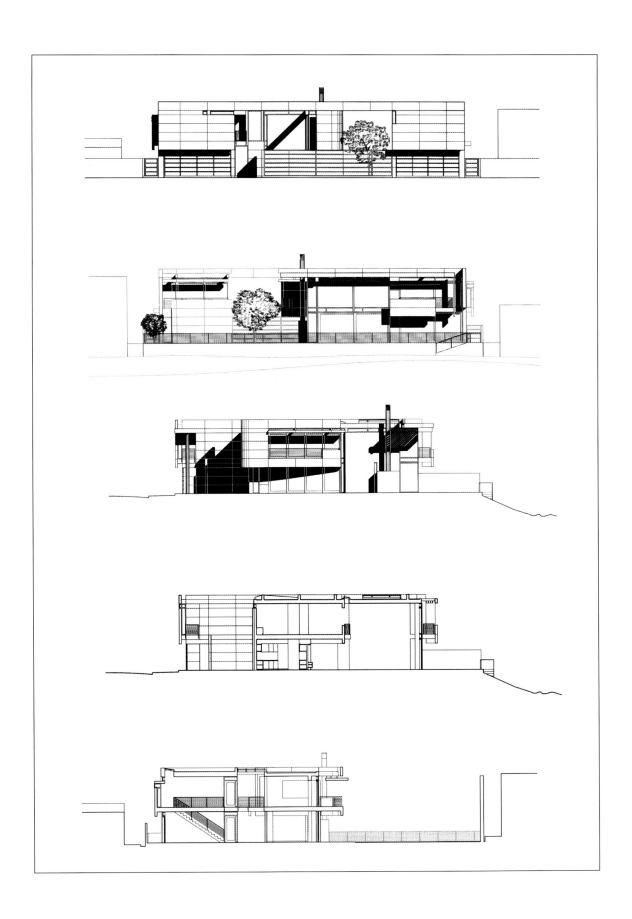

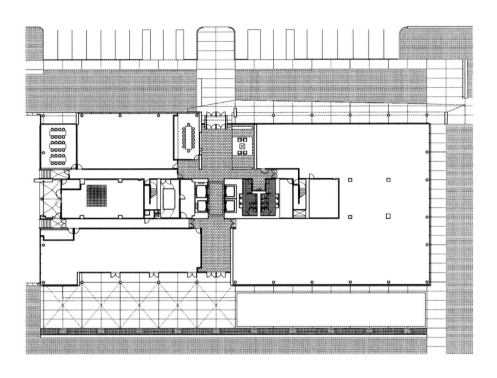

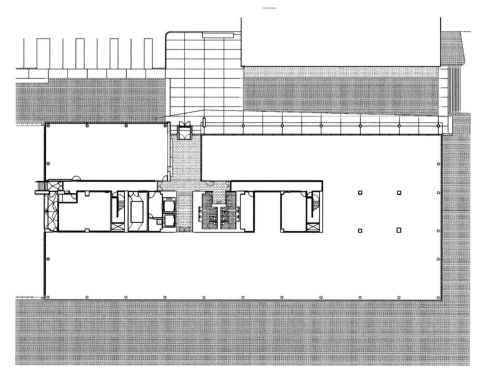

Plans of the entrance floors of the north
and south buildings.

Views of the model from the northwest
and overhead.

1999
2002

173/176 Perry Street Condominiums

Photomontages showing the towers
inserted on the urban front
of West Street.

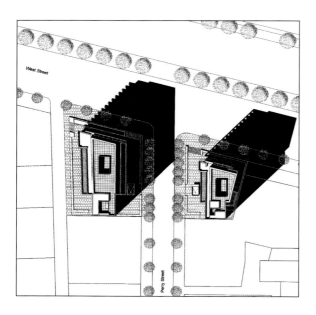

General plan.
Plans of the standard floor
and the one- and two-bedroom
apartments in the north tower.

Internal views of the digital model.
Plans of the standard floor
and the one- and two-bedroom
apartments in the south tower.

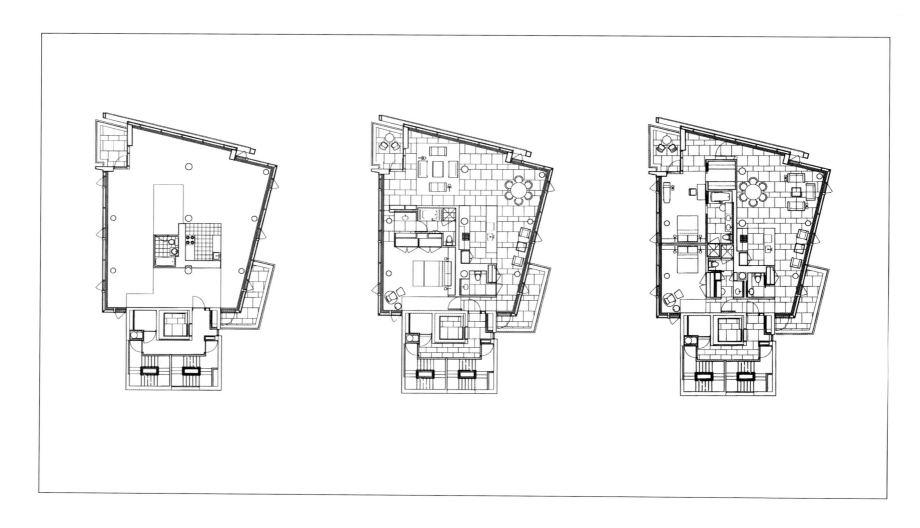

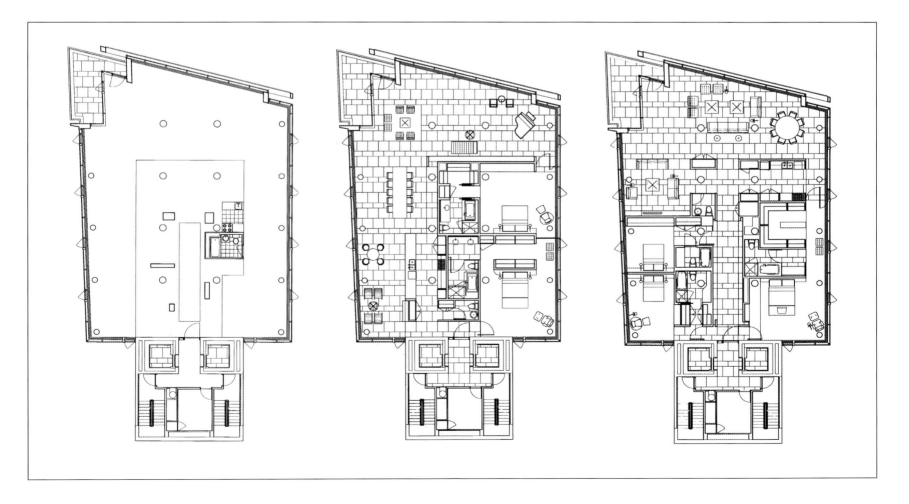

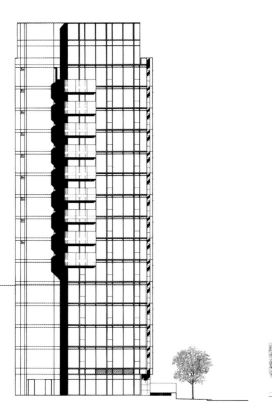
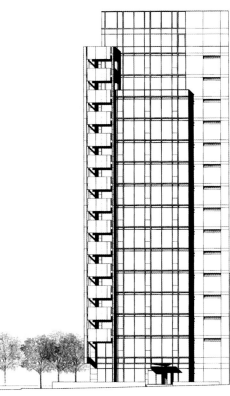
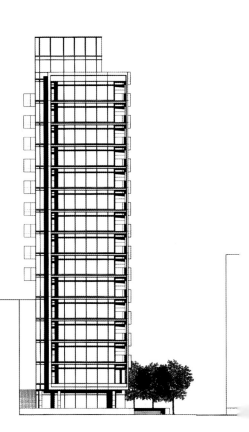

Views of the model.
North, south and west elevations
of the tower at 173 Perry Street.

North, south and west elevations
of the tower at 176 Perry Street.

Views of the digital model from
the northeast and southeast.

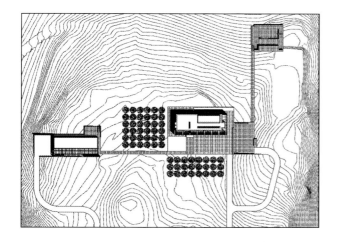

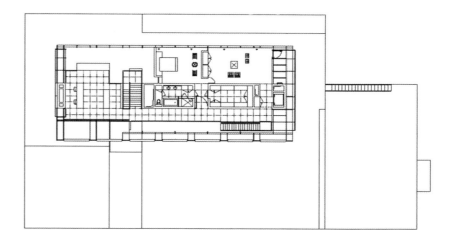

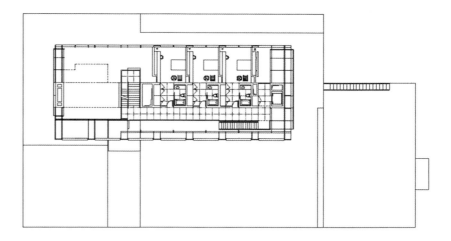

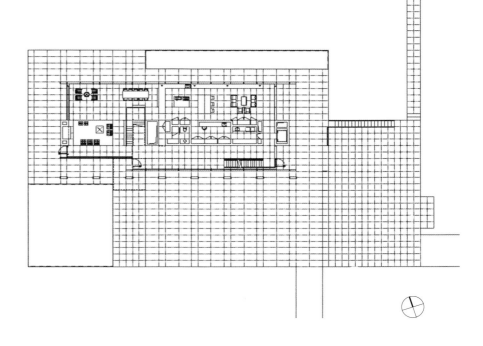

Views of the living room and the three-story-high atrium in the digital model.

General plan and plans of the third, second and ground floors.

North, south, east and west elevations
and sections.

Views of the model.

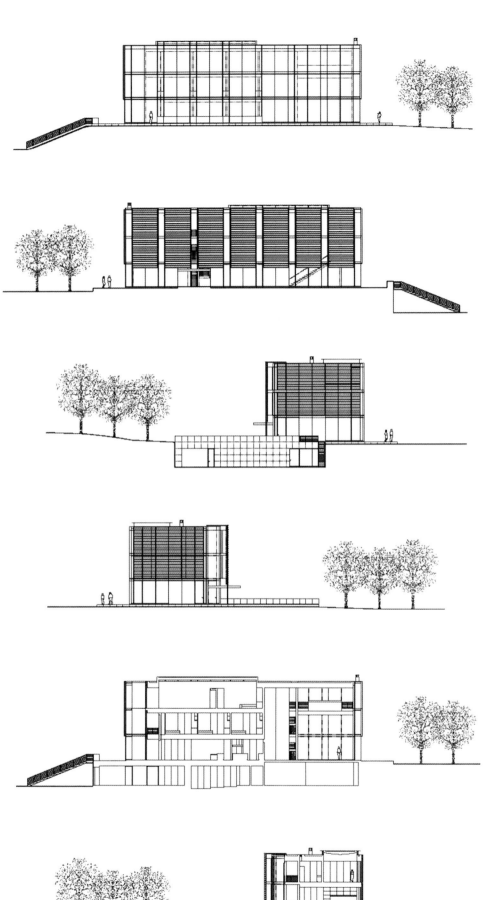

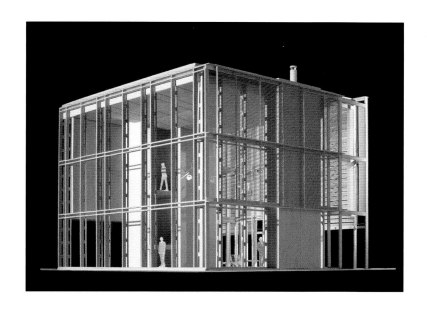

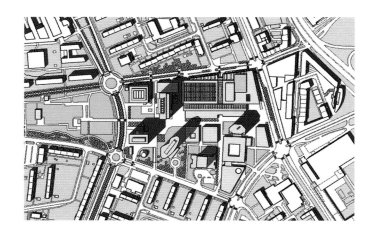

The southeast front of the complex
and general plan showing
the disposition of masses.

View of the digital model.

2001 | Project for a Performing Arts Center

Views of the model and site plan
showing the disposition of masses.

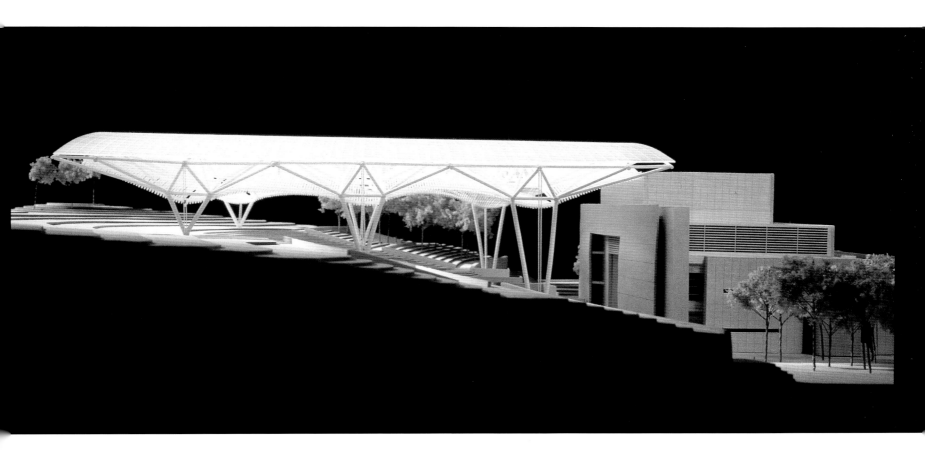

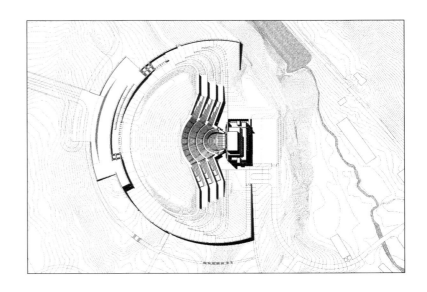

Plans of the second and stage floors.

Plans of the top and technical floors.

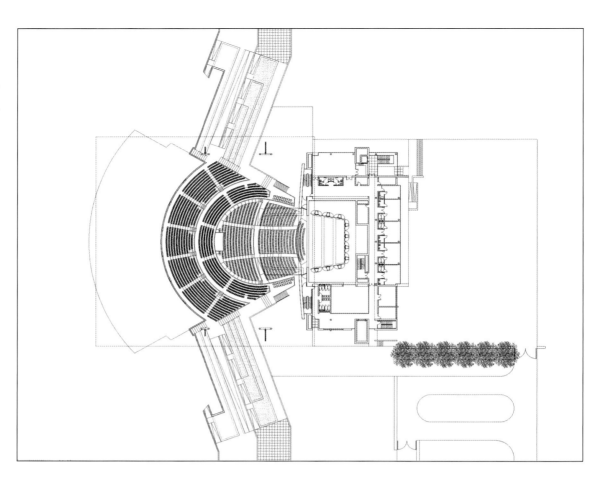

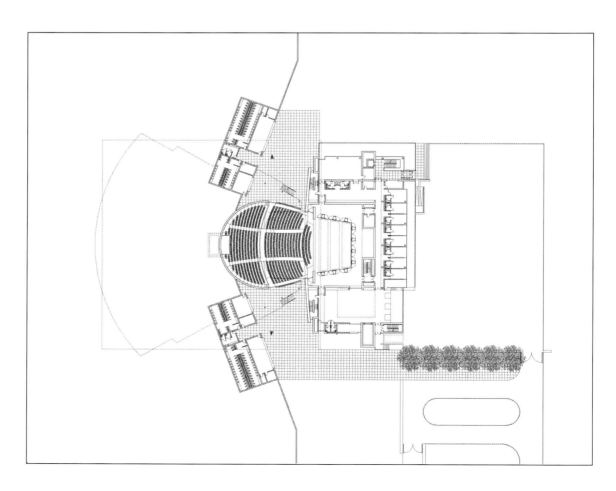

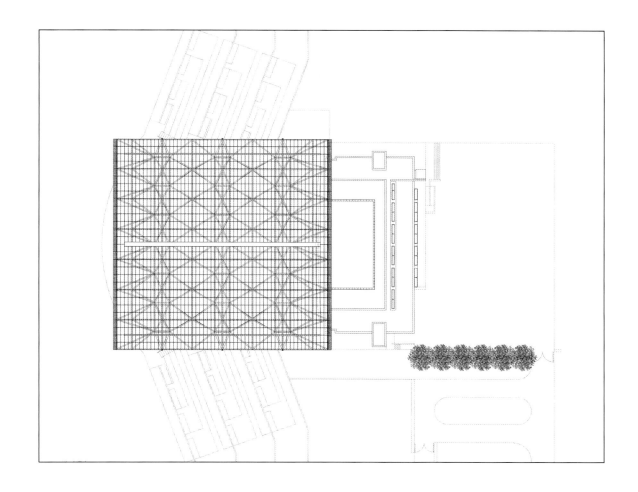

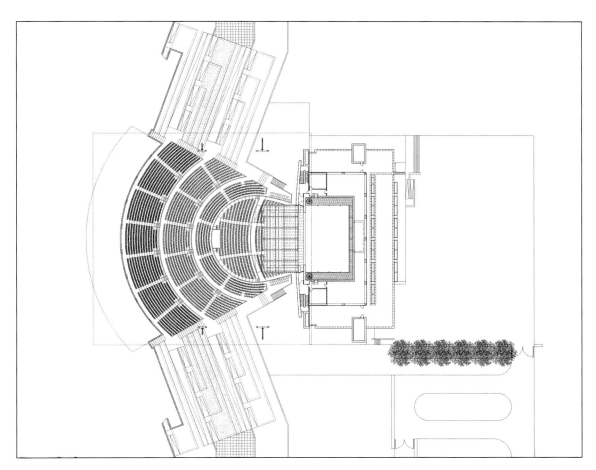

Views of the digital model.

Southeast, northeast and southwest elevations and sections.

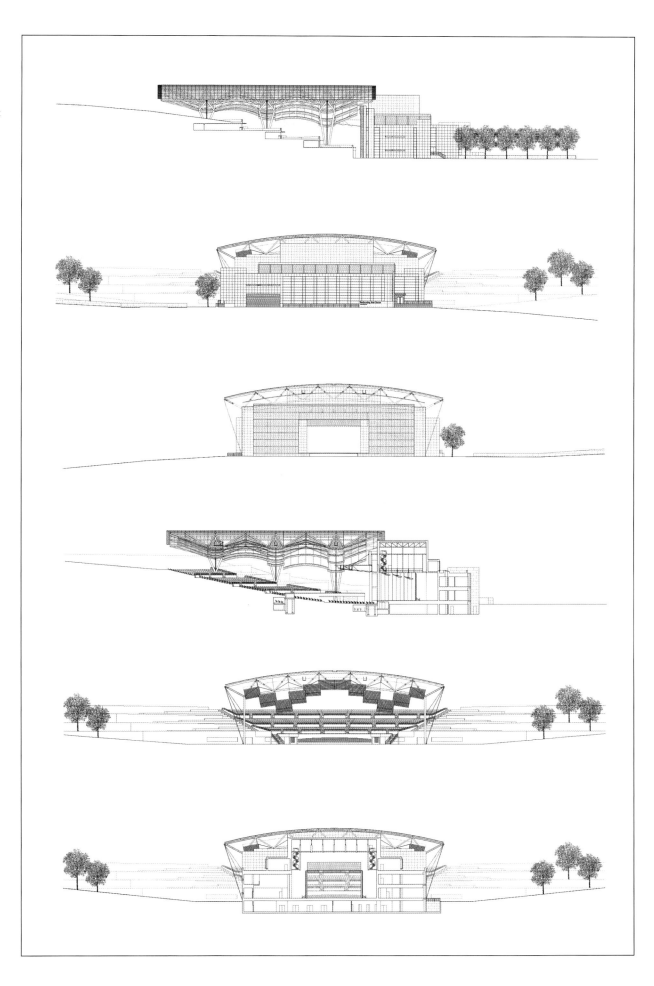

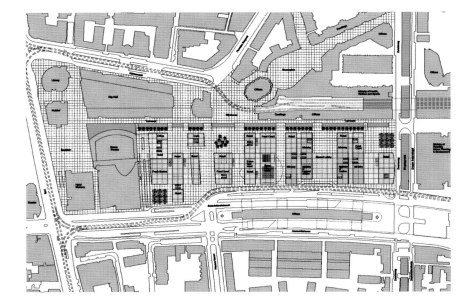

South elevation and general plan.

Perspective views of the digital model.

Views of the model from southwest,
west, northwest and east.

Plans of the ground
and basement floors.

North and south elevations.

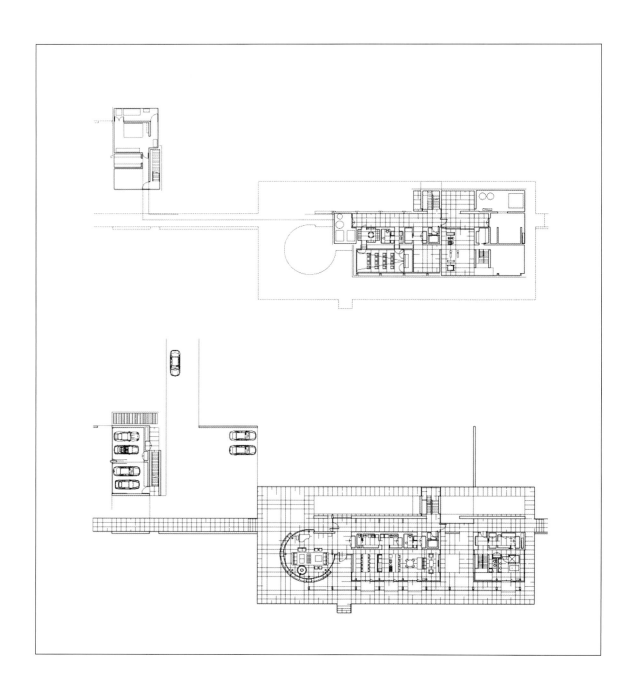

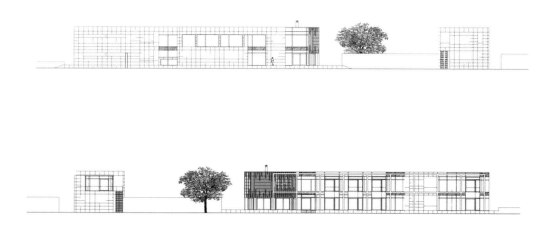

Plans of the top and second floors.

East and west elevations
and longitudinal section.

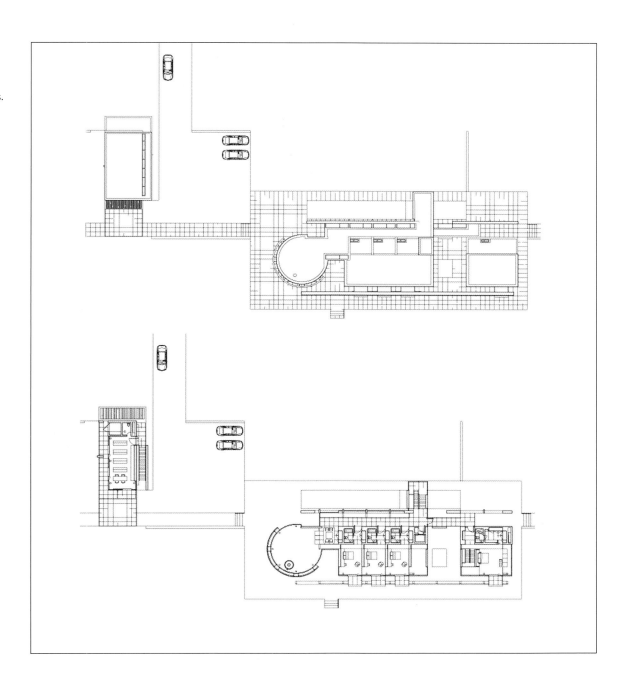

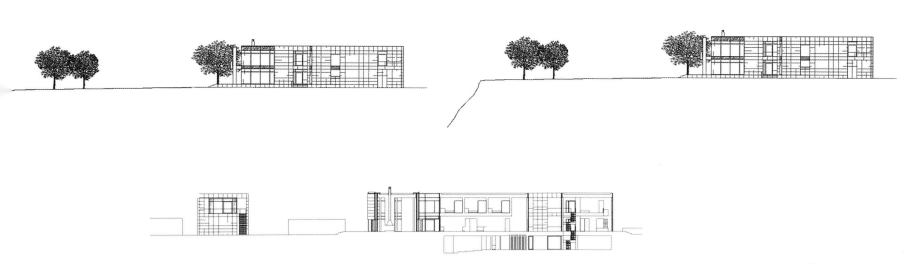

2001
2006

Yale University History of Art and Arts Library

Photomontages showing the project
alongside the building of the Art School
designed by Paul Rudolph, 1958–64.

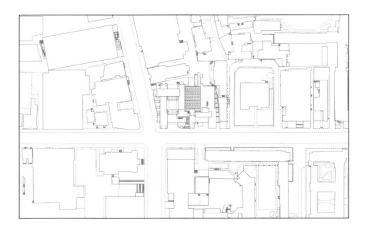

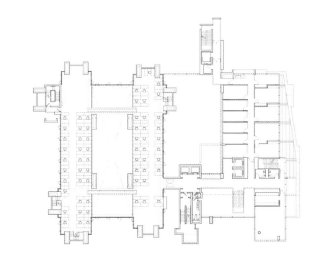

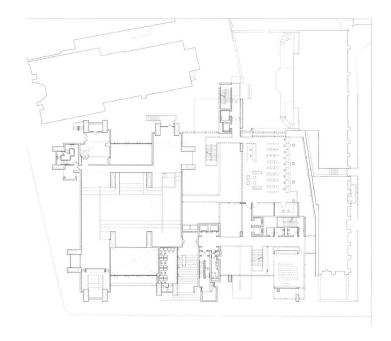

General plan and plans of the fifth,
second and ground floors.

East and west elevations
and longitudinal and cross sections.
View of the model.

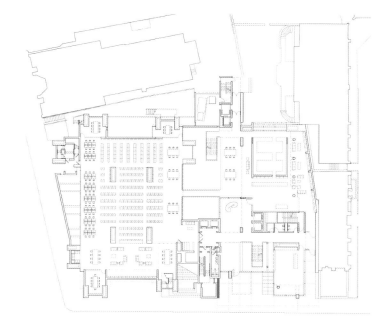

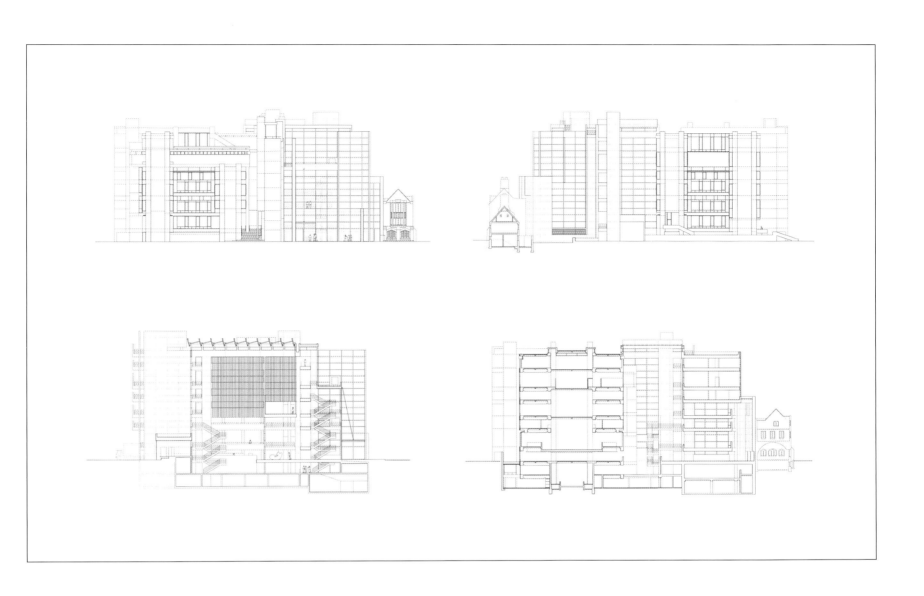

441

Burda Collection Museum

Views of the model
from the south and northeast.

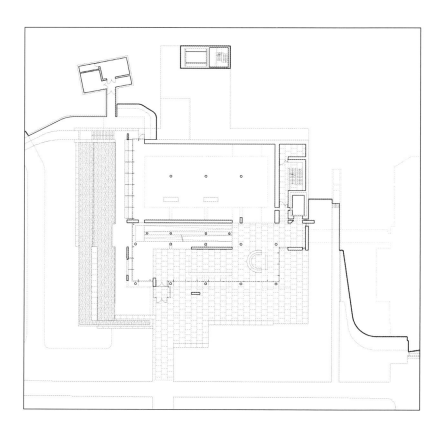

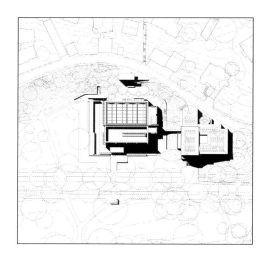

General plan and plan of the ground
floor.
Details of the structural model.

Plans of the mezzanine and second floors.
Longitudinal section through the ramp
and cross section through
the main gallery.

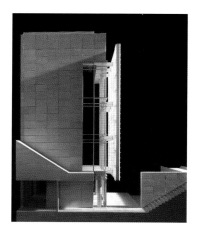

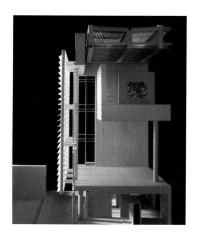

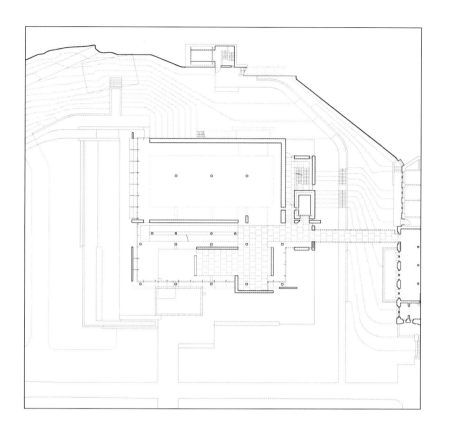

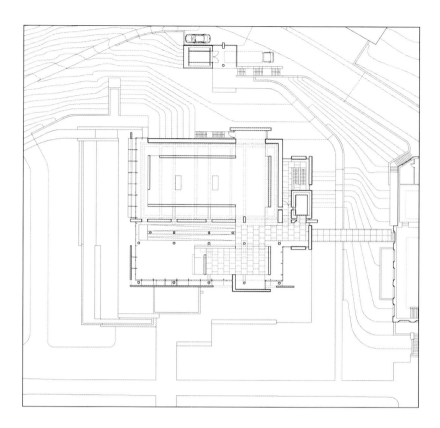

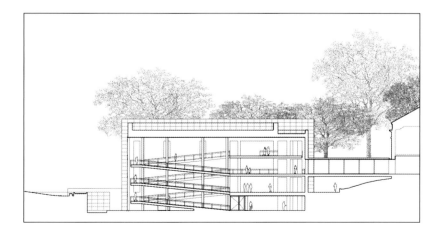

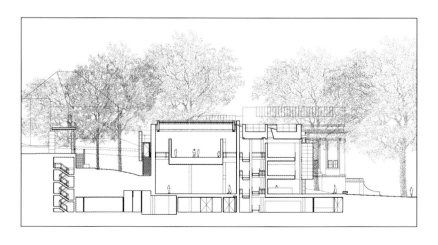

445

Perspective views of the digital model
from the east and northwest.

Plan of the ground floor.
West elevation, on Stephanienstrasse,
and east elevation, on Kurfürstenstrasse.

Plans of the penthouse
and the roofs with shadows.
Longitudinal and cross sections.

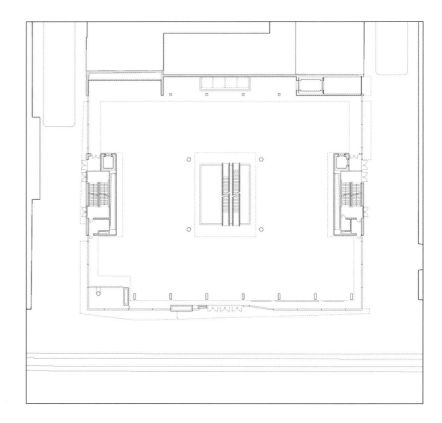

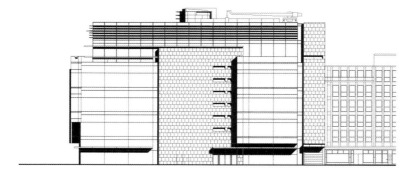

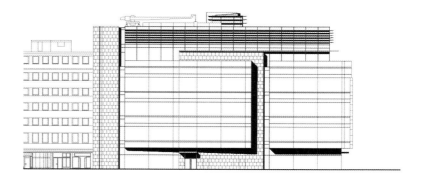

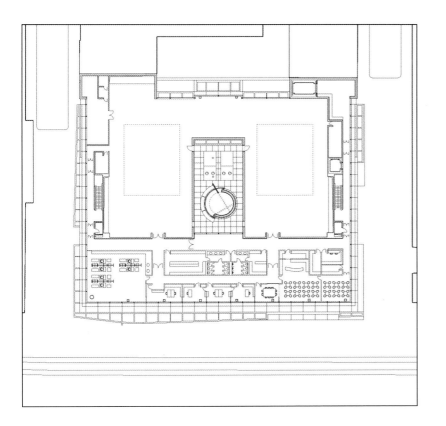

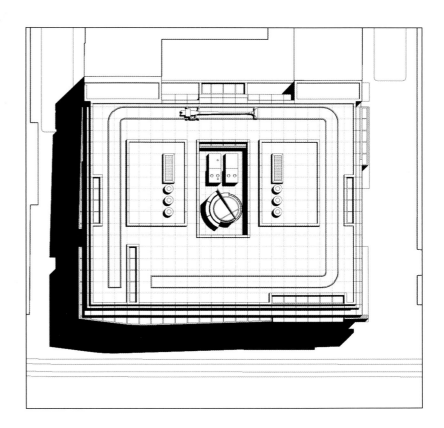

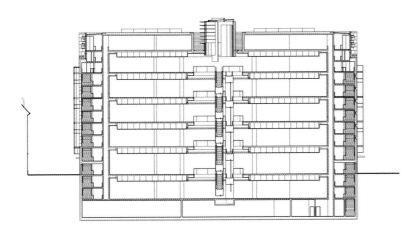

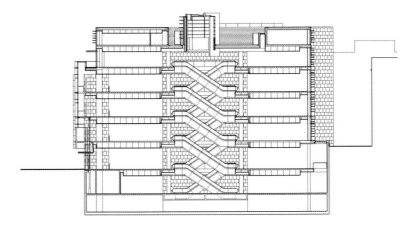

449

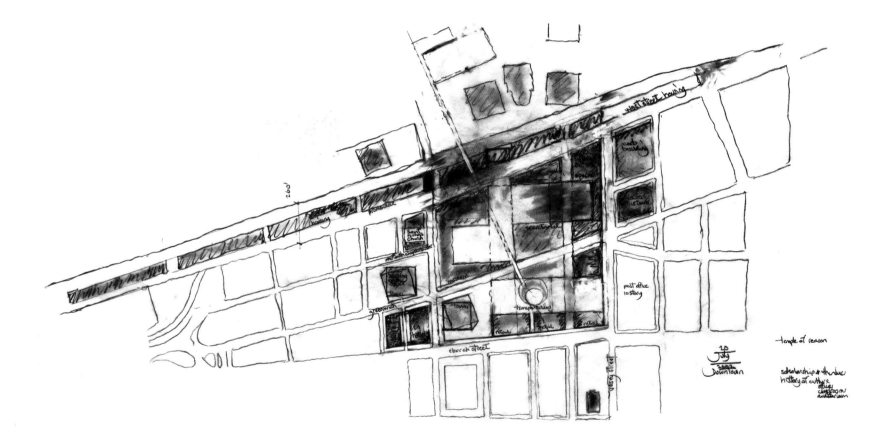

Study of site plan by Richard Meier.

Daytime and nighttime views
of the main façade.

Turning Point
Richard Meier

In my career, nothing can or will ever equal getting to be the architect for the Getty Center. Not only was it the most important event of my career, but, as things worked out, the project became inextricably linked with my children's growing up. When the Getty's Board invited leading architects to compete in 1982, they presented the Getty Center as the architect's dream of the decade—at least. And it was. The site was extraordinary—over 100 acres in the middle of Los Angeles, high above everything, untouched, with views in all directions. And the very idea of what the Center would be—museum, research institute, executive offices—was still to be formed.

The year-long selection process was grueling. One committee replaced another. The contenders were winnowed down from one hundred and ten to thirty to nine, finally to three. I flew out from New York City to L.A. over and over to answer questions. I flew to Atlanta to show them my High Museum of Art and to Frankfurt, Germany, to tour them through my Museum of Decorative Art. Then I did it again with new people. Legions of committees trooped through my Manhattan office, making it hard for us to do any other work. When, towards the end of this ordeal, I was awarded the prestigious Pritzker Prize, all I could think was, I hope this helps me get the job.

What anxiety! And so much work!

Then one Sunday night after about a year of this, I was having dinner with my children—Joseph was five, Ana was four—and the phone rang with the good news. I couldn't believe it. I said, "Kids, you have to drink champagne for the first time in your life." I tried to explain what it meant. They said, "Oh, that's nice, Dad."

In fact, it was going to mean a lot for them. I'd been recently divorced; so every summer and every vacation for the fifteen years that the design and building of the Getty took—all the time of their growing up—they spent with me in L.A. I lived next to the site there, and before construction began, we'd amble along the trails, looking at the hilltop grounds in different lights, at different times of day. It was beautiful. During construction, we'd saunter through the empty site every weekend, just the three of us. In 1997, when the throngs arrived for the big opening ceremonies, Ana, who was then seventeen, joked, "Dad, what are all these people doing here? This is our place."

Since the Getty, I've designed other buildings I'm very proud of—the Burda Museum in Baden-Baden, Germany, the Perry Street Condominium Towers, which are rising right now in New

York at the Hudson River. But the Getty will always remain a touchstone for me. I visited it a few weeks ago, and it looked great. Any time I feel depressed, all I have to do is go to the Getty, and I get undepressed. There's a lot of me in those buildings, from the very idea of the organization to the details. I was responsible for how the stone was cut and what stones were chosen, what you see and touch as you move around, the relationship of the buildings to the landscape. There's a sense of human scale that was important to me; anyone who goes can find a unique place that they feel is their own little niche.

At one point during the selection process, I was asked what materials I would use for the buildings. I spoke of using stone in a major way that could reflect and refract the unique quality of the Southern California light, that would be grounded in the earth and feel like part of the hillside. At the time, I hadn't a clue what I was talking about. But flying back and forth across the Grand Canyon, my nose to the window, I thought, "Now that's stone"—and that the Getty would have to make you feel some of that same kind of excitement.

When I visit, I look for the dozen or so giant, irregular-shaped stones I placed around to change the scale and give an accent to a place. I'd picked out each one myself in a quarry in Italy.

I remember saying, "I want this one": it was under water. I named each of these stones for someone involved in the project, like Carlo, the quarryman. Only I know their names. Of course, there's one for my son and one for my daughter.

All along, I'd wanted my kids to be part of the building of the Getty because it was part of me. But I also thought it would help them to understand how you go from nothing to something. Now, they're both in their twenties. Ana is creating her own art history/literature major at Harvard. Joseph is at Harvard too, studying to be an architect. I guess maybe they got it.

June 2002

Appendices

Chronology of Works

Lambert Beach House
Fire Island, New York
1961–62

Competion Project for a Monumental Fountain in the Benjamin Franklin Parkway
Philadelphia, Pennsylvania
1964
with Frank Stella

"Sona" Shop for Handicrafts and Handlooms
New York, New York
1964
with Elaine Lustig Cohen

"Recent American Synagogue Architecture" Exhibition Set Up
The Jewish Museum
New York, New York
1963

Dotson House
Ithaca, New York
1964

Frank Stella's Studio and Apartment
New York, New York
1965–66

House for Mr. & Mrs. Jerome Meier
Essex Fells, New Jersey
1963–65

Renfield House
Chester, New Jersey
1964–66
with Elaine Lustig Cohen

Smith House
Darien, Connecticut
1965–67

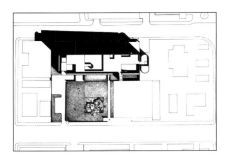

Competion Project for the University of California Arts Center
Berkeley, California
1965
with John Hejduk and Robert Slutzky

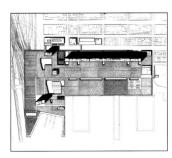

Hoboken Center Waterfront Renewal Project
Hoboken, New Jersey
1966
with John Hejduk and Robert Slutzky

Saltzman House
East Hampton, New York
1967–69

Hoffman House
East Hampton, New York
1966–67

Rubin Loft Renovation
New York, New York
1966

Fredonia Health and Physical Education Building
State University College
Fredonia, New York
1968–72

Project for a Mental Health Facilities Center for the Jewish Counseling and Service Agency
West Orange, New Jersey
1966

Westbeth Artists' Housing
Greenwich Village, New York
1967–70

Project for Charles Evans Industrial Buildings
Fairfield, New Jersey
Piscataway, New Jersey
1969

Bronx Redevelopment Planning Study
Bronx, New York
1969

Project for Robert R. Young Housing
New York, New York
1969

Bronx Developmental Center
Bronx, New York
1970–77

Project for a House in Pound Ridge
Pound Ridge, New York
1969

Monroe Developmental Center
Rochester, New York
1969–74
with Todd & Giroux, Architects

Maidman House
Sands Point, New York
1971–76

House in Old Westbury
Old Westbury, New York
1969–71

Twin Parks Northeast Housing
Bronx, New York
1969–74

Douglas House
Harbor Springs, Michigan
1971–73

Branch Office Prototypes for Olivetti
Irvine, California; Minneapolis, Minnesota;
Boston, Massachusetts; Brooklyn, New York;
Patterson, New Jersey
1971

Project for Olivetti Headquarters Building
Fairfax, Virginia
1971

Project for Paddington Station Housing
New York, New York
1973

**Modification of Olivetti Branch Office
Prototypes**
Seven Locations in the United States
1971

Project for a Housing in the East Side
New York, New York
1972
with Emery Roth, Architects

**Project for the Museum of Modern Art
at the Villa Strozzi**
Florence, Italy
1973

**Project for a Dormitory for the Olivetti
Training Center**
Tarrytown, New York
1971

Shamberg House
Chappaqua, New York
1972–74

Project for Condominium Housing
Yonkers, New York
1974

Project for the Cornell University Undergraduate Housing
Ithaca, New York
1974

Project for a Rehabilitation Warehouse for the Bronx Psychiatric Center
Bronx, New York
1975

Sarah Campbell Blaffer Pottery Studio
New Harmony, Indiana
1975–78

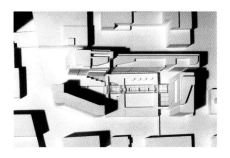

Project for a Commercial Building and Hotel
Springfield, Massachusetts
1975

The Atheneum
New Harmony, Indiana
1975–79

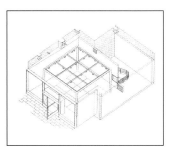

Project for the Weber-Frankel Gallery
New York, New York
1976

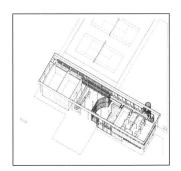

Project for the Wingfield Racquet Club
Greenwich, Connecticut
1975

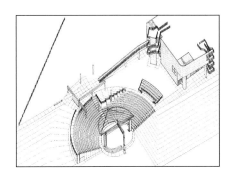

Project for The Theatrum
New Harmony, Indiana
1975

Suburban House Prototype
Concord, Massachusetts
1976

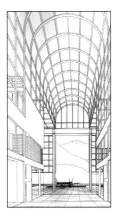

Alamo Plaza Project
Colorado Springs, Colorado
1976

The New York School Exhibition
State Museum
Albany, New York
1977

**Project for an Apartment
for Mr. and Mrs. Philip Suarez**
New York, New York
1977

**Opening Exhibition
of the Cooper-Hewitt Museum**
New York, New York
1976

Aye Simon Reading Room
Solomon R. Guggenheim Museum
New York, New York
1977–78

Clifty Creek Elementary School
Columbus, Indiana
1978–82

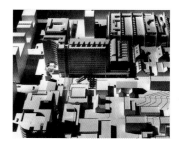

Project for Manchester Civic Center
Manchester, New Hampshire
1977

Palm Beach House
Palm Beach, Florida
1977–78
Addition to Palm Beach House
1993–95

Hartford Seminary
Hartford, Connecticut
1978–81

Giovannitti House
Pittsburgh, Pennsylvania
1979–83

Museum für Kunsthandwerk
Frankfurt am Main, Germany
1978–85

High Museum of Art
Atlanta, Georgia
1980–83

Furniture for Knoll International
1978

Project for Somerset Condominiums
Beverly Hills, California
1980

Objects for Alessi Design
1980

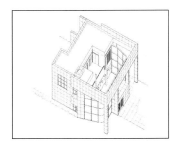

**Project for a Branch of the Irwin Union Bank
and Trust Company**
Columbus, Indiana
1979

**Competition Project
for an East 67th Street Housing**
New York, New York
1980

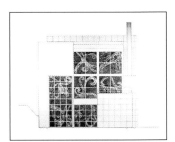

Meier/Stella Project
1980
with Frank Stella

Project for Renault Administrative Headquarters
Boulogne-Billancourt, France
1981

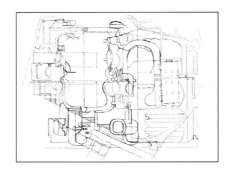

Competition Project for Parc de la Villette
Paris, France
1982

Tableware Designs for Swid Powell
1983–96

Project for International Bauaustellung Housing
Berlin, Germany
1982

Siemens Headquarters Building
Munich, Germany
1983–88

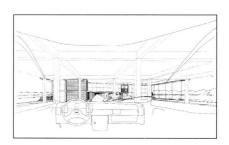

Competition Project for the Lingotto Factory Conversion
Turin, Italy
1983

Des Moines Art Center Addition
Des Moines, Iowa
1982–85

Competition Project for the Opera Bastille
Paris, France
1983

Westchester House
New York
1984–86

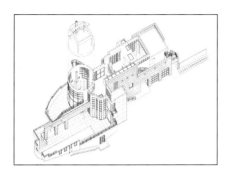

Project for the Hemlick House
Des Moines, Iowa
1984

Barnum Museum
Bridgeport, Connecticut
1984

The Getty Center
Los Angeles, California
1985–97

Ackerberg House
Malibu, California
1984–86
Addition to Ackerberg House
1993–95

Siemens Office and Research Facilities
Munich, Germany
1984–90

Offices of Richard Meier and Partners
New York, New York
Los Angeles, California
1986

Bridgeport Center
Bridgeport, Connecticut
1984–89

Grotta House
Harding Township, New Jersey
1985–89

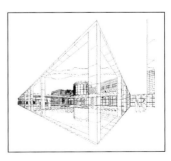

**Competition Project
for the Supreme Court Building**
Jerusalem, Israel
1986

Bicocca Competition Project
Milan, Italy
1986

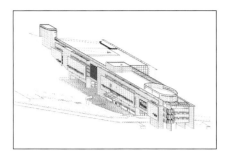

**Project for the Eye Center
for Oregon Health Sciences University**
Portland, Oregon
1986
with GBD Architects

**Competition Project for Santa Monica
Beach Hotel**
Santa Monica, California
1987

Exhibition and Assembly Building
Ulm, Germany
1986–93

Project for Naples
Naples, Italy
1987

**Competition Project for the Madison
Square Garden Site Redevelopment**
New York, New York
1987

City Hall and Central Library
The Hague, Netherlands
1989–95

**Project for the National Investment Bank
Building**
The Hague, Netherlands
1987

Weishaupt Forum
Schwendi, Germany
1987–92

Royal Dutch Paper Mill Headquarters
Hilversum, Netherlands
1987–92

Canal+ Headquarters
Paris, France
1988–92

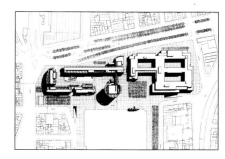

**Administrative and Maritime Center
Master Plan**
Antwerp, Belgium
1989

Museum of Contemporary Art
Barcelona, Spain
1987–95

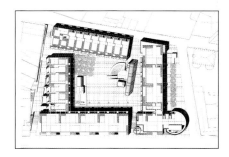

Espace Pitôt Residential Housing
Montpellier, France
1988–93

Project for CMB Headquarters Building
Antwerp, Belgium
1989

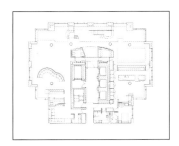

**Project for Renovating
an Apartment Interior**
Chicago, Illinois
1988

**Project for the Cornell University
Alumni and Admissions Center**
Ithaca, New York
1988

**Project for an Office Building
for Quandt**
Frankfurt am Main, Germany
1989

**Competition Project for
the Bibliothèque de France**
Paris, France
1989

Hypolux Bank Building
Luxembourg
1989–93

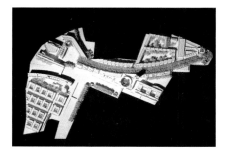

**Competition Master Plan
for the Sextius Mirabeau Area**
Aix-en-Provence, France
1990

Edinburgh Park Master Plan
Edinburgh, Scotland
1988

Project for the Museum of Ethnology
Frankfurt am Main, Germany
1989

Project for the Jean Arp Museum I
Rolandswerth, Germany
1990

Daimler-Benz Research Center
Ulm, Germany
1989–93

**Project for the Fox Inc. Studio
Expansion and Renovation**
Los Angeles, California
1990

Project for the Jean Arp Museum II
Rolandseck, Germany
1995

Euregio Office Building
Basel, Switzerland
1990–98

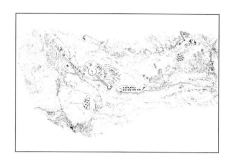

Plateau Tercier Master Plan
Nice, France
1991

Swissair North American Headquarters
Melville, New York
1991–94

Camden Medical Center
Singapore
1990–99

Light Fixtures for Baldinger
1991

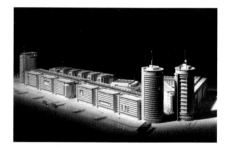

Competition Master Plan for Potsdamer Platz
Berlin, Germany
1992

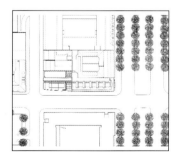

Project for Office Building
Berlin, Germany
1991

Rachofsky House
Dallas, Texas
1991–96

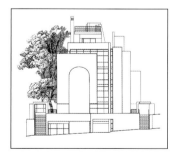

Project for a House in Wiesbaden
Wiesbaden, Germany
1992

Office Furniture for Stow Davis
1992

Museum of Television and Radio
Beverly Hills, California
1994–96

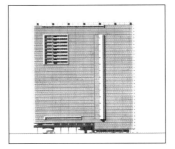

Project for Compaq Computer Administrative Manufacturing and Distribution Center
Houston, Texas
1994

United States Courthouse and Federal Building
Islip, New York
1993–2000

Gagosian Gallery
Beverly Hills, California
1994–95

Neugebauer House
Naples, Florida
1995–98

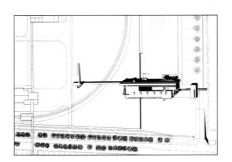

Project for an Administrative Building
Marckolsheim, France
1993

Competition Project for the Berliner Volksbank Headquarters
Berlin, Germany
1994

Sandra Day O'Connor United States Courthouse
Phoenix, Arizona
1995–2000

**Competition Project
for Swiss Re Headquarters**
Kingston, New York
1995

Jubilee Church
Rome, Italy
1996–2004

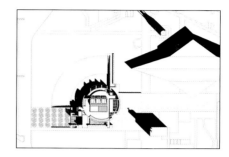

**Crystal Cathedral
Hospitality and Visitors Center**
Garden Grove, California
1996–2003

Grand Piano for Ibach Sohn
1995

Coordinated Street Furniture
New York, New York
1996

Tan House
Kuala Lumpur, Malaysia
1997–2002

Museum of the Ara Pacis
Rome, Italy
1996–

Project for Kolonihavehus Pavilion
Copenhagen, Denmark
1996

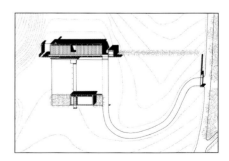

Project for the Glasgow Exhibition House
Glasgow, Scotland
1997

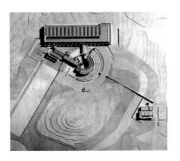

Project for Tag McLaren Headquarters
Woking, Surrey, England
1997

Competition Project for Bayer AG Headquarters
Leverkusen, Germany
1998

Project for Draycott Park Condominiums
Singapore
1998

Competition Project for the Deutsche Post Building
Bonn, Germany
1997

Competition Project for the Scottish Parliament
Edinburgh, Scotland
1998

Rickmers Reederei Headquarters
Hamburg, Germany
1998–2001

Peek & Cloppenburg Department Store
Düsseldorf, Germany
1998–2001

Westwood Promenade Master Plan
Los Angeles, California
1998

Canon Headquarters
Tokyo, Japan
1998–2002

Project for the Cittadella Bridge
Alessandria, Italy
1998

Southern California Beach House
Malibu, California
1999–2001

**Project for Office Buildings
in Chesterfield Village**
St. Louis, Missouri
1999–2003

Friesen House
Los Angeles, California
1998–2001

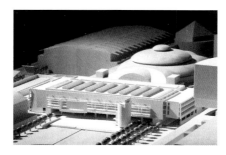

Competition Project for the Frankfurt Forum
Frankfurt am Main, Germany
1999

Swartz Residence
Laguna Beach, California
1999

San Jose Civic Center
San Jose, California
1998–2003

Project for Painted Turtle Camp
Lake Hughes, California
1999–2003

Project for Santa Ynez House
Santa Ynez, California
1999–2003

Competition Project for the Trinity College
Dublin, Ireland
1999

Competition Project for the Robert Bosch Foundation Building
Stuttgart, Germany
2000

Master Plan for Pankrac City Office Buildings
Prague, Czech Republic
2000–05

Competition Project for Canary Wharf
London, England
1999

Project for New York House
Katonah, New York
2000

Competition Project for the Habsburgerring Tower
Cologne, Germany
2001

173/176 Perry Street Condominiums
New York, New York
1999–2002

UCLA Broad Art Center
Los Angeles, California
2000–03

Viking Research Center
Greenwood, Mississippi
2001–03

Project for a Performing Arts Center
Bethel, New York
2001

**Competition Master Plan for the FSM
East River Area**
New York, New York
2001
with Peter Eisenman, Hugh Hardy & SOM

**Yale University History of Art
and Arts Library**
New Haven, Connecticut
2001–06

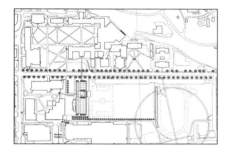

**Life Sciences Technology Building
for Cornell University**
Ithaca, New York
2001–06

Project for Santa Barbara House
Santa Barbara, California
2001

Burda Collection Museum
Baden-Baden, Germany
2001–04

Wijnhaven Kwartier Master Plan
The Hague, Netherlands
2001

**Competition Master Plan for the University
of Bologna**
Bologna, Italy
2001
with Piero Sartogo

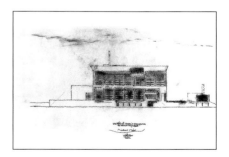

Project for Houses at Sagaponac
Long Island, New York
2001–

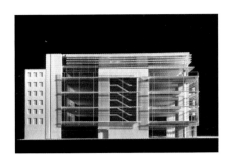

**Peek & Cloppenburg
Department Store**
Mannheim, Germany
2001–

66
New York, New York
2002–03

Joy Apartment at Perry Street
New York, New York
2002–04

**Project for Peek & Cloppenburg
Department Store**
Berlin, Germany
2002

**Project for Paris Room at the Grand Hotel
Salone**
Salone del Mobile, Fiera di Milano
Milan, Italy
2002

Kojaian Apartment at Perry Street
New York, New York
2002–03

Project of the Glimcher Yacht Interior
2002

Project for the Greenpoint Landing Housing
Brooklyn, New York
2002

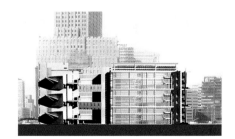

**The Urban Facility – Downtown Manhattan
Project for The New York Times**
New York, New York
2002

Biography

Richard Meier is well known and well respected around the world for his architecture and designs. He has been awarded major commissions in the United States and Europe including courthouses, city halls, museums, corporate headquarters, housing and private residences. Among his most well-known projects are the Getty Center in Los Angeles, the High Museum in Atlanta, the Museum für Kunsthandwerk in Frankfurt, Germany, the Canal+ Television Headquarters in Paris, the Barcelona Museum of Contemporary Art, The Hartford Seminary in Connecticut, and the Atheneum in New Harmony, Indiana.

Richard Meier has received the highest honors available in architecture: in 1997 he received the AIA Gold Medal as well as the Praemium Imperiale from the Japanese Government, in recognition of lifetime achievement in the arts. In 1995, he was elected Fellow of the American Academy of Arts and Sciences. He received the Deutsches Architektur Preis in 1993 and in 1992 the French Government awarded him the honor of Officier de l'Ordre des Arts et des Lettres. In 1989 the Royal Institute of British Architects, of which he is a Fellow, awarded him the Royal Gold Medal.

In 1984, Mr. Meier was awarded the Pritzker Prize for Architecture, considered the field's highest honor. He has been the youngest recipient of this award in the history of the prize. In the same year, Mr. Meier was selected architect for the prestigious commission to design the one billion dollar Getty Center in Los Angeles, California. Recently he was awarded a commission by the Archdiocese of Rome to design the Jubilee Church in Rome, Italy, which is under construction.

Since completing his architectural education at Cornell University, he has received honorary degrees from the University of Naples, New Jersey Institute of Technology, The New School for Social Research, Pratt Institute and the University of Bucharest.

Mr. Meier has given numerous lectures throughout the world and participated in many juries. He has written and been the subject of many books and monographs and innumerable newspaper and magazine articles. In addition to being on the Board of Directors of the Cooper Hewitt National Design Museum and the American Academy in Rome, he is also a Fellow of the American Academy of Arts & Science, the French and Belgian Académies d'Architecture, and a member of the Bund Deutscher Architekten and the American Academy of Arts & Letters, from which he received the Brunner Prize for Architecture in 1976.

Mr. Meier has taught at the Cooper Union, Princeton University, Pratt Institute, Harvard University, Yale University and UCLA. He currently holds the Frank T. Rhodes Class of 1956 University Professorship at Cornell University. He is a Fellow of the American Institute of Architects and received a Medal of Honor from the New York Chapter in 1980 and the Gold Medal from the Los Angeles Chapter in 1998. His numerous design awards include 21 National AIA Honor Awards and 45 New York City AIA Design Awards.

General Bibliography

Abercrombie, Stanley. "Richard Meier's Sculptures for Living." *House & Garden*, November 1976, pp. 168-71, 196.

Abercrombie, Stanley. "Bravado Variations in a Consistent Theme." *Architecture*, May 1985, p. 325.

Abercrombie, Stanley. "1997 Hall of Fame." *Interior Design*, December 1997, pp. 6-8.

Abrams, Janet. "A White Knight." *The Independent*, 25 October 1988, p. 16.

"The AD 100: Richard Meier." *Architectural Digest*, September 1995, p. 98.

Aldersey-Williams, Hugh. "Meier's magic for Europe." *The European*, 3–9 July 1997, p. 15.

Angel, Valerie Tate. "Transsubjectivity: The Space Where Psychoanalysis and Architecture Meet." *International Forum of Psychoanalysis 1-2* April 2000, pp. 76-83.

"The Architectural Digest International Directory of Interior Designers and Architects." *Architectural Digest*, January 2000, p. 92.

Architecture: Shaping the Future – A Symposium and Exhibition with Legoretta, Maki, Meier & Rogers. Introduction by Allan Temko. California: University of California, San Diego, 1990.

"Architektur: Dramatischer Dialog." *Der Spiegel*, 26 May 1980, pp. 237-41.

Arditi, Fiamma. "Lords of the Compass." *Ars* 18, June 1999, pp. 33-4, English text pp. 4-5.

Arthur, John. "Alternative Space, Richard Meier." *Art New England*, April 1986, pp. 8-9.

Barbuica, Letitia and Anca Andu Tomaeveschi. "Laudatum." *Octogon,* June 2001, pp. 65-71.

Barthelmess, Stephan. "The Collage in the Square: Art Parallel to Architecture." In Barthelmess, Stephan. *Richard Meier, Collagen.* Germany: International Creative Management, March 1993.

Bissel, Therese. "Architects' Rule." *The Robb Report Collection*, May 2002, pp. 21-25.

Blaser, Werner. *Richard Meier: Building for Art*. Basel: Birkhäuser Verlag, 1990.

Blaser, Werner. *Richard Meier Details*. Basel: Birkhäuser Verlag, 1996.

Bradaschia, Maurizio. "Benedetti Architetti: Richard Meier, quando il luogo non conta nulla." *Trieste Oggi – Il Meridiano*, 27 August 1993.

Bode, Peter M. "Im Bauhaus zu Hause: Richard Meier und sein Räume-Theater." *Frankfurter Allgemeine Magazin*, 3 June 1983, pp. 8-14.

Cassarà, Silvio. *Richard Meier*. Bologna: Zanichelli Editore S.p.A., 1995. Reprinted in German, Basel: Birkhäuser Verlag, 1996. Reprinted in Spanish, Barcelona: Editorial Gustavo Gili S.A., 1997.

Castellano, Aldo. *Architetture – D'Aria e di Luce – Una storia su Richard Meier.* Milan: Guerini Studio, 1994.

Ciorra, Pippo, ed. *Richard Meier*. Milan: Electa, 1993. Includes: "Richard Meier o la rappresentazione della modernità" by Livio Sacchi.

Ciorra, Pippo. "Richard Meier and Peter Eisenman. Talent and ideas." *Casabella*, December–January 1997, pp. 106-7.

Cohen, Alan. "Modernist Contemplations." *Architecture of Israel*, vol. 20, 1994, pp. 80-89.

Cook, Peter. "Richard Meier: Perfect Whiteness." *RIBA Journal*, June 1988, pp. 19-20.

Cooperman, Jackie. "Private Lives/Public Places: Richard Meier." *Departures*, March-April 2002, p. 50.

Costanzo, Michele, Vincenzo Giorgi and Maria Grazia Tolomeo, eds. *Richard Meier/Frank Stella: Arte e Architettura.* Exhibition catalog. Milan: Electa, 1993. Italian text with English translations. Includes "Richard Meier and Frank Stella: a conversation about architecture and art."

Dal Co, Francesco. "The 'Allusions' of Richard Meier." *Oppositions* 9, 1977, pp. 6-18.

D'Annunzio, Grazia. "Il Segno di Richard Meier." *L'Uomo Vogue*, September 1996, pp. 449-53.

Davis, Douglas. "Designs for Living: Five Frontiersmen." *Newsweek*, 6 November 1978, pp. 82-91.

De Bruyn, Gerd. *Contemporary Architecture in Germany 1970–1996*. Basel: Birkhäuser Verlag, 1997.

Diamonstein, Barbaralee. *American Architecture Now*. New York: Rizzoli, 1980, pp. 105-22.

Diamonstein, Barbaralee. "Richard Meier." In *American Architecture Now II*, New York: Rizzoli, 1985, pp. 161-68.

Di Forti, Massimo. "Meier: Roma? Città eterna, non immobile." *Il Messaggero*, 10 July 1997, p. 19.

Dimitriu, Livio. "Richard Meier: l'architettura verso il terzo millennio." *Controspazio*, March 1990, pp. 9-25.

"E-mail a: Richard Meier." *01 Taller de la Fundacion*. Fundación Museu d'Art Contemporani de Barcelona, July 2000.

"The Faces of Power." *Art & Auction*, December 1996, pp. 77-89.

Falke, Martin. "Weisse Welt." *Architektur Innenarchitektur Technischer Ausbau*, April 1995. Includes "Weiss als Dogma" by Richard Meier, p. 24.

Fernandez-Galiano, Luis, ed. "Richard Meier in Europe." *Arquitectura Viva Monografias* 59, May–June 1996. Includes "Houses and Museums: Meier in America" by Jorge Sainz; "A European America" by Tzonis Alezander and Liane Lefaivre; "Modern or Contemporary" by Joseph Giovannini; "Transparency and Perspective" by Stephan Barthelmess.

Filler, Martin. "Modernism Lives: Richard Meier." *Art in America*, May 1980, pp. 123-31.

Fischer, Volker. "Architektur-Import." *Der Architekt*, May 1990, pp. 236-37.

Five Architects: Eisenman/Graves/Gwathmey/Hejduk/Meier. New York: Wittenborn, 1972, pp. 11-13, 111-34. Introductions by Kenneth Frampton and Colin Rowe.

Five Architects NY. Rome: Officina Edizioni, 1976, pp. 24-28, 133-73. Introduction by Manfredo Tafuri.

Five Architects/Twenty Years Later. Maryland: University of Maryland, fall 1992. Includes Introduction by Steven W. Hurtt; "The Five After Twenty-Five: An Assessment" by Kenneth Frampton; "Recollections" by Ralph Bennett.

"Five on Five." *Architectural Forum*, May 1973, pp. 45-57. Articles by Romaldo Giurgola, Alan Greenberg, Charles Moore, Jaquelin Robertson, and Robert Stern.

Flagge, Ingeborg. "Richard Meier." *Häuser*, January 1989, pp. 59-74.

Flagge, Ingeborg and Oliver Hamm, eds. *Richard Meier in Europe*. Berlin: Ernst & Sohn, 1997.

Flaim, Denise. "Architecture Is Not a High L.I. Priority." *New York Newsday*, 10 April 1995, p. A25.

Fort, Jaume. "Richard Meier, la Arquitectura Blanca." *El País Semanal*, 24 November 1985, pp. 53-62.

40 under 40: An Exhibition of Young Talents in Architecture. New York: Architectural League of New York and American Federation of Arts, 1966, pp. 19-20.

Frampton, Kenneth. "Five Architects: Eisenman/Graves/Gwathmey/Hedjuk/Meier." *Lotus International* 9, 1975, pp. 147-61.

Frampton, Kenneth. "Richard Meier & Partners in Europe: Recent Work." *Casabella*, December 1990, pp. 4-10.

Frank Stella:The Moby Dick Series. Ulm: Ulmer Museum, 1993. Includes "Collaborations: Frank Stella and Richard Meier" by David Galloway; "Frank Stella's 'Moby Dick Series' in the 'Stadthaus' designed by Richard Meier" by Brigitte Reinhardt.

Frank Stella: A Vision for Public Art. Japan: Tankosha Publishing, Ltd, 1994, pp. 141-46. Includes "Broadsides" by Frank Stella; "A Relationship in the Industry of Excellence" by Earl Childress; "Richard Meier and Frank Stella: a Conversation Between Architect and Artist" edited by Peter Slatin.

Furstenberg, Rochelle. "Dreaming in White

(and Beige.)" *The Jerusalem Report*,
3 August 1998, pp. 42-43.
Futagawa, Yukio, ed. "Richard Meier." Special
issue of *Global Architecture Document Extra* 8,
1997. Includes an interview with Richard Meier.
Galloway, David. "A Heightened Urbanity:
The Recent Works of Richard Meier." *a+u –
Architecture and Urbanism*, March 1988,
pp. 27-132.
Galloway, David. "Europe's Love Affair With
an American Architect." *International Herald
Tribune*, 18–19 July 1992, p. 7.
Galloway, David. "Richard Meier, Master
Builder." *Inter Nations German-American
Cultural Review*, 6 October 1993, pp. 40-47.
Galloway, David. "Richard Meier: style
in context." *Art in America*, January 1995,
pp. 40-47.
Garcias, Jean-Claude. "Construit par Blanc."
Beaux Arts, June 1985, p. 70.
Germain, Christiane. "Le Choix de Richard
Meier." *Maison & Jardin*, July–August 1995,
pp. 18-19.
Gerosa, Mario. "Elogio della leggerezza."
*Architectural Digest: Le Più Belle Case Del
Mondo*, Italian edition, July 2000, pp. 58, 60.
Gladstone, Valerie. "A Modern Master."
Diversion, December 1993, p. 140A-140H.
Glancey, Jonathan. "As Cold, and as Passionate
as the Dawn." *World Architecture* 3, 1989,
pp. 40-51.
Gleizes, Serge. "Richard Meier: l'architecture
ocean." *Table & Cadeau*, December–January
1997, pp. 90-93.
Gleizes, Serge. "La fibre minimaliste."
L'Officiel, February 1997, p. 184.
Gleizes, Serge. "Richard Meier: ascetisme
et parfum d'epoque." *Vogue Hommes*,
spring–summer 1997, pp. 174-75.
Glusberg, Jorge, ed. *Vision of the Modern.
UIA, Journal of Architecture Theory and
Criticism*. London: Academy Editions, 1988,
pp. 88-96.
Goldberger, Paul. "Architecture's Big Five
Elevate Form." *The New York Times*,
26 November 1973, sec. 2, pp. 1, 34.
Goldberger, Paul. "Should Anyone Care
about the 'New York Five'? ... or about
Their Critics, the 'Five on Five'?"
Architectural Record, February 1974,
pp. 113-16.
Goldberger, Paul. "Review of Richard Meier,
Architect." *The New York Times Book Review*,
5 December 1976, p. 10.
Goldberger, Paul. "City Reaches Pinnacle as
Architectural Leader." *The New York Times*,
4 April 1983, pp. B1, 4.
Goldberger, Paul. "Ad-Meier-ing." *Vogue*,
June 1983, pp. 196-203, 256.

Goldberger, Paul. "Richard Meier: Form
and Function." *Goodlife*, March 1984,
pp. 34-31.
Goldberger, Paul. "Richard Meier Get the
Pritzker Prize." *The New York Times*, 18 April
1984, p. C20.
Goldberger, Paul. "A little book that led five
men to fame." *The New York Times*,
11 February 1996, sec. 2, p. 38.
Goodman, Wendy. "A Remembrance of Visions
Pure and Elegant." *The New York Times*,
3 January 1993, p. H29.
Goodman, Wendy. "Philip's Site." *Harper's
Bazaar*, October 1996, p. 189.
Graaf, Vera. "Alles Weiss in Weiss." *Männer
Vogue*, March 1986, pp. 177-81.
Graaf, Vera. "Richard Meiers Museums-Welt."
Architektur & Wohnen, June–July 1990, p. 143.
Gray, Susan, ed. *Architects on Architects*.
"Richard Meier on Frank Lloyd Wright."
New York: McGraw-Hill, 2002, p. 114-21.
Gregotti, Vittorio. "The Revival of the
Avantgarde." *Architettura*, 28 August 1988,
pp. 85-93.
Grosse Architekten – Band 2. "Richard Meier"
by Ingeborg Flagge. Hamburg: Häuserbuch,
1992.
Gubitosi, Alessandro and Ferruccio Izzo.
Richard Meier Architetture/Projects 1986–1990.
Florence: Centro Di, 1991. Exhibition catalog,
Naples, Palazzo Reale, June 21–July 21.
Includes essays by Vittorio Magnago
Lampugnani, Alberto Izzo, Camillo Gubitosi
and Ferruccio Izzo.
Haito, Masahiko and Nishizawa Midori, eds.
*Richard Meier and Frank Stella: Architecture
and Art*. Exhibition catalog. Tokyo: Akira Ikeda
Corporation, 1996. English and Japanese text.
Includes "Meier's Toad and Stella's Garden"
by David Galloway; "Richard Meier Sculpture"
by Lois Nesbitt; "Richard Meier Collage"
by Lois Nesbitt; "The Art of Abstraction,"
interview with Richard Meier by Clare Farrow;
"Ecstasy of the Artificer: On the Architecture
of Richard Meier" by Seiken Fukuda;
"Thoughts on Frank Stella" by Richard Meier;
"Walls and Frank Stella" by Masahiko Haito.
Hales, Linda. "Modernist with a Mission."
The Washington Post, Home sec., 6 February
1997, pp. 10-11, 14, 16.
Hamm, Oliver. "Fertighauser von Richard
Meier?" ("Custom Richard Meier?")
Der Architekt, April 1996, pp. 258-60.
Hansen, Jorgen Peder. "Arkitekten Richard
Meier." *Arkitekten*, March 1986, pp. 85-93.
Hanson, Bernard. "Architecture in the Abstract."
Hartford Courant, 4 May 1980, p. 2G.
Haubrich, Rainer. "Silberstelen des Kapitals."
Die Welt, 14 September 2001, p. 31.

Henning, Larson, et al. "Interview with Richard
Meier." *Skala*, August 1987, pp. 11-15.
Heydová, Eva and Jirí Horsky. "Rozhovor s
Johnem Eislerem." *Architekt* 23-24, 1996,
pp. 30-42.
Holmes, Ann. "Meier Admired Design
and a Major Architect." *Houston Chronicle*,
25 April 1981.
Horáková, Dana. "Baumeister des Papstes."
Welt am Sonntag 21, 23 May 1999, p. 41.
Hubbard, William. *Complexity and Conviction:
Steps toward an Architecture of Convention*.
Cambridge, Mass.: MIT Press, 1980,
pp. 7-9, 221-26.
Hughes, Robert. "U.S. Architects: Doing Their
Own Thing." *Time*, 8 January 1979, pp. 52-29.
Huxtable, Ada Louise. "The Gospel according
to Giedion and Gropius Is under Attack."
The New York Times, 27 June 1976, pp. 1, 29.
Huxtable, Ada Louise. "Architectural Drawings
as Art." *The New York Times*, 12 June
1977, p. 25.
Huxtable, Ada Louise. "The Troubled State
of Modern Architecture." *New York Review
of Books*, 1 May 1980, pp. 22-25.
Huxtable, Ada Louise. "Is Modern Architecture
Dead?" *New York Review of Books*, 16 July
1981, pp. 17-20.
Hyatt, Gordon. "Architects and the New York
Art Scene." *Esquire* (Japan), November 2001,
pp. 143-59.
Ivy, Robert. "Richard Meier after the Getty."
Architectural Record, September 2002, p. 100.
James, Warren A. "Meier's Opus: Richard
Meier, Architect 1965–1984." *Progressive
Architecture*, June 1985, pp. 149-55.
James, Warren A. "Interview: Richard Meier."
Arquitectura, July–August 1990, pp. 138-53.
Jencks, Charles. "Meier and the Modern
Tradition." *Architectural Design*, vol. 58
no. 9-10, 1988, pp. II-V.
Jencks, Charles. "Richard Meier and the
Modern Tradition." In *The New Moderns*.
London: Academy Edition, 1990, pp. 239-55.
*The Jerusalem Seminar in Architecture:
Megaform as the Urban Landscape*.
Proceedings, 21–23 June 1998. Jerusalem: ICC
International Convention Center, pp. 52-57.
Jodidio, Philip. *Contemporary American
Architects*. Germany: Taschen, 1993,
pp. 98-107.
Jodidio, Philip. *Richard Meier*, Köln: Benedikt
Taschen Verlag Gmbh, 1996.
Jodidio, Philip. *Contemporary American
Architects* .Vol. IV. New York: Taschen, 1998.
Jordy, William H. "Which Terrace for the
Sunset?" *The New York Times Book Review*,
17 March 1985, p. 13.
Kaplan, Sam Hall. " Getty Architect and Other."

The Los Angeles Times Book Review,
7 April 1985, p. 6.
Kay, Jane Holtz. "Right Angles, White Lines."
The Christian Science Monitor, 9 May 1984,
pp. 29-30.
Keens, William. "Dialogue and Fantasy
in White: An Interview with Richard Meier."
American Arts, September 1983, pp. 16-21.
Kelly, Lore. "Ein Gespräch mit Richard Meier."
Neue Zürchner Zeitung, 26 May 1989, p. 67.
Kupper, Eugene. "Book Review: Richard Meier,
Architect." *LA Architect*, February 1977, p. 2.
Reprinted in *Progressive Architecture*, July
1977, pp. 55-57.
Lange, Alexandra. "Richard Meier: Leaving
Los Angeles." *Graphis* 314, March–April 1998,
pp. 40-55.
Larson, Soren. "American Institute
of Architects 2000: Honors & Awards."
Architectural Record, May 2000, p. 95.
Lemos, Peter. "Richard Meier." *Northeast
Orient Magazine*, March 1985, p. 58.
Lewin, Susan Grant and Susan Hope Schraub.
"The Structure of Pace." *House Beautiful*, April
1978, pp. 79-91.
Lewis, Roger. "Another Look at the 'New York
Five'." *The Washington Post*, 12 December
1992, p. E12.
Library Builders. London: Academy Editions,
1997, pp. 126-33.
Loos, Ted. "Richard Meier's Dolce Vita." *Food
& Wine*, October 2000, pp. 192-96.
Marshall, Alex. "Let There Be Light"; "Richard
Meier: A Modernist at Heart." *Newsday*,
16 October 2000, pp. B6-B7, B10.
Marvel, Bill. "Architecture as Seen by the Eyes
of the 'Whites.'" *National Observer*, 22 June
1974, p. 20.
Mas, Jean, ed. *Richard Meier Architect* . CD
ROM. Lugano: Victory interactive Media SA,
1995. Includes commentary by Henri Ciriani;
Kenneth Frampton; Andre Rousselet; Frank
Stella; Exra Stoller.
Maurer, Caro. "A Bottle is a Bottle: The
American Architect Richard Meier likes to keep
order." *Die Welt*, 2 November 1996, pp. 52-53.
Maurer, Caro. "Ich hoffe, dass wir überzeugen
können." *Diners Club Magazine*, January 1997,
pp. 52-53.
Maxwell, Robert. "Modern Master." *Building
Design*, 16 September 1988, p. 28.
Meier, Richard. "Planning for Jerusalem."
Architectural Forum, April 1971, pp. 56-57.
Meier, Richard. "Les Heuers Claires."
In "Le Corbusier: Villa Savoye, Poissy, France,
1929–31." Ed. by Yukio Futagawa. *Global
Architecture* 13 , 1973, pp. 2-7.
Meier, Richard. "Design Strategies: Eight
Projects by Richard Meier & Associates—
Systematic Self-Description of the
Compositional Process." *Casabella*, May 1974,
pp. 17-38.
Meier, Richard. "Dialogue." With Arata
Izosaki. *a+u – Architecture and Urbanism*,
August 1976, pp. 21-38.
Meier, Richard. "Lecture in Japan." *Spazio*,
20 December 1976.
Meier, Richard. "Guest Speaker: On the Spirit

of Architecture." *Architectural Digest*, June
1981, pp. 156, 160, 162, 164.
Meier, Richard. "Remembering Breuer."
Skyline, October 1981, p. 11.
Meier, Richard. *On Architecture*. Text of Eloit
Noyes Lecture. Cambridge, Mass.: Harvard
University Graduate School of Design, 1982.
Meier, Richard. "Thoughts on Frank Stella."
In *Shards* by Frank Stella. London and New
York: Petersburg Press, 1983, pp. 1-4.
Meier, Richard. "Cultural Congress." *Skyline*,
April 1983, p. 7.
Meier, Richard. "Essay." *Perspecta 24*,
New York: Rizzoli, 1988, pp. 104-5.
Meier, Richard. Introduction to *Dante O.
Benini: Intuition and Precision*. Milano: L'Arca
Edizioni, 1998, pp. 6-7.
Meier, Richard and Sean Scully. *Espace et
Lumière: Conversation avec Michael Peppiatt*.
Paris: L'Echoppe, 1999.
Meier, Richard. "What good are critics? We
need them to excite and provoke the public."
Architectural Record, March 2000, pp. 57-8.
Meier, Richard. "Tadao Ando." *a+u –
Architecture and Urbanism*, 1 November 2001.
Meier, Richard. "A memorial of greatness."
The Daily News, 16 December 2001, p. 53.
Meier, Richard. "Reflections on the House."
Secretariat News, January–April 2002, p. 4.
Meier, Richard. "A Top Architect recalls how
he raised both a building and his kids." *Time,*
24 June 2002, p. G14.
Merkel, Jayne and Nina Rappaport. "The
Return of Four out of Five." *Oculus*, March
1996, pp. 8-9.
"The Met Grill: Interview with Richard Meier."
Metropolitan Home, September 1986, p. 24.
Micucci, Dana. "Meier: U.S. Architect With a
Feel for Europe." *International Herald Tribune*,
25–26 October 1997, p. 11.
Middleton, Faith. "Architecture's White
Tornado." *Northeast Magazine/The Hartford
Courant*, 30 September 1984, pp. 37-43.
Mik, Edvard. "Interview with Richard Meier."
Archidea, spring 1996, pp. 2-9.
Muschamp, Herbert. "Thinking Big: A Plan
for Ground Zero and Beyond." *The New York
Times Magazine*, 8 September 2002, pp. 45-58.
Myers, Linda. "Pritzker laureate Richard Meier
shares insights with CU architecture students."
Cornell Chronicle, 14 March 2002, pp. 1-6.
Nagel, Wolfgang. "The Art Banks of
Frankfurt"; Rutert, Timm. "A City Rising
in the South." *Lufthansa Bordbuch*,
March–April 1992, pp. 78-88.
Nesbitt, Lois E. *Richard Meier: Collages*.
London: Academy Editions, 1990.
Nesbitt, Lois E. "On the Road Again."
Architecture, Shaping the Future. San Diego:
University of California, 1990, pp. 25-35.
Nesbitt, Lois E. *Richard Meier: Sculpture
1992–1994*. New York: Rizzoli, 1994.
"New Buildings by Richard Meier." *Architecture*,
February 1996. Includes "Is Richard Meier Really
Modern?" and "Sculptural Sanctum"
by Joseph Giovannini; "Aloof Abstraction"
by Peter Buchanan; "The Getty Gets Ready"
by Martin Filler; "Swiss Precision" by Reed

Kroloff; "Dutch Modern" by Colin Davies;
"Meier's White Turns Green" by Raul Barreneche.
Nickson, Elizabeth. "Master Builder." *Patek
Philippe* 2, 1997, pp. 3-7.
Nobel, Philip. "Johnson & Sons." *Architecture*,
May 2000, p. 122.
Ouroussoff, Nicolai. "Building Blocks of
Culture." *Los Angeles Times*, 4 January 1997,
pp. F1, 6.
Papadakis, Andreas C., ed. *The New Modern
Aesthetic*. London: Art and Design, 1990,
pp. 10-19, 30-31, 45-46. Includes "Richard Meier
and the City in Miniature" by Kenneth
Frampton; "The Tate Gallery Discussion"
with Richard Meier, Charles Jenks, Daniel
Libeskind and Conrad Jameson; a transcript
of the lecture given by Richard Meier
at The Annual Architecture Forum.
Pehnt, Wolfgang. "Enkelsohn der Moderne.
Die Farbe Weisse: Der Architekt Richard Meier
wird Sechzig Jahre alt." *Frankfurter
Allgemeine Zeitung*, 12 October 1994.
Peppiatt, Michael. "AD Exclusif." *Architectural
Digest,* July–August 2000, pp. 36-38.
Perego, Francesco. "Sono le cattedrali d'oggi."
L'Espresso 30, 1 August 1993, pp. 124-25.
Pettena, Gianni, et al. *Richard Meier*. Venice:
Marsilio, 1981.
Pick, Eric J. "Meier for hire." *Architectural
Record*, May 2000, p. 30.
Plaut, Jeannette. "Arquitectura en interaccion
con el entorno." *Ambientes*, August 2001,
pp. 44-49.
Postmaa, Casper. "Gemeente: Madonna
onteigenen"; "Meiers Manhattan"; "Hilhorst:
Nu kan het, nu moet je het doen" (Interview
with Richard Meier). *Haagsche Courant*,
19 June 2001, pp. A1, B3.
Powell, Kenneth. "The Famous Five."
Perspectives on Architecture, February–March
1997, pp. 34-40.
*Progetto Architettura, Richard Meier
The Getty Center*. Exhibition catalog, Trento,
Galleria Civica Di Arte Contemporanea,
9 June–18 July 1998. Includes "Richard Meier
and the Museum as a Metaphor" by Aldo
Colonetti; "Absolut LA The Getty Center"
by Florencia Costa.
Rappaport, Mariana. "Estaos en un Perisodo
de Resonstruccion Modernista."
Clarin, November 1987, p. 4.
"Reflections on Artificial Light: Richard Meier
on Light in Architecture." *Siemens Design
and Light*, February 1993, pp. 16-19.
Rice Jackson, Paula. "Richard Meier."
Museum Highlights, pp. 11-14.
Richard Meier. Great Britain: Academy
Editions, 1990. Reprinted in German,
Stuttgart: Deutsche Verlags-Anstalt GmbH,
1990. Includes "Richard Meier and the City
in Miniature" by Kenneth Frampton;
"Richard Meier Interviews 1980–1988"
by Charles Jencks; "RIBA Royal Gold Medal
Address 1988" by Richard Meier.
Richard Meier Architect. Exhibition catalog.
New York: The Monacelli Press; Los Angeles:
The Museum of Contemporary Art, 1999.
Foreword and acknowledgments by Richard

Koshalek and Dana Hutt. Introduction by Dana Hutt. Essays by Stan Allen, Kenneth Frampton, Jean-Louis Cohen, and Lisa J. Green.
Richard Meier Architect 1964–1984. New York: Rizzoli, 1984. Reprinted in Spanish, Barcelona: Editorial Gustavo Gili S.A., 1995. Includes Preface by Richard Meier; Introduction by Joseph Rykwert; Postscript by John Hejduk.
Richard Meier Architect 1985–1991. New York: Rizzoli, 1991. Reprinted in Spanish, Barcelona: Editorial Gustavo Gili S.A. Includes Preface by Richard Meier; Postscript by Frank Stella; "Works in Transition" by Kenneth Frampton; "The Second Installment" by Joseph Rykwert.
Richard Meier Architect 1992–1999. New York: Rizzoli, 1999. Includes Preface by Richard Meier; "Three Tropes in the Later Work of Richard Meier" by Kenneth Frampton; "The Third Installment" by Joseph Rykwert; Postscript by Arata Isozaki.
Richard Meier, Architect: Buildings and Projects 1966–1976. New York: Oxford University Press, 1976. Includes Introduction by Kenneth Frampton; Postscript by John Hejduk.
Richard Meier: The Art of Architecture. Exhibition Catalogue. Hartford: Wadsworth Atheneum, 1980.
"Richard Meier a Beverly Hills." *Abitare*, July–August 1996, p. 135.
"Richard Meier, l'Exposition." *Connaissance des Arts* 141, July 1999, special issue on the occasion of the MOCA/Jeu de Paume Exhibition, 13 July–26 September 1999. Includes Preface by Richard Koshalek and Dana Hutt; "Justesse et Lumière" by Philip Jodidio.
"Richard Meier and Frank Gehry." *Vanity Fair*, December 1997, p. 264.
Richard Meier Houses. New York: Rizzoli, 1996. Reprinted in Italian, Milan: RCS Libri & Grandi Opere S.p.A., 1996. Reprinted in Great Britain, London: Thames & Hudson, 1996. Includes "The Dance of Composition" by Paul Goldberger; "Richard Meier's Ideal Villas" by Sir Richard Rogers.
Richard Meier: Matrix 58. Exhibition catalog. Hartford: Wadsworth Atheneum, 1980.
"Richard Meier: 'Die Postmoderne ist Passe.'" *Ambiente*, March 1985, p. 160.
"Richard Meier: Wesentlich in Weiss." *Wohn! Design*, 4/96–1/97, pp. 88-93.
"Richard Meier: Zetströmungen in der Architektur—Einige Vauten." *Deutsches Architektenblatt*, 1 September 1981, pp. 1251-60.
Richards, Ivor. "The Meier Way." *The Architects' Journal*, 23 May 1990, p. 73.
Richards, Ivor. "Master of space and form." *The Architects' Journal*, 11 September 1997, pp. 28-29.
Riding, Alan. "Celebrating an Architect, Hailing an Artist." *New York Times Sunday*, 8 August 1999, p. 34 AR. Reprinted as "Paris Fetes Richard Meier, Architect and Artist." *International Herald Tribune*, 10 August 1999.
Rudolph, Karen. "Museum of Contemporary Art, Barcelona"; "Light is a Transient Medium." *ERCO Lichtbericht 52*, August 1996, pp. 4-11.

Rudolph, Karen. "Richard Meier: Light as a Transient Medium." *Architectural Design*, March–April 1997, vol. 67, pp. 54-59.
Russell, James. "Electronic persuasion." *Architectural Record*, May 1995, pp. 36-43.
Sabisch, Christian and David Galloway. "Visionen in Weiss." *Expression*, February 1986, pp. 54-57.
Sartogo, Piero and Nathalie Grenon. *Architecture in Perspective.* New York: The Monacelli Press, 1998. Includes Foreword by Richard Meier, pp. 7-8.
Seward, Keith. "Richard Meier, Leo Castelli Gallery." *ArtForum*, December 1994, pp. 82-83.
Siola, Uberto and Rosaldo Bonicalzi. "Architettura e razione: Appunti sulla Internazionale di Architettura della XV Triennale." *Controspazio*, December 1973, pp. 16-24.
Slatin, Peter. "Interview with Richard Meier." *Omni*, September 1993, p. 67.
Solomon, Deborah. "From the Rubble, Ideas for Rebirth." *The New York Times*, 30 September 2001, p. 37.
"Spatial Structure of Richard Meier." *a+u – Architecture and Urbanism*, April 1976, pp. 45-120. Includes "Lyricism in Whiteness" by Arata Izosaki; "My Statement" by Richard Meier; "Analysis: Richard Meier's Work" by Mario Grandelsonas; "Recent Work of Richard Meier" by Rosemarie Bletter, "Meier's Whiteness" by Ching-Yu Chang; "Five Projects"; "Bibliography."
Steele, James. *Museum Builders.* London: Academy Editions, 1994. Includes "The Museum as Public Architecture" by Ian Ritchie, pp. 130-45.
Stephens, Suzanne. "The Individual: Richard Meier." *Progressive Architecture*, May 1977, pp. 60-62.
Stephens, Suzanne. "Richard Meier Architect 2." Review, NYC/AIA *Oculus*, December 1991, p. 7.
Stoller, Ezra. *Modern Architecture.* New York: Harry N. Abrams, Inc., 1990, pp. 188-202, 210-13.
Tafuri, Manfredo. "L'Architecture dans le Boudoir." *Oppositions 3*, 1974, p. 52.
Tafuri, Manfredo. "'European Graffiti': Five X Five = Twenty-five." *Oppositions* 5, 1976, pp. 35-74.
Tafuri, Manfredo. "Les Cendres de Jefferson." *L'Architecture d'Aujourd'hui*, August–September 1976, pp. 53-69.
Tempest, Rone. "America's Designs on Europe." *Los Angeles Times*, August 25, 1992, p. 1.
Thorndike, Joseph. Jr., ed. *Three Centuries of Notable American Architects.* New York: American Heritage, 1981. Essay by Paul Goldberger, pp. 338-41.
Toy, Maggie, ed. *Aspects of Minimalism in Architecture.* London: Academy Editions, 1994, pp. 50-57.
Trends in Contemporary Architecture. Exhibition catalog. Athens: National Gallery, Alexander Soutzos Museum, Ministry of Culture and Sciences, pp. 17-18, 72-87. Introduction by Kenneth Frampton.

Trescott, Jacqueline and Benjamin Forgey. "White on White." *The Washington Post*, 16 May 1984, pp. B1, B13.
Tung, Roseanne. "Architecture Alumni Lectures about Museums. Modernism. *Cornell Daily News*, 21 February 1986, p. 7.
Vaudou, Valerie, ed. *Richard Meier.* Paris: Electa Moniteur, 1986. Reprinted in Italian, Milan: Electa, 1986. Includes "Avant-propos" by Richard Meier; "La Modernité comme seuil" by Hubert Damisch; "Radieuse modernité" by Henri Ciriani; "Sur Richard Meier" by Diane Lewis; "La capture du regard" by Jean Mas.
Viladas, Pilar. "Lost in the Stacks." *The New York Times Magazine*, 5 October 1997, pp. 66-67.
Von Hossli, Peter. "Jedes Land Hat die Architektur." *Interior*, May 2002, pp. 16-22.
Waisman, Marina. "Richard Meier: Del objecto al entorno." *Summarios*, April 1977, pp. 2-32. Includes Introduction by Kenneth Frampton; Interview with Richard Meier.
Ward, Meghan, ed. "Q&A with Richard Meier." *The West LA Chronicle*, May 2000, pp. 4-22.
Webb, Michael. "King of the Hill." *Buzz*, February–March 1991, pp. 64-68.
Webb, Michael. "Romantic Modernist." *Korean Architects* 153, May 1997, pp. 60-67.
Webb, Michael. "Blueprints for Success." *Robb Report*, June 1999, pp. 100-102.
Weinstein, Richard. "Richard Meier Collages." *UCLA Collage Exhibition Catalogue*, February 1993.
"White Existence: Richard Meier, 1961–77." *Space Design*, January 1978, pp. 3-158. Includes "A Word From Richard Meier"; "Dialogue: On Architecture" by Richard Meier and Fumihiko Maki; "A Personal View on R. Meier" by Yukio Tominaga; "Architecture of Pleasure" by Hiromi Fujii; "Works: Private Buildings and projects"; "Richard Meier's Works Chronologically Scanned."
Williams, Hugh Aldersey. "The White Knight." *Blueprint*, October 1988, pp. 51-52.
Wilmotte: réalisations et projets. Paris: Editions du Moniteur, 1993. Includes Avant-Propos by Richard Meier, p. 9.
Wolf, Deborah. "Dit Is De Meest Opinwindende Opdacht Sinds Het Parthenon." *Avenue*, May 1985.
Zabalbeascoa, Anatxu. *The House of the Architect.* New York: Rizzoli International, 1995, pp. 118-21.
Zabalbeascoa, Anatxu. *The Office of the Architect.* New York: Rizzoli International, 1995, pp. 112-15.
Zabalbeascoa, Anatxu. "Doy lo que se espera de mi." *El País*, 11 March 1995, p.17.
Zevi, Bruno. "Richard Meier and the Language of Baalbek." *L'Architettura – cronache e storia*, November 1993.

Project Bibliography

Smith House, Darien, Connecticut, 1965–67
Blake, Peter. "Movement, Space, Direction." *Daily Telegraph Magazine*, October 1973, pp. 102-5.
Demoriane, Hélène. "Chaque soir fuir la ville." *Connaissance des Arts*, March 1970, pp. 90-91.
Eisenman, Peter. "Letter to the Editor: Meier's Smith House." *Architectural Design*, August 1971, p. 52.
Futagawa, Yukio, ed. "Houses in U.S.A." *Global Interiors 1*, 1971, pp. 144-51.
Futagawa, Yukio, ed. "Smith House, Darien, Connecticut, 1967." Text by David Morton. *Global Architecture* 22, 1973. Reprinted in *Global Architecture Book 3: Modern Houses*, A.D.A. Edita Co., Tokyo 1981.
Futagawa, Yukio, ed. "Smith House, Darien, Connecticut, 1967." *Global Architecture Detail* 2, 1976, pp. 7-25.
"Habitation à Darien, Connecticut." *L'Architecture d'Aujourd'hui*, February–March 1968, pp. 92-94.
"Houses in Darien." *Toshi-Jutaku*, April 1969, pp. 65-70.
"House Opens 180 Degrees." *Architectural Forum*, December 1967, pp. 66-71.
Kulski, Julian. *Architecture in a Revolutionary Era*. Nashville: Aurora, 1971, pp. 295, 298.
"Le due Americhe." *Abitare*, October 1969, pp. 14-19.
Lee, Sarah Tomerlin. "Transparent Geometry." *House Beautiful*, September 1968, pp. 106-112.
"Mit der Aussicht wohnen." *Bauen und Wohnen*, November 1968, pp. 392-94.
Pearson, Clifford, ed. *Modern American Houses*. New York: Harry Abrahms, Inc., Publishers, 1996.
Plumb, Barbara. "Taking the Long View." *The New York Times Magazine*, 23 March 1969, pp. 96-97.
"Record Houses of 1968." *Architectural Record*, mid-May 1968, pp. 52-57.
"Un sogno americano." *Domus*, April 1968, pp. 20-23.
Yagi, Koji. *Transformation of American Houses*. Kodansha, 1994, pp. 86-87.
Zevi, Bruno. "Un sogno americano." *L'Espresso*, 10 March 1974.

Hoffman House, East Hampton, New York, 1966–67
Chester, Marjorie. "Adding on to a Meier House." *The East Hampton Star*, 14 August 1997, p. III-8.
"Hoffman House." *a+u – Architecture and Urbanism*, November 1983, pp. 128-33.
Plumb, Barbara. "White on White." *The New York Times Magazine*, 23 March 1969, pp. 96-97.

"Record Houses of 1969." *Architectural Record*, mid-May 1969, pp. 76-79.
"Top 20 House Designs Emphasize 'Great Spaces.'" *The New York Times*, 22 June 1969, sec. 8, p. 1.

Westbeth Artists' Housing, Greenwich Village, New York, 1967–70
"Artists: Lofty Solutions." *Time,* 18 August 1967, p. 60.
Berkeley, Ellen Perry. "Westbeth: Artists in Residence." *Architectural Forum*, October 1970, pp. 44-49.
Blake, Peter. "Downtown Dakota." *New York Magazine*, 3 August 1970, pp. 54-57.
Fowler, Glenn. "Low Budget Building Fare Well in AIA Awards." *The New York Times*, 30 May 1971, sec. 8, p. 1.
Huxtable, Ada Louise. "Bending the Rules." *The New York Times*, 10 May 1970, sec. 2, p. 23.
Kahn, Eve M. "Westbeth at 20: Artist's Utopia Still A-Bowing." *The New York Times*, 2 February 1989.
Rozhon, Tracie. "Retouching the Vision." *The New York Times*, 25 May 2000, pp. F1, F11.
Rozhon, Tracie. "Richard Meier Builds in Manhattan. At Last." *The New York Times*, 25 May 2000, pp. F1, F11.
"Westbeth." *The New Yorker*, 8 June 1968, pp. 26-28.
"Westbeth Artists' Housing." *Space Design*, June 1972, pp. 17-28.
"Westbeth's Rehabilitation Project: A Clue to Improving our Cities." *Architectural Record*, March 1970, pp. 44-49.

Saltzman House, East Hampton, New York, 1967–69
"Bianca e spettacolare." *Domus*, June 1970, pp. 16-17.
Futagawa, Yukio, ed. "Houses in U.S.A." *Global Interiors 1*, 1971, pp. 152-69.
Giovannini, Joseph. "Renny Saltzman: Complementing Contemporary Volumes in East Hampton." *Architectural Digest*, September 1996, pp. 140-47.
Gordon, Alastair. "Weekend Utopia: The Modern Beach House on Eastern Long Island (1960–1973)." Booklet of the exhibition held at the *Guild Hall Museum*, 26 June–3 August 1999. New York: Triangle Press, 1999, pp. 8-9.
Gordon, Alastair. "The 10 Best Houses in the Hamptons." *The Observatory*, 2–9 July 2001, p. 13.
"House in East Hampton." *a+u – Architecture and Urbanism*, November 1972, pp. 107-14.
Raggi, Franco. "Templi e roulottes." *Casabella*, October 1974.

"Villa bei New York, U.S.A." *Bauen und Wohnen*, December 1970, pp. 448-49.
"Villa Saltzman." *Progressive Architecture*, April 1970, pp. 100-105.

Fredonia Health and Physical Education Building, State University College, Fredonia, New York, 1968–72
"Fredonia's Athletic Center: Legible Design in Steel." *Architectural Record*, August 1971, pp. 105-7.
"Health and Physical Education Facility at S.U.N.Y., Fredonia, New York." *a+u – Architecture and Urbanism*, April 1975, pp. 57-64.

Charles Evans Industrial Buildings, Fairfield & Piscataway, New Jersey, 1969
Rykwert, Joseph. "The Very Personal Work of Richard Meier and Associates." *Architectural Forum*, March 1972, pp. 30-37.

Project for a House in Pound Ridge, Pound Ridge, New York, 1969
"House in Pound Ridge." *a+u – Architecture and Urbanism*, November 1972, pp. 31-34.
Rykwert, Joseph. "The Very Personal Work of Richard Meier and Associates." *Architectural Forum*, March 1972, pp. 30-37.

House in Old Westbury, New York, 1969–71
"The Arts in America—the Forgotten Home." *Newsweek*, 24 December 1973, p. 76.
"Casa a Long Island." *Domus*, December 1972, pp. 14-16.
Davern, Jeanne. *Architecture 1970–1980: A Decade of Change*. New York: McGraw-Hill, 1980, pp. 56-57.
Futagawa, Yukio, ed. "House in Old Westbury, Long Island, New York, 1971." Text by David Morton. *Global Architecture* 22, 1973. Reprinted in *Global Architecture Book 3: Modern Houses*. Tokyo: A.D.A. Edita Co., 1981.
Futagawa, Yukio, ed. "Houses in U.S.A." *Global Interiors 6,* 1974, pp. 72-80.
Futagawa, Yukio, ed. "Houses in Old Westbury." *1970–1980*, special issue of *Global Architecture Document*, 1980, pp. 46-49.
"Habitation in Old Westbury, Long Island." *L'Architecture d'Aujourd'hui*, August–September 1971, pp. 68-69.
Morgan, James D. "A House that Glows with Crystalline Transparency." *Architectural Record*, April 1972, pp. 97-104.
Owens, Mitchell. "Step by Step." *Elle Decor*, October 1991, p. 62.
"A Sculptured Machine for Living." *House & Garden*, March 1972, pp. 68-77, 115.

Twin Parks Northeast Housing, Bronx, New York, 1969–74

Cliff, Ursula. "U.D.C. Scorecard." *Design and Environment*, September 1972, pp. 54-63.
Cohen, Stuart. "Physical Context/Cultural Context: Including It All." *Oppositions 2*, 1974, pp. 14-21, 30-37.
Davern, Jeanne. *Architecture 1970–1980: a Decade of Change*. New York: McGraw-Hill, 1980, pp. 92-93.
Frampton, Kenneth. "Twin Parks as Typology." *Architectural Forum*, June 1973, pp. 56-61.
Goldberger, Paul. "Twin Parks, an Effort to Alter the Problem of Public Housing." *The New York Times*, 27 December 1973, p. 39.
Goldberger, Paul. "Two Cheers for Eight Winners." *The New York Times Magazine*, 2 June 1974, pp. 62-64.
Goldberger, Paul. "U.D.C.'s Architecture Has Raised Public Standard." *The New York Times*, 5 March 1975, p. 43.
Hoyt, Charles. "Richard Meier: Public Space and Private Space." *Architectural Record*, July 1973, pp. 89-98.
"Learning from Twin Parks." *Architectural Forum*, June 1973, pp. 62-64.
Mackay, David, and Roger Sherwood. "La obra de Richard Meier en Bronx." *Arquitecturas Bis*, May 1974, pp. 1-7.
Pommer, Richard. "The Architecture of Urban Housing in the U.S. during the Early 1930s." *Journal of the Society of Architectural Historians*, December 1978, p. 263.
"Twin Parks Northeast." *a+u – Architecture and Urbanism*, June 1973, pp. 55-68.
"U.D.C. Twin Parks Northeast." *L'Architecture d'Aujourd'hui*, August–September 1976, pp. 4-7.
Weintraub, Myles and Mario Zicarelli. "Tale of Twin Parks." *Architectural Forum*, June 1973, pp. 54-55.

Bronx Developmental Center, Bronx, New York, 1970–77

"Bronx Developmental Center." *a+u – Architecture and Urbanism*, November 1977, pp. 3-29. Includes "Bronx Developmental Center" by Paul Goldberger; "A Comparative Study – Bronx Developmental Center and Gunma Prefectural Museum of Modern Art" by Arata Isozaki; "The Modern Language of Architecture and Richard Meier" by Francesco Dal Co.
"Bronx State School." *a+u – Architecture and Urbanism*, June 1973, pp. 55-68.
Cassarà, Silvio. "Bronx Developmental Center." *Parametro*, May 1977, pp. 37-39.
Futagawa, Yukio, ed. "Bronx Developmental Center." *1970–1980*, special issue of *Global Architecture Document*, 1980, pp. 240-43.
Goldberger, Paul. "Bronx Developmental Center: Is it a Masterwork or a Nightmare?" *The New York Times*, 3 May 1977, pp. 43, 46.
Huxtable, Ada Louise. "The Latest Style Is Jeweler's Mechanical." *The New York Times*, 27 June 1976, pp. 1, 29.
Huxtable, Ada Louise. "A Landmark before Its Doors Open." *The New York Times*, 8 May 1977, sec. 2, p. 1.
Iovine, Julie. "A New Bronx Sweeps a Meier Design Clean." *The New York Times*, 23 May 2002, p. E1.
Kulterman, Udo. *Architecture of the Seventies*. Boston: Architectural Book Publishing Co., 1980, pp. 4-7.
Makovsky, Paul. "Richard Meier's Late-Modern Merits another look." *Docomomo*, spring 2002.
Martin, Douglas. "An Architectural Milestone Loses Its Pedigree." *The New York Times*, 1 February 2002.
"Rieducazione a New York." *Domus*, April 1977, pp. 6-9.
Rykwert, Joseph. "The Very Personal Work of Richard Meier and Associates." *Architectural Forum*, March 1972, pp. 30-37.
Stephens, Suzanne. "Architecture Cross-examined." *Progressive Architecture*, July 1977, pp. 43-54.
Stevens, Mark. "Living in a Work of Art." *Newsweek*, 30 May 1977, p. 59.
Turner, Judith. *Five Architects*. New York: Rizzoli, 1980, pp. 107-27.
"Two New York Schools for the Retarded." *L'Architecture d'Aujourd'hui*, February–March 1971, pp. 96-97.

Maidman House, Sands Point, New York, 1971–76

Futagawa, Yukio, ed. "House in Sands Point." *Global Architecture Houses 5*, winter 1978, pp. 116-23.
Lewin, Susan Grant and Susan Hope Schraub. "The Structure of Space." *House Beautiful*, April 1978, pp. 79-91.
"Meier's Meisterwerk." *Häuser*, February 1981, pp. 14-19, 54.

Douglas House, Harbor Springs, Michigan, 1971–73

Davis, Douglas and Mary Rourke. "Architecture: Real Dream Houses." *Newsweek*, 4 October 1976, pp. 66-69.
Futagawa, Yukio, ed. "Douglas House, Harbor Springs, Michigan. 1974." Text by Paul Goldberger. *Global Architecture 34*, 1975. Reprinted in *Global Architecture Book 3: Modern Houses*. Tokyo: A.D.A. Edita Co., 1981.
Futagawa, Yukio. "Douglas House." *1970–1980*, special issue of *Global Architecture Document*, 1980, pp. 106-9.
Goldberger, Paul. "Purism on the Lake." *The New York Times Magazine*, 22 September 1974, pp. 72-74.
Goldberger, Paul. "Honors for Uncertainty." *The New York Times Magazine*, 2 May 1976, pp. 68-69.
Goldberger, Paul. "Architecture: Richard Meier." *Architectural Digest*, December 1988, pp. 186-91.
"House in Harbor Springs." *a+u – Architecture and Urbanism*, November 1972, pp. 27-30.
Hoyt, Charles. "Richard Meier: Public Space and Private Space." *Architectural Record*, July 1973, pp. 89-98.
"L'Ultima Villa from the U.S.A." *Domus*, January 1975, pp. 19-22.
Morton, David. "Douglas House." *Progressive Architecture*, July 1975, pp. 58-61.
"Vorsicht Glashaus." *Häuser* no. 3, 1980, pp. 71-75.
"Wohnhaus am Michigan-See, U.S.A." *Baumeister*, July 1977, pp. 617-19.

Branch Office Prototypes for Olivetti, Irvine, California; Minneapolis, Minnesota; Boston, Massachusetts; Brooklyn, New York; Patterson, New Jersey, 1971
Project for a Dormitory for the Olivetti Training Center, Tarrytown, New York, 1971
Project for Olivetti Headquarters Building, Fairfax, Virginia, 1971

Allen, Gerald. "Traditional Image for Olivetti." *Architectural Record*, February 1974, pp. 117-24.
Moneo, Rafael. "Proyectos no realizados para Olivetti." *Arquitecturas Bis*, July 1975, pp. 10-14.
"Olivetti." *Architecture Plus*, September 1973, pp. 20-27.
"Olivetti Dormitory in Tarrytown." *a+u – Architecture and Urbanism*, March 1974, pp. 40-43.
"Olivetti Prototype, Olivetti Washington & Olivetti Tarrytown." *a+u – Architecture and Urbanism*, August 1974, pp. 29-50.
"Prototyp für Olivetti." *Bauen und Wohnen*, February–March 1976, pp. 56-58.
Schwarting, Jon Michael. "Richard Meier & Associates: quattro progetti per la Olivetti in U.S.A." *Domus*, March 1974, pp. 2-8.

Shamberg House, Chappaqua, New York, 1972–74

Futagawa, Yukio, ed. "House in Mount Kisco, New York." *Global Architecture Houses 1*, 1976, pp. 92-97.

Goldberger, Paul. "Architecture: Richard Meier." *Architectural Digest*, September 1978, pp. 150-55, 180.

Hoyt, Charles. "4 Projects by Richard Meier: Change and Consistency." *Architectural Record*, March 1975, pp. 111-20.

Meier, Richard. "Tre recenti progetti." *Controspazio*, September 1975, pp. 38-47.

"Record Houses of 1977." *Architectural Record*, mid-May 1977, pp. 68-71.

"Shamberg Pavilion." *a+u – Architecture and Urbanism*, April 1975, pp. 57-64.

Project for the Museum of Modern Art at the Villa Strozzi, Florence, Italy, 1973
"Dortmunder Architekturausstellung 1979. Museumsbauten: Entwürfe und Projekte seit 1945." *Dortmunder Architekturhefte* no. 15, 1979.

Hoyt, Charles. "4 Projects by Richard Meier: Change and Consistency." *Architectural Record*, March 1975, pp. 111-20.

Meier, Richard. "Tre recenti progetti." *Controspazio*, September 1975, pp. 38-47.

Morton, David. "MOMA, Italian Style." *Progressive Architecture*, March 1975, pp. 58-61.

"Museum in der Villa Strozzi, Florenz." *Baumeister*, May 1975, pp. 416-17.

Project for the Cornell University Undergraduate Housing, Ithaca, New York, 1974
Hoyt, Charles. "4 Projects by Richard Meier: Change and Consistency." *Architectural Record*, March 1975, pp. 111-20.

Meier, Richard. "Tre recenti progetti." *Controspazio*, September 1975, pp. 38-47.

The Atheneum, New Harmony, Indiana, 1975–79
Abercrombie, Stanley. "A Vision Continued." *AIA Journal*, mid-May 1980, pp.126-37.

"The Architecture of the Promenade: The Atheneum." *International Architect* 3, 1980, pp. 13-24.

Cassarà, Silvio. "Richard Meier: Intrinsic Qualities of Remembrances. The Atheneum at New Harmony, Indiana." *Parametro*, July–August 1976, pp. 16-19, 59.

Cohen, Arthur. "Richard Meier, Creator of New Harmony: An Architect Builds a Classic Meeting Hall for the Nation's Heartland." *United Mainliner*, March 1980, pp. 69-71.

Futagawa, Yukio. ed. "Collage and Study Sketches for the Atheneum." *Global Architecture Document* 1, 1980, pp. 25-65. Includes "Meier's Atheneum" by Kenneth Frampton; "Richard Meier, An American Architect" by Arthur Cohen; "The Atheneum, New Harmony, Ind. (First Scheme)"; "The Atheneum (Executed Scheme)."

Futagawa, Yukio. "The Atheneum, New Harmony, Indiana. 1975–1979." Text by Paul Goldberger. *Global Architecture* 60, 1981. Reprinted in *Global Architecture Book 6: Public Buildings*. Tokyo: A.D.A. Edita Co., 1981.

Goldberger, Paul. "The Atheneum: Utopia

Lives." *Vogue*, February 1980, pp. 250-51, 296.

Haker, Werner. "New Harmony und das Athenaeum von Richard Meier." *Werk, Bauen+Wohnen*, December 1980, pp. 44-53.

"Harmonious Museum for New Harmony." *Life*, February 1980, pp. 60-62.

Huxtable, Ada Louise. "A Radical New Addition for Mid-America." *The New York Times*, 30 September 1979, sec. 2, pp. 1, 31.

Klotz, Heinrich, ed. "Das Atheneum." Text by Richard Meier. *Jahrbuch für Architektur: Neues Bauen, 1980–1981*, 1981, pp. 53-64.

Magnago Lampugnani, Vittorio. *Architecture of Our Century in Drawings: Utopia and Reality.* Stuttgart: Verlag Gerd Hatje, 1982, pp. 106-7.

Marlin, William. "Revitalizing Architectural Legacy of an American 'Camelot.'" *The Christian Science Monitor*, 16 April 1976, p. 26.

Marlin, William. "Dissonance in New Harmony." *Inland Architect*, December 1981, pp. 20-28.

Meier, Richard. "The Atheneum, New Harmony, Indiana; Manchester Civic Center, Manchester, New Hampshire – Comments." *Harvard Architecture Review*, spring 1981, pp. 176-87. Reprinted in French in *Les Cahiers de la Recherche Architecturale*, November 1982, pp. 66-73.

Rykwert, Joseph. "New Harmony Propylaeon." *Domus*, February 1980, pp. 12-17.

Shezen, Roberto. "La via storica: l'Atheneum di New Harmony nell'Indiana di Richard Meier." *Gran Bazaar*, January–February 1982, pp. 128-35.

Stephens, Suzanne. "Emblematic Edifice: The Atheneum, New Harmony, Indiana." *Progressive Architecture*, February 1980, pp. 67-75.

Zevi, Bruno. "Un UFO nel campo di grano." *L'Espresso*, 6 April 1980, p. 124.

Suburban House Prototype, Concord, Massachusetts, 1976
Meier, Richard. "College Suburb." *La Biennale di Venezia 1976*. Venice: Edizioni La Biennale di Venezia, 1978, vol. 2, pp. 134-40.

Project for Manchester Civic Center, New Hampshire, 1977
"Manchester Center, Manchester, U.S.A." *L'Architecture d'Aujourd'hui*, September 1978, pp. 68-69.

Meier, Richard. "The Atheneum, New Harmony, Indiana; Manchester Civic Center, Manchester, New Hampshire – Comments." *Harvard Architecture Review*, spring 1981, pp. 176-87. Reprinted in French in *Les Cahiers de la Recherche Architecturale*, November 1982, pp. 66-73.

The New York School Exhibition, State Museum, Albany, New York, 1977
Hess, Thomas B. "Art: The Big Picture." *New York Magazine*, 24 October 1977, pp. 68, 71.

"La Maison Nouvelle." *Connaissance des Arts*, July–August 1999, pp. 106-12.

Nobuyuki,Yoshida, ed. "Neugebauer House."

a+u Architecture and Urbanism 371, August 2001, pp. 40-51.

Aye Simon Reading Room, Solomon R. Guggenheim Museum, New York, New York, 1977–78
Filler, Martin. "Splendid Spin-off." *Progressive Architecture*, October 1978, pp. 68-71.

Goldberger, Paul. "New Room at the Guggenheim." *The New York Times*, 15 June 1978, p. C17.

Clifty Creek Elementary School, Columbus, Indiana, 1978–82
"Clifty Creek Elementary School." *a+u – Architecture and Urbanism*, November 1984, p. 27.

Croset, Pierre-Alain. "Elementary School in Columbus." *Casabella*, May 1984, pp. 4-13.

Futagawa, Yukio, ed. "Clifty Creek Elementary School, Columbus Ohio." *Global Architecture Document* 9, February 1984, pp. 114-21.

Knight, Carleton. "Shiplike School on a Sea of Grass." *Architecture*, June 1984, pp. 44-48.

Hartford Seminary, Hartford, Connecticut, 1978–81
Arriola, Ricardo Contreras. "Richard Meier: Dos proyectos recientes." *ARS* (Revista del Centro de Estudios de la Arquitectura, Santiago), August 1981, pp. 75-79.

Brenner, Douglas. "Two Projects in Context." *Architectural Record*, April 1981, pp. 87-97.

Brenner, Douglas. "A Progression into Light: The Hartford Seminary by Richard Meier & Partners." *Architectural Record*, January 1982, pp. 65-73.

Canty, Donald. "Shining Vessel of Religious Thought." *AIA Journal*, mid-May 1982, pp. 124-33.

Davern, Jeanne. *Architecture 1970–1980: A Decade of Change.* New York: McGraw-Hill, 1980, pp. 254-55.

Doubilet, Susan. "Seminary, Hartford, Connecticut." *The Architectural Review*, May 1982, pp. 25-31.

Fumagalli, Paolo. "Hartford Seminary, Hartford, Connecticut, 1978–1981." *Werk, Bauen+Wohnen*, January–February 1983, pp. 12-17.

Futagawa, Yukio, ed. "The Hartford Seminary Foundation." *Global Architecture Document* 1, 1980, pp. 66-69.

Futagawa, Yukio. "The Hartford Seminary, Hartford, Connecticut"; Gill, Theodore. "First Sight: The Hartford Seminary." *Global Architecture Document* 4, 1981, pp. 50-67.

"Hartford Seminary." *a+u – Architecture and Urbanism*, February 1983, pp. 31-46.

Hoyet, Jean-Michel. "Made in U.S.A.: Trois conceptions récentes de Richard Meier & Associés." *Techniques & Architecture*, November 1982, pp. 140-47.

Huxtable, Ada Louise. "Architecture View: Moving into a New Realm." *The New York Times*, 27 September 1981, sec. 2, p. 33.

Kay, Jane Holtz. "Echo of the 1920's: Architect Richard Meier Teams Up with the Sun."

The Christian Science Monitor, 22 January 1982, p. 15.
Margolies, Linda. "The Hartford Seminary Gets a New Look." *Hartford Courant Magazine*, 13 January 1980, pp. 4-6, 13.
Pettena, Gianni. "A Whiter Shade of Pale." *Domus*, June, 1982, pp. 2-12.
"Richard Meier at Hartford and Atlanta." *L'Architecture d'Aujourd'hui*, February 1982, pp. 59-68.
Vidler, Anthony. "Deconstructing Modernism." *Skyline*, March 1982, pp. 21-23.

Furniture for Knoll International, 1978
Abercrombie, Stanley. "Furnishings." *AIA Journal*, December 1980, pp. 62-63.
Emery, Marc. *Furniture by Architects*. New York: Harry N. Abrams, pp. 204-7.
"Everything for the House: Furniture Drawings." *Express*, December 1980, p. 9.
Goldberger, Paul. "Furniture by Architects: Vitality and Verve." *The New York Times*, 14 October 1982, pp. C1, 8.
Halliday, Sarah. "Inside Furniture: Meier and Gwathmey/Siegel at Knoll." *Skyline*, April 1983, pp. 1, 21.
Koltz, Heinrich, ed. "Möbelentwürfe." *Jahrbuch für Architektur: Neues Bauen 1980–1981*, 1981, pp. 85-86.
Philips, Lisa. *Shape and Environment: Furniture by American Architects*. New York: Whitney Museum, 1982, pp. 19, 42-43.
"Richard Meier's Furniture Collection." *Domus*, Feb. 1983, p. 64.
Wintour, Anna. "Design: Reserved Seating." *New York Magazine*, 27 September 1982, pp. 56-57.

Giovannitti House, Pittsburgh, Pennsylvania, 1979–83
De Stefano, Pierluigi. "New Architecture: a house in Pittsburgh." *Abitare*, December 1985, pp. 30-37.
Filler, Martin. "Facets of Perfection." *House & Garden*, December 1984, pp. 142-214.
Gandee, Charles. "What to do with the T.V." *House & Garden*, September 1991, p. 163.
"Giovannitti House." *a+u – Architecture and Urbanism*, June 1985, pp. 34-42.
"Jeux de Transparence." *L'Architecture d'Aujourd'hui*, December 1984, p. 22.
Lacerte, Pierre. "Les Formes Apprivoiseés." *Decormng*, April 1985, p. 56.

Museum für Kunsthandwerk, Frankfurt am Main, Germany, 1978–85
Allégret, Laurence. *Musées, tome 2*. Paris: Editions du Moniteur, 1992, pp. 18-23.
"Architektur: Ein 'Juwel' für Frankfurt." *Der Spiegel*, 20 July 1981, pp. 132-34.
"Arts and Crafts Museum, Frankfurt." *The Architectural Review*, October 1980, pp. 196-97.
Brawne, Michael. *Architecture in Detail: Museum für Kunsthandwerk*. London: Phaidon Press Ltd., 1992.
Brenner, Douglas. "The Frankfurt Museum for the Decorative Arts: Theme and Variations."

Architectural Record, April 1981, pp. 87-95.
Canon-Brooks, Peter. "Frankfurt and Atlanta: Richard Meier as a Designer of Museums." *The International Journal of Museum Management and Curatorship*, vol. 5, no. 1, March 1986, pp. 39-64.
Cobb, Henry N. and Richard Meier. "Richard Meier's Museum für Kunsthandwerk." *Express*, April 1981, p. 7.
Cook, Peter. "White Magic." *Interiors*, July 1985, pp. 202-5, 217-18, 231.
Cook, Peter. "Meier Handwerk." *The Architectural Review*, November 1985, pp. 48-57.
"Crafts Museum, Frankfurt." *Space Design*, February 1986, pp. 29-44.
Dean, Andrea Oppenheimer. "Serene, Ordered Presence in a Park." *Architecture*, January 1986, pp. 56-63.
De Bruyn, Gerd. *Contemporary Architecture in Germany 1970–1996*. Basel: Birkhäuser Verlag, 1997, pp. 98-99.
"Die Erste Skizze/The First Sketch." *Daidalos*, 15 September 1982, pp. 46-47.
"Einfach Reinlatschen." *Der Spiegel*, 22 April 1985, pp. 202-7.
Fernandez-Galiano, Luis, ed. "Richard Meier in Europe." *Arquitectura Viva Monografias* 59, May–June 1996, pp. 33-39. Includes "Modern or Contemporary" by Joseph Giovannini.
Flagge, Ingeborg. "Museum für Kunsthandwerk, Frankfurt." *Lichtbericht*, June 1985, pp. 64-71.
Frampton, Kenneth. "Il Museo come Mescolanza." *Casabella*, July–August 1985, pp. 11-17.
Futagawa, Yukio. "New Museum Graces Frankfurt's Cultural Skyline." *International Herald Tribune*, 11–12 May 1985, p. 7.
Futagawa, Yukio, ed. "Winning Scheme, Museum for the Decorative Arts Competition, Frankfurt am Main, West Germany." *Global Architecture Document 2*, 1981, pp. 66-71
Futagawa, Yukio, ed. "Museum für Kunsthandwerk." *Global Architecture Document* 13, September 1985, pp. 4-41.
Goldberger, Paul. "New Museums Harmonize with Art." *The New York Times*, 14 April 1985, sec. 2, p. 1.
Goldberger, Paul. "Harmonizing Old and New Buildings." *The New York Times*, 2 May 1985, p. C23.
Hoyet, Jean-Michel. "Made in U.S.A.: Trois conceptions récentes de Richard Meier & Associés." *Techniques & Architecture*, November 1982, pp. 140-47.
Huse, Norbert. *Richard Meier Museum für Kunsthandwerk, Frankfurt am Main*. Berlin: Wilhem Ernst & Sohn Verlag für Architektur und Technische Wissenschaften, 1985.
Irace, Fluvio. "Radiant Museum." *Domus*, June 1985, pp. 2-11.
Jaeger, Falk. "Schimmernde Perle." *Deutsche Bauzeitung*, August 1985, pp. 28-33.
Jodidio, Philip. "Quand Les Cathedrales Etaient Blanches." *Connaissances des Arts*, July–August 1985, p. 20.
Klemm, Gisela. "Museum für Kunsthandwerk."

Detail, September–October 1985, pp. 457-66.
Klotz, Heinrich, ed. *Jahrbuch für Architektur: Neues Bauen 1980–1981*, 1981. Includes "Der Wettbewerb für das Museum für Kunsthandwerk in Frankfurt am Main" by Frank Werner, pp. 22-39.
Knobel, Lance. "Meier Modules." *The Architectural Review*, July 1981, pp. 34-38.
Lemos, Peter. "Museum as Masterpeice." *Pan Am Clipper*, September 1985, pp. 57-62.
Maas, Tom. "Een Bron Van Architectonisch Genoegen." *de Architect*, June 1985, p. 33.
Magnago Lampugnani, Vittorio. "The Jewel with All Qualities." *Lotus International 28*, 1980, pp. 34-38.
Magnago Lampugnani, Vittorio. *Architecture of Our Century in Drawings: Utopia and Reality*. Stuttgart: Verlag Gerd Hatje, 1982, p. 108.
Magnago Lampugnani, Vittorio. *Museums Architektur in Frankfurt 1980–1990*. Munich: Prestel-Verlag, 1990. Includes "Magnificent Chaos" by Kenneth Frampton, pp. 106-115.
Ministry of Culture and Sciences. *Trends in Contemporary Architecture*. Athens: National Gallery, Alexander Soutzos Museum, 1982, pp. 76-83.
Montaner, Josep M. and Jordi Oliveras. "Museum of Arts and Crafts, Frankfurt." *The Museums of the Last Generation*. Barcelona: Gustavo Gili, S.A., 1986, pp. 102-9.
Murray, Peter. "Frankfurt's Carbuncle." *RIBA Journal*, June 1985, pp. 23-25.
"Musée de l'Artisanat et des Métiers d'Art Francfort." *Techniques et Architecture*, April–May 1985, pp. 103-8.
"Musée des Arts Décoratifs, Francfort." *L'Architecture d'Aujourd'hui*, September 1980, pp. XI-XII.
"Museum für Kunsthandwerk." *Werk, Bauwen+Wohnen* 12, December 1984, pp. 36-41.
"The Museum für Kunsthandwerk." *a+u – Architecture and Urbanism*, September 1985, pp. 15-48.
"Museum für Kunsthandwerk in Frankfurt." *Baumeister*, August 1980, pp. 767-73.
"Museum für Kunsthandwerk in Frankfurt." *Baumeiester*, August 1985, pp. 22-33.
"Neue Tempel fur die Kunst." *Stern*, 25 April 1985, pp. 46-66.
Papadakis, Andreasc, ed. "Richard Meier: A Personal Manifesto"; "Museum for the Decorative Arts, Frankfurt, West Germany." *Architectural Design*, vol. 55, no. 1/2, 1985, pp. 56, 58-69.
"Richard Meier: Museum für Kunsthandwerk." *AMC*, December 1985, pp. 20-33. Includes "Décalages et Dynamisme: an Interview with Richard Meier" by Henri Ciriani and Jacques Lucan; "Le Musée de Francfort: 'Apprendere à voir l'architecture'" by Jacques Lucan.
"Roth fur Ausstellungsetats." *Rhein-Main-Zeitung*, 11 May 2000, pp. 59-60.
Rumpf, Peter. "Museum für Kunsthandwerk, Frankfurt am Main." *Bauwelt*, May 1985, pp. 766-77.
Ruthenfranz, Eva. "Nobler Kultur-Park für die Bürger." *Art das Kunstmagazin*,

September 1983, pp. 68-74.
Sabisch, Christian. "Kein Manhattan in 'Manhattan.'" Der Apotheker, July 1985, p. 5.
Schilgen, Jost. Neue Hauser für die Kunst. Dortmund: Harenberg Kommunikation, 1990, pp. 82-105.
Schreiber, Mathias. "Weisses Bauhaus Schloss." Frankfurter Allgemeine Zeitung, 27 April 1985.
Stephens, Suzanne. "Frame by Frame." Progressive Architecture, June 1985, pp. 81-91.
Stock, Wolfgang Jean. "Richard Meier: Museum für Kunsthandwerk in Frankfurt am Main." Bauen in Beton, November 1988, pp. 32-41.
"Ten Star Museums: White on White." Monografias de Arquitectura y Vivienda 18, 1989, pp. 57-63.
Van Dijk, Hans. "Richard Meier in Duitsland: Museum für Kunsthandwerk, Frankfort." Wonen Tabk, 15 July 1985, pp. 20-28.
Wilson, William. "Germany's Grand Designs." The Los Angeles Times, 3 November 1985, pp. 74-77.
Zardini, Mirko. "Il Bianco e Il Grigio." Casabella, July–August 1985, pp. 4-10.

High Museum of Art, Atlanta, Georgia, 1980–83

Balfour, Alan. "High Museum, Atlanta, Georgia." The Architectural Review, February 1984, pp. 20-27.
Betsky, Aaron. "New Museums." Horizon, June 1984, pp. 45-52.
Birmingham, Stephen. "Richard Meier's Framework for the Decorative Arts at the High Museum." Architectural Digest, September 1984, pp. 125-32.
Campbell, Robert. "Forms 'Exploding' from a Drum." Architecture: The AIA Journal, May 1984, pp. 222-29.
Cannon-Brooks, Peter. "Frankfurt and Atlanta: Richard Meier as a Designer of Museums." The International Journal of Museum Management and Curatorship, vol. 5, no. 1, March 1986, pp. 39-64.
Cassarà, Silvio. "Richard Meier: The New Museum of Atlanta. 'Ratio' and 'Inclusive' Dimensions.'" Parametro, August–September 1982, pp. 44-51.
Chaslin, François. "Le virtuose aux pieds nus." Le Monde Aujourd'hui, 26–27 February 1984, p. XV.
Davis, Douglas. "Making Museums Modest." Newsweek, 26 July 1982, pp. 66-67.
"Ein Kunstmuseum als Kunst der Museums-Architektur." Werk, Bauen+Wohnen, April 1984, pp. 4-10.
Filler, Martin. "Sneak Preview of a Dazzling New Museum." House & Garden, August 1980, p. 6.
Fox, Catherine. "The New High 'A Work of Art.'" The Atlanta Journal/Constitution, 7 October 1983, pp. 1A, 13A.
Fox, Catherine. "A New High for Atlanta." Artnews, November 1983, pp. 102-6.
Fox, Catherine, et al. "A New High: An Introduction to Atlanta's Museum." Supplement to The Atlanta

Journal/Constitution, 9 October 1983.
Frampton, Kenneth. "High Museum of Art at Atlanta." Casabella, November 1982, pp. 50-61.
Freeman, Allen. "80's Retrospective: Demanding Showcase." Architecture, December 1989, pp. 51-53.
Furer, Rene. "MACBA." Architektur & Technik, July 2001, pp. 6-8.
Futagawa, Yukio. "The High Museum of Art, Atlanta, Georgia." Global Architecture Document 9, February 1984, pp. 100-113.
Futagawa, Yukio, ed. "The High Museum of Art, Atlanta, Georgia." Global Architecture Document 6, 1983, pp. 78-85.
Gaskie, Margaret. "Atlanta High." Architectural Record, January 1984, pp. 118-31.
Giovannini, Joseph. "La Sofia del Gusto Americano." Architectural Digest, November 1984, p. 66.
Goldberger, Paul. "Designing a Proper Environment for Art." The New York Times, 4 July 1982, sec. 2, pp. 19-20.
Goldberger, Paul. "Architecture: New Atlanta Museum." The New York Times, 5 October 1983, p. C21.
Griffith, Helen C. "Atlanta's New Museum of Art – A Striking Balance between Architecture and Art." Southern Accents, March–April 1984, pp. 112-18.
"High Museum of Art." a+u – Architecture and Urbanism, February 1983, pp. 47-50.
"The High Museum of Art, Atlanta." Architectural Design, November–December 1984, pp. 36-39.
"High Museum of Art, Atlanta, Georgia, 1983." a+u – Architecture and Urbanism, February 1984, pp. 19-32.
Irace, Fulvio and Catherine Fox. "Art Games/Atlanta High Museum." Domus, May 1984, pp. 14-19.
Jodidio, Philip. "Quand Les Cathedrales Etaient Blanches." Connaissance des Arts, July–August 1985, p. 20.
Kuhn, Irene Corbally. "Atlanta's High Museum." Gourmet, December 1984, p. 48.
Lewis, Roger. "High Expectations." Museum News, March–April 1993, pp. 34-37.
Limsky, Drew. "A Hub for Corporations and Upscale Nightlife." The New York Times, 3 September 2002, p. C5.
Maxwell, Robert. "The High Museum, Atlanta, Georgia." AA Files 7, 1984, pp. 68-74.
Mettler, Alexandra. "Reaching for a New High." Atlanta, January 1981, pp. 31-34.
Middleton, Faith. "Architecture's White Tornado." Northeast Magazine/The Hartford Courant, 30 September 1984, pp. 37-43.
Pestalozzi, Manuel. "Weiss im Grun." Architektur & Technik, July 2001, pp. 10-14.
Pettena, Gianni. "A Whiter Shade of Pale." Domus, June 1982, pp. 2-12.
Plattus, Alan J. "Il museo e la città: la geografia della cultura." Casabella, January–February 1992, pp. 71-77.
"Richard Meier at Hartford and Atlanta." L'Architecture d'Aujourd'hui, February 1982, pp. 59-68.

Russell, John. "Atlanta's New Museum Has Spaces to Fill." The New York Times, 13 November 1983, sec. 2, p. 29.
Searing, Helen. "New American Art Museums." Skyline, June 1982, pp. 16-21.
Searing, Helen, ed. New American Art Museums. New York: Whitney Museum/University of California Press, 1982. Includes statements by Gudmund Vigtel and Richard Meier, pp. 106-13.
Tighe, Mary Ann. "A New High for Atlanta." House & Garden, November 1983, pp. 148-53.
"Un Atrium de Lumière." Le Moniteur, December 1984, p. 44.
Vaudou, Valérie. "Une Architecture de Synthèse." Techniques & Architecture, February–March 1984, pp. 124-36.
Vigtel, Gudmund, Richard Meier and Anthony Ames. High Museum of Art, The New Building: A Chronicle of Planning, Design and Construction. Atlanta: High Museum of Art, 1983.
Wernick, Robert. "Atlanta's New High Museum Is a Jewel for a Queenly City." Smithsonian, January 1984, pp. 38-47.

Project for Renault Administrative Headquarters, Boulogne-Billancourt, France, 1981

Brenner, Douglas. "An American in Paris." Architectural Record, October 1982, pp. 116-23.
Futagawa, Yukio, ed. "Renault Administrative Headquarters, Boulogne-Billancourt, France." Global Architecture Document 6, 1983, pp. 86-93.
Hoyet, Jean-Michel. "Made in U.S.A.: Trois conceptions récentes de Richard Meier & Associés." Techniques & Architecture, November 1982, pp. 140-47.
"L'Image d'une enterprise: Renault." La modernité: Un Projet inarcheve. Exhibition Catalogue. Paris: Editions du Moniteur, 1982, pp. 102-7.
Architecture Intérieure/Crée, October 1982, pp. 90-91.
"Projet pour le Nouvel Immeuble Administratif de la Régie Renault." L'Architecture d'Aujourd'hui, September 1982, pp. 23-27.
"Renault." a+u – Architecture and Urbanism, February 1983, pp. 51-54.

Project for International Bauausstellung Housing, Berlin, Germany, 1982

Futagawa, Yukio, ed. "Housing Project, Berlin." Global Architecture Document 9, February 1984, pp. 122-25.

Des Moines Art Center Addition, Iowa, 1982–85

Blunk, Mark, E. "An Experiment in Contextual Evolution." Inland Architect, May–June 1989, pp. 70-73.
Dean, Andrea Oppenheimer. "Eliel Saarinen, Then Pei, Now Meier." Architecture, October 1985, pp. 32-41.
Demetrion, James T. "Des Moines Art Center." Iowa Architect, March–April 1984, pp. 16-25.
"The Des Moines Art Center." a+u –

Architecture and Urbanism, September 1985, pp. 44-70.
"Des Moines Art Center: One Museum with Three Architects." *Baumeister*, January 1987, pp. 52-56.
Futagawa, Yukio, ed. "Des Moines Art Center Addition." *Global Architecture Document* 13, September 1985, pp. 4-41.
Goldberger, Paul. "Museums Designed for Tight Quarters." *The New York Times*, 20 October 1985, p. 28.
Jodidio, Philip, "Quand Les Cathedrales Etaient Blanches." *Connaissance des Arts*, July–August 1985, p. 20.
Lucas, Mary. "The Richard Meier Addition." *Des Moines Magazine*, April 1985, p. 43.
Magnago Lampugnani, Vittorio. "Des Moines Art Center Addition." *Domus*, April 1986, pp. 37-43.
Meier, Richard. "Des Moines Art Center." *Iowa Architect*, March–April 1984, pp. 21-25.
Metrick, Lenore. "Grand space." *Des Moines Sunday Register*, 11 January 1998, pp. 4Q-5Q.
Nusbaum, Eliot. "Revised scorecard: Art Center wing 'mostly brilliant.'" *Des Moines Sunday Register*, 7 August 1988, sec. F, p. 7.
Papadakis, Andreasc, ed. "Richard Meier: A Personal Manifesto"; "Des Moines Art Center Addition, Des Moines, Iowa." *Architectural Digest*, vol. 55, no.1/2, 1985, pp. 56, 58-69.

Siemens Headquarters Building, Munich, Germany, 1983–88
Backs, Stefanie. "High-Tech unter Glas und Alu." *Münchner Mercur* 226, 30 September 1999, p. 13.
Futagawa, Yukio, ed. "Siemens Office Building, Munich." *Global Architecture Document* 9, February 1984, pp. 126-31.
Herwig, Oliver. "Transzendenz am Tunnelmund." *Süddeutsche Zeitung* 225, 29 September 1999, p. 21.
Horschig, Jola. "Siemens setzt Zeichen." *IndustrieBAU*, January–February 2000, pp. 76-79.
Office Building and Siemens Forum, Oskar-von-Miller-Ring, Munich. Munich: Siemens Immobilien Management GmbH & Co. OHG, 1999. Includes Introduction and "Aims of the Design" by Richard Meier.
Thomas, Christian. "Ermessensspielräume, Richard Meiers Siemens-Hauptzentrale in München." *Frankfurter Rundschau* 226, 29 September 1999, p. 8.

Tableware Designs for Swid Powell, 1983–96
Barbee, Pat. "Through a Glass, Purely." *Beverly Hills Magazine*, 20 January 1993, pp. 14-15.
Bass, Judy. "Drawing a Full House." *The Robb Report*, September 1985, pp. 34-40.
Brolin, Brent C. "At Swid Powell, the Architects' Collection of Tableware." *The New York Observer*, 13 May 1991, p. 20.
Catoir, Barbara. "Architektur in Schwar." *Frankfurter Allgemeine Zeitung*, 26 March 1996.
Clyde, Amy. "Cheeky Chairs." *House Beautiful*, March 1993, p. 66.

Cowie, Denise. "Architect turns skills to more than buildings." *The Philadelphia Inquirer*, 25 October 1996, pp. F1, F10-11.
Dreyer, Clemens, ed. "Der Konzertflügel-Ibach." *Deutsche Standards*, Edition Arcum, 1996, pp. 80-81.
Dunlap, David W. "Street Furniture Designs Stuck in Gridlock." *The New York Times*, 9 August 1998, sec. 11, pp. 1, 24.
Gleizes, Serge. "Richard Meier: l'architecture ocean." *Table & Cadeau*, December 1996–January 1997, pp. 90-93.
Gleizes, Serge. "La fibre minimaliste." *L'Officiel*, February 1997, pp. 184-89, 190.
Gleizes, Serge. "Richard Meier: ascetisme et parfum d'époque." *Vogue Hommes*, spring–summer 1997, pp. 174-75.
Goodman, Wendy. "Home Plate." *New York*, 21 September 1998, pp. 42-45.
High Styles: Twentieth Century American Design. Exhibition catalogue. New York: Whitney Museum, Summit Books, 1985, p. 194.
Jay, Hilary. "Eminent Domain." *The Philadelphia Inquirer Magazine*, 27 October 1996, pp. 30-31.
Maurer, Caro. "A Bottle is a Bottle: The American Architect Richard Meier likes to keep order." *Die Welt*, 2 November 1996.
Maurer, Caro. "Ich hoffe, dass wir überzeugen können." *Diners Club Magazine*, January 1997, pp. 52-53.
Nerot Mitzvah (Contemporary Ideas for Light in Jewish Ritual). Exhibition Catalogue. Jerusalem: The Israel Museum, 1986, pp. 33 ff.
"On and off the avenue." *New Yorker*, 26 November 1984, p. 91.
Posner, Ellen. "Designs for Sitting: New Furniture by Living Architects." *The Wall Street Journal*, 20 November 1984, p. 28.
Rico, Diana. "Personal Style/Design Dinnerware? Painter's Perfume?" *Republic*, January 1996, p. 12.
Schön, Wolf. "Man müßte Klavier spielen können." *Rheinischer Merkur*, 16 February 1996, p. 19.
Shear, Michael D. "Name is Big, Work is Small: Famous Architect Adapts His Vision to Bus Shelter." *The Washington Post*, 13 September 1999, pp. B1-2.
"Swid-Powell Tableware." *Time Magazine*, 17 December 1984, p. 90.

Competition Project for the Lingotto Factory Conversion, Turin, Italy, 1983
"Consultazione internazionale per la fabbrica FIAT-Lingotto: Meier."*L'Architettura*, May 1984, pp. 338-39.
Pelissier, Alan. "Metamorphoses d'une Barre Industrielle (à propos de la consultation internationale pour la reconversion de l'une Fiat-Lingotto)." *Techniques & Architecture*, June–July 1984, pp. 10-18.
Rumpf, Peter. "Fiat-Lingotto: Chance oder Danaergeschenk für Turin?" *Bauwelt*, 4 May 1984, pp. 722-33.
Venti progetti per il futuro del Lingotto. Milan: Etas Libri, 1984, pp. 120-27.

Westchester House, New York, 1984–86
Adam, Peter. "Ein Meister der Moderne." *Ambiente*, July 1987, pp. 44-52.
Boidi, Sergio. "Moderno Ma Non Troppo." *Costruire*, April 1991, pp. 184-88.
Filler, Martin. "Eminent Domain." *House & Garden*, April 1987, pp. 162-69. Reprinted as "Precision au Sommett." *Vogue Decoration*, September 1987, pp. 114-17, 212.
"Formas Blancas." *Architectural Houses*, May 1992, vol. 8, pp. 144-56.
Futagawa, Yukio, ed. "Westchester House." *Global Architecture Houses* 22, December 1987, pp. 22-33.
James, Warren. "Casa en Westchester, Neuva York 1984–87." *Arquitectura*, November–December 1987, pp. 80-89.
Rykwert, Joseph. "Richard Meier: Two New Houses in USA." *Domus*, March 1987, pp. 29-45.
Van den Dungen, Mabel. "Richard Meier." *Avant Garde*, October 1990, pp. 120-25.
Vogel, Carol. "Classic Modern." *The New York Times Magazine*, 1 February 1987, pp. 60-64.

Ackerberg House, Malibu, California, 1984–86 Addition to Ackerberg House, 1993–95
Ackerberg House+Addition. New York: Monacelli Press, 1996.
Biagi, Marco. "Rigore e Nitore." *VilleGiardini* 340, October 1998, pp. 34-43.
Contal, Marie-Helene. "Meier à Malibu." *Architecture Intérieure Crée*, February–March 1989, pp. 92-97.
Futagawa, Yukio, ed. "Ackerberg House." *Global Architecture Houses* 22, December 1987, pp. 6-21.
Graaf, Vera. "Luxusdampfer am Strand." *Architektur & Wohnen*, June–July 1990, pp. 22-28.
Hollenstein, Roman. "Eine Hymne an Südkaliforniens Licht." *Nzz Folio* 2, February 1992, pp. 62-63.
Hubeli, Ernst. "Unsichtbare Konstruktion als Allegorie." *Werk, Bauen+Wohnen*, December 1988, pp. 9-11.
Hughes, Robert. "Architecture: Richard Meier." *Architectural Digest*, October 1987, pp. 152-59.
Mulard, Claudine. "La Maison Blanche." *Maison & Jardin*, March 1991, pp. 132-39.
Papadakis, Andreas C., ed. "Richard Meier, Ackerberg House, Malibu, 1984-86." *Architectural Design*, vol. 58, no. 7/8, 1988, pp. 24-33.
Prichett, Jack. "Richard Meier's Ackerberg House: Beauty at the Beach." *Inside*, vol. 6, February–March 1990, pp. 5-13.
Rykwert, Joseph. "Richard Meier: Two New Houses in USA." *Domus*, March 1987, pp. 29-45.
Stephens, Suzanne. "Malibu Modernism." *Progressive Architecture*, December 1987, pp. 94-101.
Van den Dungen, Mabel. "Richard Meier." *Avant Garde*, October 1990, pp. 120-25.
Von Uthmann, Jorg. "Das weltliche Kloster van Malibu." *Frankfurter Allgemeine Zeitung*, 29 October 1991.

Webb, Michael. "Shelter for the Soul." *Guest Informant*, winter 2000, pp. 18-23.

Bridgeport Center, Connecticut, 1984–89
Berman, Karen. "There's a new kid on the block." *Bridgeport Post Telegram*, 23 April 1989, sec. H, pp. 1, 2.
Branch, Mark Alden. "Bridgeport Center." *Progressive Architecture*, July 1989, pp. 19, 24.
"Bridgeport Center." *a+u – Architecture and Urbanism*, April 1990, pp. 8-24.
Canella, Guido, ed. "Bridgeport Center." *Zodiac 1*. Milan: Rizzoli, 1989, pp. 92-107.
Dietsch, Deborah. "New Directions." *Architectural Record*, August 1989, pp. 70-77.
Dimitriu, Livio, ed. "Bridgeport Center." *New York Architects 3*. New York: U.S.A. Books, 1990, pp. 173-77.
Futagawa, Yukio, ed. "Bridgeport Center." *Global Architecture Document* 24, August 1989, pp. 76-91.
Goldberger, Paul. "A Short Skyscraper with a Tall Assignment." *The New York Times*, 26 March 1989, p. 32.
Hartoonian, Gevork. "Bridgeport Center: Re-Minding Richard Meier." *Journal of Architectural Education*, November 1990, pp. 33-36.

Siemens Office and Research Facilities, Munich, Germany, 1984–90
Fernandez-Galiano, Luis, ed. "Richard Meier in Europe." *Arquitectura Viva Monografias* 59, May–June 1996, pp. 40-43.

Grotta House, Harding Township, New Jersey, 1985–89
"Amor a la Geometría." *Architectural Houses*, May 1992, vol. 7, pp. 116-27.
Balint, Juliana. "Det Perfekta Samspelet." *Sköna Hem*, March 1990, pp. 94-101.
Balint, Juliana. "Kokoelmien koti." *Avotakka* 2, 1993, pp. 56-63.
Blanckaert, Marie-Claire. "La Modernité est Dans le Pré" *Elle Decoration*, March 2001, pp. 158-65.
Borghi, Ruggero. "Prova D'Artista." *VilleGiardini*, April 1992, pp. 2-11.
Doubilet, Susan and Boles Daralice. *American House Now*. New York: Universe, 1997, pp. 136-47.
Fernandez-Galiano, Luis. "The Ten Best Houses in the World." *El País Semanal*, pp. 42-47.
Filler, Martin. "Modern Idyll." *House & Garden*, June 1990, pp. 150-57.
Filler, Martin. "Ideal Villa." *Vogue Living/Australian*, June–July 1991, pp. 110-15.
Futagawa, Yukio, ed. "Grotta House." *Global Architecture Houses* 28, March 1990, pp. 46-47.
Futagawa, Yukio, ed. "Grotta Residence." *Global Architecture Houses* 30, December 1990, pp. 8-31.
"Grotta House." *a+u – Architecture and Urbanism*, December 1990, pp. 16-23.
Izzo, Ferruccio. "Richard Meier & Partners Grotta Residence, New Jersey." *Domus*, April 1991, pp. 64-71.
Murphy, Jim. "A Collaboration." *Progressive Architecture*, November 1990, pp. 90-95.
Oberlerchner, Karl. "Ansichts sache." *Wohnen*, May 1992, pp. 28-35.
Rasch, Horst. "Herr Meier Und Die Lubeb Zur Geometric." *Häuser*, May 1990, pp. 16-23.
Shields, Jody. "A Change in the Atmosphere." *The New York Times Magazine*, 11 October 1992, pp. 16-17.

The Getty Center, Los Angeles, California, 1985–97
Aberg, Lars. "Caesar's Palace." *Scanorama*, February 1998, pp. 46-51.
"Acropole d'Art: The J. Paul Getty Center, Los Angeles." *Techniques & Architecture* 408, June 1993, pp. 54-59
"Acropolis moderna." *Clarin*, 22 December 1997, pp. 6-8.
"Amerikas Bastion der Kunst." *Berliner Morgenpost*, 13 September 1997.
Amery, Colin. "Getty's Acropolis: any colour but white." *Financial Times*, 4 November 1991.
Andersen, Kurt. "A Grand New Getty." *Time*, 21 October 1991, p. 100.
Andersen, Kurt. "A City on a Hill." *The New Yorker*, 29 September 1997, pp. 66-72.
Antoniades, Anthony. "The Getty Center." *The World of Buildings* 24, 2000, pp. 72-94.
"Architettura: Getty Center, Los Angeles." *OFX* 6, November–December 1998, pp. 40-63. Includes "Al centro dell'arte prevale l'architettura" by Corrado Gavinelli; "La filosofia del progetto" by Roberta Mutti.
Armstrong, David. "Building a Blockbuster." *San Francisco Examiner*, 29 July 1997, pp. C1, C4.
Arnaboldi, Mario Antonio. "Il Getty Center a Los Angeles." *L'Arca*, March 1992, pp. 4-11.
Bachmann, Wolfgang. "The Getty Center in Los Angeles." *Baumeister*, February 1998, pp. 16-27.
Banham, Reyner. "Who's the King of the Mountain?" *California*, August 1984, pp. 94-103, 120-121.
Basso Peressut, Luca. "The Getty Center." *Musei Architetture 1990–2000*. Milan: Motta, 1999, pp. 166-81.
Berthelsen, Christian. "Watchful neighborhood." *The Outlook*, 16 December 1997, pp. A1, 6.
Betsky, Aaron. "American Acropolis." *Condé Nast Traveler*, October 1997, pp. 156-59, 201-202.
"Blasts Now Past." *The Los Angeles Times*, 29 December 1997, pp. E1, 4.
Boaga, Giorgio. "J. Paul Getty Center a Los Angeles di Richard Meier." *Casabella*, April 1990, pp. 32-33.
Bonetti, David. "Triumph of the Will." *San Francisco Examiner*, 7 December 1997, pp. 18-22, 24, 36-39.
Book, Jeff. "Edifice Complex." *Departures*, November–December 1997, pp. 216-23, 273-76.
Boschmann, Hella. "Wie Getty Millionen Berge versetzten." *Die Welt*, 8 April 1997, p. 3.
Bradaschia, Maurizio. "Meier per 'Getty.'" *L'Architettura* 8, 1993, pp. 54-58.
Brawne, Michael. *The Getty Center, Architecture in Detail*. London: Phaidon Press Ltd., 1998.
Bransburg, Pablo. "Recorrida por 'la encomienda del siglo.'" *El Cronista Arquitectura*, 4 February 1998, pp. 1-4, 12.
Campbell, Robert. "A Critical Tour of the Getty." *Architectural Record*, November 1997, pp. 106-7, 197.
Campbell, Robert. "The Getty's Beautiful Mess." *The Boston Globe*, 21 December 1997, pp. N1, 4.
Canedo, Patricia. "Richard y su nino mimado." *La Nacion*, 14 January 1998, pp. 5-7.
Caotorta, Francesca. "Il Giardino del Getty Center." *Abitare 412*, December 2001, pp. 82-87.
Caruso, Jorge. "Media go to mountaintop for tour of Getty." *The Outlook*, 10 December 1997, pp. A1, 7.
Caruso, Michelle. "New crest for culture in Getty Center." *Daily News*, 17 December 1997, pp. 16-17.
Cerami, Charles A. "Controversial Getty Center Worth Billion-Dollar Billing." *Insight*, 29 June 1998, pp. 38-39.
Chazanor, Mathis. "Architect Vows Getty Museum will Blend into Brentwood Hills." *The Los Angeles Times*, 23 February 1986, sec. W, part IX, p. 5.
Colacello, Bob. "Meier's Moment." *Vanity Fair*, April 1997, pp. 332-39, 376-79.
Colybes, Annick. "The cultural citadel of the Getty Center in Los Angeles." *Les Echos Immobilier*, 24 October 1996, p. 48.
Conover, Kirsten A. "Scholars Make a Case for Artistic Values." *The Christian Science Monitor*, 28 June 1996.
Cooper, Frederick. "El Centro Getty." *Arkinka*, February 1998, pp. 14-50.
Cornwell, Tim. "Getty takes high art to Hollywood." *The Independent*, 9 December 1997, p. 9.
Cosin, Elizabeth. "L.A. Life." *Daily News*, 10 August 1996, pp. 12-14.
Cosin, Elizabeth. "The Getty Buildup." *Daily News*, 18 August 1996, p. 14.
Costa, Florencia. "Richard Meier a Los Angeles: The Getty Center." *Abitare*, March 1998, pp. 146-53, 182.
Crane, Brian. "Out and About: The J. Paul Getty Museum." *To the Trade*, April–May 2000, pp. 56-61.
D'Arcy, David. "Lights, Camera, Getty." *Los Angeles Times*, November 1997, pp. 84-91, 169-70.
D'Arcy, David. "Billion Dollar Getty Opens." *The Art Newspaper*, December 1997, pp. 1, 29-33.
Deal, Joe. *Between Nature and Culture: Photographs of the Getty Center*. Los Angeles: Getty Trust Publications, 1999. Includes Preface by Richard Meier.
Decker, Andrew. "Gettyworld." *ARTnews*, May 1996, pp. 110-16.
De Michelis, Marco. "The Getty Center, Los Angeles." *Domus*, December 1997, pp. 38-49.
de Xaxas, Xavier Mas. "La Fundacion Getty

acaba su nuevo museo, un centro de 146.000 millones que abrira Clinton." *La Vanguardia*, 16 November 1997, p. 57.

de Xaxas, Xavier Mas. "La Herencia Getty se Hace Museo." *La Vanguardia Magazine*, 14 December 1997, pp. 86-93.

Diamonstein, Barbaralee. "Designer of the Decade." *Vanity Fair*, January 1985, pp. 86-88.

Doehne, Eric. "Travertine Stone at the Getty Center." *The Getty Conservation Institute Newsletter*, vol. XI no. 2, summer 1996.

Drewes, Frank F. "Revolution à la Richard Meier." *Deutsche Bauzeitschrift*, July 1998, p. 18.

Duncan, Michael. "Live from the Getty." *Art in America*. May 1998, pp. 98-101.

"Dulwich, California. Michael Brawne interviews Richard Meier." In Woodward, Christopher, ed. *Inspired by Soane*. London: Sir John Soane's Museum, 1999, pp. 14-21.

"Farbwechsel: Getty-Stiftung in Los Angeles." *AIT*, March 1997, p. 26.

Filler, Martin. "Meier's Marvel." *Harper's Bazaar*, October 1995, pp. 208-11.

Filler, Martin. "The Getty Gets Ready." *Architecture*, February 1996, pp. 80-87.

Filler, Martin. "The Citadel of Light." *House Beautiful*, December 1997, pp. 100-3, 140.

Filler, Martin. "The Big Rock Candy Mountain." *The New York Review of Books*, 18 December 1997, pp. 29-34.

Forgey, Benjamin. "The Getty Center Sets its Site." *The Washington Post*, 27 October 1991, pp. G1, G5.

Forgey, Benjamin. "Getty's Big Address." *The Washington Post*, 14 December 1997, pp. G1, 4.

Frampton, Kenneth. "Una acrópolis cultural." *Arquitectura Viva*, May–June 1992, pp. 18-23.

Futagawa, Yukio, ed. "Getty Center." *Global Architecture Document* 55, July 1998, pp. 8-49.

Gandee, Charles. "Modern Man." *Vogue*, December 1997, pp. 284-89, 346.

"The Getty Center." *Architecture*, December 1997. Includes "Art vs. Architecture" by Allan Schartzman; "Faulty Towers" by Aaron Betsky; "Ready for Art?" by Dave Hickey.

The Getty Center Design Process. Los Angeles: The J. Paul Getty Trust, 1991. Includes an Introduction by Harold Williams; "The Architect Selection and Design" by Bill Lacy; "The Architectural Program" by Stephen D. Rountree; "The Design Process" by Richard Meier.

"Getty Unveils Mega-Museum." *Art in America* 12, December 1991, p. 136.

Ghirado, Diane. "Invisible Acropolis." *The Architectural Review*, June 1990, pp. 92-95.

Gillette, Jane Brown. "Western Civ." *Landscape Architecture Magazine*, December 1997, pp. 52-61.

Giovannini, Joseph. "Getty v. Guggenheim, A Paradigm Apart." *Art in America*, July 1998, pp. 80-85.

Gitlin, Todd. "Getty's Modernist Palace." *The New York Observer*, 8 June 1998, p. 4.

Glionna, John M. "A Magic Kingdom for Art Lovers." *The Los Angeles Times*, 17 December 1997, pp. B1, 8.

Glueck, Grace. "From Quirky Little Gallery to Behemoth." *New York Times*, 13 October 1991, sec. 2, pp. 31, 34.

Glusberg, Jorge. "Centro Paul Getty." *Buenos Aires bellas artes* 2, 1999, pp. 70-73.

Goldberger, Paul. "Architect Chosen for Getty Complex." *The New York Times*, 27 October 1984, sec. 1, p. 13.

Goldberger, Paul. "A Romantic Modernist Wins a Plum from the Getty." *The New York Times*, 11 November 1984, sec. 2, pp. 32, 34.

Goldberger, Paul. "Can the Getty Buy Design Happiness?" *New York Times*, 13 October 1991, sec. 2, pp. 1, 31.

Goldberger, Paul. "The People's Getty." *The New Yorker*, 23 February–2 March 1998, pp. 178-81.

Goodale, Gloria. "New Getty Center Shouts Strong Message from Mountaintop." *The Christian Science Monitor*, 28 June 1996, p. 10.

Goodwin, Betty. "A-List Attends Getty's Opening Gala." *The Los Angeles Times*, 10 December 1997, p. B3.

Gordon, Larry. "A Blueprint for Workers' Pride." *The Los Angeles Times*, 9 December 1997, pp. B1, 2.

Graaf, Vera. "Ihr Lebenwerk, Richard Meier?" *Architektur & Wohnen*, August–September 1997, pp. 102-5.

Graaf, Vera. "Piazza mit allem, bitte!" *Süddeutsche Zeitung*, 13–14 December 1997, p. 14.

Grossberg, Josh. "Ready, Getty, Go!" *The Outlook*, 16 December 1997, pp. A1, 6.

Gruber, Michael. "A Look at Making in the Meier-Getty Model Shop." *Architecture California*, 1994, pp. 32-41.

Gura, Judith. "Modernism at the millennium." *Echoes*, fall 1999, p. 71.

Haithman, Diane. "Moving Up." *The Los Angeles Times*, 13 August 1996, pp. B1, B8.

Hales, Linda. "The Getty: Views on Architecture, Views of Los Angeles." *The Washington Post*, Home Section, 6 February 1997, p. 15.

Hamm, Oliver G. "Die Alte und die Neue Welt." *Bauwelt*, 13 February 1998, pp. 302-13.

Henderson, Justin. *Museum Architecture, Glouchester, MA*: Rockport Publishers, 1998, pp. 82-89.

Herrera, Philip. "Lights, Camera, Action!" *Town & Country*, December 1997, pp. 178-87, 210-214.

Hoetzel, Holger. "GroBer, heller, teurer." *Focus*, 1 December 1997, pp. 154-58.

Hohmeyer, Jurgen. "Tempelstadt fur die Kunst." *Der Spiegel* 50, 1997, pp. 235-39.

Hollenstein, Roman. "Eine Alhambra fur Los Angeles." *Neue Zurcher Zeitung*, 15 November 1991, p. 65.

Hughes, Robert. "The Beauty of Big." *Time*, Special Issue, spring 1997, p. 54.

Hughes, Robert. "Bravo! Bravo!" *Time*, 3 November 1997, pp. 98-105.

"Interview: John Walsh, Director, The J. Paul Getty Museum." T*he Karsten/Hutman Margolf Project Management Report*,

winter 1996, pp. 2-4.

Irace, Fulvio. "Nell'Olimpo dei saperi." *Il Sole 24 Ore*, 7 December 1997, p. 35.

Jacobs, Karie. "Fleshing out the Getty." *Los Angeles Times Calendar*, 25 August 1996, pp. 5, 85-86.

Januszczak, Waldemar. "Getty's white elephant." *The Sunday Times*, 28 December 1997, pp. 10-11.

Jarmusch, Ann. "Satisfied Meier soaks up work, awaits verdict." *San Diego Union Tribune*, 30 November 1997, pp. H1, 6.

Jarmusch, Ann. "Modern master makes museum a site to behold"; Pinkus, Robert. "Promised landmark." *San Diego Union Tribune*, 14 December 1997.

Jodidio, Philip. "Le Monastére de Brentwood." *Connaissance des Arts*, November 1994, pp. 124-51.

Kaplan, Sam Hall. "Getty Designer Stresses Flexibility." *The Los Angeles Times*, 16 December 1984, sec. I, IV.

Ketcham, Diana. "Chaste Geometry in Los Angeles." *Metropolis*, October 1987, p. 26.

Ketcham, Diana. "No garland for Getty garden." *San Francisco Examiner*, 17 December 1997, pp. B1, 6.

Kieran, Kevin, et al. "The Getty Trust and the Process of Patronage." *The Harvard Architecture Review* 6. New York: Rizzoli, 1987, pp. 122-31.

Kimmelman, Michael. "The New Getty, Dream and Symbol." *The New York Times*, 16 December 1997, pp. E1, 3.

Kippoff, Petra. "Ein Gipfel namens Getty." *Die Zeit*, 12 December 1997, p. 55.

Knight, Christopher. "Modernist Delivers the Unimaginable." *Los Angeles Times*, 2 December 1997, pp. A1, 21.

Knight, Christopher. "An Artwork That Will Grow on You." *The Los Angeles Times*, 17 December 1997, pp. F1, 4.

Knight, Christopher. "Playing to the Gallery." *The Los Angeles Times*, 6 December 1998, Calendar pp. 4-5, 63.

Koenig, Gloria. *Iconic L.A., California*: Los Angeles: Gloria Koenig, 2000, pp. 99-105.

Körte, Peter. "Arkadien unterm Smogschleier." *Frankfurter Rundschau*, 18 December 1997.

Laisné, Jean C. "La Colline Magique." *ArchiCréé*, September 199 283, pp. 34-39.

Lange, Alexandra. "In Print Setting Sail." *New York Magazine*, 1 December 1997, p. 142.

Laube, Helene. "Meiers Musentempel am Pazifischen Ozean." *Cash* 28, 11 July 1997, pp. 38-39.

Leeds, Jeff. "Getty May Limit Attendance Through Jan. 4." *The Los Angeles Times*, 30 December 1997, sec. B1, p. 8.

Lefevre, Peter. "Building the Getty." *Beverly Hills 213*, 10 December 1997, pp. 8-9.

Lerano, Giorgio. "Usa e Getty: la via miliardaria ai beni culturali." *Panorama*, 1 August 1996, pp. 112-15.

Lewis Joanne, et. al. "Art 2001." *Hemispheres*, December 1997, pp. 74-79.

Lloyd, Stephen. "Get ready for Getty." *The Scotsman*, 28 November 1997, p. 21.

Lutterbeck, Claus. "Das Erbe des alten

Knausers." *Stern* 52, 1997, pp. 162-65.

Macdonald, Marianne. "If God is in the detail..." *Observer Life*, 7 December 1997, pp. 12-17.

McGuigan, Cathleen and Emily Yoffe. "A Place in the Sun." *Newsweek*, 21 October 1991, p. 64. Reprinted in Newsweek international ed., 11 November 1991, pp. 72-74.

McGuigan, Cathleen and Emily Yoffe. "A Place in the Sun." *Newsweek*, 13 October 1997, pp. 72-74.

Mack, Gerhard. "Eine Festung als kulturelles Symbol." *St. Gallo Tagblatt*, 17 December 1997.

Mack, Gerhard. "Zu wenig sexy fur private Sponsoren." *Cash* 51/52, 19 December 1997, pp. 60-61.

McKenna, Kristine. "Uncommon Grounds." *The Los Angeles Times*, 7 April 1996, p. 3.

McKenna, Kristine. "As Ideas Take Root." *The Los Angeles Times*, 25 August 1998, pp. F1, F8.

MacRitchie, Lynn. "The Getty citadel of culture opens its doors." *The Financial Times*, 29-30 November 1997, p. VII.

Madigan, Nick. "Cultural Monument." *The Outlook*, 7 June 1996, p. A3.

Madigan, Nick. "Gardens and Galleries." *The Outlook*, 14 October 1996, p. A1.

Making Architecture. Los Angeles: The J. Paul Getty Trust, 1997. Includes an Introduction by Harold Williams; "The Clash of Symbols" by Ada Louise Huxtable; "A Concert of Wills" by Stephen D. Rountree; "A Vision for Permanence" by Richard Meier.

Mead, Rebecca. "Pecking Order." *The New Yorker*, 22 & 29 December 1997, pp. 49-50.

Meier, Richard. *Building the Getty.* New York: Alfred A. Knopf Inc., 1997.

"Meier's Magic Mountain." *The Architectural Review*, February 1998, pp. 30-51. Includes "Getty Genesis" by Ivor Richards; "Playing to the Gallery" by Michael Brawne.

"Meier's Museums: A Tale of Two Cities." *The Journal of Art*, April 1989, pp. 50-53.

Meisler, Stanley. "The House that Art Built." *Smithsonian Magazine*, December 1997, pp. 82-92.

Mejias, Jordan. "Atemraubende Perspektiven Fur Die Kunst: Das Getty Center." *FAZ Magazin*, 12 December 1997, pp. 50-55.

Minervino, Fiorella. "Getty in Olimpo per l'arte." *Corriere della Sera*, 10 December 1997, p. 22.

Minetti, Maria Giulia. "L'Acropoli della California." *Specchio*, 31 January 1998, pp. 54-66.

Montaner, Josep M. *Museos Para el Nuevo Siglo*. Barcelona: Gustavo Gili S.A., 1995, pp. 132-35.

Moore, Rowan. "Getty's shining city on a hill." *The Daily Telegraph*, 6 June 1997, p. 25.

Morgenstern, Joe. "Getty Opens Mammoth Hilltop Center to Public." *The Wall Street Journal*, 16 December 1997, p. A16.

Moro, Ginger. "The Getty: This billion dollar beacon." *Echoes,* winter 1998, p. 20.

Muchnic, Suzanne. "Catching up with the Getty Center." *The Los Angeles Times*, 22 October 1990, pp. F1, 12.

Muchnic, Suzanne. "Getty Trust Reaches Out." *The Los Angeles Times*, 3 June 1996, p. A1.

Muchnic, Suzanne. "The Year of the Getty." *The Los Angeles Times*, 1 January 1997, pp. F1, F24.

Muchnic, Suzanne. "A Getty Chronicle: The Malibu Years"; "T Minus Five Months." *The Los Angeles Times* Calendar, 6 July 1997, pp. 4-5, 55.

Muchnic, Suzanne. "Getty Center Is More Than Sum of Its Parts." *The Los Angeles Times*, 30 November 1997, pp. A1, 40.

Mulard, Claudine. "Le Getty Trust construit à Los Angeles le plus grand complexeculturel privé du monde." and "Le grand œuvre de l'architecte Richard Meier." *Le Monde*, 16 October 1996, p. 26.

Mulas, Antonio. *Richard Meier: The Getty Center.* Tolentino: Poltrona Frau, 1998.

Muschamp, Herbert. "Herbert Muschamp on California Architecture." *Art Forum*, October 1990, pp. 31-33.

Muschamp, Herbert. "A Mountaintop Temple Where Art's Future Worships Its Past." *The New York Times*, 1 December 1997, pp. A1, 18.

Muschamp, Herbert. "The Getty Center, Distilled From Slices of Time." *International Herald Tribune*, 2 December 1997, p. 24.

Neffe, Jürgen. "Eine Affäre mit dem Licht." *Der Spiegel* 17, 1997, pp. 206-210.

"The New Getty." Special issue of *The Los Angeles Times Magazine*, 7 December 1997. Includes "Shining City on a Hill" by Nicolai Ouroussoff; "His Defining Moment" by Steve Proffitt.

Newman, Morris. "Raising the Getty." *Progressive Architecture*, January 1995, pp. 63-75.

Ouroussoff, Nicolai. "West Coast Showdown." *Harper's Bazaar*, November 1996, pp. 256-58, 268.

Ouroussoff, Nicolai. "Building Blocks of Culture." *The Los Angeles Times*, 4 January 1997, pp. F1, 6.

Ouroussoff, Nicolai. "Realizing a Utopian Goal in Center that Doesn't Cohere." *Los Angeles Times*, 1 December 1997, pp. A1, 23.

Ouroussoff, Nicolai. "High Above It All." *The Los Angeles Times*, Calendar Section, 6 December 1998, pp. 5-6, 63.

Ouroussoff, Nicolai. "So Where's the Art?" *The Los Angeles Times,* 31 March 2002.

"Outside Voices on the Getty Center." *Los Angeles Business Journal*, 22 December 1997, p. 39.

Pacheo, Patrick. "Museums Face the Millenium." *Art & Antiques*, January 1997, pp. 54-59.

Parkes, Christopher. "Getty extravaganza makes play for new." *Financial Times*, 14 May 1996.

Pastier, John. "J. Paul Getty Museum Unveils Preliminary Scheme by Meier." *Architecture*, July 1987, p. 18.

Pastier, John. "Getty Center Design Unveiled in Los Angeles." *Architecture*, November 1991, pp. 21-22.

Pearson, Clifford. "Unveiling a Modern Classic." *Architectural Record*, October 1991, pp. 80-87.

Peers, Alexandra. "How the Getty Lost Its Buzz." *The Wall Street Journal*, 6 October 2000, p. W14.

Perl, Jed. "Acropolis Now." *The New Republic*, 26 January 1998, pp. 25-31.

"Perspectives: Richard Meier's Getty Center." *Progressive Architecture,* February 1992, pp. 103-7.

Plagens, Peter. "Another Tale of Two Cities." *Newsweek*, 3 November 1997, pp. 82-84.

Plattus, Alan J. "Il museo e la città: la geografia della cultura." *Casabella*, January–February 1992, pp. 71-77.

Pringle, Paul. "Giddy for the Getty." *Santa Monica Daily Breeze*, 5 October 1997, pp. A1, A4.

Pristin, Terry. "Getty Center Challenges a Premier U.S. Architect." *The Los Angeles Times*, 19 May 1989, pp. 1, 28-30.

Purdum, Todd S. "An L.A. Star Shines Anew." *The New York Times*, 12 October 1997, p. 10.

Purdum, Todd S. "Up on a Hill: The Getty Learns to Weather the Crowds." *The New York Times*, 2 May 2001, p. 12.

Raulff, Ulrich. "The Acropolis of Hollywood." *Frankfurter Allgemeine Zeitung*, 28 October 1995.

Raulff, Ulrich. "The California Monks of Mount Pathos." *Frankfurter Allgemeine Zeitung*, 16 December 1997, p. 41.

Reese, Thomas F. "The Architectural Politics of the Getty Center for the Arts." *Lotus 85*, 1995, pp. 6-43.

Reese, Thomas and Carol McMichael Reese. "Richard Meier's New Getty Center in Los Angeles." *a+u – Architecture and Urbanism*, January 1998, pp. 6-69.

Reeves, Phil. "Dream Without a Theme." *The Independent*, 30 October 1991, p. 17. Reprinted in *The New York Times*, Los Angeles ed., 10 October 1991, p. B3; and in *International Herald Tribune*, weekend ed., 19–20 October 1991, p. 6, as "At Last, Meier's Vision for the Getty."

"Richard Meier – The Getty Center." *a+u – Architecture and Urbanism*, special issue, November 1992. Includes "A Citadel for Los Angeles and an Alhambra for the Arts" by Kurt Foster; "Richard Meier's Getty Center" by Henri Ciriani.

"Richard Meier – Getty Center Los Angeles," *Casabella*, February 1997, pp. 76-77.

Richards, Ivor. "Californian Acropolis." *World Architecture* 19, September 1992, pp. 54-57.

Riedle, Gabriele. "Schöner als das Taj Mahal." *DieWoche*, 19 Dec 1997.

Rikola, Taina. "California Perspective." *Building Design*, 16 September 1988, pp. 30-33.

Rimanelli, David. "The Cutting Edge." *Travel & Leisure*, November 1997, pp. 188-89.

Rocco, Andrea. "Usa e Getty." *Carnet*, November 1997, pp. 147-55.

Rosenbaum, Lee. "View from the Getty: What Its Billions Bought." *Art In America*, May 1998, pp. 92-97, 138.

Rosenberg, Howard. "A Candid Look at Monument Making." *The Los Angeles*

Times, 17 December 1997, pp. F1, 10.
Russell, James S. "The Xanadu of Art." *The Philadelphia Inquirer*, 2 November 1997, pp. F1, F6.
Rykwert, Joseph. "Acropolis with hover-tram." *London Times Literary Supplement*, 9 January 1998, pp. 15-16.
Saulnier, Beth. "Come & Getty." *Cornell Magazine*, January–February 1998, pp. 32-37.
Schulz, Bernhard. "Die Akropolis des Westens." *Tages Spielgel*, 11 Dec 1997.
Sherman, Chris. "Hilltop Masterpiece." *St. Petersburg Times*, 18 January 1998, pp. F1, 3.
Sobral, Sandra and Inez Sobral Meehan. "Pátios espaços íntimos e humanos em meio à grandiosidade do centro cultural mais rico do mundo." *Projeto* 219, April 1998, pp. 32-39.
Soran, Patrick. "My Oh Meier." *OutPosts*, November–December 1997, pp. 22-24.
Sorkin, Michael. "Come and Getty." *Metropolis*, June 1998, pp. 45, 47.
Stecyk, CR. "Museum Architecture." *Juxtapoz*, spring 1998, pp. 86-87.
Stein, Karen D. "The Getty Center, Los Angeles, California." *Architectural Record*, November 1997, pp. 72-105.
Stephens, Suzanne. "Assessing the State of Architectural Criticism in Today's Press." *Architectural Record*, March 1998, pp. 64-69, 194.
Stephens, Suzanne. "Richard and Famous." *House & Garden*, February 1985, p. 54.
Sterngold, James. "Already, the Getty Has a Full Agenda." *The New York Times*, 13 December 1997, pp. B7-15.
Stevens, Mark and Douglas Davis. "The Golden Eye of Los Angeles." *Newsweek*, 26 November 1984, pp. 80-82, 87-89.
Streisand, Betsy. "A new Getty for the people." *U.S. News & World Report*, 22 December 1997, pp. 58-59.
Stromme, Elizabeth. "Something About Azaleas." *Buzz*, April 1998, pp. 30-32.
Tasset, Jean-Marie. "Naissance du plus grand musée privé du monde." *Le Figaro*, 12 December 1997, p. 4.
Taylor, Jennifer. "Art, Architecture and Los Angeles." *Design Book Review*, winter 1994, pp. 67-73.
Ter Borg, Lucette. "Een berg van licht." *De Volkskrant*, 12 December 1997, p. 21.
Thompson, Angel. "Getting into the Getty." *Feng Shui*, December 2001, pp. 34-41.
Trebay, Guy. "L.A.'s Museum Complex." *Village Voice*, 15 April 1997, p. 30.
Tuner, Jim. "My Oh Meier." *Detour*, December–January 1997, pp. 64-68.
Tyrnauer, Matthew. "A Meier Calling." *Vanity Fair*, April 1996, p. 212.
"Una Bienal en dos Tiempos, con todos los invitados." *CP67 News: Publication de Arquitectura y diseno*, 1998, pp. 20-21.
"The unrepentent modernist." *The Economist*, 7 February 1998, pp. 87-88.
Vagheggi, Paolo. "Un'Acropoli per Hollywood." *La Repubblica*, 11 December 1997, p. 41.
Van der Meer, Ron and Deydan Sudjic. *Das Architektur-Paket*. Van der Meer

Publishing, 1997, p. 14.
Vercelloni, Matteo. "Getty Center." *Interni 8*, 23 June 2000, pp. 19-21.
Vidler, Anthony. "Architecture as Spectacle." *Los Angeles Times*, 3 May 1998, pp. M1, M6.
Vogel, Carl. "The Getty's Hidden World of Wizardry." *The New York Times*, 10 February 1998, pp. B1, 4.
Von Eckardt, Wolf. "Taking on an Imperial Task." *Time*, 12 November 1984, p. 111.
Wallach, Amei. "Getty Museum Expands." *New York Newsday*, 11 October 1991.
Warnod, Jeanine. "Le Louvre présente le nouveau Getty." *Le Figaro*, 15 October 1996.
Watson, Peter. "King of the Hill." *Buzz*, February–March 1991, pp. 64-68.
Watson, Peter. "Getty's World." *Blueprint* 82, November 1991, pp. 28-30.
Watson, Peter. "Bastion of high culture." *The Daily Telegraph Magazine*, 15 February 1997, pp. 40-45.
Watson, Peter. "The cultural high ground." *The Sunday Times*, 14 December 1997.
Webb, Michael. "The Getty Center." *Interiors*, December 1997, pp. 72-77.
Weeks, Janet. "The house Getty oil built"; Wark, Tammy. "Paintings, photos and furniture." *USA Today*, 12 December 1997.
Whiteson, Leon. "The Man who got the Getty Job." *The Los Angeles Herald Examiner*, 6 December 1984, p. B1.
Whiteson, Leon. "Put-Up-Or-Shut-Up Time at the Getty." *The Los Angeles Herald Examiner*, 23 March 1986, pp. E1-6.
Whiteson, Leon. "Center of Attention." *Elle Decor*, December–January 1997, pp. 130-33.
Woo, Elaine. "The Getty as Teacher." *The Los Angeles Times*, 10 December 1997, p. B2.
Wooldridge, Adrian. "Shining Getty on a hill." *The World in 1997*, special issue of *The Economist*, pp. 66, 69.
"Work in Progress." *The Los Angeles Times*, Calendar Section, 29 December 1996.
Wyszpolski, Bondo. "Getty while it's hot." *Easy Reader*, 18 December 1997, p. 20.
Yook, Euna. "Richard Meier: Getty Center." *Space*, March 1998, pp. 34-63.

Exhibition and Assembly Building, Ulm, Germany, 1986–93
Bächer, Max. "The Stadthaus at Ulm and the Cathedral Square." *Domus*, February 1995, pp. 7-22.
Barthelmess, Stephan. "Richard Meiers Stadhaus." *Schwäbische Zeitung*, 27 May 1992.
Canella, Guido, ed. "Exhibition and Assembly Building, Ulm, Germany." *Zodiac 9*, March–April 1993, pp. 180-96.
"The Civic Center in Ulm." *Lichtbericht 47*, November 1994, pp. 10-13.
"Exhibition-Assembly Hall, Munsterplatz, Ulm, West Germany." *Progressive Architecture*, February 1988, p. 39.
Fernandez-Galiano, Luis, ed. "Richard Meier in Europe." *Arquitectura Viva Monografias* 59, May–June 1996, pp. 96-99.
Futagawa, Yukio, ed. "Exhibition-Assembly Building, Ulm, West Germany." *Global*

Architecture Document 18, April 1987, pp. 7-12.
Galloway, David. "Richard Meier, Master Builder." *Inter Nations German-American Cultural Review*, 6 October 1993, pp. 40-47.
Jodidio, Philip. "La Quadrature du Cercle." *Connaissance des Arts*, December 1994, pp. 96-105.
Magnago Lampugnani, Vittorio "Richard Meier: Davanti alla Cattedrale di Ulm." *Domus*, October 1987, pp. 8-9.
Metz, Tracy. "A Circle in the Square." *Architectural Record*, October 1995, pp. 90-99.
Montaner, Josep M. *Nuevos Museos*. Barcelona: Gustavo Gili, S.A., 1990, pp. 44-49.
"Neuggestaltung des Musterplatzes in Ulm." *Architektur+Wettewerbe*, December 1987, pp. 52-58.
Richard Meier: Stadthaus Ulm. Germany: International Creative Management, 1993. Includes "Richard Meier and the Urban Context" by David Galloway; "The Urbanization of Architecture" by Stephan Barthelmess. Richards, Ivor. "Square Deal," *The Architectural Review*, June 1995, pp. 38-45.
Rumpf, Peter. "Square of Circles." *Bauwelt*, 14 January 1994, pp. 96-101.
Sack, Manfred. "Luxury? Why not." *Die Zeit*, 19 November 1993, p. 63.
Sack, Manfred. *Richard Meier Stadhaus Ulm*. Stuttgart: Axel Menges, 1994.
Schuster, Jan-Richard. "Ulm […] Die Schöne Wae? e Welt du Richard Meier in der Region." *Schwabischer Zeitung*, 11 March 1989, p. 59.
Ullman, Gerhard. "Vergnugliches Schauen." *Werk, Bauen+Wohnen*, 6 June 1994, pp. 14-15.

City Hall and Central Library, The Hague, Netherlands, 1989–95
Buddingh, Hans. "Directeur De Ridden Velvaat Planbureau." *NRC Handelsblad*, 1 December 1988, p. 1.
Casciato, Maristella. "The Hague City Hall: Anywhere But Here." *Progressive Architecture*, September 1995, p. 27.
"City Hall and Library." *Architecture in the Netherlands*, Rotterdam: NAi Uitgevers Publishers, 1996, pp. 42-49.
Davies, Colin. "Dutch Modern." *Architecture*, February 1996, pp. 98-107.
Diaz, Tony. "El sentido de la práctico: Richard Meier en La Haga." *Arquitectura Viva* 388, March 1989, pp. 17-19.
Dorigati, Remo. "The Hague Townhall." *L'Arca*, December 1997, pp. 40-47.
Fernandez-Galiano, Luis, ed. "Richard Meier in Europe." *Arquitectura Viva Monografias* 59, May–June 1996, pp. 52-59.
Futagawa, Yukio, ed. "City Hall and Central Library." *Global Architecture Document* 46. February 1996, pp. 56-77.
"Hague City Hall." *SD* 31, 1998, pp. 32-35.
Hamm, Oliver G. "Der wahre weiße Riese." *Bauwelt*, 11 August 1995, pp. 1635-41.
Lambert, Donald. "La Haye Grands Projets, *L'Architecture d'Aujourd'hui*, June 1988, pp. 22-24.

Library Builders. London: Academy Editions, 1997, pp. 126-33.
Magnago Lampugnani, Vittorio "City Hall/Central Library, The Hague." *Domus*, November 1987, pp. 25-31.
Melet, Ed. "De onaantastbare perfectie." *de Architect*, June 1995, pp. 43-47.
Melis, Liesbeth. "Publiksforum mist intermediaire schaal." *de Architect*, June 1995, pp. 28-32.
"Rathaus mit Zentralbibliothek in Den Haag, Neiderlande." *Architektur+Wettbewerbe*, September 1988, pp. 28-38.
Richards, Ivor. "Heart of the Hague." *The Architectural Review*, January 1996, pp. 40-49.
Rossman, Andreas. "Contemplation Under the Sky of Den Haag." *Frankfurter Allgemeine Zeitung*, 21 September 1995.
Stadhuis Bibliotheek: The City Hall/Library Complex by Richard Meier in The Hague. Den Haag: 1988. Includes an interview with Richard Meier; Introduction by Adri Duivesteijn; "Who is Richard Meier?" by Thomas Hines.
Van de Bilderdijkstraat Naar Het Spui: De Geboorte Van Een Nieuwe Centrale Openbare Bibliotheek. Den Haag: Dienst Openbare Bibliotheek, 1992.
Van Heuvel, Wim J. "Drie varianten stahuis-ontwerp Meier." *Architectuur/Bouwen*, January 1989, pp. 41-44.
Vantisphout, Wouter. "Richard Meier in Holland." *ANY Magazine* 16, pp. 40-44.
Vermeulen, Paul. "Verzengend." *Archis*, September 1995, pp. 16-27.
Weisser, Riese. *Architektur Innenarchitektur Technischer Ausbau*. December 1995, pp. 68-75.
Westerman, Maks. "De giest van Berlage: Richard Meier over zijn Haagse Stadhuis." *Elseviers*, 23 May 1987, pp. 23-25.

Project for the Eye Center for Oregon Health Sciences University, Portland, Oregon, 1986
Monstrasi, Fabio. "Centro Oculistico a Portland, Oregon, di Richard Meier." *Casabella*, April 1989, pp. 30-32.
"Portland Eye Center." *Progressive Architecture*, January 1989, pp. 100-2.

Competition Project for the Madison Square Garden Site Redevelopment, New York, New York, 1987
Cassarà, Silvio. "Le Torri della Ragione: Richard Meier ed il Madison Square Garden." *Paesaggio Urbano*, October 1996, pp. 104-111.
Dimitriu, Livio, ed. "Madison Square Garden Site Redevelopment." *New York Architects 3*. New York: U.S.A. Books, 1990, pp. 178-81.
Futagawa, Yukio, ed. "Madison Square Garden." *Global Architecture Document* 23, April 1989, pp. 7-11.
"Madison Square Garden Site Redevelopment." *OZ*, vol. 11, 1989, pp. 40-41.

Weishaupt Forum, Schwendi, Germany, 1987–92
Barthelmess, Stephan. "Perfektes Beispiel Für 'Corporate Culture.'" *Heidenheimer Neue Presse*, 16 May 1992.
Barthelmess, Stephan. "In Germania un museo privato di Meier." *Il Giornale Dell'Arte* 102, July–August 1992, p. 20.
Blaser, Werner. *Weishaupt Forum*. Published on the occasion of the opening of Weishaupt Forum. Schwendi, Germany: Max Weishaupt, May 1992.
Blaser, Werner. *Weishaupt Forum/Richard Meier*. Schwendi, Germany: Max Weishaupt, 1993. Includes Introduction by Richard Meier; "Essay" by Claudia Rudeck.
"Due edifici europei di Richard Meier." *Casabella*, April 1993, pp. 12-19.
Fernandez-Galiano, Luis, ed. "Richard Meier in Europe." *Arquitectura Viva Monografias* 59, May–June 1996, pp. 60-67.
Futagawa, Yukio, ed. "Canal+; Weishaupt Forum; Royal Dutch Paper Mills Headquarters." *Global Architecture Document* 34, September 1992, pp. 8-57.
Galloway, David. "Europe's Love Affair With an American Architect." *International Herald Tribune*, 18–19 July 1992, p. 7.
Glusberg, Jorge. "Tecnica, estetica y creacion." *Arquitectura*, 18 January 1995, pp. 2-3.
Hamm, Oliver. "Meier IV." *Deutsche Bauzeitung*, 6 June 1992, pp. 8-9.
Kipphoff, Petra. "Prazision doppelt." *Die Zeit*, 15 May 1992, p. 80.
"Richard Meier – Royal Dutch Papermills Headquarters, Weishaupt Forum." *a+u – Architecture and Urbanism* 275, August 1993, pp. 54-72.
Richards, Ivor. "Visionary Weishaupt." *The Architectural Review*, March 1994, pp. 53-57.
Sebastien, Stephanie. "Strict Strategy." *AIT*, March 1996, pp. 60-61.
"Weishaupt Forum." *Bauwelt*, 5 June 1992, p. 1200.
"Wenn Schwarz und Weiss Zusammenfinden." *Häuser*, May 1992, pp. 8-9.

Royal Dutch Paper Mills Headquarters, Hilversum, Netherlands, 1987–92
"Due edifici europei di Richard Meier." *Casabella*, April 1993, pp. 12-19.
Fernandez-Galiano, Luis, ed. "Richard Meier in Europe." *Arquitectura Viva Monografias* 59, May–June 1996, pp. 68-75.
Futagawa, Yukio, ed. "Canal+; Weishaupt Forum; Royal Dutch Paper Mills Headquarters." *Global Architecture Document* 34, September 1992, pp. 8-57.
Gubitosi, Alessandro. "The Dialectics of Image." *L'Arca*, March 1994, pp. 4-11.
Kloos, Maarten. "Presence, not illusion: Richard Meier in Hilversum." *Archis*, July 1992, p. 3.
Metz, Tracy. "Richard Meier Builds a 'Big House' for KNP." *NRC Handelsblad*, 2 June 1992, p. 15.
Pearson, Clifford. "Working Couple."

Architectural Record, March 1993, pp. 52-61.
"Royal Dutch Paper Mills Headquarters." *Architektur+Wettbewerbe*, June 1994, pp. 10-11.
Sicuso, Francisco. "El Juego de Escalas de Richard Meier." *La Prensa*, Buenos Aires, 18 April 1995, p. 223.
Staal, Gert. *KNP Corporate Office Hilversum*. Hilversum: KNP, June 1992.
Toy, Maggie, ed. "Aspects of Minimal Architecture." *Architectural Design* 64, July–August 1994, pp. 54-57.

Museum of Contemporary Art, Barcelona, Spain, 1987–95
Arnaboldi, Mario Antonio. "The Museum of Contemporary Art." *L'Arca*, April 1996, pp. 6-15.
Audusseau, Martine. "Meier a Barcelone." *d'Architectures,* December 1995.
"The Barcelona Museum for Contemporary Art." *World Architecture*, February 1998, pp. 42-44.
Bartolucci, Marisa. "Museum or object?" *Metropolis*, July–August 1996, pp. 65, 99.
Bevan, Roger. "A White Cube Distorted." *The Art Newspaper* 54, December 1995.
Bohigas, Oriol. "El Museu d'Art Contemporani de Barcelona." *La Municipal de Barcelona*, March 1993, p. 23-27.
Bohigas, Oriol. "Museum of Contemporary Art of Barcelona." *Diseño Interior* 53, 1996, pp. 56-67.
Buchanan, Peter. "Aloof Abstraction." *Architecture*, February 1996, pp. 70-79.
Cabeza, Elisabet. "El MACBA, favorit dels premis FAD 96." *AVUI*, 22 March 1996, p. B3.
Canella, Guido, ed. "Museum of Contemporary Art, Barcelona." *Zodiac 6*. Milan: Rizzoli, 1991, pp. 136-51.
Capella, Juli and Quim Larrea. "Barcelone et Richard Meier." *L'Architecture d'Aujourd'hui*, December 1995, pp. 40-41.
Capella, Juli and Quim Larrea. "Eine unerwartete Liebergeschichte..." *Architektur*, April 1996, pp. 42-53.
Cervello, Marta. "Museum of Contemporary Art." *Domus*, December 1995, pp. 7-17.
Cohn, David. "A Fine Romance." *World Architecture* 41, 1995, pp. 96-99.
"Coup de blanc dans les vieux quartiers de Barcelone." *Connaissance des Arts*, February 1996, pp. 52, 56-59.
Fernandez-Galiano, Luis. "Catedral y Museo: Meier en Barcelona." *El País Babelia*, 25 November 1995, pp. 20-21.
Fernandez-Galiano, Luis. "Museum of Contemporary Art, Barcelona." *Arquitectura Viva Monografias* 57-58, January–April 1996, pp. 34-37.
Fernandez-Galiano, Luis, ed. "Richard Meier in Europe." *Arquitectura Viva Monografias* 59, May–June 1996, pp. 88-95.
Furer, Rene. "MACBA"; Pestalozzi, Manuel. "Weiss im Grun." *Architektur & Technik*, July 2001, pp. 6-8, 10-14.
Futagawa, Yukio, ed. "Museum of Contemporary Art." *Global Architecture*

Document 46, February 1996, pp. 8-43.
Galloway, David. "In Barcelona, a 'Cathedral' of Art Awaits Definition." *International Herald Tribune*, 8 December 1995, p. 11.
Guardia, Maria Asuncion. "Philip Johnson says that MACBA is Meier's best work." *La Vanguardia*, 10 May 1996, p. 39.
Gubitosi, Alessandro. "Metamorfosi e continuità." *L'Arca*, April 1992, pp. 60-63.
Hoyet, Jean-Michel, ed. *Techniques & Architecture*, June–July 1996. Includes "An American Dream"; "Transformations in Ciutat Vella," pp. 33-37, 38-41.
Jodidio, Philip. *Contemporary American Architects: Volume III*. Cologne: Taschen, 1997, pp. 98-103.
Lagos, Roberto G. "Meier en Barcelona: el Museo de Arte Contemporaneo." *Bienal de Arquitectura*, October 1995, p. 33.
Massot, Josep. "MACBA: Barcelona abre su museo mas contemporaneo." *La Vanguardia Magazine*, 12 November 1995, pp. 34-51.
"Museo de Arte Contemporáneo." In *Barcelona: Arquitectura y Ciudad 1980–1992*. Barcelona: Editorial Gustavo Gili, S.A., 1990, pp. 124-29. Includes essays by Oriol Bohigas, Peter Buchanan, Vittorio Magnago Lampugnani.
Museos y arquitectura; nuevas perspectivas. Exhibition catalog. Barcelona: Ministerio de Obras Publicas, Transportes y Medio Ambiente, 1994, pp. 86-93. Includes "Museo de arte contemporaneo en Barcelona" by Richard Meier; "El Museo" by Joseph Rykwert; Introduction by Martha Thorne.
"Museum of Contemporary Art." *Progressive Architecture*, January 1991, pp. 94-95.
Permanyer, Lluis. "Im Dienste der Kunst?" *Bauwelt*, May 1996, pp. 1010-17.
Rambert, Francis. "Richard Meier: 'Les Architectes ne peuvent pas changer la ville!'" *Le Figaro*, 5 December 1995, p. 23.
Richards, Ivor. "Interactive Languages." *The Architectural Review*, April 1993, pp. 22-37.
Richards, Ivor. "White City." *The Architectural Review*, March 1997, pp. 34-41.
Riding, Alan. "A Modern 'Pearl' Inside Old Barcelona." *The New York Times*, 10 May 1995, p. C13.
Rudolph, Karen. "Museum of Contemporary Art, Barcelona"; "Light is a transient medium." *ERCO Lichtbericht 52*, August 1996, pp. 4-9, 10-11.
Rudolph, Karen. "Light is a Transient Medium." *Architectural Design 67*, March–April 1997, pp. 54-59.
Schwarz, Michael. "Light Rooms by Contemporary Artists." *Licht & Architektur*, July–September 1996, pp. 82-85.
Serra, Catalina. "La perla del Raval." *El País Quadern*, 27 April 1995, pp. 1-3.
Von Peininger, Enrique. "Richard Meier White"; "FMRS and the Museum of Contemporary Art " *Licht & Architektur*, July–September 1996, pp. 74-77, 78-80.
Von Peininger, Enrique. "Richard Meier." *ERCO Lichtbericht 52*, August 1996, pp. 4-11.

Zeitz, Rudiger. "Mensch, Meier." *Design Report*, April 1996, pp. 62-65.

Canal+ Headquarters, Paris, France, 1988–92
Beaudouin, Laurent. "Canal+ Building in Paris." *a+u - Architecture and Urbanism*, January 1993, pp. 46-71.
"Cadrage Sur La Ville." *Architecture Interieure Cree*, November 1992, pp. 115-21.
"Canal Plus." *Bauwelt*, October 1989, p. 1910.
"Canal+ Headquarters." *Progressive Architecture*, January 1990, pp. 92-93.
Canella, Guido, ed. "The Canal+ Headquarters, Paris." *Zodiac 4*. Paris: September 1990, pp. 204-223.
Cohen, Jean-Louis. "The Message in the Medium"; Vonier, Thomas. "Bien Venue." *Progressive Architecture*, December 1992, pp. 44-53.
Fernandez-Galiano, Luis, ed. "Richard Meier in Europe." *Arquitectura Viva Monografias* 59, May–June 1996, pp. 80-87.
Fillion, Odile. "La Leçon de Canal+." *Le Moniteur*, 26 June 1992, pp. 80-81.
Forster, Kurt W. "Stella televisiva sul palcoscenico urbano." *Domus* 741, September 1992, pp. 29-41.
Forster, Kurt W. "Carácter corporativo: nuevo sede de Canal+ en Paris." *Arquitectura Viva* 30, May–June 1993, pp. 90-95.
Futagawa, Yukio, ed. "Canal+; Weishaupt Forum; Royal Dutch Paper Mills Headquarters." *Global Architecture Document* 34, September 1992, pp. 8-57.
Gubitosi, Alessandro. "Architecture with a Plus." *L'Arca*, February 1993, pp. 50-59.
Loriers, Marie-Christine. "Precision Audiovisuelle: Canal+." *Techniques & Architecture*, November 1992, pp. 18-28.
Mas, Jean. "Siège de Canal Plus: Richard Meier." *L'Architecture d'Aujourd'hui*, September 1989, pp. 64-65.
Mas, Jean. "La Lumière en Mouvement." *L'Architecture d'Aujourd'hui*, June 1992, pp. 111-14.
Moore, Rowan. "A Vision in White, by an American in Paris." *The Independent*, 14 April 1993, p. 13.
Muschamp, Herbert. "On a Clear Day, You Can Watch Television." *The New York Times*, 7 February 1993, p. 32.
Régnier, Nathalie. "Canal Plus: Un Scenario Bien Orchestre." *Le Moniteur*, 8 February 1991, pp. 68-71.
Slessor, Catherine. "White Heat." *The Architectural Review*, December 1994, pp. 58-62.

Espace Pitôt Residential Housing, Montpellier, France, 1988–93
Brausch, Marianne. "Montpellier. L'Enprente de Richard Meier." *Le Moniteur*, 26 May 1989, pp. 110-13.
"Espace Pitôt." *Bauwelt*, 6 October 1995, pp. 2126-31.
Montpellier Architectures 1977–1992. Ville de Montpellier, 1993, pp. 32-33.

"Montpellier: Folie de la Ville." *d'Architectures*, March 1994, pp. 33-38.

Competition Project for the Bibliothèque de France, Paris, France, 1989
Pelissier, Alain. "Concours Pour La Bibliothèque de France." *Techniques & Architecture*, October 1989, pp. 34-45.
Welsh, John. "Salon de Refusees: Speaking Volumes." *Building Design*, 6 October 1989, pp. 18-29.

Daimler-Benz Research Center, Ulm, Germany, 1989–93
"Daimler-Benz Forschungszentrum." *Bauwelt*, 19 November 1993, pp. 2358-59.
Flagge, Ingeborg. *Richard Meier: Daimler-Benz*. Stuttgart: Gerd Hatje, 1994.
Futagawa, Yukio, ed. "Daimler-Benz Research Center." *Global Architecture Document* 40, July 1994, pp. 8-23.

Hypolux Bank Building, Luxembourg, 1989–93
Barthelmess, Stephan. "Zwei Amerikaner in Europa: Richard Meier und Frank Stella mit Projekten in Luxemburg, Rom und Ulm." *CCHeidenheimer Neue Presse – Neue Wurttembergische Zeitung* 168, 24 July 1993.
Barthelmess, Stephan. "Zinseszins: Richard Meiers Hypolux-Bank." *AIT*, December 1993, pp. 22-29.
Davies, Colin. "Spatial Assets." *Architecture*, June 1994, pp. 74-83.
Delluc, Manuel. "Siege de Banque au Luxembourg." *Architecture d'Aujourd'hui*, February 1994, pp. 64-67.
"Dialog zwischen menschlicher Tätigkeit und Kultur." *Wirtschaft-Finanzen Luxembourg* 152, 6 July 1993, p. 9.
Dibar, Carlos L. "Meier: Impecable Inserción Urbana." *La Nacion*, 26 October 1994, pp. 1-2.
"Erfolgreiche Kombination von Architektur, Kunst und Kommerz." *Wirtschaft-Finanzen Luxembourg*, 6 July 1993.
Fernandez-Galiano, Luis, ed. "Richard Meier in Europe." *Arquitectura Viva Monografias* 59, May–June 1996, pp. 100-7.
Futagawa, Yukio, ed. "Hypolux Bank Building, Luxembourg." *Global Architecture Document* 40, July 1994, pp. 34-47.
Galloway, David. *Der Dialog Als Program Die Hypobank in Luxemburg*. Luxembourg: Hypobank International S.A., 1993.
Gazzaniga, Luca. "Richard Meier: Edificio per una banca, Lussemburgo." *Domus 755*, December 1993, pp. 25-35.
Hollenstein, Roman. "Zeitgenössische Architektur in der Bankenfestung: Bauten zwischen Banalität and Kunst in Luxemburg." *Neue Zurchner Zeitung* 191, 20 August 1993.
Illies, Florian. "Hier ist dein Geld." *Frankfurter Allgemeine Zeitung*, 28 January 1994.
Knapp, Gottfried. "Die Macht des kleinen Unterscheids; wie fremdes Geld ein Land verändert: Luxemburg und seine neuen Bankpaläste." *Suddeutsche Zeitung München* 176, 3 August 1993, p. 11.
Reuter, Monika. "Die Kathedralen des Geldes:

In Luxemburg profilieren sich die Banken mit ehrgeiziger Architektur." *TZ* 154, 8 July 1993.
Stungo, Naomi. "Modern markitecture?" *RIBA Journal*, November 1993, pp. 38-39.
"Weise Bank fürs schwarze Geld: die Neue Hypobank von Richard Meier." *Baumeister*, 10 October 1993, p. 8.

Project for the Museum of Ethnology, Frankfurt am Main, Germany, 1989
Freiling, Frank-Dieter. "Der Herr Der Museen." *Männer Vogue*, June 1992, pp. 84-87.
Futagawa, Yukio, ed. "Richard Meier, Museum of Ethnology." *Global Architecture Document International 1993*, April 1993, pp. 60-63.
Magnago Lampugnani, Vittorio. *Museums Architecktur in Frankfurt 1980–1990*. Munich: Prestel-Verlag, 1990, pp. 116-23. Includes "Unity in Diversity" by Dieter Bartetzko.
Peters, Paulhans. "Museum für Völkerkunde in Frankfurt." *Baumeister*, June 1990, pp. 40-45.

Euregio Office Building, Basel, Switzerland, 1990–98
Allenspach, Christoph. "Ganz in Weiss." *Facts*, 26 March 1998, pp. 146-51.
Barreneche, Raul. "Meier's White Turns Green." *Architecture*, February 1996, p. 136.
Hollenstein, Roman. "Pittoreske Spätmoderne." *Neue Zürcher Zeitung*, 10 July 1998.
"Kein 'Fast-Building'-dafür ein Qualitätsbau." *Basler Zeitung*, 4 April 1997, p. 29.
Windhöfel, Lutz. "Der Lichtendurchflutet Boulevard." *Basel Landschaftliche Zeitung*, 2 April 1998.

Camden Medical Center, Singapore, 1990–99
Hassell, Richard. "Meier Tower." *The Architectural Review Australia*, summer 1999, pp. 100-3.
"Richard Meier & Partners; Camden Medical Center." *Space*, July 2001, p. 110-14.
Turner, Nicole. "Urban Resistance." *World Architecture* 89, September 2000, pp. 60-61.

Rachofsky House, Dallas, Texas, 1991–96
Biagi, Marco and Kay Von Westernsheimb. "Arte e funzione." *VilleGiardini* 361, September 2000, pp. 2-15.
Dietsch, Deborah K. "Howard's House." *Architecture*, July 1997, pp. 72-79.
Dillon, David. "Meier's design achieves utopian ideal, if not ease." *The Dallas Morning News*, 10 November 1996, pp. C1-6.
"Edifice Rex: The Ultimate Home is the Sum of Many Parts." *The Robb Report*, April 2002, pp. 63-81.
Frankel, Claire. "Mr. Rachofsky's Dream House." *Art & Antiques*, October 1997, pp. 76-81.
Futagawa, Yukio, ed. "Rachofsky House II." *Global Architecture Houses* 37 *Project 1993*, March 1993, pp. 90-93.
Futagawa, Yukio. "Rachofsky House." *Global Architecture Houses* 51, March 1997, pp. 70-85.
Giovanelli, Francesca. "White Cube." *Moebel*

Interior Design, March 1998, pp. 36-41.
Hines, Thomas. "Bridging the public and private realms in a Dallas House." *Architectural Digest*, April 1997, pp. 118-25, 214.
Kutner, Janet. "Owner's modern works are worthy of a museum." *The Dallas Morning News*, 10 November, 1996, pp. C1-6.
Mostaedi, Arian. "Rachofsky House." In *The American House Today*. Barcelona: Carles Broto & Josep Ma Minguet, 2000, pp. 10-19.
"New digs get the smart art." *The Dallas Morning News*, 4 October 1996.
Nobel, Philip. "Mixed Media for an Artist: Lawn, Light and House." *The New York Times*, 15 June 2000, pp. F1-8.
Rojas, Vincente. "Un Meier, Domestico." *Arquitectura Contemporanea,* May–June 2000, pp. 12-21.
Von Westersheimb, Kay. "Bauen fur die Kunst." *Architektur Aktuell*, January–February 1998, pp. 54-65.

Swissair North American Headquarters, Melville, New York, 1991–94
Anastasi, Nick. "SwissAir USA HQ Heads to Market." *Long Island Business News*, 18 June 2002.
Colwell, Carolyn. "School of Design." *New York Newsday*, 30 October 1993, pp. 30-31.
Dunlap, David. "For Swissair, Modernism on the Long Island Expressway." *The New York Times*, 22 April 1992, p. D25.
Futagawa, Yukio, ed. "Swissair North American Headquarters." *Global Architecture Document* 46, February 1996, pp. 44-55.
Kroloff, Reed. "Swiss Precision." *Architecture*, February 1996, pp. 92-97.
Muschamp, Herbert. "A Reason to Rubberneck on the Expressway." *The New York Times*, 26 February 1995, p. 42.

United States Courthouse and Federal Building, Islip, New York, 1993–2000
Bradford, Hazel. "Read Their List: No New Courts." *Engineering News Record*, 3 July 1995, p. 7.
Brown, Bay. "'Great White' Strikes Again." *World Architecture*, November–December 2000, p. 28.
Dillon, David. "Courthouse can be Justly Praised." *The Dallas Morning News*, 26 November 2000.
Dunlap, David W. "Putting a New Face on Justice." *The New York Times*, 19 July 1998, sec. 11, pp. 1, 18.
Forgey, Benjamin. "Judicial Buildings Earn GSA Awards." *The Washington Post*, 30 March 2001, p. C2.
Futagawa, Yukio, ed. "US Courthouse and Federal Building, Islip, New York." *International* 1995, special issue of *Global Architecture Document* 43, 1995, pp. 74-77.
Futagawa, Yukio. "United States Courthouse and Federal Building." *Global Architecture Document* 64, March 2001, pp. 10-27.
Gibson, Eric. "Medico and Mellons, Make Way: A New Patron Has Arrived." *The Wall Street*

Journal, 27 October 2000, p. W17.
Giovannini, Joseph. "Ardor in the Court." *New York*, 9 October 2000, pp. 94-96.
Giovannini, Joseph. "United States Courthouse and Federal Building, Central Islip, New York." *Architecture*, January 2001, pp. 78-89.
Goldberger, Paul. "Suburban Grandeur." *The New Yorker*, 9 October 2000, pp. 94-96.
Gragg, Randy. "Monuments to a Crime-Fearing Age." *The New York Times*, 28 May 1995, pp. 36-39.
Kessler, Robert E. "New Courthouse Debuts This Week." *Long Island Newsday*, 20 August 2000, p. A8.
Landecker, Heidi. "Court Houses." *Architecture*, January 1996, pp. 64-85.
Marshall, Alex. "Let There Be Light"; Meier, Richard. "A Modernist at Heart." *Newsday*, 16 October 2000, pp. B6-B7, B10.
Martin, Natalia. "GSA to honor 7 Projects where Quality Shows." *The Washington Times*, 24 March 2001, p. D3.
Muschamp, Herbert. "A Rational Vision That Lets you know Who's Boss." *The New York Times*, 19 November 2000, pp. 39-40.
"Order in the Courthouse." *Time Magazine,* 4 September 2000, p. 74.
Ouroussoff, Nicolai. "A Hall of Justice That's Actually Sexy." *The Los Angeles Times*, 11 December 2000, p. F9.
Ouroussoff, Nicolai. "Order in the Court?" *The Los Angeles Times*, 11 December 2000, pp. F1, F8.
Paquette, Carole. "Courthouse and Tree House win Architects' Awards." *The New York Times*, 2 December 2001, p. 9.
Rappaport, Nina. "New Courthouses Around New York." *Oculus*, April 1996, pp. 6-7.
"Richard Meier & Partners, Federal Building and United States Courthouse Central Islip." *Space,* July 2001, pp. 94-109.
Stern, Seth. "Building halls of Justice." *Christian Science Monitor*, 22 February 2001, pp. 12-13.
"U.S. Courthouse & Federal Building." *Zodiac* 14, January–February 1996, pp.110-17.
Wise, Michael. "Architecture on Trial." *Metropolis*, May 1995, pp. 99-151.

Museum of Television & Radio, Beverly Hills, California, 1994–96
Dietsch, Deborah K. "Broadcast News." *Architecture*, November 1996, pp. 100-7.
Futagawa, Yuiko, ed. "Museum of Television & Radio, Beverly Hills, California, USA." *Global Architecture Document* 49, November 1996, pp. 50-61.
Goldberger, Paul. "And now, live from Beverly Hills, a new museum." *The New York Times*, 7 April 1996, sec. 2, p. 32.
Mills, Rochelle Dynes. "Beverly Hills Duo." *Southland*, spring–summer 1999, pp. 66-75.
"Museum of Television & Radio." *Paesaggio urbano*, July–October 1997, pp. 112-19.
Toy, Maggie, ed. "Richard Meier & Partners: Museum of Television & Radio." *Architectural Design*, November–December 1997, pp. 42-45.
Whiteson, Leon. "TV Museum Both Formal

and Inviting." *The Los Angeles Times*, 2 June 1996, pp. K1, K5.
Whiteson, Leon. "Richard Meier in Beverly Hills." *Bauwelt*, 25 October 1997, pp. 2302-05.

Gagosian Gallery, Beverly Hills, California, 1994–95
Futagawa, Yukio, ed. "The Gagosian Gallery." *Global Architecture Document 46*, February 1996, pp. 78-81.
"The Gagosian Gallery." *a+u – Architecture and Urbanism*, January 1998, pp. 70-77.
Giovannini, Joseph. "Sculptural Sanctum." *Architecture*, February 1996, pp. 88-91.
Haden-Guest, Anthony. "Of dealers and players." *The New Yorker*, 2 October 1995, pp. 36-7.
Iovine, Julie V. "State of the art gallery." *The New York Times Magazine*, 10 December 1995, pp. 94-95.
"Richard Meier a Beverly Hills." *Abitare*, July–August 1996, p. 135.
Whiteson, Leon. "Gallery Talk." *Elle Decor*, December 1995, pp. 50-53.

Project for the Jean Arp Museum II, Rolandseck, Germany, 1995–
"Arp-Museum 1999 eröffnet." *Bonner Generalanzeiger*, 2 April 1997.
"Arp-Museum Rolandseck." *Bauwelt*, 1 March 1996, p. 426.
"Federal Government is giving green light for their millions." *General Anzeiger*, 7 July 2000.
"Ganz in Weiß." *Sudwest Presse*, 12 February 1996.
"Hans Arp-Museum in Rolanseck." *Kunstzeitung* 6, February 1997.
Maurer, Caro. "Beautiful View: Richard Meier and the Arp Museum." *General Anzeiger*, 12–13 November 1996.
"The New Arp Museum Comes Into Being." *Art Magazine*, August 1997, p. 112.
Parade, Heidi. "Rose Götte: Es soll beim Arp-Museum bleiben." *Bonner General Anzeiger*, 22 May 1997, p. 5.
"Projekt: Hans Arp-Museum in Rolandseck." *Kunstzeitung*, 6 February 1997, p. 16.
Werner, Klaus and Peter Guth. *Räume Für Kunst*. Exhibition catalogue in the European museums, September 1992–January 1993, pp. 40-41.

Neugebauer House, Naples, Florida, 1995–98
Chestnut, Cathy. "Meier 2000," and "White Light." *Naples Illustrated*, January 2000, pp. 76-81, 122, 124, 126.
Dal Co, Francesco, ed. "Un aliante di fronte al mare." *Casabella* 646, June 1997, pp. 22-27.
Goldberger, Paul. "Architecture: Millenial Modernism." *Architectural Digest*, March 1999, pp. 96-107, 184. Reprinted in German as "Ein Tempel Für Das Licht." *Architectural Digest* 18, German ed., February–March 2000, pp. 64-73.
Goldberger, Paul. "La Villa sur la Baie." *Architectural Digest* 4, July–August 2000, pp. 43-53.
Futagawa, Yukio, ed. "Neugebauer House." *Global Architecture Houses Projects 1997*,

April 1997, pp. 104-7.
"La Maison Nouvelle." *Connaissance des Arts*, July–August 1999, pp. 106-112.
Nobuyuki, Yoshida, ed. "Neugebauer House." *a+u – Architecture and Urbanism 371*, August 2001, pp. 40-51.
"Villa in Florida." *VilleGiardini*, September 1997.

Sandra Day O'Connor United States Courthouse, Phoenix, Arizona, 1995–2000
Barreneche, Raul. "Meier's White Turns Green." *Architecture*, February 1996, p. 137.
Carter, Brian. "Meier's green shift." *Ecotech*, March 2001, pp. 14-17.
Davey, Peter. "Open Court." *The Architectural Review*, August 2001, p. 99.
Fearnow, Dawson. "Top 10 of the Last 20 Years." *City AZ*, March–April 2002, p. 69.
Forgey, Benjamin. "Judicial Buildings Earn GSA Awards." *The Washington Post*, 30 March 2001, p. C2.
Futagawa, Yukio, ed. "US Courthouse and Federal Building, Phoenix, Arizona." *Global Architecture Document 58 – International 1999*, pp. 68-71.
Futagawa, Yukio, ed. "Sandra Day O'Connor United States Courthouse." *Global Architecture Document 64*, March 2001, pp. 28-37.
Lebow, Edward. "Building History." *Phoenix New Times*, 23 November 2001.
Martin, Natalia. "GSA to honor 7 Projects where Quality Shows." *The Washington Times*, 24 March 2001, p. D3.
"Progressive Architecture Awards." *Architecture*, May 1996, pp. 118-21.
Stephens, Suzanne. "Sandra Day O'Connor United States Courthouse, Phoenix." *Architectural Record*, March 2001, pp. 9-99.
Unali, Maurizio. "Federal Building & United States Courthouse"; Sacchi, Livio. "Architetture invulnerabili." *Progetto* 1, July 1997.

Museum of the Ara Pacis, Rome, Italy, 1996–
Casalini, Simona. "Il segno di Meier sull'Ara Pacis." *la Repubblica*, 15 May 1996, p. 5.
Casalini, Simona. "Rinascimento in chiave romana." *la Repubblica*, 21 June 1996, p. 5.
Casciani, Stefano. "Richard Meier: museo dell'Ara Pacis." *Domus*, November 2001, pp. 144-145.
Ceen, Allan. "No Peace for the Ara Pacis." *Studiumuris.org*, fall 2001.
Cinanni, Maria Teresa. "Ara Pacis, riprendono i lavori." *Il Nuovo*, May 2002.
Colonelli, Lauretta. "Ara Pacis, le modifiche di Meier." *Corriere della Sera*, 11 April 2002.
Diehl, Ute. "Shadow Plays and Architectural Light." *Frankfurter Allgemeine Zeitung*, 13 June 1996.
Fitzgerald, Ian. "Augustus' Resting Place." *History Today*, May 1998, pp. 29-30.
Madeo, Liliana. "Provinciale, devastante, troppo costoso: il critico d'arte boccia il progetto di Meier a Roma." *La Stampa*, 8 March 1998, p. 23.
Maestosi, Danilo. "Un museo di vetro per l'Ara Pacis." *Il Messaggero*, 20 June 1996, p. 25.

"Meier scopre l'Ara Pacis del 2000, un nuovo museo da 21 miliardi." *La Repubblica*, 20 June 1996, p. 1.
Muratore, Giorgio. "Roma non è l'America: troppo disimpegno storico nel progetto di Meier per l'Ara Pacis." *Il Messaggero*, 10 March 1998.
Muschamp, Herbert. "A Visionary Has Become A Builder." *The New York Times*, 23 June 2002, p. 31.
Pearson, Albert and Catherine Siphron. "A Modern Classic." *SOMA*, December 2001–January 2002, p. 42.
Pullara, Giuseppe. "L'Ara Pacis 'made in Usa.'" *Corriere della Sera*, 20 June 1996, p. 49.
Quintavalle, Arturo. "Ara Pacis, più leggerezza per il progetto Meier." *Corriere della Sera*, 5 December 2001, p. 37.
Sainz, Jorge. "El castillo blanco." *CCA & V*, February 1993, pp. 108-12.
"Sistemazione museale dell'Ara Pacis, Roma." *Zodiac 17*, May 1997, pp. 128-33.
Stanley, Alessandra. "Colorful Characters Lurk Around Monuments." *The New York Times*, 29 June 2001, p. A4.
Wise, Michael. "Dictator by Design." *Travel & Leisure*, March 2001, pp. 102-8.
Wise, Michael. "Feud Over Fascist Legacy." *ARTnews*, April 2001, p. 76.

Jubilee Church, Rome, Italy, 1996–2004
Bagini, Alessandro G. "A vele spiegate nella periferia romana." *Bergamo 15*, 31 March 1997.
Bell, Jonathan. "Faith and the Future." *Blueprint*, March 2002, pp. 60-63.
Borgese, Giulia. "E domani l'incontro col 'committente': Giovanni Paolo II." *Corriere della Sera*, 24 February 1997, p. 18.
Brzobohat, Petr et al. "Rozhovor s Johnem Eislerem." *Architekt*, 23-24, 1996, pp. 30-42.
Bugatti, Angelo. "Nel segno del cemento." *Costruire*, November 1997, pp. 26-27.
Burdett, Ricky. "Rome: the Mayor and His Architects." *Domus*, December 2000, pp. 70-83.
Bussel, Abby. "Meier & Partners Wins Vatican Church Competition." *Architectural Record*, August 1996, p. 11.
Campanelli, Alessandro Pergoli. "A Roma non si può sfuggire alla storia." *La Voce Repubblicana*, 18–19 July 1997, p. 4.
Caretto, Ennio. "Meier: l'anno 2000 in una chiesa." *Corriere della Sera*, 24 February 1997, p. 18.
Castellano, Aldo. "The Church of the Year 2000." *Ecclesia*, August–September 1996, pp. 44-67.
Castellano, Aldo. "The Church of the Year 2000." *l'Arca*, September 1996, pp. 12-17.
"C'è anche Verona nella chiesa dove il Papa aprirà il Giubileo." *L'Arena*, 5 April 1998, p. 11.
"Chiesa del 2000 e il cemento bianco." *L'industria italiana del cemento*, November 1996, pp. 813-20.
Chung, Karen. "Miracle Work." *Wallpaper Magazine*, p. 78.

"The Church of the Year 2000." *a+u – Architecture and Urbanism* 319, April 1997, pp. 40-53.

"The Church of the Year 2000." *Politecnico*, 25 February 1997, pp. 13-23.

Cialini, Giulio. "La Chiesa del 2000? Rivoluzionaria." *Il Giorno*, 1 March 1998.

Ciorra, Pippo. "Richard Meier and Peter Eisenman. Talent and ideas"; Garofalo, Francesco. "The Church of the Year 2000." *Casabella*, December–January 1997, pp. 106-107, 88.

Curtis, Eleanor. "Rome reborn will not be built in a day." *Financial Times/Weekend*, 6–7 March 1999, p. 26.

"Designs on the Future: Monuments to the Millennium." *Newsweek, European ed.*, 11 January 1999, p. 4.

Diehl, Ute. "Carrying new churches to Rome: Fifty new churches, one of them by Richard Meier." *Frankfurter Allgemeine Zeitung*, 27 June 1996.

Di Forti, Massimo. "Meier: Roma? Città eterna, non immobile." *Il Messaggero*, 10 July 1997, p. 19.

Dignola, Carlo. "Una chiesa modernista per il Giubileo." *L'eco di Bergamo*, 25 February 1997, p. 18.

Dignola, Carlo. "La chiesa trasparente." *Avvenire*, 25 February 1997, p. 18.

Dillenberger, John and Daniela Ford. "Richard Meier's Church of the Year 2000." *Faith and Form*, vol. XXXI, no. 2, 1998, pp. 7-11.

Dives in Misericordia Church, Rome, Project by Richard Meier. Rome: Italcementi Group, Edita, 2001.

Doig, Allan. "Richard Meier's Church for the Year 2000 in Rome." *Church Building* 44, March–April 1997, pp. 14-15.

Early, Tracy. "Jewish Architect calls chance to design Catholic church an honor." *Catholic News Service* (Internet).

"Estetyka logiki." *Architektura & Biznes*, July–August 1996, pp. 11-13.

"Etwas Modernes für Rom." *Werk, Bauen+Wohnen*, March 1997, p. 66.

Fernandez-Galiano, Luis. "Iglesias de Autor." *El País*, 28 September 1996, p. 23.

Fontanarosa, Aldo. "Un architetto di religione ebraica costruirà un santuario per il Papa." *La Repubblica*, 29 May 1996.

Fontechiari, Giovanni. "Il tempo del nuovo millennio." *Architettura & Ambiente*, April 1997, pp. 5-6.

Freund, Anthony Barzilay. "Ten Rising Stars." *Town & Country*, November 2000, pp. 173-81.

Futagawa, Yukio, ed. "Church of the Year 2000." *Global Architecture Document* 51, *Global Architecture International 1997*, pp. 63-65.

Gandini, Manuela. "La mia chiesa tutta di Luce." *Il Giorno*, 1 March 1998.

Garofalo, Francesco. "The Church of the Year 2000." *Casabella*, December 1996–January 1997.

Gattinara, Fonti Morelli. "An A to Z of the Jubilee." *The Art Newspaper*, February 2001, p. 6.

Gersony, Marina. "L'architetto del Giubileo incanta alla Triennale." *Il Giornale*, 4 March 1998.

Gibson, David. "Church design crosses new frontiers." *Bergen County Sunday Record*, 21 March 1999, p. NJ-3.

Gould, Kira L. "Cooling Rome's Millennial Church." *Oculus*, vol. 61, no. 8, April 1999, p. 24.

Grasso, Giacomo. "The Church of the Year 2000." *L'Architettura* 484, July 1996, pp. 68-80.

Hager, June. "Rome's Jubilee Church for the Year 2000." *Inside the Vatican*, November 1998, pp. 62-65.

Hart, Sara. "Dynamic Concrete in the 21st Century." *Architectural Record*, October 2001, pp. 175-82.

Hartmann, Rahel. "Richard Meier baut die Jubilaumskirche in Rom." *Kunst in Judentum*, November 1996, pp. 274-79.

Heathcote, Edwin. "Richard Meier: Church for the Year 2000, Rome." *Architectural Design*. January 2000, pp. 78-79.

"Heaven's window." *The New Yorker*, 27 April 1998, pp. 116-17.

Hovey, Richard. "Meier building church in Rome." *The Artistic Traveler*, May–June 1997, p. 3.

Iacoboni, Jacopo. "La chiesa del nuovo millennio? La facciamo senza croce." *Il Mattino*, 2 March 1998.

"Invited International Competition for the Church of the Year 2000." *Compe & Contest* 52, May 1997, pp. 18-22.

Irace, Fulvio. "Pregare nel nuovo Millennio." *Il Sole 24 Ore*, 2 March 1997.

"Jew to design Catholic Church." *The Daily Telegraph*, 14 June 1996, p. 18.

"Jubileo simbólico." *Arquitectura Viva* 58, January–February 1998, pp. 52-55.

"Kirche in Tor Tre Teste, Rom." *Bauwelt*, 1996, p. 1506.

Lotito, Piero. "Tre grandi vele traghettano la Chiesa nel terzo millennio." *Il Giorno*, 26 February 1997.

Louie, Elaine. "Church for the Third Millenium." *New York Times*, 20 June 1996, p. C1.

Maestosi, Danilo. "A Tor Tre Teste una chiesa 'americana.'" *Il Messaggero*, 29 May 1996.

Malin, Navad. "What? No Air Conditioning in this Building?" *Architectural Record*, May 2000, pp. 281-90.

Mantegna, Gianfranco. "Architects Present Rome with 'The Church of the Year 2000.'" *Graphis*, July–August 1997, p. 14.

Mays, John Bentley. "Vatican's 'cold' disdain chills locals near avant-garde church." *National Post*, 18 December 1999 (Internet).

Mazzoleni, Emilio. "La chiesa? Va a gonfie vele." *Carnet*, August 1997, pp. 110-19.

"Meier designs Jubilee Church." *Art in America*, January 2001, p. 25.

"Meier hara en Roma la iglesia del ano 2000." *La Vanguardia*, 29 May 1996, p. 40.

Melvin, Jeremy. "The Shock of the New." *RIBA Journal*, January 2000, pp. 22-30.

Meyer, Gudrun and Oliver Herwig. "Helige Neubauten." *Focus*, December 1999, pp. 88-91.

Mornement, Adam. "Almighty Achievement." *Condé Nast Traveler*, September 2000, p. 28.

Muolo, Mimmo. "Verso il Giubileo con le vele di Meier." *L'Avvenire*, 1 March 1998.

Muschamp, Herbert. "Architecture of Light and Remembrance." *The New York Times,* 15 December 1996, sec. 2, pp. 1, 44.

Muschamp, Herbert. "A Visionary Has Become A Builder." *The New York Times*, 23 June 2002, p. 31.

Noris, Sara. "La chiesa del Giubileo parla bergamasco." *Il Giorno*, 25 February 1997, p. 26.

Perego, Francesco. "Sono le cattedrali d'oggi." *L'Espresso* 30, 1 August 1993, pp. 124-25.

Pretzlik, Charles. "Jew to Design Catholic Church." *The Daily Telegraph*. 14 June 1996, p. 18.

"Progetti per la Chiesa del 2000, Roma." *Zodiac 17*, May 1997, pp. 116-27.

"Progetto Marmo Builds the Church of the Year 2000." *Architectural Stone*, October–December 1997, pp. 82-91.

"Project: Kirche des Jahres 2000 in Rom, Italien." *Architektur+Wettbewerbe*, June 1998, pp. 402-3.

"Richard Meier & Partners, Chiesa del 2000." *Abitare*, January 2000, p. 115.

"Richard Meier: Wesentlich in Weiss." *Wohn! Design*, April 1996–January 1997, pp. 88-93.

Rosso, Renata. "Whiter than white." *World Architecture* 54, March 1997, pp. 58-59.

Sangiorgi, Michele. "Strutture e linee architettoniche emblematiche della nostra epoca." *L'Osservatore Romano*, 12 March 1997.

Schisa, Brunella. "Mostri sacri." *Il Venerdì di Repubblica*, 21 November 1997, pp. 56-66.

Sebastini, Cinzia. "White sails in the Roman suburbs." *Ecclesia*, January–February 1998, pp. 24-31.

Sebastino, Umberto. "The White Sails of the Third Millennium." *Design Diffusion News*, June 1998, p. 67.

Shannon, Kelly. "Meier for Church of the Year 2000." *World Architecture*, p. 33.

Smith, Karen Sue. "Church of the Year 2000." *Church*, fall 1998, p. 44.

"Spazio e Luce." *Marie Claire*, April 1999, pp. 118, 120, 122.

Stroik, Duncan G. "Modernism Triumphs in the Eternal City: American Architect Richard Meier wins a Church competition to design the Church for the Third Milennium." (Internet).

Tretiack, Philippe. "De Sacres Eglises." *Elle Decoration*, December 1999, pp. 125-26.

"Una Chiesa per il Duemila." *Exhibition*, September 1996, pp. 8-13.

"Una chiesa per il Duemila: La Moltiplicazione degli spazi." *Chiesa Oggi: Architettura e comunicazione*, vol. 22, 1996, pp. 16-19.

"Una chiesa per il Giubileo." *Focus*, November 1999, pp. 28-9.

Vrancic, Tanja. "Crkva za 2000 godinu." *Graditelj*, April 1999, pp. 42-4.

Wang, Tseng-jung. "Too heavy to call it

Millennium." *Chinese Architect*,
January 2000, pp. 144-53.
Ward, Beatriz Montero. "Iglesia de la Luz."
El Mercurio: Vivienda y Decoracion,
30 September 2000, pp. 76-79.
Warda, Arlene. "Church of the Year 2000."
Chiesa Oggi, vol. XXII, 1996.
Waugh, Jamie. "Holy Communion." *Madison*,
March–April 2000, pp. 110-17.
"White light for Rome's millennium church."
Concrete Quarterly, fall 1999, pp. 6-7.
Zabalbeascoa, Anatxu. "Templos Modernos."
El País Semanal, 20 February 2000, pp. 36-39.
Zevi, Bruno. "Richard Meier in Bramante's
Place." *L'Architettura – cronache e storia* 7,
1995, pp. 66-67.
Zevi, Bruno. "Kostel pro rok 2000." *Architekt*,
January–February 1997, pp. 13-21.

**Crystal Cathedral Hospitality and Visitors
Center, Garden Grove, California, 1996–2003**
Ouroussoff, Nicolai. "Love thy Neighbor,
Modern Style." *The Los Angeles Times*,
13 May 2001, pp. 55-56.
Takahama, Valerie. "Dr. Schuller
and the Architects." *The Orange County
Register*, 9 March 2001 pp. 1-2.

**Peek & Cloppenburg Department Store,
Dusseldorf, Germany, 1998–2001**
"Imagepflege." *Architektur Innenarchitektur
Technischer Ausbau,* September 2001,
pp. 108-13.
"Shopping-Ara." *German Vogue*,
May 2001, p. 40.

**Rickmers Reederei Headquarters, Hamburg,
Germany, 1998–2001**
Arnaboldi, Mario Antonio. "Rickmers Reederei
Headquarters." *L'Arca*, April 2002, pp. 26-29.
Barton, Patrick. "Des Reeders feines
Buroschiff." *Frankfurter Allgemeine Zeitung*,
21 May 2001, p. 57.
Boschmann, Hella. "Glashaus furr
Prominente." *Die welt*, 23 April 2001, p. 32.
Futagawa, Yukio, ed. "Rickmers Reederei
Headquarters." *Global Architecture Document*
61, *Global Architecture International 2000*,
April 2000, pp. 52-55.
Maak, Niklas."Ruckkehr der Urmotive:
Burogebaude der Reederei Rickmer Rickmers."
Architektur in Hamburg, Jahrbuch 2001,
pp. 12-17.

**Canon Headquarters, Tokyo, Japan,
1998–2002**
"Canon Headquarters, Tokyo, 1997–2002."
Global Architecture Japan 57, July–August
2002, pp. 88-93.
"Canon Headquarters, Tokyo 1997–2002."
Obayashi Design Department, March 2001,
pp. 58-63.

**Project for the Cittadella Bridge, Alessandria,
Italy, 1998**
Gerosa, Mario. "Elogio della leggerezza."
*Architectural Digest: Le Più Belle Case
Del Mondo*, Italian ed., July 2000, pp. 58-60.

**Friesen House, Los Angeles, California,
1998–2001**
Giovannini, Joseph. "Friesen Outside."
Elle Décor, April–May 1995.
Futagawa Yukio, ed. "Friesen Residence."
Global Architecture Houses 59: *Project 1999*,
February 1999, pp. 124-26.

San Jose Civic Center, California, 1998–2003
Adams, Gerald D. "A New Face on San Jose."
San Francisco Examiner, 23 November 1998,
pp. D1-2, D7.
Bartindale, Becky and David Beck. "Getty
Center architect favored for S.J. City Hall."
San Jose Mercury News, 27 October 1998,
pp. A1, A10.
Hess, Alan. "The building blocks of City Hall."
Silicon Valley Life, 23 November 1998,
p. 2G.
Hess, Alan. "Plan will set stage for new City
Hall." *Silicon Valley Life*, 21 March 1999,
p. 2G.
Hess, Alan. "Will S.J. officials rise to the challenge
of new City Hall design?" *San Jose Mercury
News*, 11 July 1999, p. 1G.
Hess, Alan. "S.J. wrestles with the notion
of a 'true civic center.'" *San Jose Mercury
News*, 23 January 2000.
Hess, Alan. "Cooperative efforts spurred
improvements in S.J. City Hall design."
San Jose Mercury News, 16 April 2000.
Hess, Alan. "Ornate Dome Anchors Strong City
Hall Design." *San Jose Mercury News*,
24 June 2001.
Levey, Noam. "New City Hall would feature
dome and plaza." *San Jose Mercury News*,
5 February 2000.
Levey, Noam. "City Hall gets dash of daring."
San Jose Mercury News, 21 March 2000.
Levey, Noam. "S.J. Council approves modern
City Hall design." *The San Jose Mercury News*,
20 September 2000, pp. B1-4.
Witt, Barry. "City Stall: Officials Stalemate
on Design." *San Jose Mercury News*,
11 December 1999, pp. A1, A9.
Witt, Barry. "City Hall to be Whittled Down."
San Jose Mercury News, 1 February 2001,
pp. B1, B4.

**Southern California Beach House, Malibu,
California, 1999–2001**
Frank, Peter. "For Art's Sake." *UCLA Magazine*,
winter 2000, p. 45.
Futagawa, Yoshio. "Southern California Beach
House." *Project 2002*, special issue of *Global
Architecture Houses* 70, March 2002, pp. 124-29.

**Project for Office Buildings in Chesterfield
Village, St. Louis, Missouri, 1999–2003**
Duffy, Robert W. "Modernism's in again."
St. Louis Post-Dispatch, 9 September 2001,
pp. H6-H7.

**173/176 Perry Street Condominiums, New
York, New York, 1999–2002**
Berger, Philip. "15 Rooms, Riverview." *Town
& Country,* July 2001, pp. 102-7.
Boschmann, Hella. "Glashaus für Prominente."

Die welt, 23 April 2001, p. 32.
Buonamici, Stefano. "Ritorno a New York."
Costruire, February 2001, pp. 36-37.
Cerio, Gregory. "On the block: Mr. Meier Builds
His Dreamhouse." *House & Garden*,
March 2001, pp. 86-90.
Columbia, David. "Social Diary." *Avenue*,
September 2000, p. 18.
Ebeling, Ashlea. "The Glamour Factor." *Forbes*,
11 June 2001, pp. 224-26.
Futagawa, Yukio. "Richard Meier."
International 2001, special issue of *Global
Architecture Document* 65, May 2001,
pp. 37-38.
Gardner, James. "A Welcome Enhancement."
The New York Sun, 15 July 2002, p. 10.
Gray, Kevin. "Building Envy." *Details*,
January–February 2001, pp. 108-15.
Iovine, Julie. "Solving Modern's Midlife Crisis."
The New York Times, 7 February 2002,
pp. F1-F6.
Keil, Braden. "Sun Exec Latest to Join Heavy
Hitters in Perry St. Towers." *New York Post*,
3 December 2000.
Kolker, Robert. "Gotham Glass Houses."
New York Magazine, 19 June 2000, pp. 13-14.
Pittel, Christine. "Ice Palaces." *House Beautiful*,
September 2000, p. 114.
"Real Estate Market: Extraordinary Properties
for Sale." *Architectural Digest*, July 2000,
pp. 76, 78.
"Richard Meier." *Casa Brutus*, March 2002, p. 41.
Rozhon, Tracie. "Retouching the Vision."
The New York Times, 25 May 2000, pp. F1, F11.
Rozhon, Tracie. "Richard Meier Builds
in Manhattan. At Last." *The New York Times*,
25 May 2000, pp. F1, F11.
Shoeneman, Deborah. "Richard Meier Builds
Perry Street Palace for Calvin and Martha."
The Financial Observer, 4 December 2000,
pp. 29, 32.
Sullivan, Paul. "All abuzz over a brace
of buildings." *Financial Times*, 2 July 2000,
p. 21.
Suqi, Rima. "Wonder Twin Towers Activate."
Paper, October 2000, p. 42.
Tang, Jean. "Is this the Next Park Avenue?"
Avenue, December 2001, pp. DT2-DT6.

**Project for New York House, Katonah,
New York, 2000**
Futagawa, Yoshio. "New York House." *Project
2002*, special issue of *Global Architecture
Houses* 7, March 2002, pp. 124-29.

**UCLA Broad Art Center, Los Angeles,
California, 2000–03**
Anderton, Frances. "The Suavely Familiar
vs. the Daring of the Internet Age."
The New York Times, 21 September 2000,
p. F3.
Brinkmann, U. "Fakultat der Kunste
und Architektur des UCLA." *Bauwelt*,
October 2000, p. 2.
Ouroussoff, Nicolai. "The Mark of Meier Will
Make UCLA Arts Center Very Visual."
The Los Angeles Times, September 8, 2000,
pp. F1, F22.

Project for a Performing Arts Center, Bethel, New York, 2001
Hu, Winnie. "Progress in the Long, Strange Trip Toward a Monument to Woodstock." *The New York Times*, 15 June 2001, pp. B1, B5.
Israel, Steve. "Arts Center Design Gets Raves." *The Times Herald Record*, 13 June 2001, p. 17.
Israel, Steve. "Bravo: New York Philharmonic commits to region's performing arts center." *The Times Herald Record*, 12 July 2001, pp. 1, 3.
Kreye, Andrian. "Glas und Stahl am Woodstock-Gelande." *Suddeutsche Zeitung*, 11 July 2001.

Life Sciences Technology Building, Cornell University, Ithaca, New York, 2001–2006
Brand, David. "New Building promises to be 'magnet' providing connectivity and education." *Cornell Chronicle*, 1 February 2002.
"Trustees approve Alumni Field as site for new life science technology building." *Cornell Chronicle*, 1 February 2002.

Wijnhaven Kwartier Master Plan, The Hague, Netherlands, 2001
Chao, Jennifer. "White beacons to oust Black Madonna." *Het Financieele Dagblad*, 14 August 2001, p. 8.
Postmaa, Casper. "Gemeente: Madonna onteigenen"; "Meiers Manhattan"; "Hilhorst: Nu kan het, nu moet je het doen." *Haagsche Courant*, 19 June 2001, pp. A1, B3.
Postmaa, Casper. "Meier's Manhattan." *Haagsche Courant*, 20 June 2001, p. 6.
Schoorl, John. "Den Haag wordt 'Manhattan op z'n Madurodams.'" *De Volkskrant*, 21 June 2001.

Competition Master Plan for FSM East River Area, New York, New York, 2001
Cummings, Mary. "Architects Invited to Share Visions of a New East End." *The Southampton Press*, 15 March 2001, pp. B1, B5.
Muschamp, Herbert. "Fireworks or Fallbacks for a New River City?" *The New York Times*, 5 March 2001, pp. E1, E3.
Muschamp, Herbert. "2 Architectural Firms Chosen to Design East River Tract." *The New York Times*, 9 June 2001, p. B3.
Muschamp, Herbert. "A Team with More Smoke than Fire," *The New York Times*, 24 June 2001, pp. 31-32.

Burda Collection Museum, Baden-Baden, Germany, 2001–2004
"Burda stellt Plane vor." *Badisches Tagblatt* 239, 16 October 2001.
"Der Neubau von Richard Meier." *Sammlung Frider Burda, Autoren*, 27 September 2002. Groundbreaking Catalogue.
Hartmann, Serge. "Baden s'offre Burda qui s'offre Meier." *Dernieres Nouvelles D'Alsace*, 16 October 2001, p. 6.
Hubl, Michael. "Transparenz aus dem Gestus der Bescheidenheit." *Badisch Neues Nachrichten, Kultur*, 16 October 2001.
Noll, Albert. "Star-Planer verspricht 'Juwel':

Rat begeistert." *Badisches Tagblatt* 239, 16 October 2001.
Noll, Albert. "'Stadtbild' bleibt bei Ablehnung." *Badisches Tagblatt*, 17 October 2001.
Von Jutta Manz. "'Leichtes' Gebaude fur eine groBe Sammlung." *Offenburger Tagblatt*, 16 October 2001.
Von Lenhardt, Christiane. "Neue MaBstabe fur Museumswelt." *Badisches Tagblatt* 239, 16 October 2001.
Von Lenhardt, Christiane. "Impulse für Zukunft"; "Im Herbst 2004 gibt es einen neuen Treffpunkt für die Kunstfrende: Museum für die Sammling Frieder Burda." *Badisches Tagblatt* 225, 27 September 2002, p. 2.
Walter, Karin. "Kunstwerk Allee erhalt zusatzliches Kunstwerk." *Badisches Neueste Nachrichten*, 16 October 2001.

Project for Houses at Sagaponac, Long Island, New York, 2001
Cummings, Mary. "Architects Invited to Share Visions Of a New East End." *The Southampton Press*, 15 March 2001, pp. B1, B5.
Czarnecki, John E. "34 Top Architects Selected for Hamptons Houses" and "Hamptons Development, According to Meier." *Architectural Record*, April 2001, pp. 27-32.
Deitz, Paula. "View." *The Architectural Review*, July 2001, pp. 18-19.
Gordon, Alastair. "The 10 Best Houses in the Hamptons." *The Observatory*, 2–9 July 2001, p. 13.
Pavarini, Stefano. "Houses at Sagaponack." *L'Arca*, English ed., June 2002, pp. 14-25.

66, New York, New York, 2002–03
"66 Leonard Street Restaurant". *The New York Times – Restaurant Section,* 8 May 2002, p. F10.

Project for Paris Room at the Grand Hotel Salone, Salone del Mobile, Fiera di Milano, Italy, 2002
Bauzano, Gianluca. "Quando un designer entra al Grand Hotel." *Corriere della Sera*, 10 April 2002.
Futagawa, Yoshio. "Grand Hotel Salone." *Global Architecture Houses* 71, May 2002, pp. 10-31, 52.
Hinchcliffe, Rob. "A room of one's own." *Blueprint*, April 2002, pp. 30-31.
Iovine, Julie. "Baby and Hotels Star at Milan Fair." *The New York Times*, 11 April 2002.
Moretti, John. "Architects have clean fun with hotel design." *Italy Daily*, 12 April 2002, pp. 1-2.
"The 'Parisian' Room." Design Diffusion News, October 2002, pp. 96-7.
Paul, Donna. "Grand Hotel Milano." *Interior Design*, June 2002, pp. 186-90.

Other Projects
Arnott, Ian. "Meier at Maybury." *Prospect*, spring 1990, pp. 40-41.
Aronson, Steven M.L. "Can This Vacation Be Saved?" *Travel & Leisure*, March 1999, pp. 164-71, 213-15.
Ash, Jennifer and Alex McLean. *Private Palm Beach*. New York: Abbeville Press, 1992, pp. 40-47.
Avins, Mimi. "The New Hamptons." *The Los Angeles Times*, 8 March 2001, pp. E1, E3.
Barthelmess, Stephan. *Richard Meier, Collagen*. Germany: International Creative Management, March 1993. Includes "The Collage in the Square: Art Parallel to Architecture" by the author.
The Bauhaus: A Japanese Perspective. Tokyo: Aiko Hasegawa, 1992.
"Beach House, Fire Island, New York." *Arts and Architecture*, January 1964, pp. 22-23.
Borg, Alan. "Ten Lessons from a Superb House." *American Home*, March 1967, pp. 82-87.
Borras, Maria Lluisa. "Los Collages de Richard Meier." *La Vanguardia*, 26 July 1988, p. 38.
"Business Park: Maybury." *The Architectural Review*, March 1991, pp. 66-67.
Carli, Fabrizio. "Bianco Meier." *Il Giornale*, 18 July 1993.
Catoir, Barbara. "Architektur in Schwar." *Frankfurter Allgemeine Zeitung*, 26 March 1996.
Chapman, Irv. "Alumni Profiles: Richard Meier: Celebrated architect, Cornell ready for each other again." *Cornell '87*, summer 1987, p. 3.
Ciorra, Pippo. "Vite artistiche parallele di Richard Meier and Frank Stella in mostra al Palazzo delle Esposizioni di Roma." *Il Manifesto*, 9 July 1993, p. 12.
Clyde, Amy. "Cheeky Chairs." *House Beautiful*, March 1993, p. 66.
Cohen, Edie Lee. "Richard Meier & Partners: Two Offices by and for the Architectural Firm." *Interior Design*, May 1988, pp. 278-84.
Collins, Glenn. "A Showplace for a Showman." *The New York Times*, 6 June 1989, pp. 15-16.
Cowie, Denise. "Architect turns skills to more than buildings." *The Philadelphia Inquirer*, 25 October 1996, pp. F1, F10-11.
Cummings, Mary. "Architects Invited to Share Visions of a New East End." *The Southampton Press*, 15 March 2001, pp. B1, B5.
De Candia, Mario. "L'architetto e il post-pittore." *La Repubblica – Trovaroma*, 8–14 July 1993, p. 34.
Diamonstein, Barbaralee. "New York Apartment Renovation." *Global Architecture* 5, winter 1978, pp. 110-15.
Diamonstein, Barbaralee, ed. *Collaboration: Artists and Architects*. New York: Whitney Library of Design, 1981, pp. 104-8.
"Diseños y realizaciones de maestros de la arquitectura." *Ambito Financiero*, 5 October 1993, p. 2.
Dreyer, Clemens, ed. "Ibach – Der Konzertflugel." *Deutsche Standards: Die Klassiker von Morgen*. Cologne: Edition Arcum, 1996, pp. 80-81.
Duffy, Robert W. "Modernism's in again."

St. Louis Post-Dispatch, 9 September 2001, pp. H6-H7.

Dunlap, David W. "Street Furniture Designs Stuck in Gridlock." The New York Times, 9 August 1998, sec. 11, pp. 1, 24.

Edwards, Brian. "Meier's Maybury Master Plan." RIBA Journal, September 1989, pp. 28-29.

Firlotte, Gregory. "Intent or Smut: Conversing with Richard Meier, Ed Ruscha and DeWain Valenlal." Designer's West, January 1988, pp. 114-15.

Fortier, Bruno. "Il Concorso Per Il Quartiere Sextius-Mirabeau a Aix en Provence." Casabella, October 1990, pp. 62-69.

Frank Stella: A Vision for Public Art. Japan: Tankosha Publishing, Ltd, 1994. Includes "Broadsides" by Frank Stella; "Richard Meier and Frank Stella: a Conversation Between Architect and Artist" edited by Peter Slatin; "A Relationship in the Industry of Excellence" by Earl Childress, pp. 141-46.

Futagawa, Yukio, ed. "Apartment in New York." Global Architecture Houses 6, 1979, pp. 90-92.

Futagawa, Yukio, ed. "Palm Beach House." Global Architecture Houses 56, April 1998, pp. 134-47.

Genauer, Emily. "New Styles in Synagogues." The New York Times, 5 October 1963, p. 22.

Giordano, Paolo. "Progetti per Napoli." Domus, March 1987, pp. 79-84.

Giovannini, Joseph. "Design Notebook: Tea Services with the Touch of an Architect." The New York Times, 17 November 1983, p. C18.

Goldberger, Paul. "Architecture: Townhouse Rows." The New York Times, 16 June 1980, p. C15.

Goldberger, Paul. "A Meeting of Artistic Minds." The New York Times Magazine, 1 March 1981, pp. 70-80.

Grossman, Luis J. "Pelli, Jahn, Meier y Mayne, en una Muestra fuera de serie." La Nacion, Arquitectura, 15 September 1993, p. 7.

Gubitosi, Alessandro. "La città in miniatura." L'Arca, July–August 1992, pp. 26-31.

Gueft, Olga. "House with Sky Inside." Interiors, August 1964, pp. 58-62.

Gueft, Olga. "Sona the Golden One." Interiors, September 1965, pp. 150-53.

"Habitation à Essex Falls, New Jersey." L'Architecture d'Aujourd'hui, September–October 1965, pp. 82-83.

Huxtable, Ada Louise. "Designs for American Synagogues." The New York Times, 5 October 1963, p. 22.

Iovine, Julie. "A-List Alternatives to Hamptons Hulk." The New York Times, 8 March 2001, pp. F1, F7.

Izzo, Alberto, et al. Progetti per Napoli. Napoli: Guida Edition, 1987.

Jay, Hilary. "Eminent Domain." The Philadelphia Inquirer Magazine, 27 October 1996, pp. 30-31.

Kay, Andrew. "Duplex Complex." Quest, May 1998, pp. 18-22.

Keysers, Paul. "Waarom een Wereldberoem de Architect Antwerpen Vervloekt." Panorama de Post 24, 11 June 1993, pp. 38-40.

Lambertini, Luigi. "Insieme, alla scuola del Barocco." Corriere della Sera, 25 July 1993, p. 23.

Larson, Soren. "American Institute of Architects 2000: Honors & Awards." Architectural Record, May 2000, pp. 95, 134-35.

"Lexus LS430" Advertisement, Architectural Digest, November 2000.

Meier, Richard. Recent American Synagogue Architecture. New York: The Jewish Museum, 1963.

Michelson, Annette. "An Art Scholar's Loft." Vogue, 15 March 1967, pp. 136-42, 154-55.

Muschamp, Herbert. "New Jersey House of Contrasts Wins a Design Award." The New York Times, 4 July 1965, sec. 8, p. 1.

Muschamp, Herbert. "2 Architectural Firms Chosen to Design East River Tract." The New York Times, 9 June 2001, p. B3.

O'Brien, George. "Living in an Art Form." The New York Times Magazine, 22 March 1964, pp. 94-95.

Papadakis, Andreas C., ed. "Richard Meier: The Art of Abstraction." Art and the Tectonic. Art and Design, 1990, pp. 86-91.

Pasti, Daniela. "Ditta Stella & Meier." La Repubblica, 7 July 1993, p. 34.

Pica, Agnoldomenico. "Sona: Un centro di artigianato indiano a New York." Domus, December 1966.

Pittel, Christine. "Color, Color, Color." Elle Décor 21, February–March 1992, pp. 57-62.

Plumb, Barbara. "Remodeling on a Grand Scale." The New York Times Magazine, 24 September 1966, pp. 170-72.

Plumb, Barbara. "One of a Kind." The New York Times Magazine, 24 September 1967.

Pratesi, Ludovico. "La Pelle d'acciaio della città-museo." La Repubblica, 8 July 1993, p. 9.

"Record Houses of 1964." Architectural Record, mid-May 1964, pp. 68-71.

"Richard Meier al Palazzo Delle Esposizioni di Roma." L'Industria Delle Costruzioni, vol. 297, January 1994, pp. 60-61.

"Richard Meier, Frank Stella, Palazzo delle Esposizioni." Flash Art 178, October 1993, p. 112.

"Richard Meier, l'Exposition." Connaissance des Arts 141, July 1999. Special issue on the occasion of the MOCA/Jeu de Paume Exhibition, 13 July–26 September. Includes Preface by Richard Koshalek and Dana Hutt; "Justesse et Lumière" by Philip Jodidio.

Riding, Alan. "Celebrating an Architect, Hailing an Artist." New York Times Sunday, 8 Aug 1999, p. 34. Reprinted as "Paris Fetes Richard Meier, Architect and Artist." International Herald Tribune, 10 Aug 1999, p. 34.

Rinaldi, Rosamaria. "Due Studi d'Architettura: Da New York a Los Angeles." Interni, March 1989, pp. 8-13.

Robbins, Jack. "Architects own offices." World Architecture, October 1998, pp. 80-93.

Schön, Wolf. "Man müßte Klavier spielen können." Rheinischer Merkur, 16 February 1996, p. 19.

Seward, Keith. "Richard Meier, Leo Castelli Gallery." ArtForum, December 1994, pp. 82-83.

Shaw, Dan. "Memory Mania." House & Garden, May 2000, p. 40.

Shear, Michael D. "Name is Big, Work is Small: Famous Architect Adapts His Vision to Bus Shelter." The Washington Post, 13 September 1999, pp. B1-2.

Stephens, Suzanne. "Design Deformed." Artforum, January 1977, pp. 44-47.

"Stirling e Meier: costruire a Manhattan." Domus, July 1980, p. 32.

Strappa, Giuseppe. "L'Architetto e il post-pittore." La Repubblica, 14 July 1993, p. 34.

Sverbeyeff, Elizabeth. "For the New Horizon: A Sculptured Profile." House Beautiful, September 1967, pp. 140-45.

Timmerman, Jacques. "Antwerpen: Den Entrepot." A+Architektuur, February 1990, pp. 40-44.

"Una intensa semana con la arquitectura: La V Bienal en marcha." El Cronista Arquitectura & Diseño, 22 September 1993, pp. 1-8.

Weinstein, Richard. "Richard Meier Collages." UCLA Collage Exhibition Catalogue, February 1993.

Zabalbeascoa, Anatxu. The House of the Architect. New York: Rizzoli International, 1995, pp. 118-21.

Zabalbeascoa, Anatxu. The Office of the Architect. New York: Rizzoli International, 1995, pp. 112-15.

Zevi, Bruno. "Richard Meier and the Language of Baalbek." L'Architettura – cronache e storia, November 1993, pp. 754-55.

Collaborators

Acknowledgements

A book of this scale and ambition could never have been realized without the involvement, dedication and assistance of a great number of people. I am deeply grateful to all of them for the generosity and good will with which they have participated in this endeavor. Withouth their involvement this substantial book would be significantly less rich and less beautiful. I am particularly indebted to Francesco Dal Co, for this book is his idea and he has been responsible for its realization.

Special thanks go to Lisetta Koe, the master organizer of this book, and her staff, Esther Kim, Elizabeth Lee and Stella Lee. I also wish to thank Giovanna Crespi and Gabriella Cursoli at Mondadori Electa for their invaluable organizational assistance. Most sincere thanks go to Kenneth Frampton, one of the finest architectural critics of our generation, for his illuminating insight.

Above all, my sincere thanks to all of the collaborators listed here who worked with me to create a wonderful legacy of creativity and inspiration.

Richard Meier
March 2003

New York

Kimberly Ackert
Paul Aferiat
Maria Alataris
Dorothy Alexander
Stanley Allen
Philip Babb
Jeff Barber
Roy Barris
Stuart Basseches
Margaret Bemiss
Susan Berman
Thomas Bish
Peter Bochek
Karl Born
Patricia Bosch Melendez
Michel Bourdeau
Wolfgang Brandl
Alfred Brice
Karin Bruckner
Jason Buchheit
Andrew Buchsbaum
Annie Luise Buerger
Peter Burns
Amedee Butt
Mary Buttrick
Michael Calvino
John Carhart
Ron Castellano
Pablo Castro Estevez
Paul Cha
Christine Chang Hanway
Renee Cheng
Christopher Chimera
John Chimera
Eva Chiu
Mark Cigolle
Miles Cigolle
John Clappi
Nancy Clark
Adam Cohen
John Colamarino
Clayton Collier
Carlos Concepcion
Jon Cooksey
Peter Coombe
Donald Cox
Charles Crowley
Adam Cwerner
Benjamin Darras
Richard Davies
Susan Davis-McCarter
Stephen Dayton
Allan Denenberg
David Diamond
Mark Dizon
Pamela Donnelly
Alfonso D'Onofrio
Amy Donohue
Timothy Collins Douglas
Michael Duncan
Bernd Echtermeyer
Robert Edwards
John Eisler

Karin Elliot
Nikolaus Elz
Murray Emslie
David Estreich
Donald Charles Evans
Martin Falke
Peter Felix
Manfred Fischer
Renate Fischer
Frank Fitzgibbons
Patrick Flynn
Diederik Fokkema
Christopher Ford
Steven Forman
Kenneth Frampton
Nina Freedman
Jonathan Friedman
Axel Gaede
Robert F. Gatje
Sudipto Ghosh
Laurent Gilson
Hans Goedeking
Kevin Gordon
Mark Goulthorpe
William Gravely
Lisa J. Green
W. Jeffrey Greene
Gerald Gurland
Kornel Gyarmathy
Marc Hacker
Ronnie K. Hamlett
Ireneus Harasymiak
Frank Harmon
Stephen Harris
Price Harrison
Christopher Haynes
Brian Healy
Daniel Heuberger
Daniel Heyden
Abigail Hopkins
Katharine Huber
Irene Hui
Julienne Icart
Raphael Justewicz
Thomas Juul-Hansen
Gunter Kaesbach
Douglas Kahn
Bernhard Karpf
Lucy Kelly
George Kewin
Isaac Khabie
Nadia Khan
Andrew Kim
Jeffrey King
Julian King
Marcus Klein
Grace Kobayashi
Lisetta Koe
Christina Kohm
Jah-Hee Koo
Tobias Kraus
Robert Krawietz
Sherman Kung
Beat Kuttel

Marianne Kwok
Thierry Landis
Ulrike Lauber
Kevin Lee
Stella Lee
Stephen Lesser
Robert Lewis
Hans Li
Eric Liebman
David Ling
Barbara Littenberg
Annie Lo
John Locke
L. Reynolds Logan
James Luhur
Knut Luscher
Bernhard Lutz
Era Malewitsch
Richard Manna
Joachim Mantel
David Martin
Jonathan Marvel
Jacopo Mascheroni
Mark Mascheroni
Jean Mas
Paul Masi
Siobhan McInerney
Petra Meerkamp
Carl Meinhardt
Ada Karmi Melamede
Brian Messana
Claude Meyers
Jean-Michel Meunier
Edward Mills
Michael Misczynski
Richard Morris
Katsu Muramoto
Bruce Nagel
Jun-ya Nakatsugawa
Marc Nelen
Alex Nussbaumer
Michael O'Boyle
Ana O'Brien
Sean O'Brien
Richard Oliver
Matthias Oppliger
Douglas Pancoast
Alfonso Peña
Alfonso Perez-Mendez
Matteo Pericoli
Matthew Petrie
Thomas Phifer
Katherine Platis
Vincent Polsinelli
Stephen Potters
Susan Price
Gundula Proksch
Hans Put
John Quale
Jurgen Raab
Mihai Radu
J. Woodson Rainey, Jr.
Robert Ramirez
Gilbert N. Rampy, Jr.

J. Gregory Reaves
John Reed
James Richards
Eric C. Richey
Rijk Rietveld
David Robins
Peter Robson
Marc Rosenbaum
François Roux
Madeleine Sanchez
Arndt Sänger
Thomas Savory
James Sawyer
Stefan Scheiber
John Schneider
Rainer Scholl
Alan Schwabenland
Jon Michael Schwarting
Ralph Schwarz
Sandra Schwartz
Leonard Segel
Suzanne Sekey
Carl Shenton
Joseph Shields
Erin Shih
David Shilling
David Shultis
James Smith
Kimberly Smith
Henry Smith-Miller
Gunter Standke
Ralph Stern
James R. Stephenson
Jennifer Stevenson
Daniel Stuver
Harley Swedler
Peter Szilagyi
Leland Taliaferro
William Talley
Carlos Tan
Michael Thanner
Steven Theodore
Joerg Thorissen
Stephen Tobler
Jean-Christophe Tougeron
Adrian Ulrich
Orestes Valella
Valerie Vaudou
Michael Vinh
David Walker
Greta Weil
Birgit Werner
Tod Williams
Wolfram Wöhr
Geoffrey Wooding
David Woolf
Evan Yassky
Dukho Yeon
Michael G. Yusem
François Zajdela
Birgit Zwanhuizen

Los Angeles
Amy Alper
Robert J. Ashley
Gregory Baker
John H. Baker
Donald E. Barker
Michele Baron
Roger Barrett
John Bender
Daniel Benjamin
Therese Bennett
Donald Berges
Peter Berman
Michael Bessner
Steve Billings
Manuel Bouza
Karen Bragg
Shari Brukman
Peter Burns
Noel Carriere
David Chang
Steven Chung
Christopher Coe
Florencia Costa
Angelo Costas
James Crawford
David Davis
Rhonna Del Rio
Carlos Dell'Acqua
Victor De Santis
Maurice Edwards
Tom Farrell
Nils C. Finne
Eric Fisher
Francis Freire
E. Jon Frishman
Rozan Gacasan
Shekar Ganti
Tami Gam
Dean Geib
Pavel Getov
Estabrook Glosser
Derek Gonzales
Paul Goodenough
Rick Gooding
Stefan Gould
Tom Graul
Michael Gruber
Jason Haim
Gavin Harris
Jeff Heller
Dennis Hickok
Bradley James Hill
Tom Hoos
Michael Hootman
Glen Irani
Richard Kent Irving
Glen Ishida
James Jackson
Bijoy Jain
Gudlaug Jonsdottir
Kamyar Kamran
Anne Katata
Kathy Kikuno

Christine Kilian
Yunghee Kim
Philip Koss
Caroline Kreiser
Bernard Kummer
Willis Kusuma
Robert Larson
Mark Lawrence
Paul Lee
Jean Lem
Stephen Levine
Mario Madayag
Stuart Magruder
James Matson
Hiroshi Matsubara
James Mawson
Neil McLean
Mark McVay
Paul Mitchell
Mark Moreno
Milena Murdoch
John Murphey
Ronald J. Musser
Lonnie Nakasone
Alexis Navarro
Susan Nelson
James Noh
Kevin O'Brien
Olivia Ocampo
Shuji Otsuki
Carlo Paganuzzi
Michael Palladino
David Scott Parker
Martin Pease
John Petro
Eric Randolph
Renaldo Raya
Averill Vic Schnider
Rivka Schoenfeld
Joanne Scott
Anne Seol
Timothy Shea
Lilia Skutnik
Mark Sparrowhawk
Bruce Stewart
Richard Stoner
Krishna Suharnoko
David Swartz
Timothy Swischuk
Aram Tatikian
Phillip Templeton
John Thomann
Russell N. Thomsen
Norman Title
George Todorovich
Jeffrey Turner
Flora Vara
Stephen Vitalich
Laszlo Vito
Thomas Vitous
Michael Volk
Philip Warde
J.F. Warren
Bruce Weinstein

Lori Welsh
Malvin Whang
John Woell
Harry Wolf
Alex Wuo
Terrence Yuan Young
James Yu
David Yuguchi
Tom Zook
John Zorich

Photograph Credits

We wish to thank Studio Meier for having kindly supplied the material illustrated in this book.

The photographs published herein are by:

Richard Bryant/Arcaid: pp. 18, 222, 224
Richard Bryant/Esto: pp. 216, 223, 304, 305, 386
Barbara Burg, Oliver Schuh/Palladium Photodesign: pp. 152, 153, 154, 155, 156, 157
Louis Checkman: pp. 74 (top and right hand corner), 76, 86, 87
Klaus Frahm: pp. 372, 373, 388, 389, 390, 391, 392, 393
Scott Frances/Esto: pp. 10, 13, 17, 21, 23, 28, 29, 30, 31, 40, 41, 42, 66, 67, 68, 69, 70, 121 (top), 122, 123 (right), 124, 170, 171, 172-173, 174 (right), 175, 180, 181, 182-183, 184, 192, 193, 194, 195, 196-197, 198, 199, 200, 201, 202, 203, 204, 205, 206, 217, 218, 219, 240, 241, 242, 243, 246, 247, 248, 249, 252, 253, 254, 255, 256, 257, 262, 263, 264, 274, 275, 276, 284, 285, 286, 287, 288, 289, 312, 313, 314, 315, 316, 317, 320, 321, 322, 323, 324, 330, 331, 332, 333, 334, 338, 339, 340, 342, 343, 348, 349, 350, 351, 352, 356, 357, 358-359, 360, 361, 362, 400, 404, 405, 406, 407
Jeff Goldberg/Esto: pp. 178, 179
Tim Griffith/Esto: pp. 308, 309
Wolfgang Hoyt/Esto: pp. 102, 103, 162, 163, 164, 165, 174 (left), 233
Go Kamochi: p. 396
Dieter Leistner: p. 168
Peter Mauss/Esto: p. 229
Richard Meier: pp. 96, 97
Jock Pottle/Esto: pp. 278, 280, 281, 292, 293, 294, 298, 300, 328, 374, 375, 398, 399, 411, 416, 423, 426, 427, 434, 435, 441, 444
Uwe Rau: p. 145
Christian Richters/Esto: p. 225
Michael Rutchik: pp. 210, 211
Ezra Stoller/Esto: pp. 14, 25, 36, 38, 46, 47, 50, 51, 52, 54, 55, 58, 59, 60, 61, 64, 65, 74 (bottom left), 77, 80, 82, 83, 88, 89, 90, 91, 92, 100, 104, 105, 106, 108, 109, 110, 111, 114, 115, 116, 117, 120, 121 (bottom), 123 (left), 130, 131, 132, 133, 134, 135, 136, 140, 141, 146, 147, 148, 234, 235, 236, 260, 261
Luca Vignelli: p. 478
Josh White: p. 383
Oliver Wogenscky: pp. 268, 269